STORY BY
HYUNG MIN KIM

ART BY
KYUNG IL YANG

MARCH STORY

1

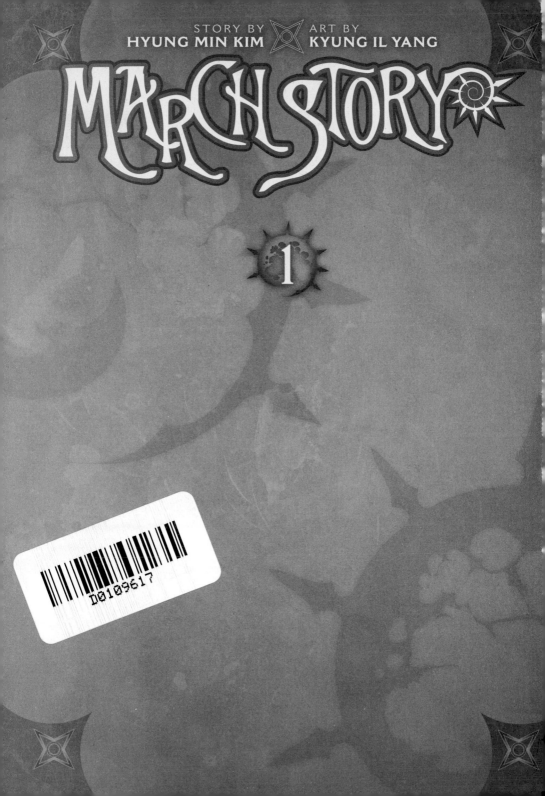

CONTENTS

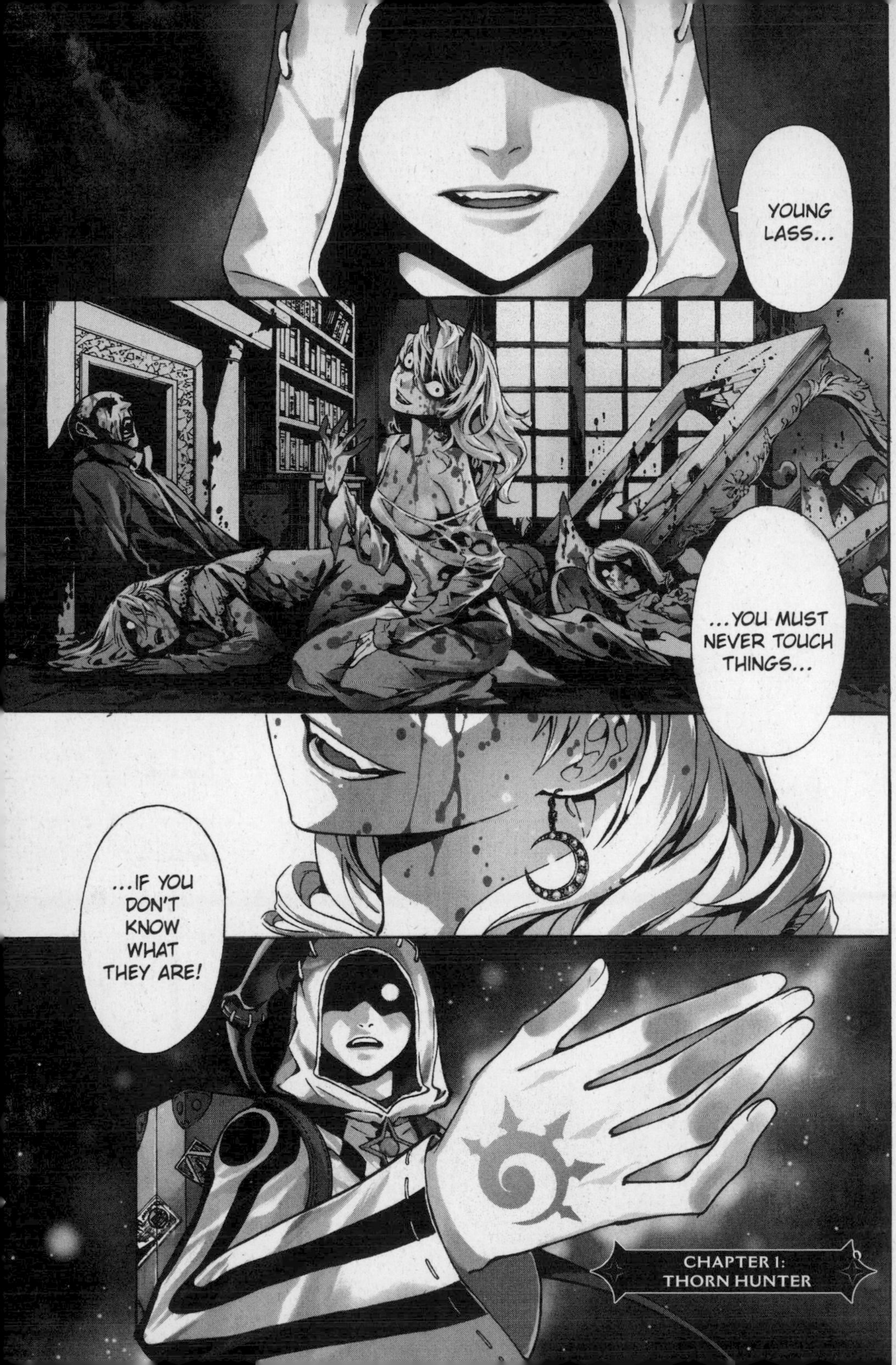
YOUNG LASS...
...YOU MUST NEVER TOUCH THINGS...
...IF YOU DON'T KNOW WHAT THEY ARE!
CHAPTER 1: THORN HUNTER

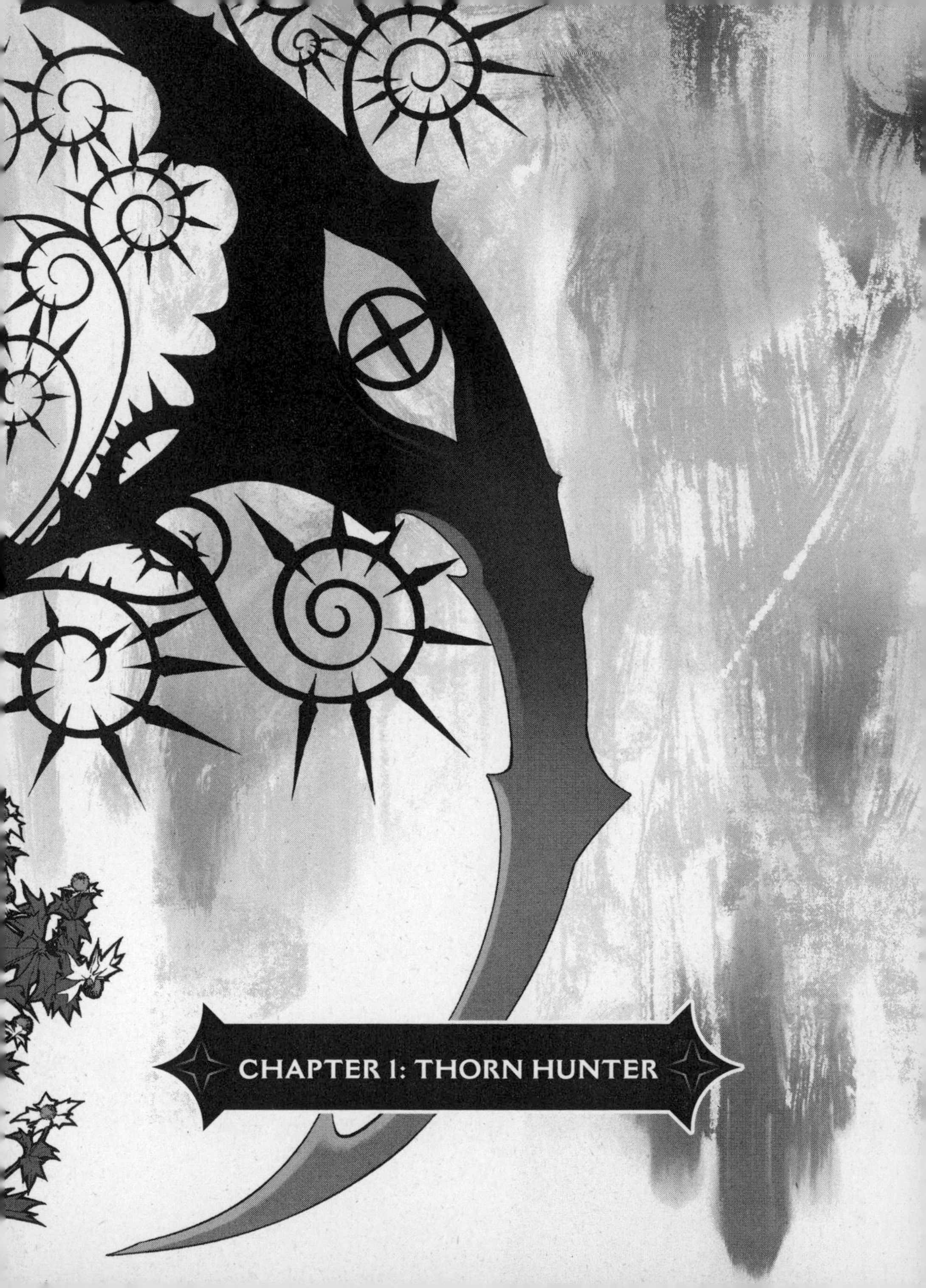

CHAPTER 1: THORN HUNTER

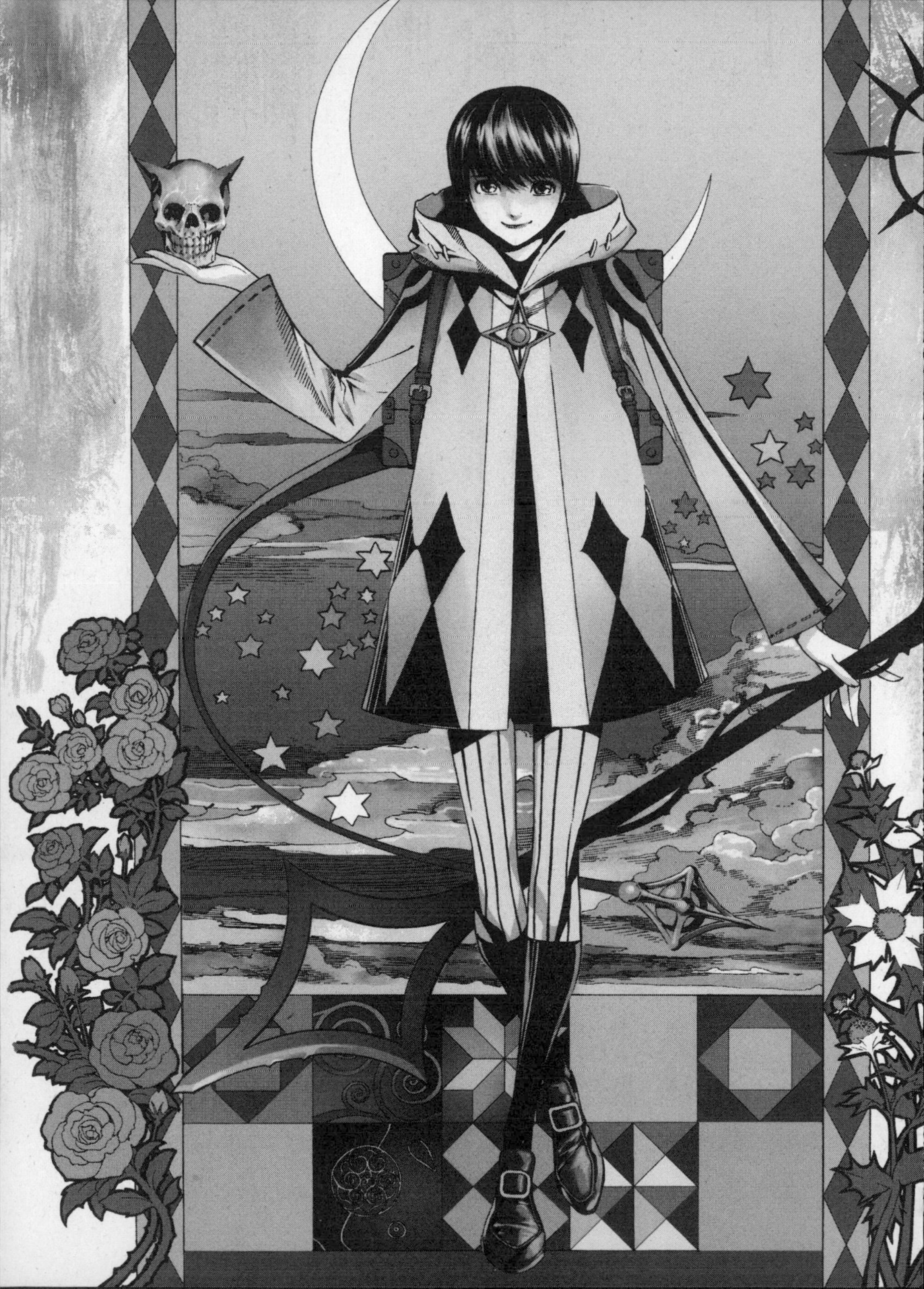

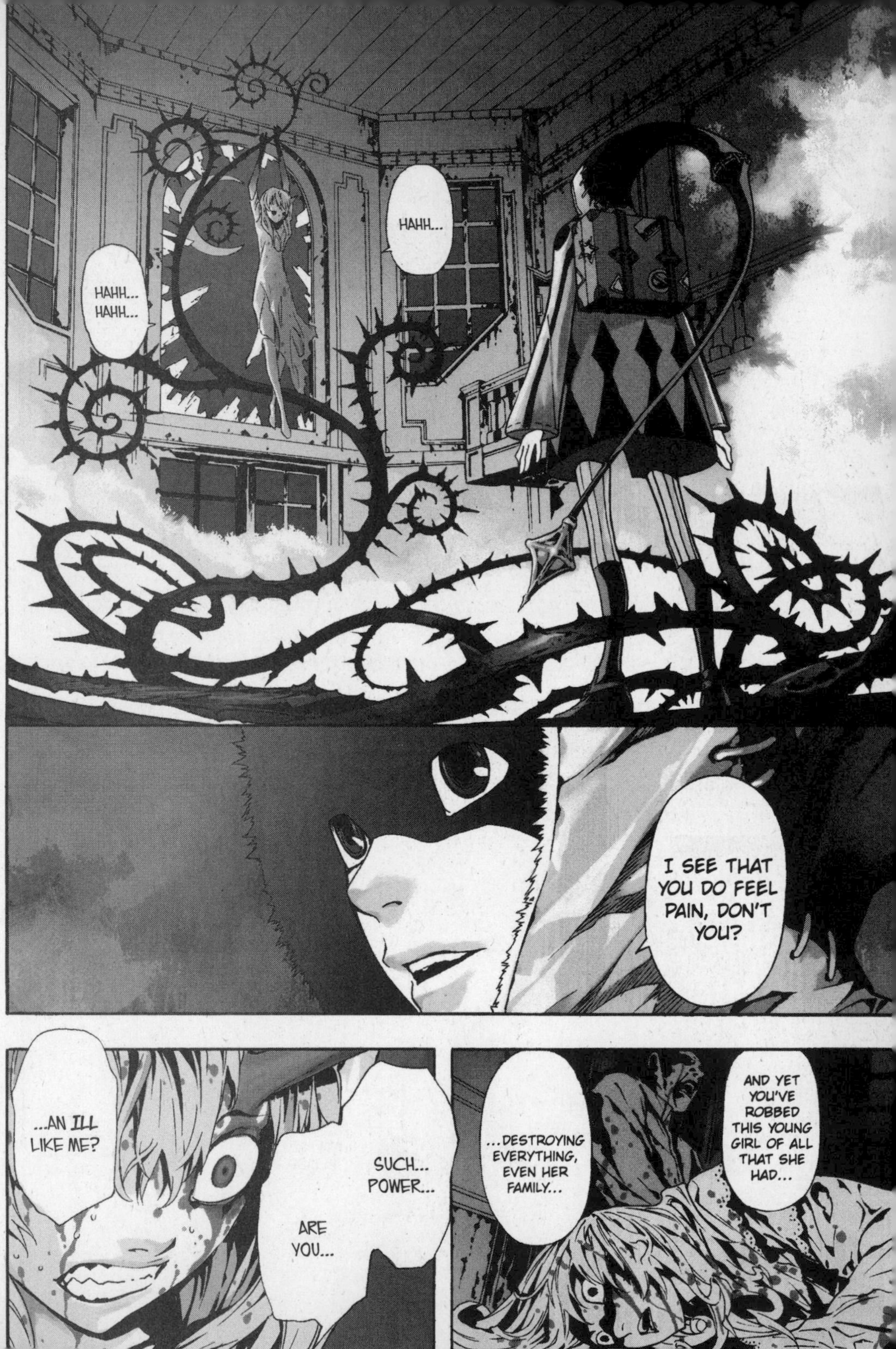
HAHH...
HAHH... HAHH...
I SEE THAT YOU DO FEEL PAIN, DON'T YOU?
AND YET YOU'VE ROBBED THIS YOUNG GIRL OF ALL THAT SHE HAD...
...DESTROYING EVERYTHING, EVEN HER FAMILY...
SUCH... POWER...
ARE YOU...
...AN ILL LIKE ME?

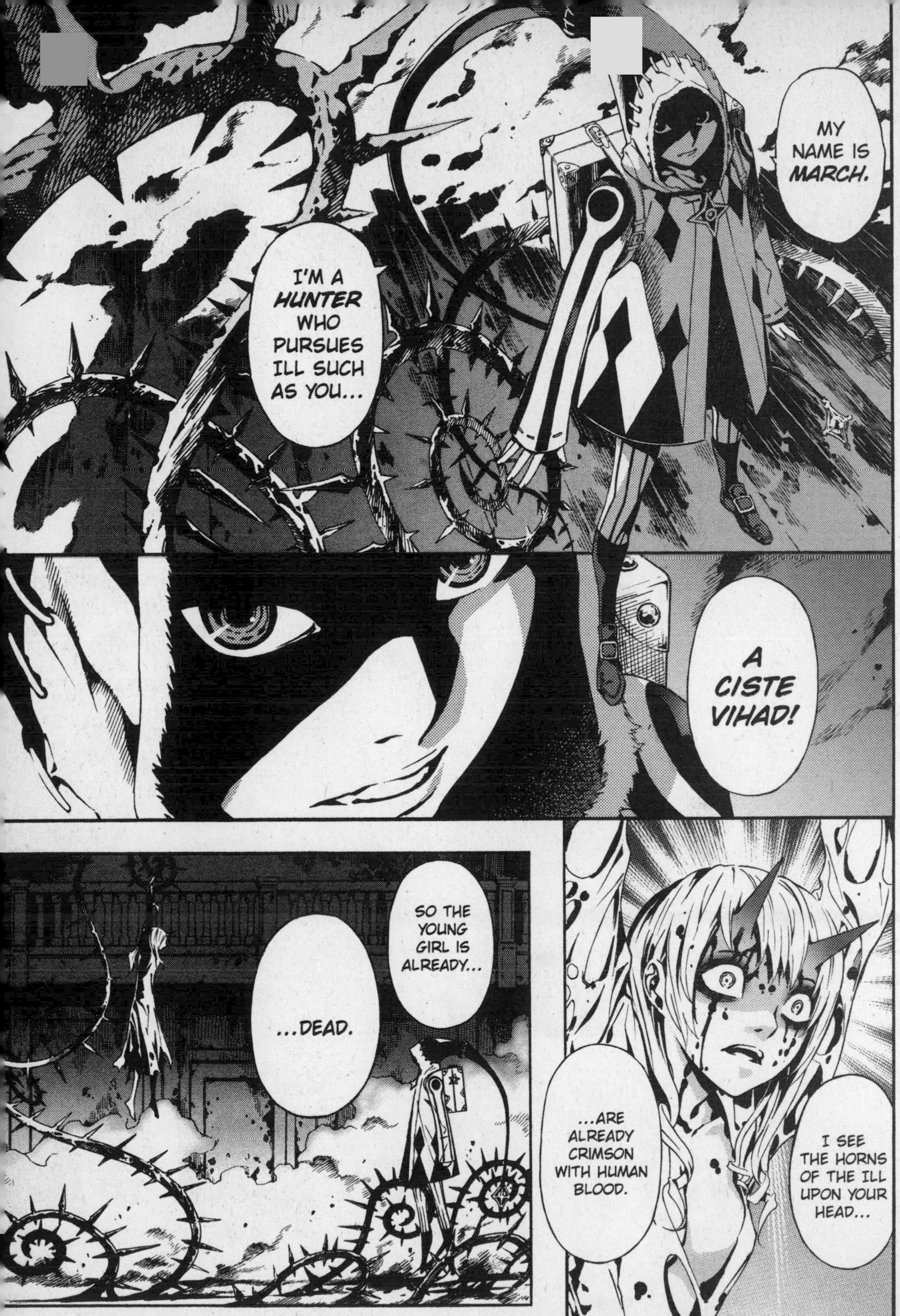
MY NAME IS MARCH.
I'M A HUNTER WHO PURSUES ILL SUCH AS YOU...
A CISTE VIHAD!
I SEE THE HORNS OF THE ILL UPON YOUR HEAD...
...ARE ALREADY CRIMSON WITH HUMAN BLOOD.
SO THE YOUNG GIRL IS ALREADY...
...DEAD.

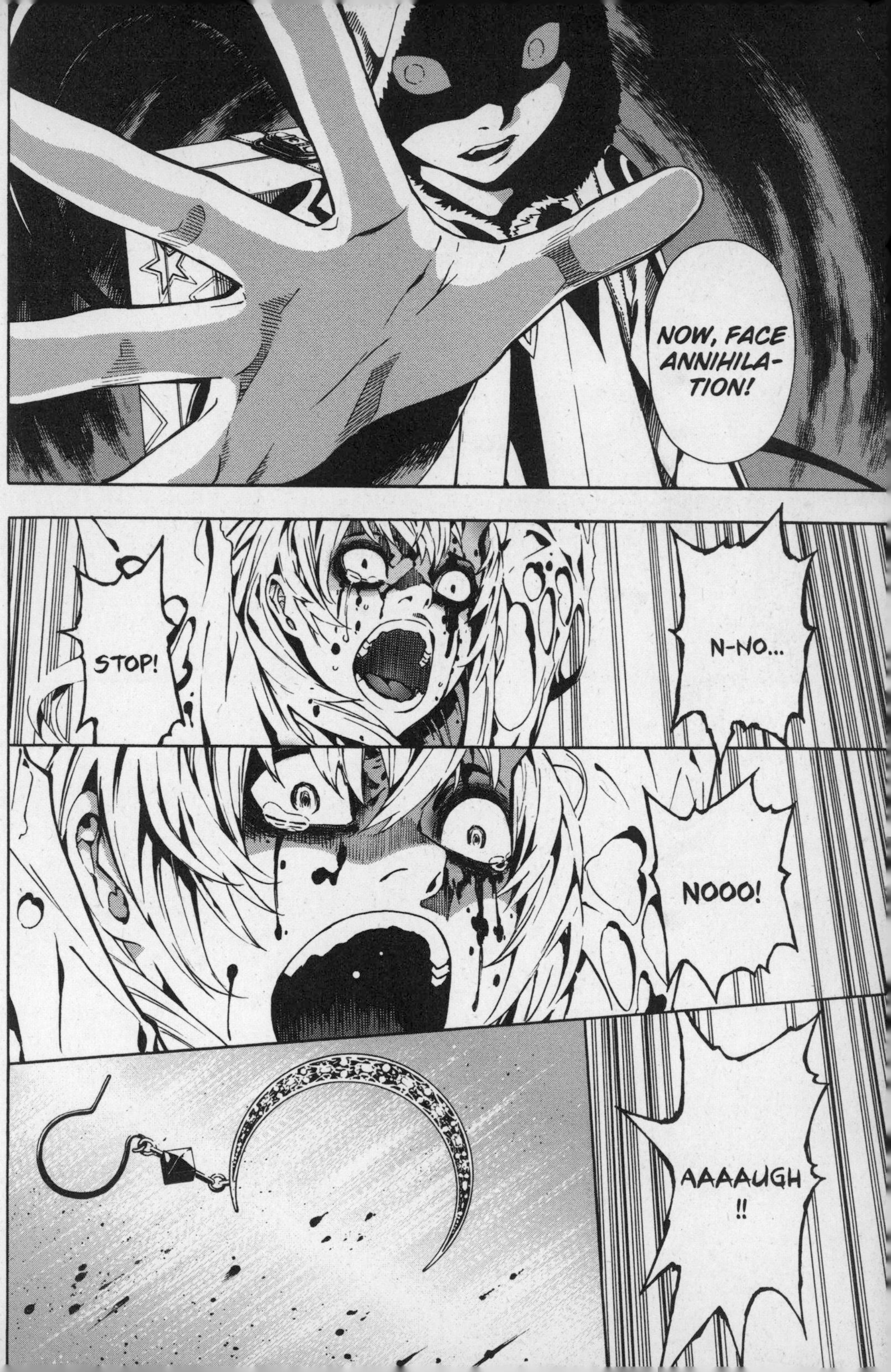
NOW, FACE ANNIHILA- TION!
N-NO...
STOP!
NOOO!
AAAAUGH !!

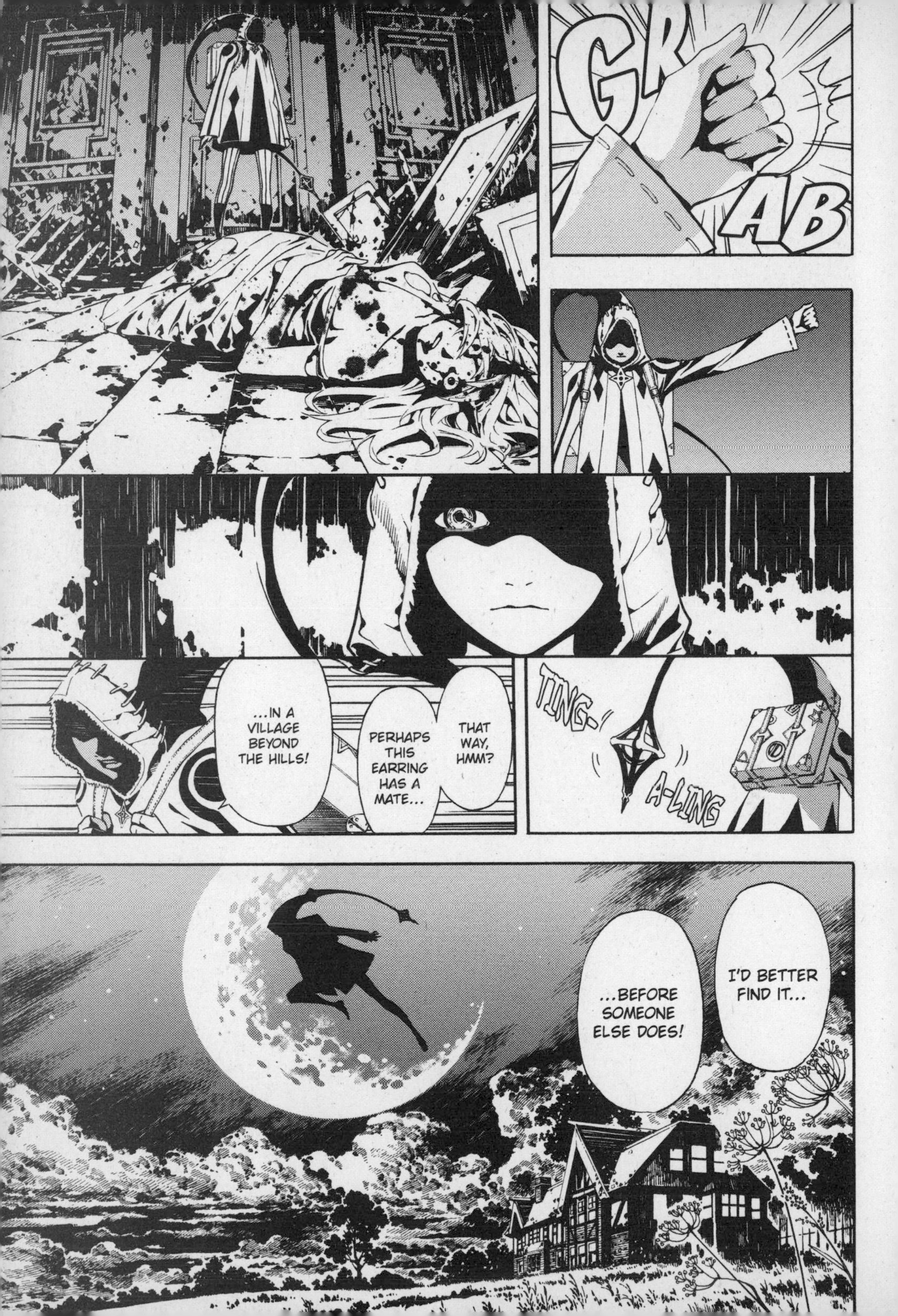
GRAB
TING-A-LING
THAT WAY, HMM?
PERHAPS THIS EARRING HAS A MATE...
...IN A VILLAGE BEYOND THE HILLS!
I'D BETTER FIND IT...
...BEFORE SOMEONE ELSE DOES!

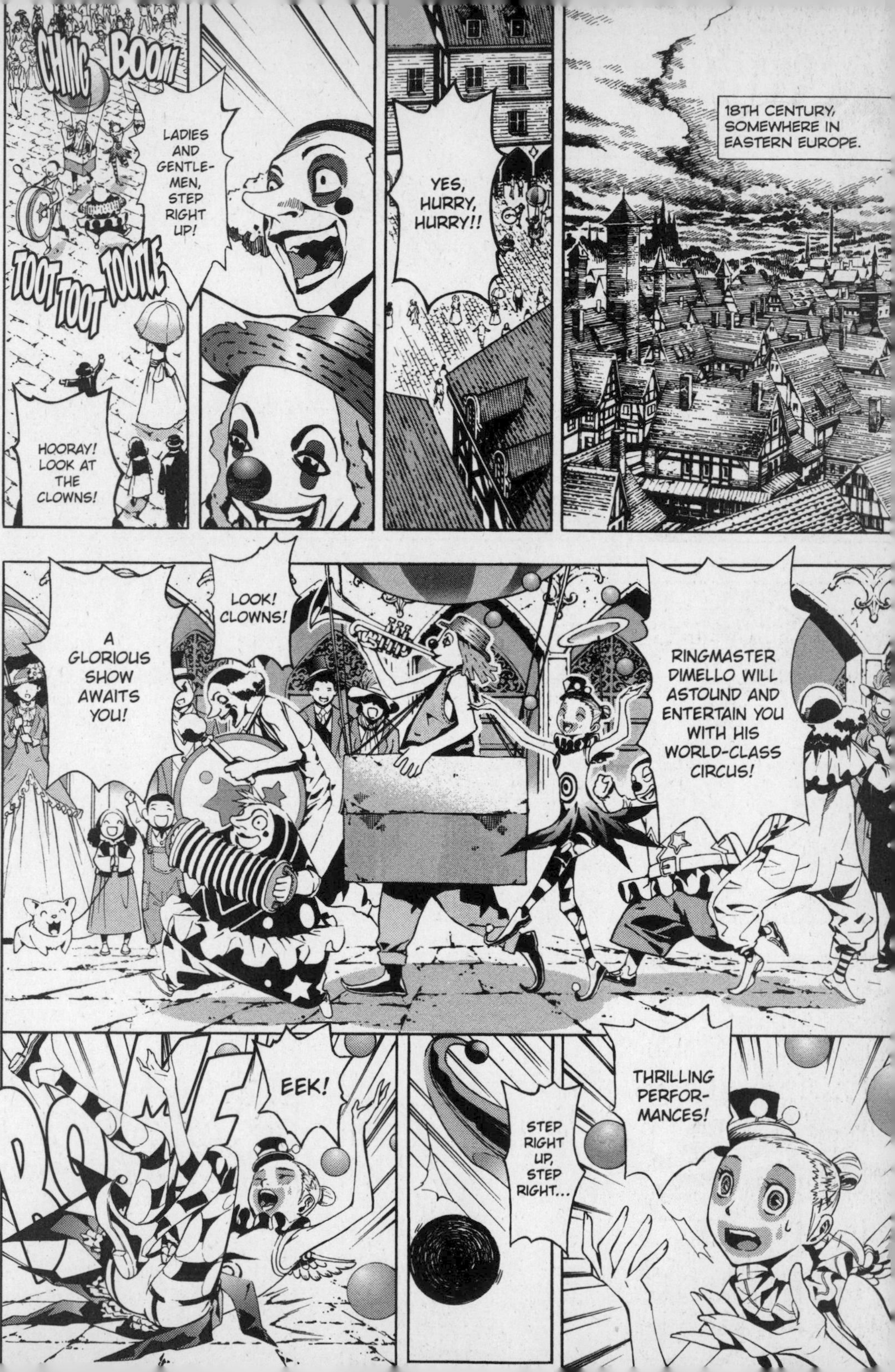
18TH CENTURY, SOMEWHERE IN EASTERN EUROPE.
YES, HURRY, HURRY!!
LADIES AND GENTLE-MEN, STEP RIGHT UP!
CHING BOOM
TOOT TOOT TOOTLE
HOORAY! LOOK AT THE CLOWNS!
RINGMASTER DIMELLO WILL ASTOUND AND ENTERTAIN YOU WITH HIS WORLD-CLASS CIRCUS!
LOOK! CLOWNS!
A GLORIOUS SHOW AWAITS YOU!
THRILLING PERFOR-MANCES!
STEP RIGHT UP, STEP RIGHT...
EEK!

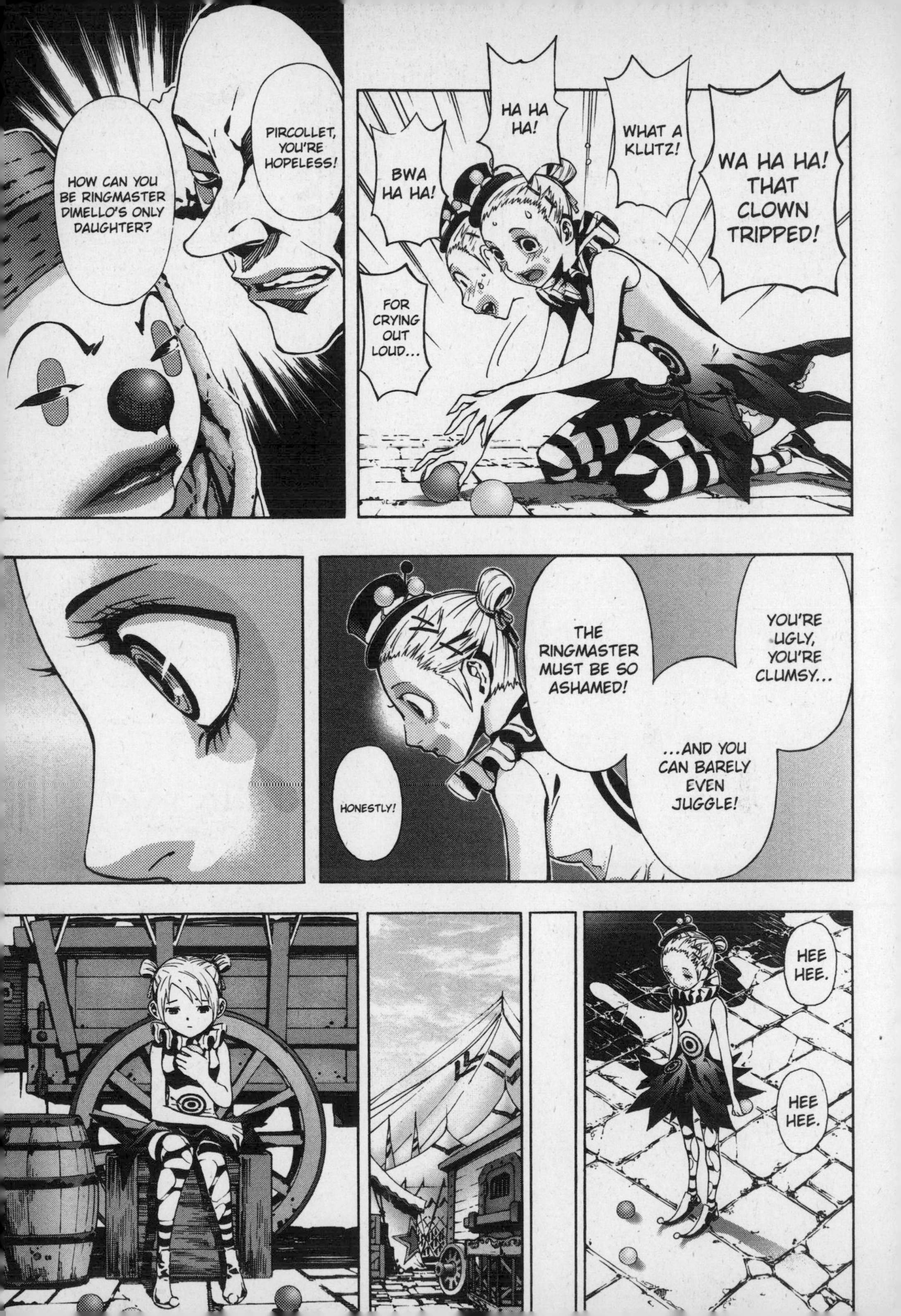
WA HA HA! THAT CLOWN TRIPPED!
WHAT A KLUTZ!
HA HA HA!
BWA HA HA!
FOR CRYING OUT LOUD...
PIRCOLLET, YOU'RE HOPELESS!
HOW CAN YOU BE RINGMASTER DIMELLO'S ONLY DAUGHTER?
YOU'RE UGLY, YOU'RE CLUMSY...
THE RINGMASTER MUST BE SO ASHAMED!
...AND YOU CAN BARELY EVEN JUGGLE!
HONESTLY!
HEE HEE.
HEE HEE.

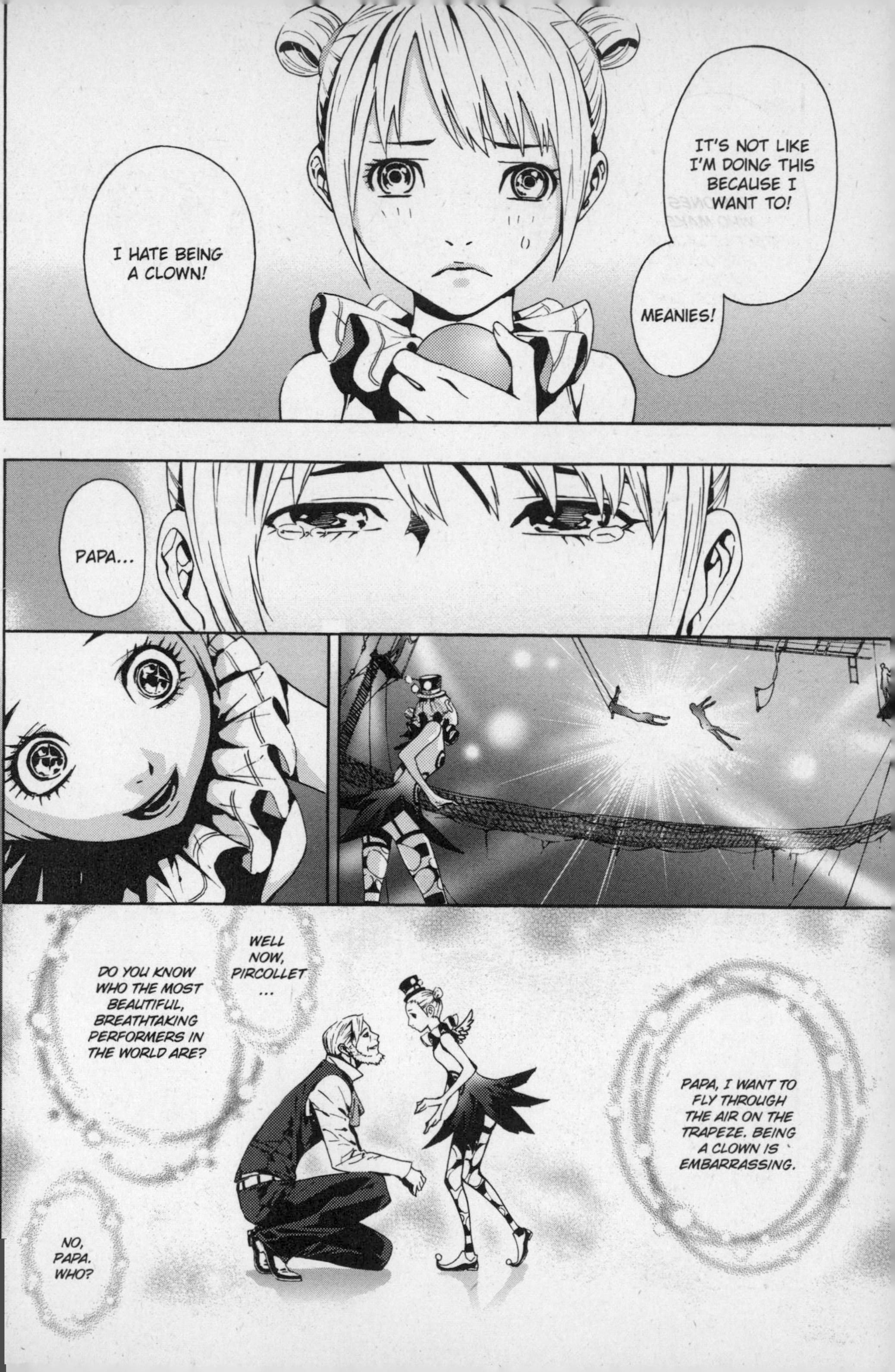
IT'S NOT LIKE I'M DOING THIS BECAUSE I WANT TO!
MEANIES!
I HATE BEING A CLOWN!
PAPA...
PAPA, I WANT TO FLY THROUGH THE AIR ON THE TRAPEZE. BEING A CLOWN IS EMBARRASSING.
WELL NOW, PIRCOLLET...
DO YOU KNOW WHO THE MOST BEAUTIFUL, BREATHTAKING PERFORMERS IN THE WORLD ARE?
NO, PAPA. WHO?

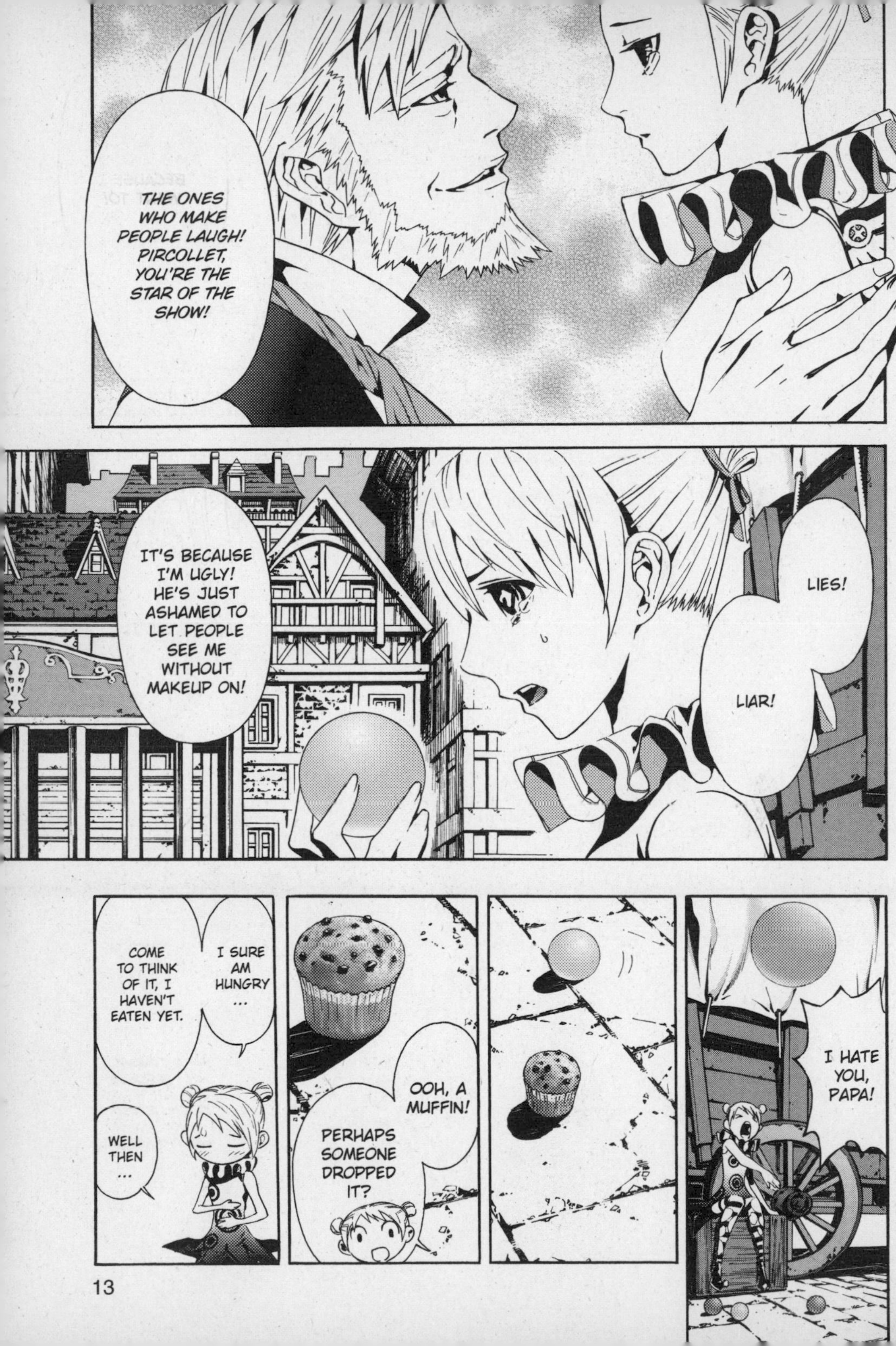
THE ONES WHO MAKE PEOPLE LAUGH! PIRCOLLET, YOU'RE THE STAR OF THE SHOW!
LIES!
LIAR!
IT'S BECAUSE I'M UGLY! HE'S JUST ASHAMED TO LET PEOPLE SEE ME WITHOUT MAKEUP ON!
I HATE YOU, PAPA!
OOH, A MUFFIN!
PERHAPS SOMEONE DROPPED IT?
I SURE AM HUNGRY ...
COME TO THINK OF IT, I HAVEN'T EATEN YET.
WELL THEN ...

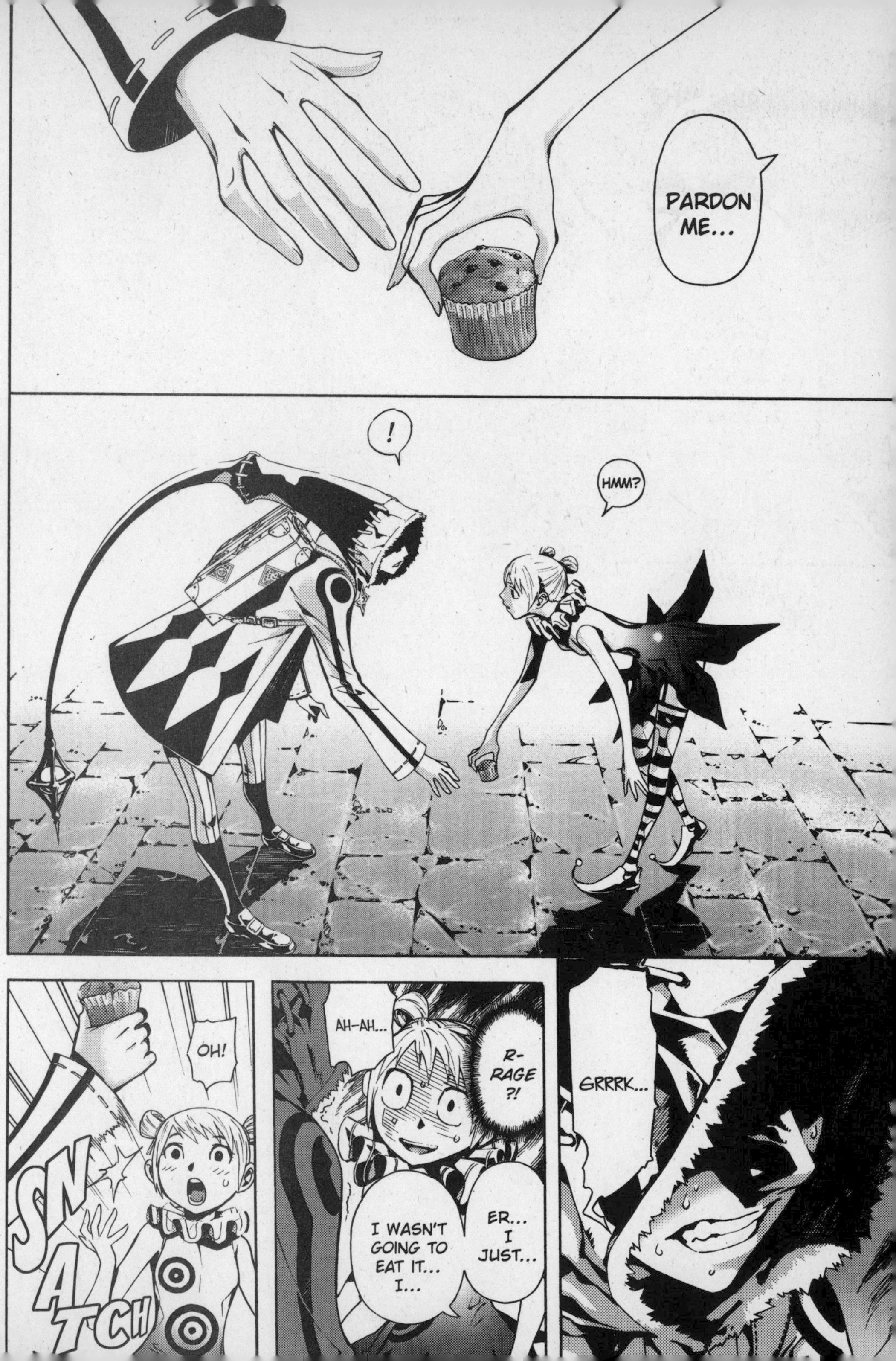
PARDON ME...
HMM?
!
GRRRK...
R-RAGE?!
AH-AH...
ER... I JUST...
I WASN'T GOING TO EAT IT... I...
OH!
SNATCH

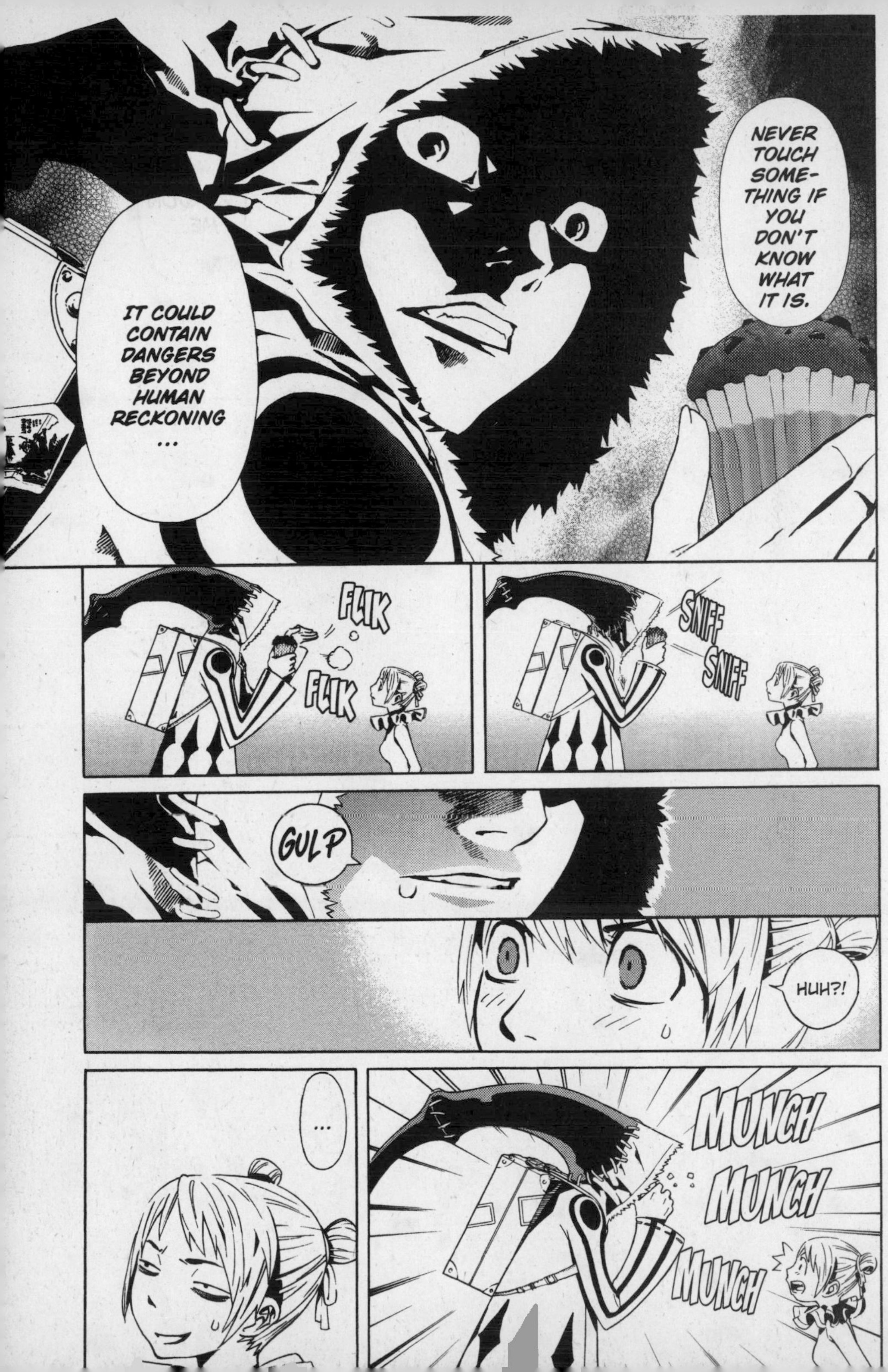
NEVER TOUCH SOME-THING IF YOU DON'T KNOW WHAT IT IS.
IT COULD CONTAIN DANGERS BEYOND HUMAN RECKONING ...
SNIFF
SNIFF
FLIK
FLIK
GULP
HUH?!
MUNCH
MUNCH
MUNCH
...

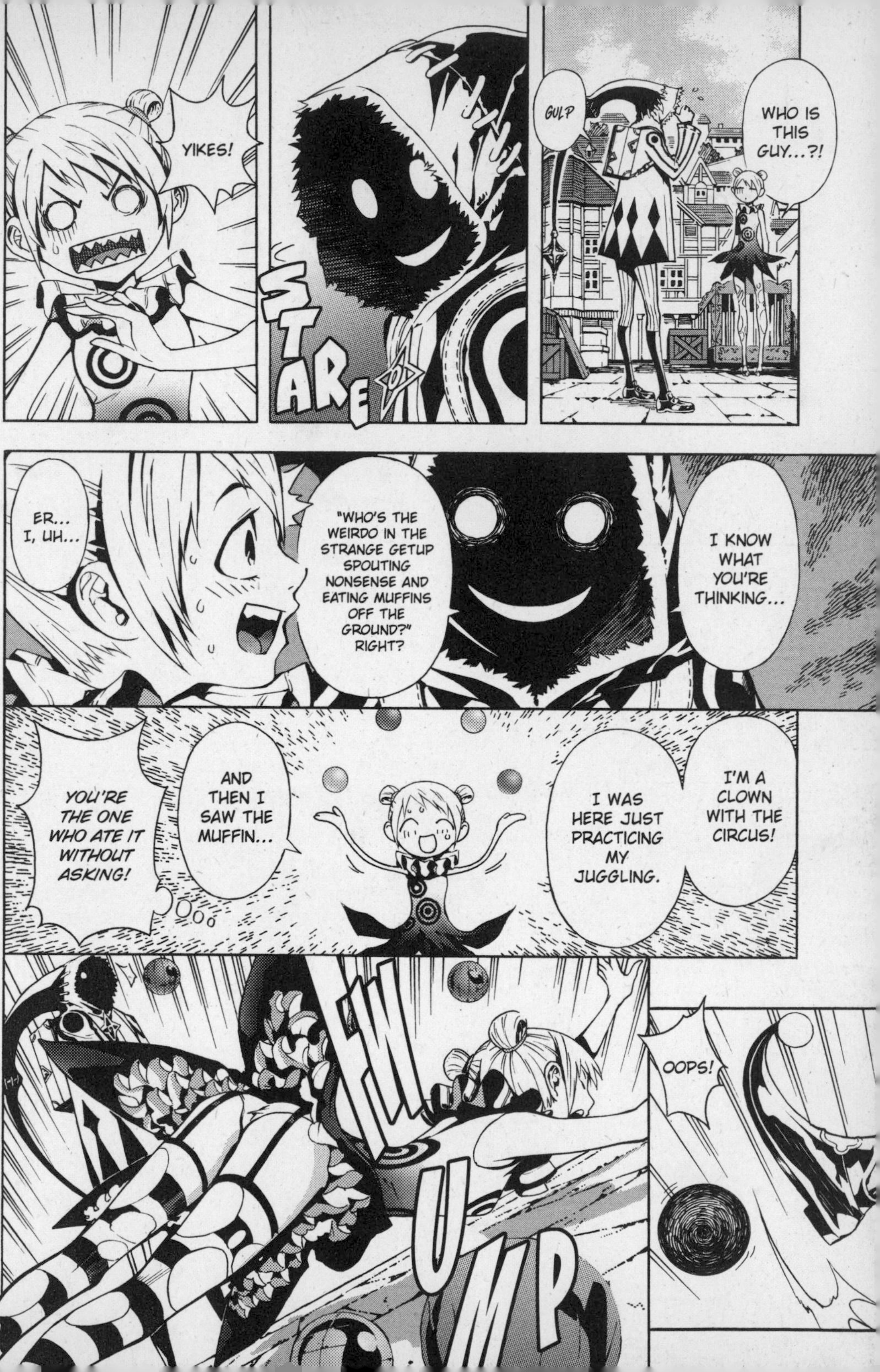
WHO IS THIS GUY...?!
GULP
STARE
YIKES!
I KNOW WHAT YOU'RE THINKING...
"WHO'S THE WEIRDO IN THE STRANGE GETUP SPOUTING NONSENSE AND EATING MUFFINS OFF THE GROUND?" RIGHT?
ER... I, UH...
I'M A CLOWN WITH THE CIRCUS!
I WAS HERE JUST PRACTICING MY JUGGLING.
AND THEN I SAW THE MUFFIN...
YOU'RE THE ONE WHO ATE IT WITHOUT ASKING!
OOPS!
THUMP

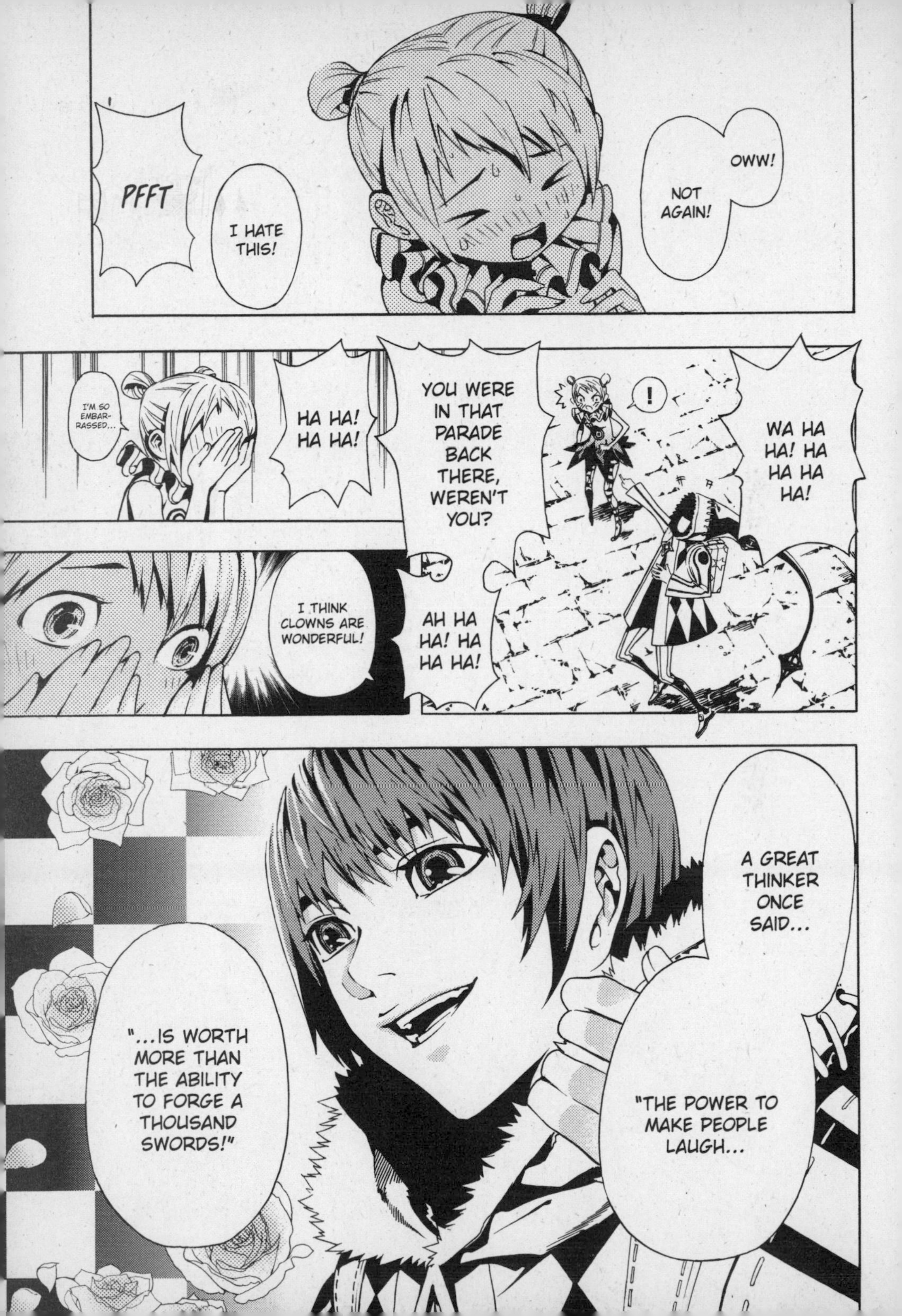
OWW!
NOT AGAIN!
I HATE THIS!
PFFT
WA HA HA! HA HA HA HA!
!
YOU WERE IN THAT PARADE BACK THERE, WEREN'T YOU?
AH HA HA! HA HA HA!
HA HA! HA HA!
I'M SO EMBARRASSED...
I THINK CLOWNS ARE WONDERFUL!
A GREAT THINKER ONCE SAID...
"THE POWER TO MAKE PEOPLE LAUGH...
"...IS WORTH MORE THAN THE ABILITY TO FORGE A THOUSAND SWORDS!"

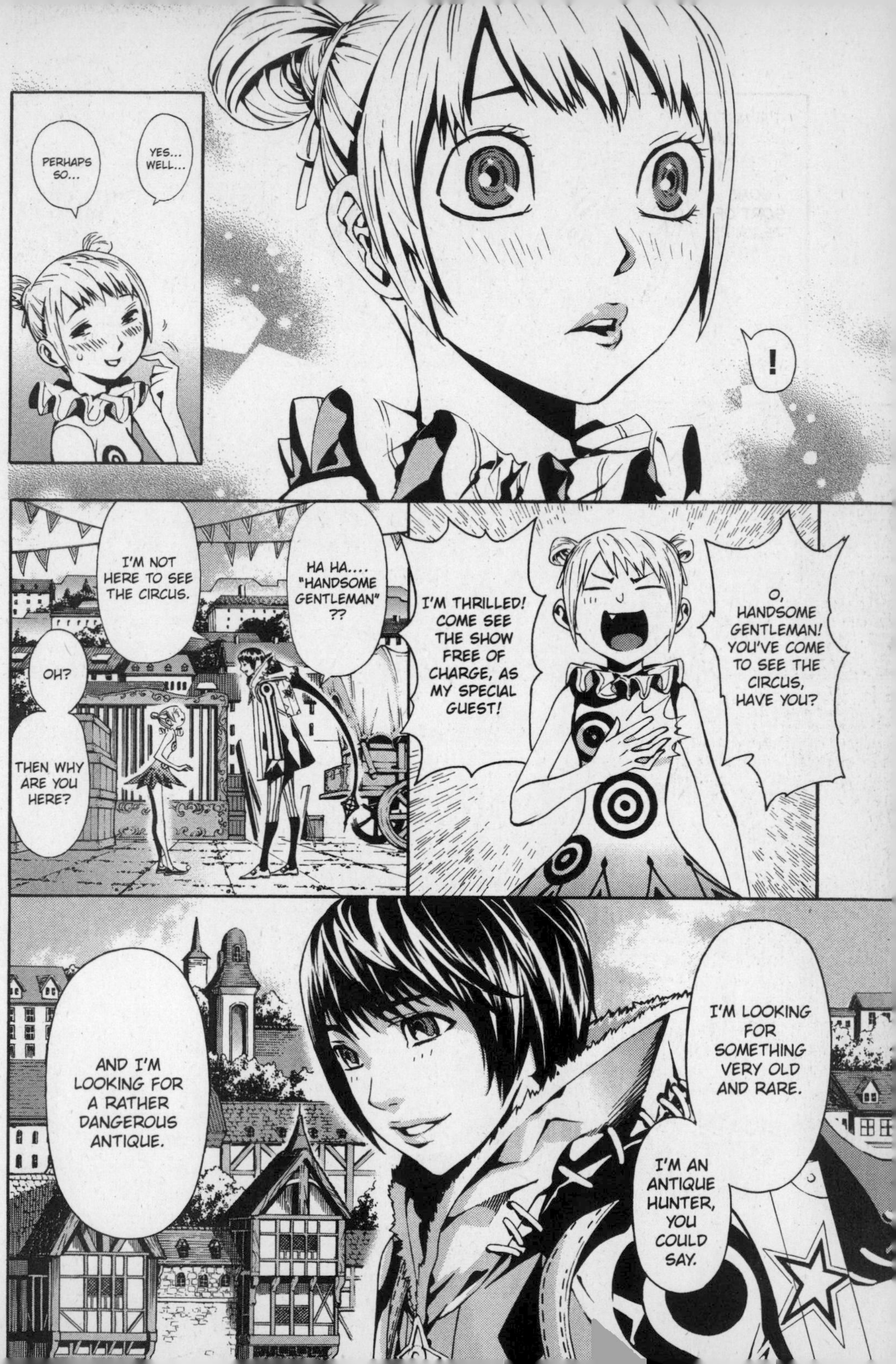
!
YES... WELL...
PERHAPS SO...
O, HANDSOME GENTLEMAN! YOU'VE COME TO SEE THE CIRCUS, HAVE YOU?
I'M THRILLED! COME SEE THE SHOW FREE OF CHARGE, AS MY SPECIAL GUEST!
HA HA.... "HANDSOME GENTLEMAN" ??
I'M NOT HERE TO SEE THE CIRCUS.
OH?
THEN WHY ARE YOU HERE?
I'M LOOKING FOR SOMETHING VERY OLD AND RARE.
I'M AN ANTIQUE HUNTER, YOU COULD SAY.
AND I'M LOOKING FOR A RATHER DANGEROUS ANTIQUE.

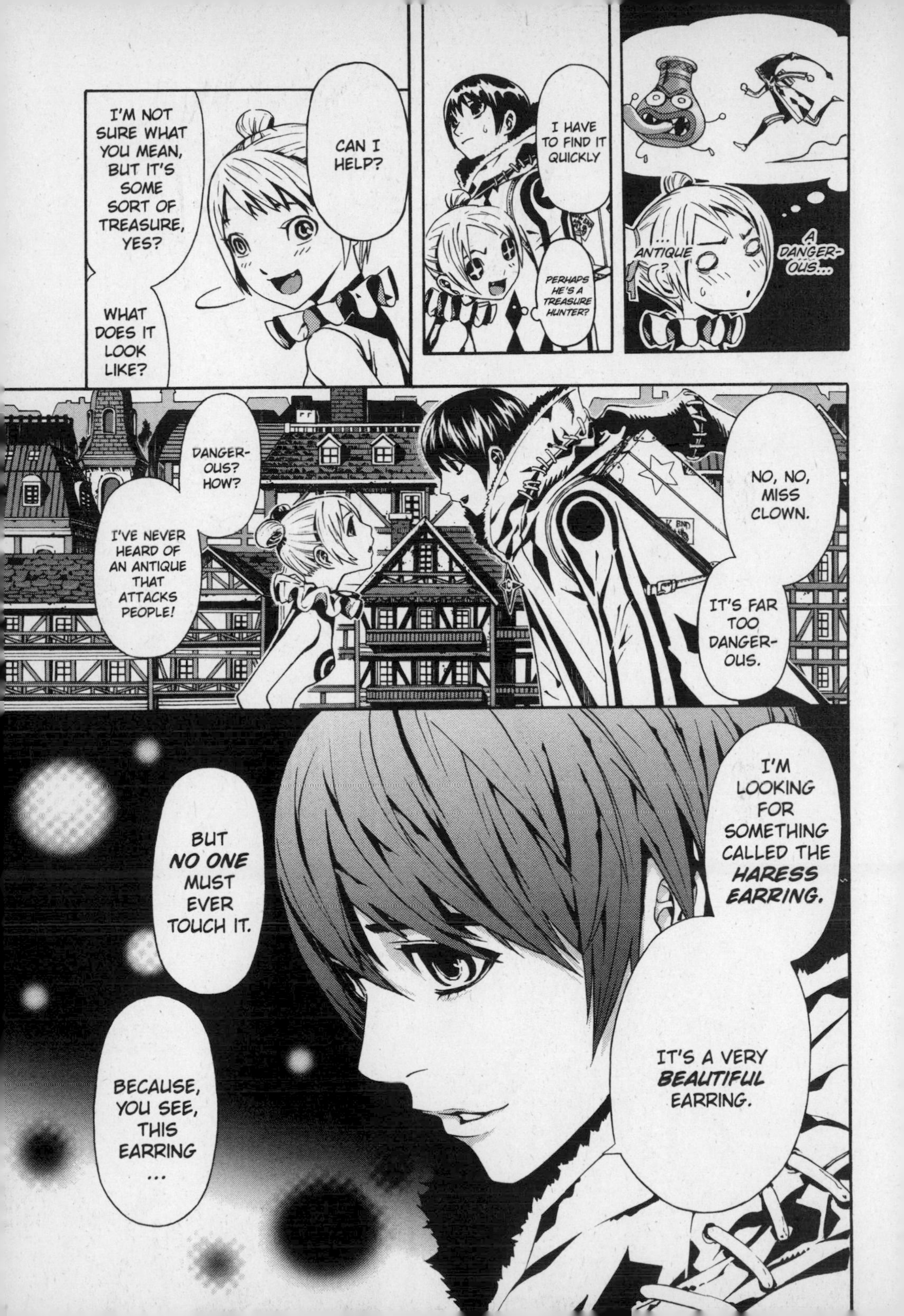
A DANGER-OUS...
...ANTIQUE?
I HAVE TO FIND IT QUICKLY
PERHAPS HE'S A TREASURE HUNTER?
CAN I HELP?
I'M NOT SURE WHAT YOU MEAN, BUT IT'S SOME SORT OF TREASURE, YES?
WHAT DOES IT LOOK LIKE?
NO, NO, MISS CLOWN.
IT'S FAR TOO DANGER-OUS.
DANGER-OUS? HOW?
I'VE NEVER HEARD OF AN ANTIQUE THAT ATTACKS PEOPLE!
I'M LOOKING FOR SOMETHING CALLED THE HARESS EARRING.
IT'S A VERY BEAUTIFUL EARRING.
BUT NO ONE MUST EVER TOUCH IT.
BECAUSE, YOU SEE, THIS EARRING ...

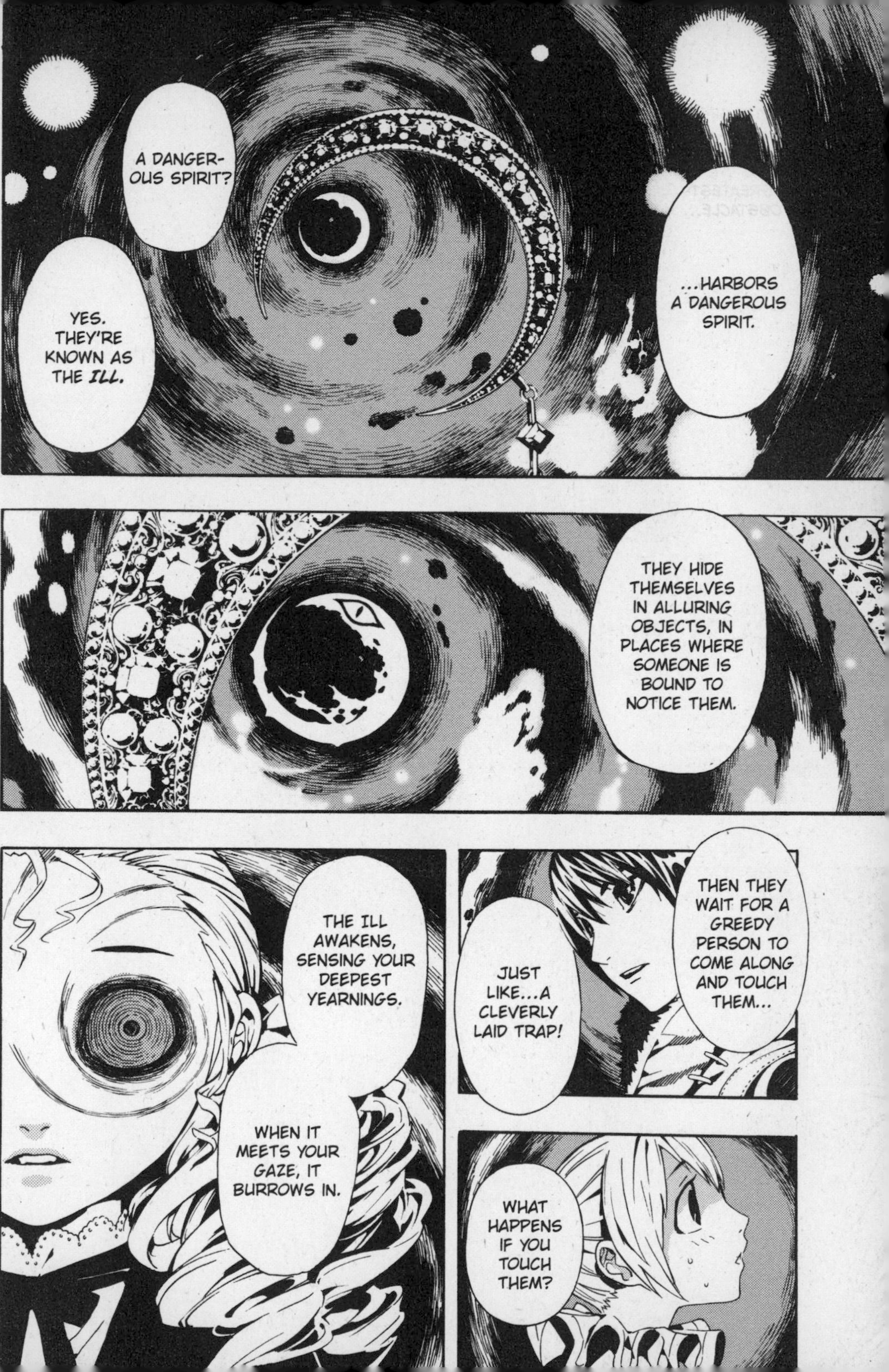
...HARBORS A DANGEROUS SPIRIT.
A DANGER-OUS SPIRIT?
YES. THEY'RE KNOWN AS THE *ILL*.
THEY HIDE THEMSELVES IN ALLURING OBJECTS, IN PLACES WHERE SOMEONE IS BOUND TO NOTICE THEM.
THEN THEY WAIT FOR A GREEDY PERSON TO COME ALONG AND TOUCH THEM...
JUST LIKE...A CLEVERLY LAID TRAP!
WHAT HAPPENS IF YOU TOUCH THEM?
THE ILL AWAKENS, SENSING YOUR DEEPEST YEARNINGS.
WHEN IT MEETS YOUR GAZE, IT BURROWS IN.

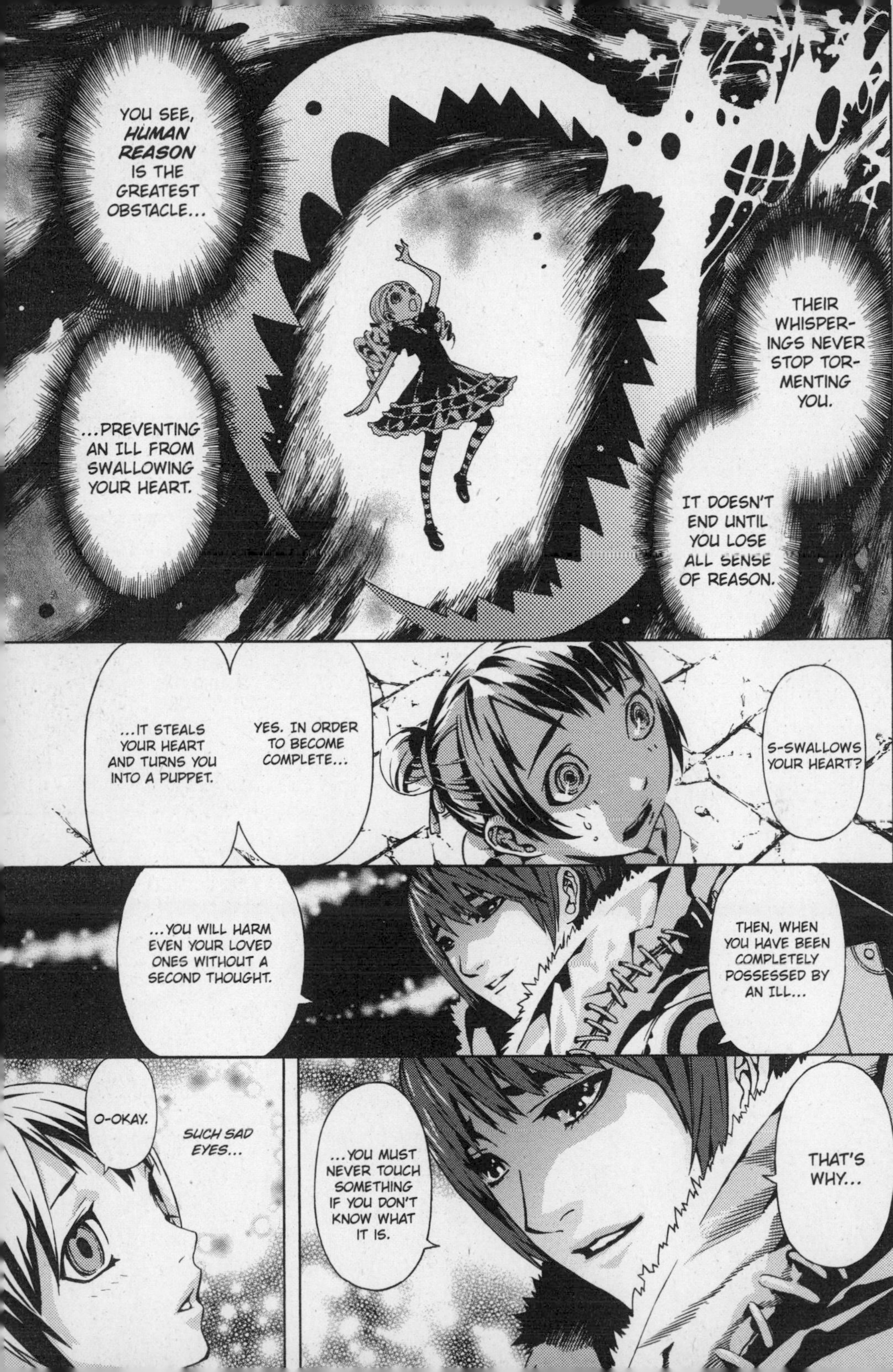
THEIR WHISPERINGS NEVER STOP TORMENTING YOU.
IT DOESN'T END UNTIL YOU LOSE ALL SENSE OF REASON.
YOU SEE, *HUMAN REASON* IS THE GREATEST OBSTACLE...
...PREVENTING AN ILL FROM SWALLOWING YOUR HEART.
S-SWALLOWS YOUR HEART?
YES. IN ORDER TO BECOME COMPLETE...
...IT STEALS YOUR HEART AND TURNS YOU INTO A PUPPET.
THEN, WHEN YOU HAVE BEEN COMPLETELY POSSESSED BY AN ILL...
...YOU WILL HARM EVEN YOUR LOVED ONES WITHOUT A SECOND THOUGHT.
THAT'S WHY...
...YOU MUST NEVER TOUCH SOMETHING IF YOU DON'T KNOW WHAT IT IS.
O-OKAY.
SUCH SAD EYES...

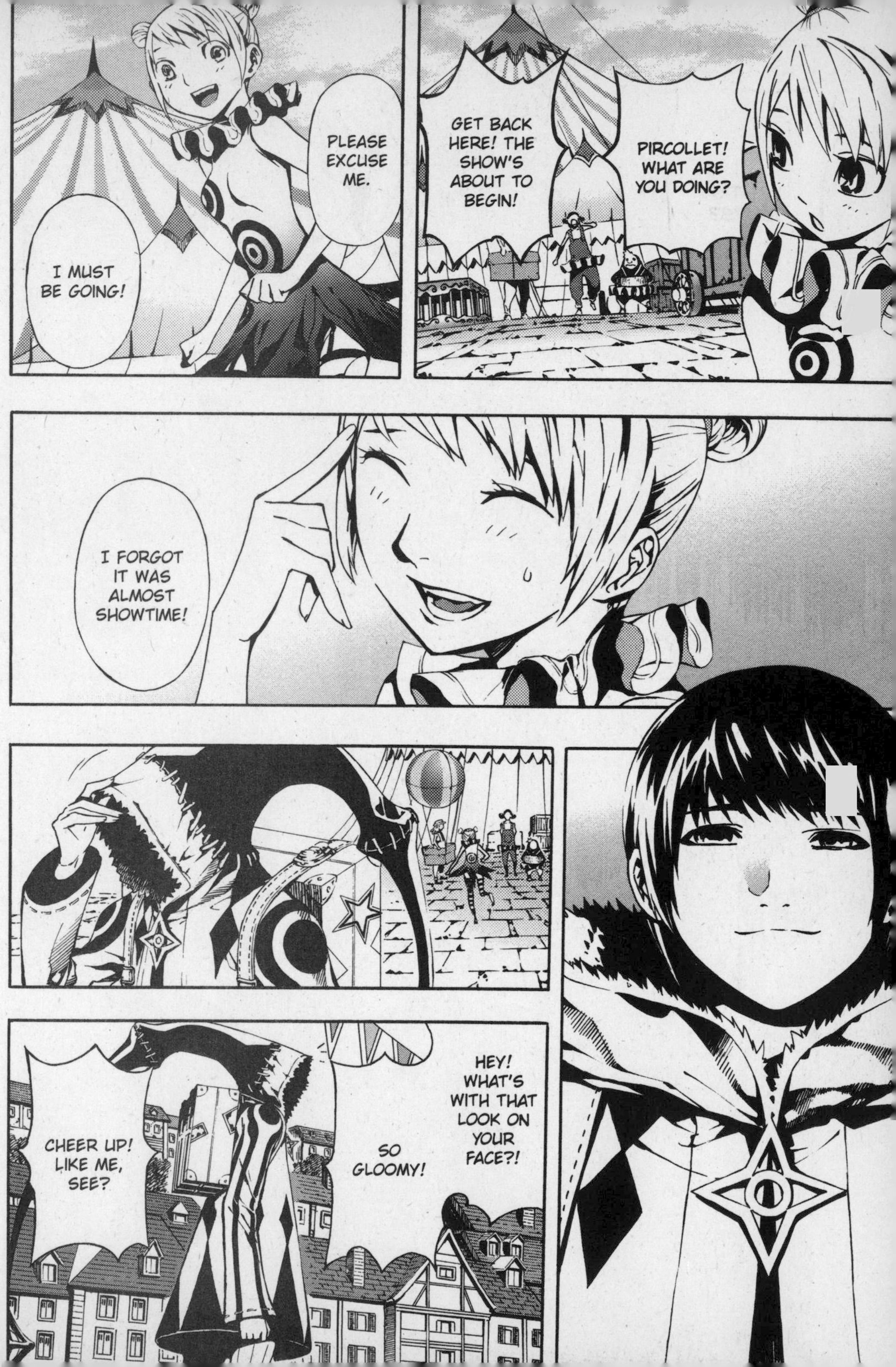
PIRCOLLET! WHAT ARE YOU DOING?
GET BACK HERE! THE SHOW'S ABOUT TO BEGIN!
PLEASE EXCUSE ME.
I MUST BE GOING!
I FORGOT IT WAS ALMOST SHOWTIME!
HEY! WHAT'S WITH THAT LOOK ON YOUR FACE?!
SO GLOOMY!
CHEER UP! LIKE ME, SEE?

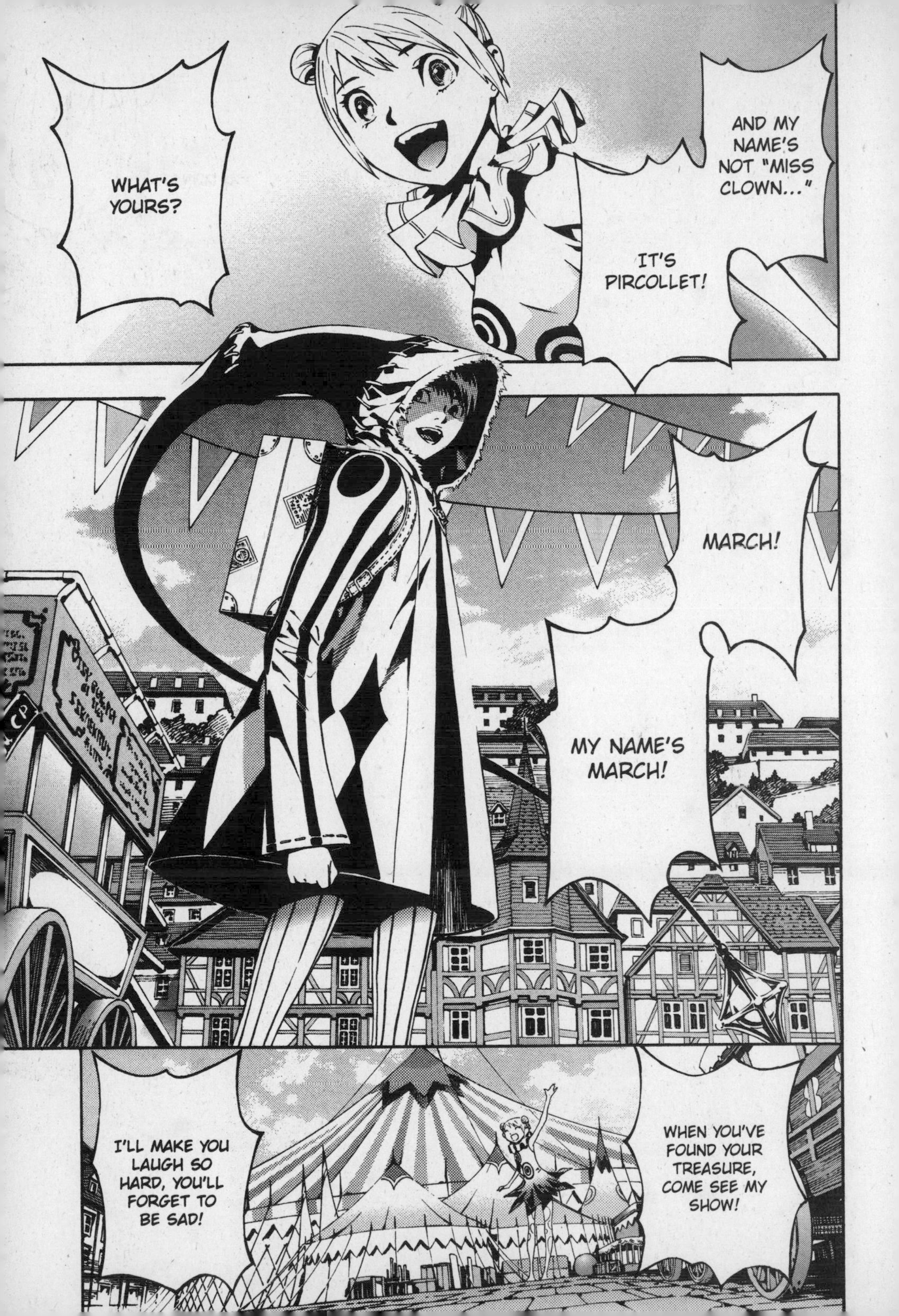
AND MY NAME'S NOT "MISS CLOWN..."
IT'S PIRCOLLET!
WHAT'S YOURS?
MARCH!
MY NAME'S MARCH!
WHEN YOU'VE FOUND YOUR TREASURE, COME SEE MY SHOW!
I'LL MAKE YOU LAUGH SO HARD, YOU'LL FORGET TO BE SAD!

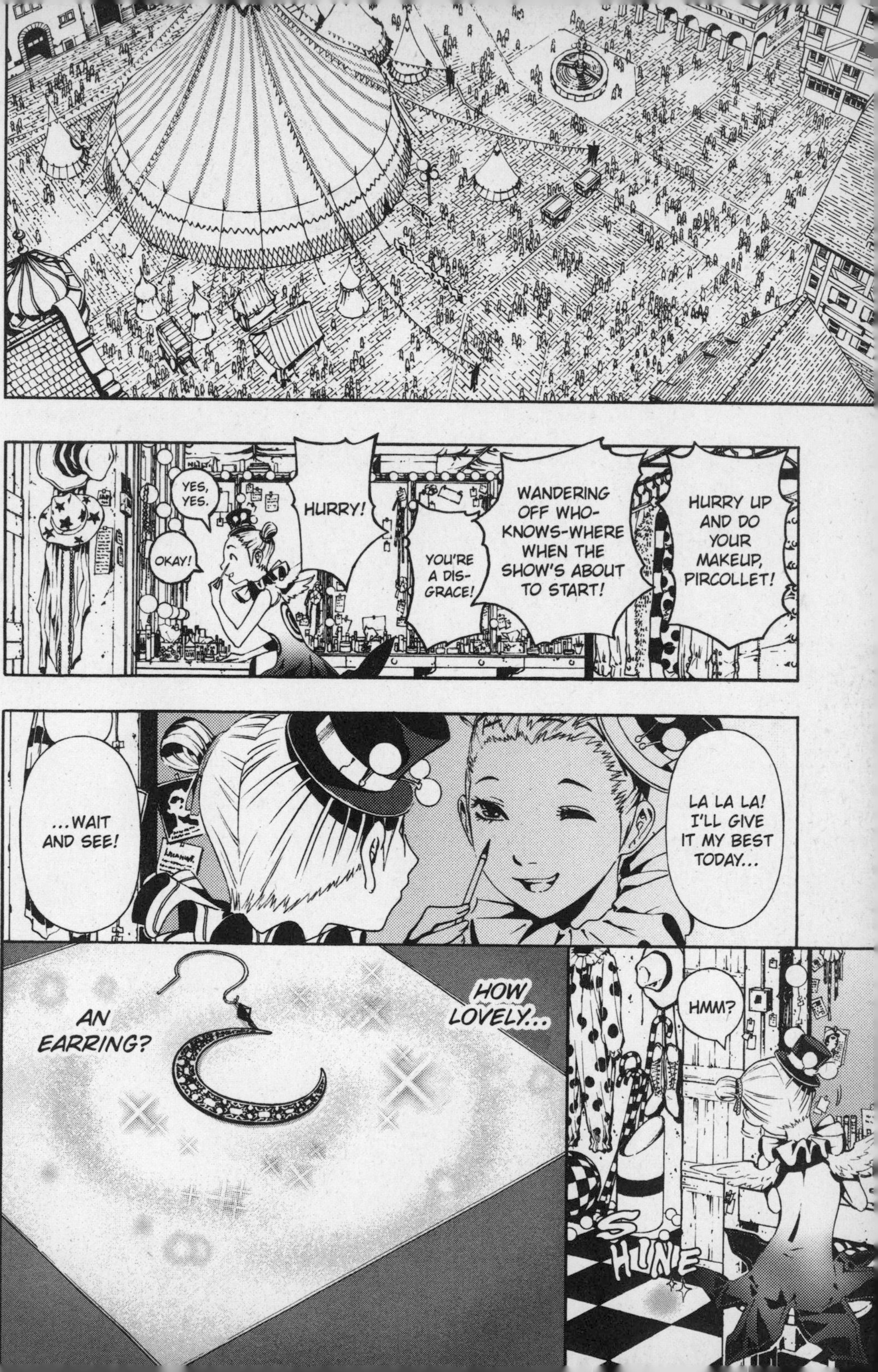
HURRY UP AND DO YOUR MAKEUP, PIRCOLLET!
WANDERING OFF WHO-KNOWS-WHERE WHEN THE SHOW'S ABOUT TO START!
YOU'RE A DIS-GRACE!
HURRY!
YES, YES.
OKAY!
LA LA LA! I'LL GIVE IT MY BEST TODAY...
...WAIT AND SEE!
HMM?
SHUNE
HOW LOVELY...
AN EARRING?

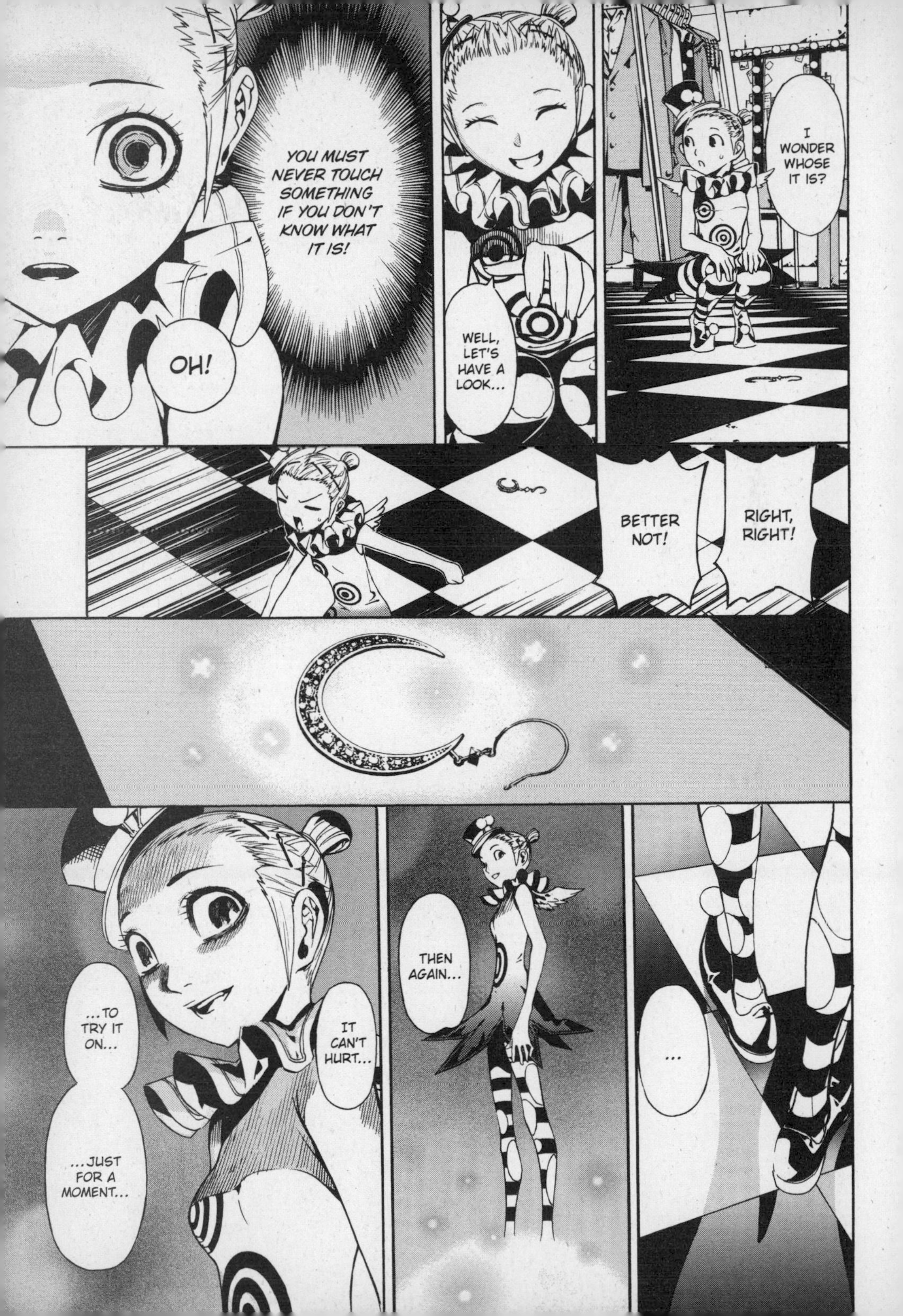
I WONDER WHOSE IT IS?
WELL, LET'S HAVE A LOOK...
YOU MUST NEVER TOUCH SOMETHING IF YOU DON'T KNOW WHAT IT IS!
OH!
RIGHT, RIGHT!
BETTER NOT!
...
THEN AGAIN...
IT CAN'T HURT...
...TO TRY IT ON...
...JUST FOR A MOMENT...

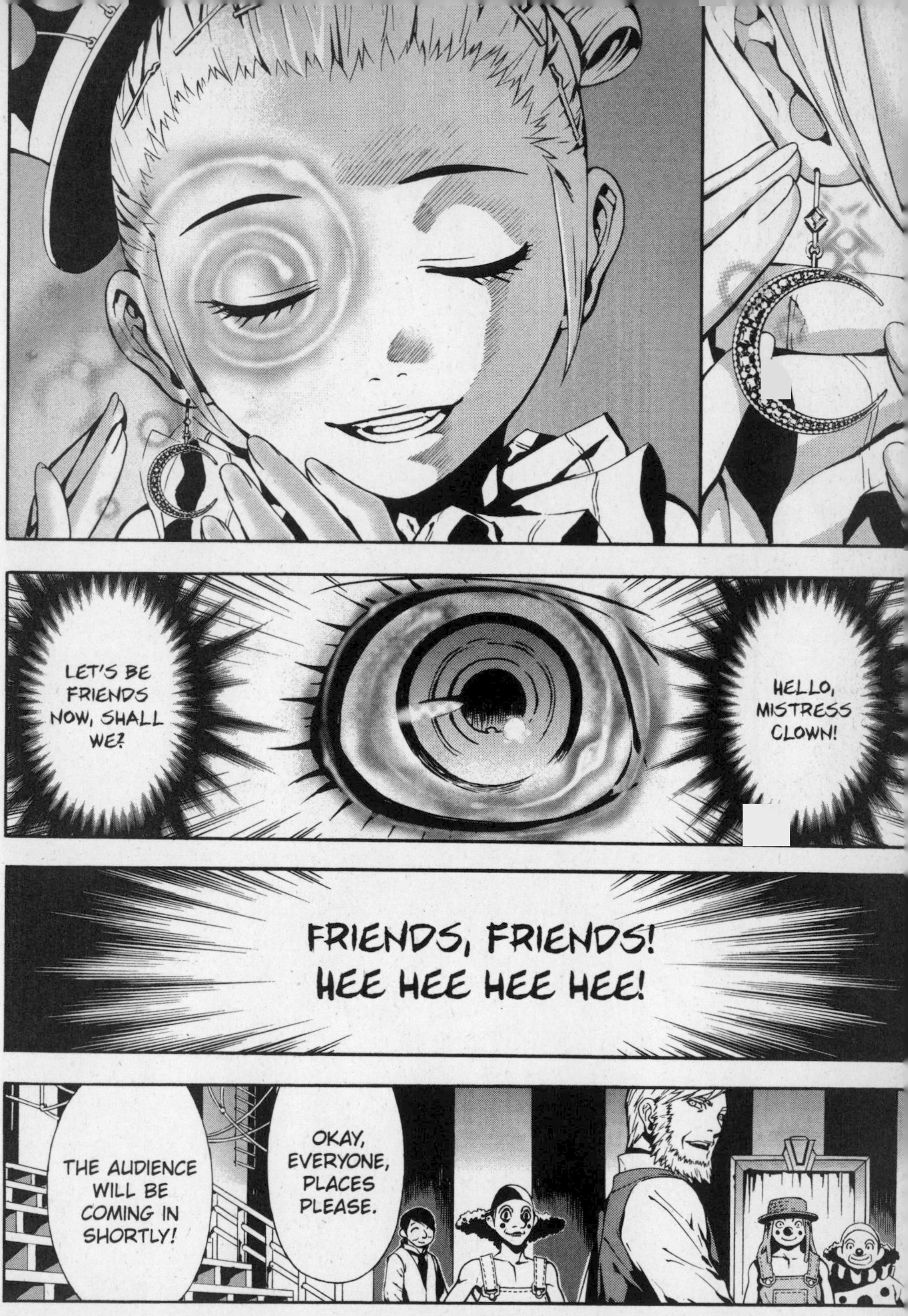
HELLO, MISTRESS CLOWN!
LET'S BE FRIENDS NOW, SHALL WE?
FRIENDS, FRIENDS! HEE HEE HEE HEE!
OKAY, EVERYONE, PLACES PLEASE.
THE AUDIENCE WILL BE COMING IN SHORTLY!

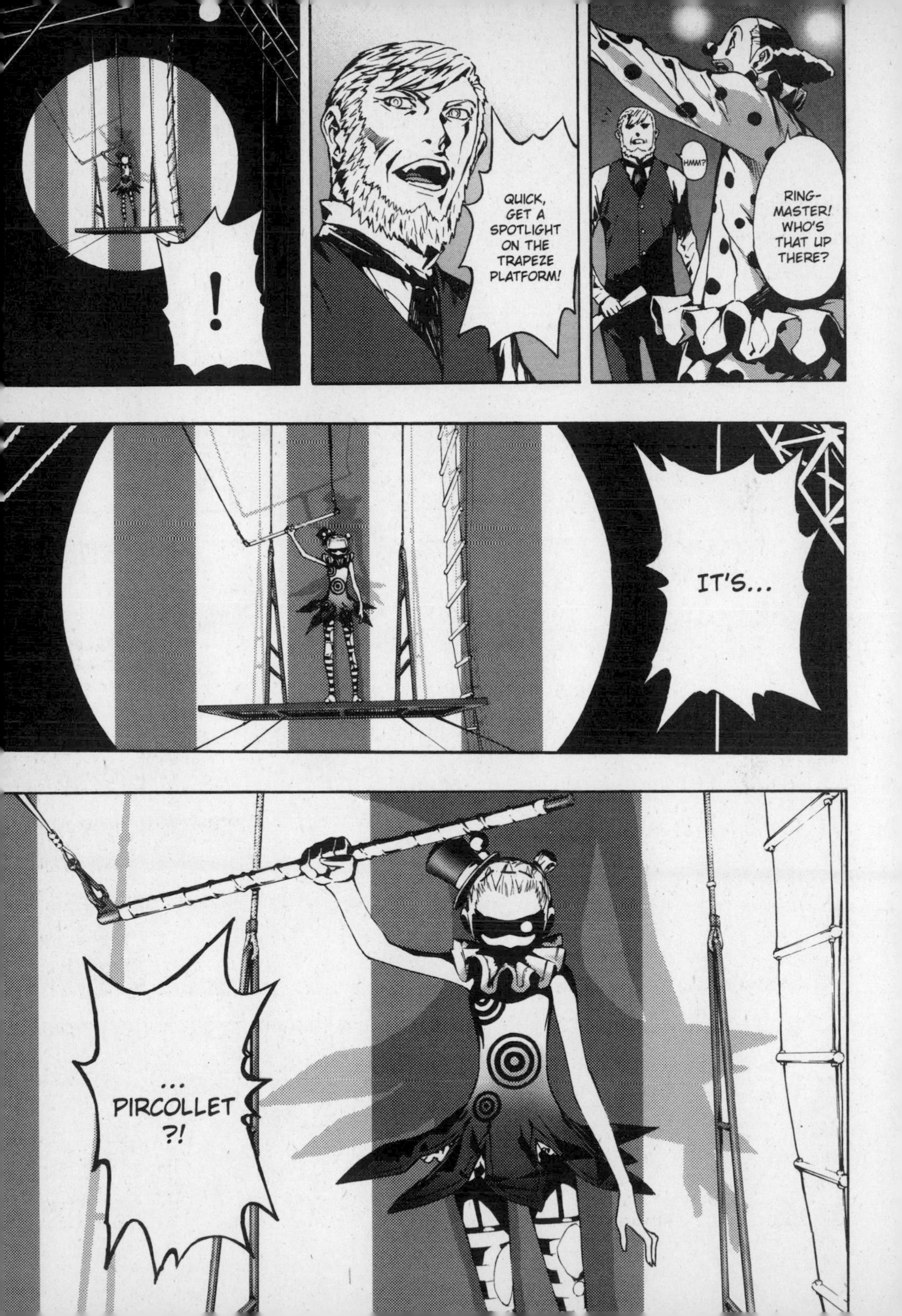
RING-MASTER! WHO'S THAT UP THERE?
HMM?
QUICK, GET A SPOTLIGHT ON THE TRAPEZE PLATFORM!
!
IT'S...
...PIRCOLLET ?!

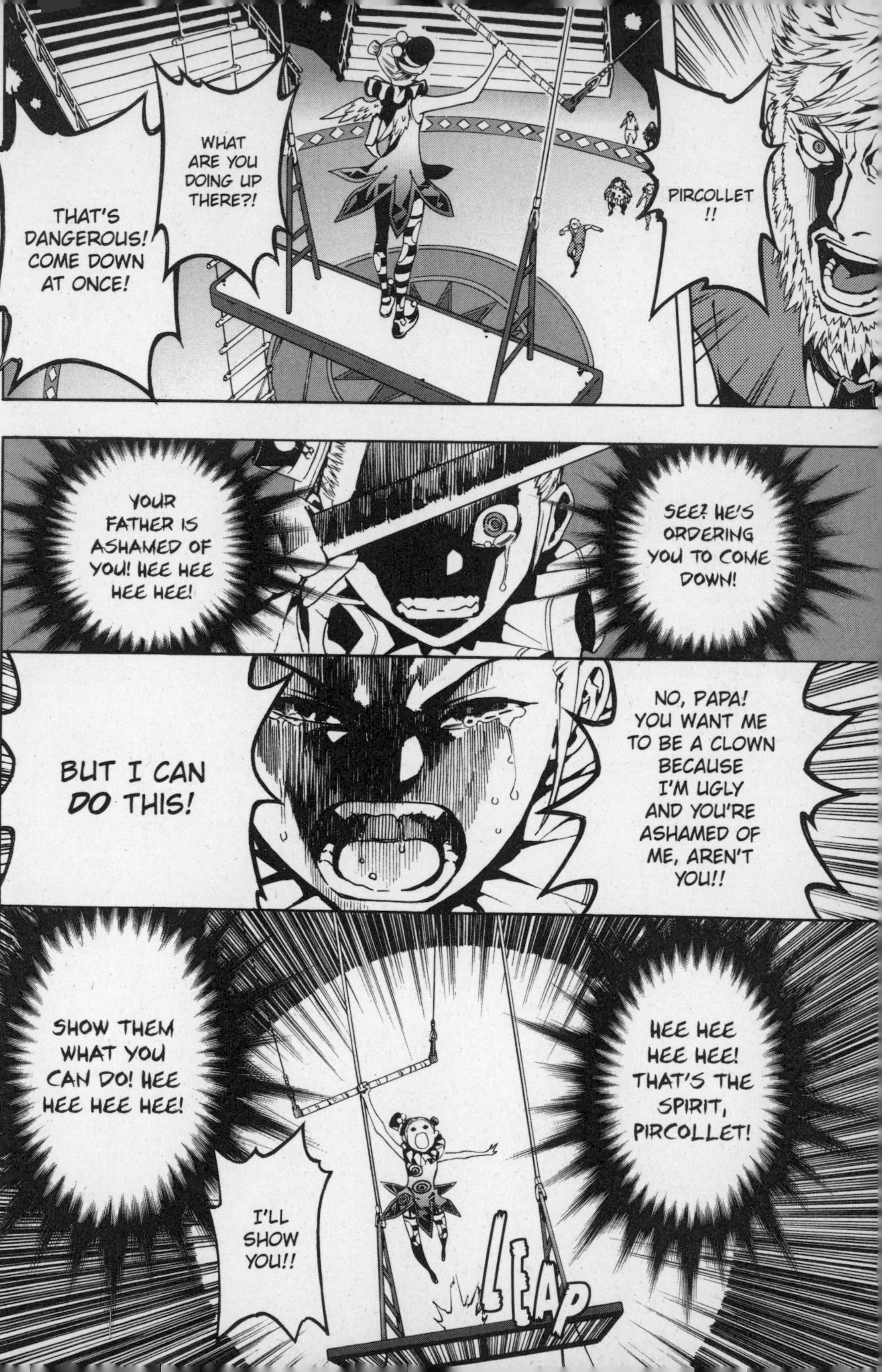
PIRCOLLET !!
WHAT ARE YOU DOING UP THERE?!
THAT'S DANGEROUS! COME DOWN AT ONCE!
SEE? HE'S ORDERING YOU TO COME DOWN!
YOUR FATHER IS ASHAMED OF YOU! HEE HEE HEE HEE!
NO, PAPA! YOU WANT ME TO BE A CLOWN BECAUSE I'M UGLY AND YOU'RE ASHAMED OF ME, AREN'T YOU!!
BUT I CAN *DO* THIS!
HEE HEE HEE HEE! THAT'S THE SPIRIT, PIRCOLLET!
SHOW THEM WHAT YOU CAN DO! HEE HEE HEE HEE!
I'LL SHOW YOU!!
LEAP

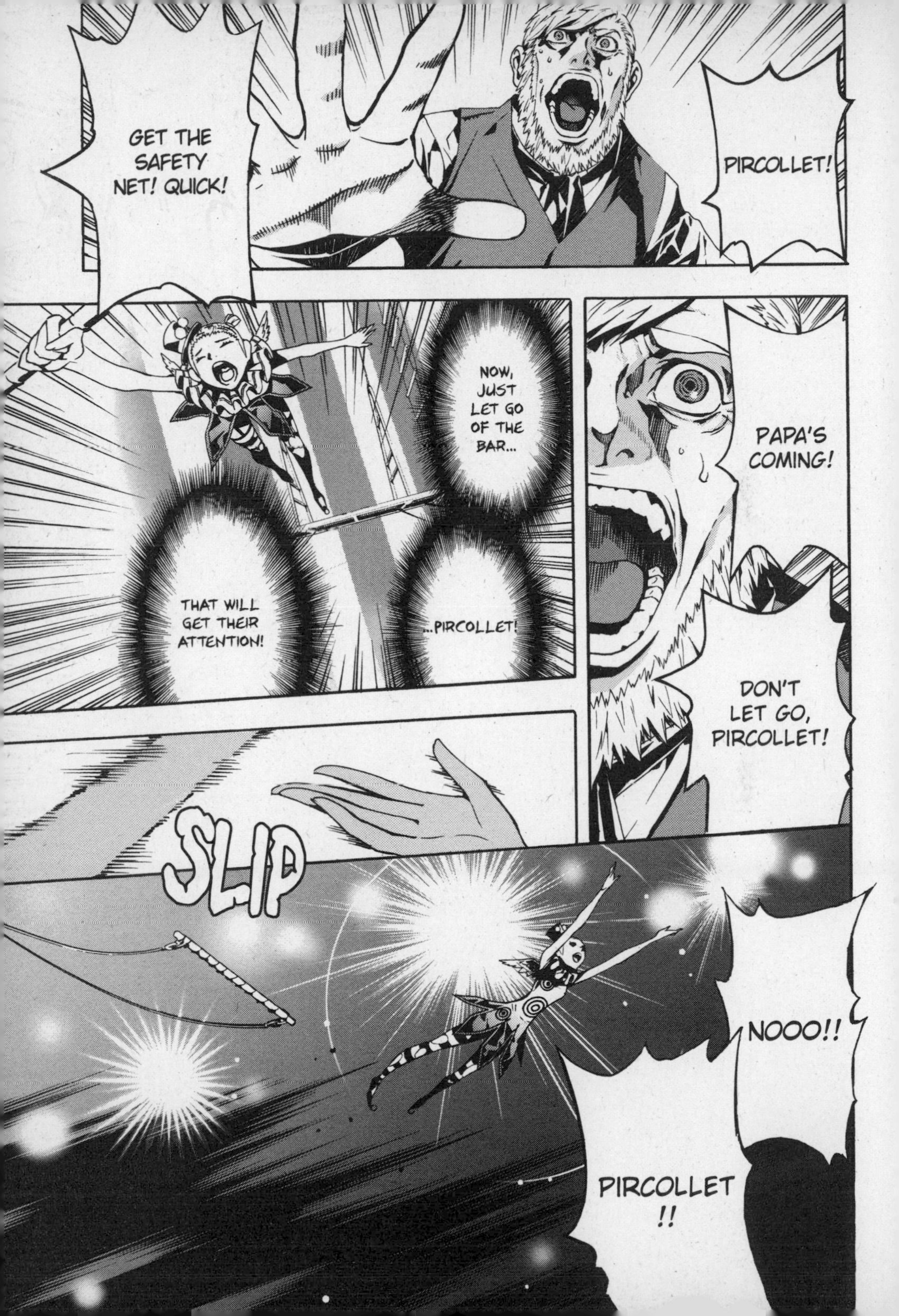
PIRCOLLET!
GET THE SAFETY NET! QUICK!
PAPA'S COMING!
DON'T LET GO, PIRCOLLET!
NOW, JUST LET GO OF THE BAR...
...PIRCOLLET!
THAT WILL GET THEIR ATTENTION!
SLIP
NOOO!!
PIRCOLLET !!

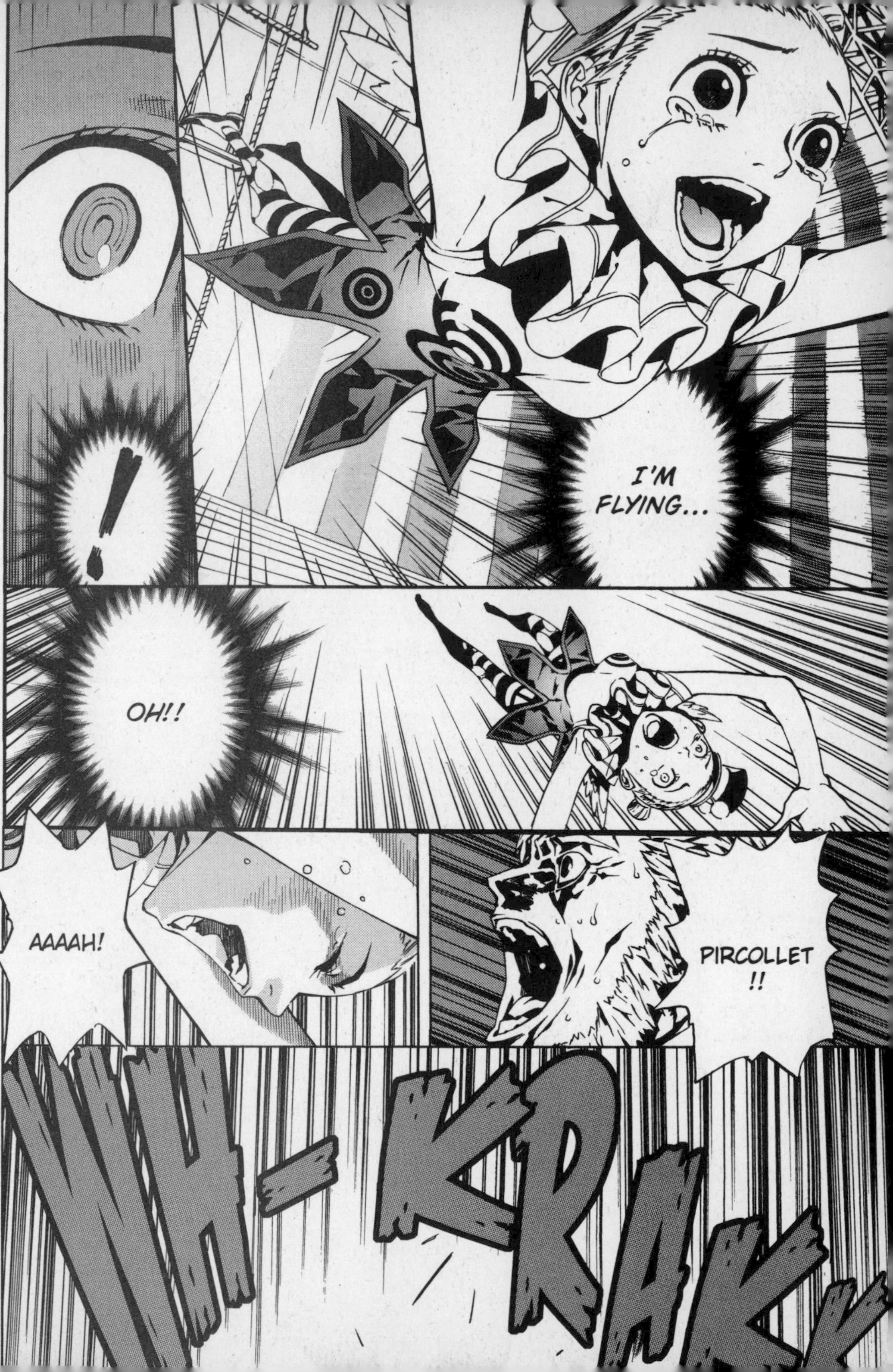
I'M FLYING...
!
OH!!
PIRCOLLET !!
AAAAH!
WH-KRAK

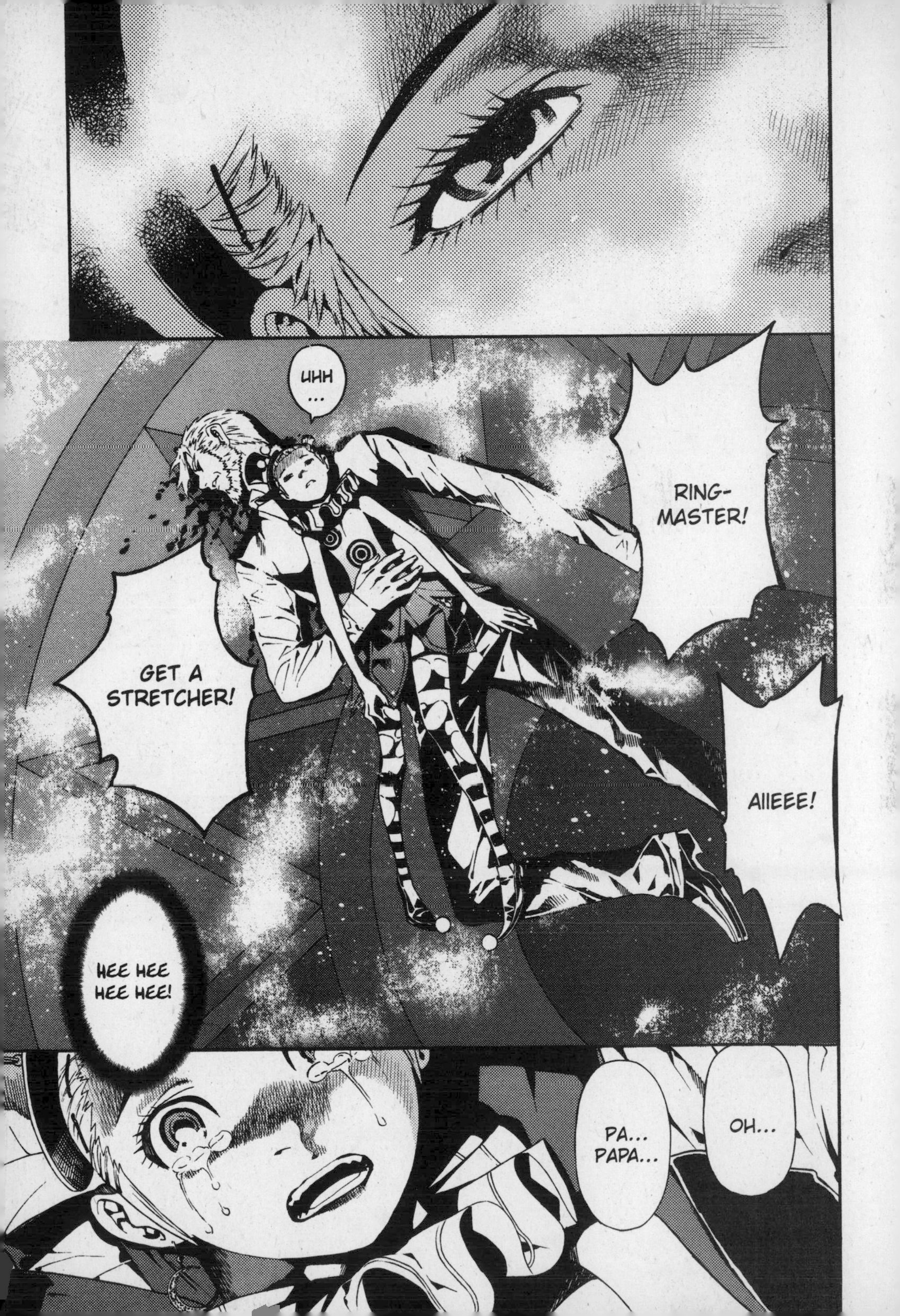
RING-MASTER!
UHH ...
AIIEEE!
GET A STRETCHER!
HEE HEE HEE HEE!
OH...
PA... PAPA...

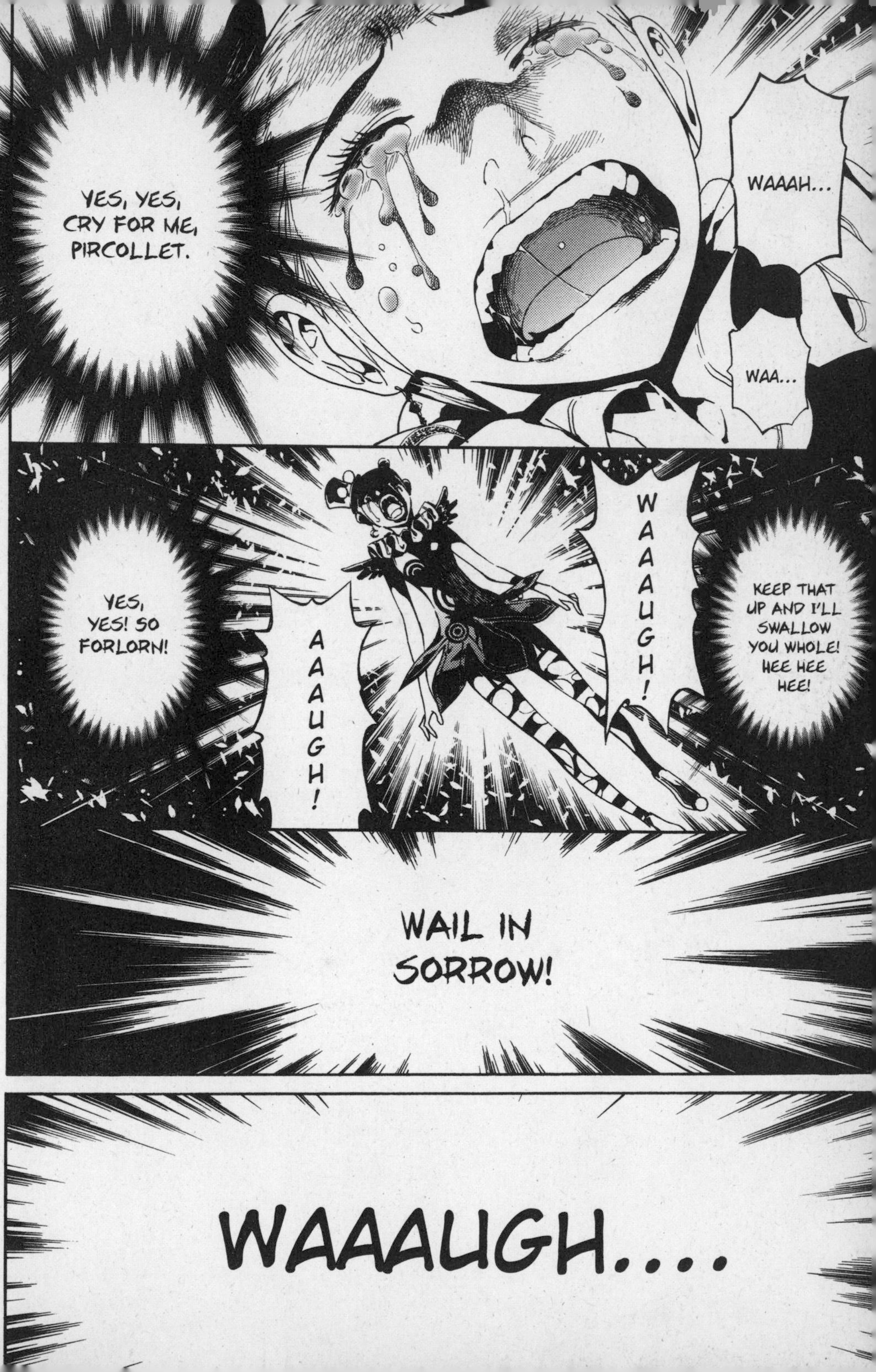
WAAAH...
WAA...
YES, YES, CRY FOR ME, PIRCOLLET.
KEEP THAT UP AND I'LL SWALLOW YOU WHOLE! HEE HEE HEE!
WAAAAUGH!
AAAAUGH!
YES, YES! SO FORLORN!
WAIL IN SORROW!
WAAAUGH....

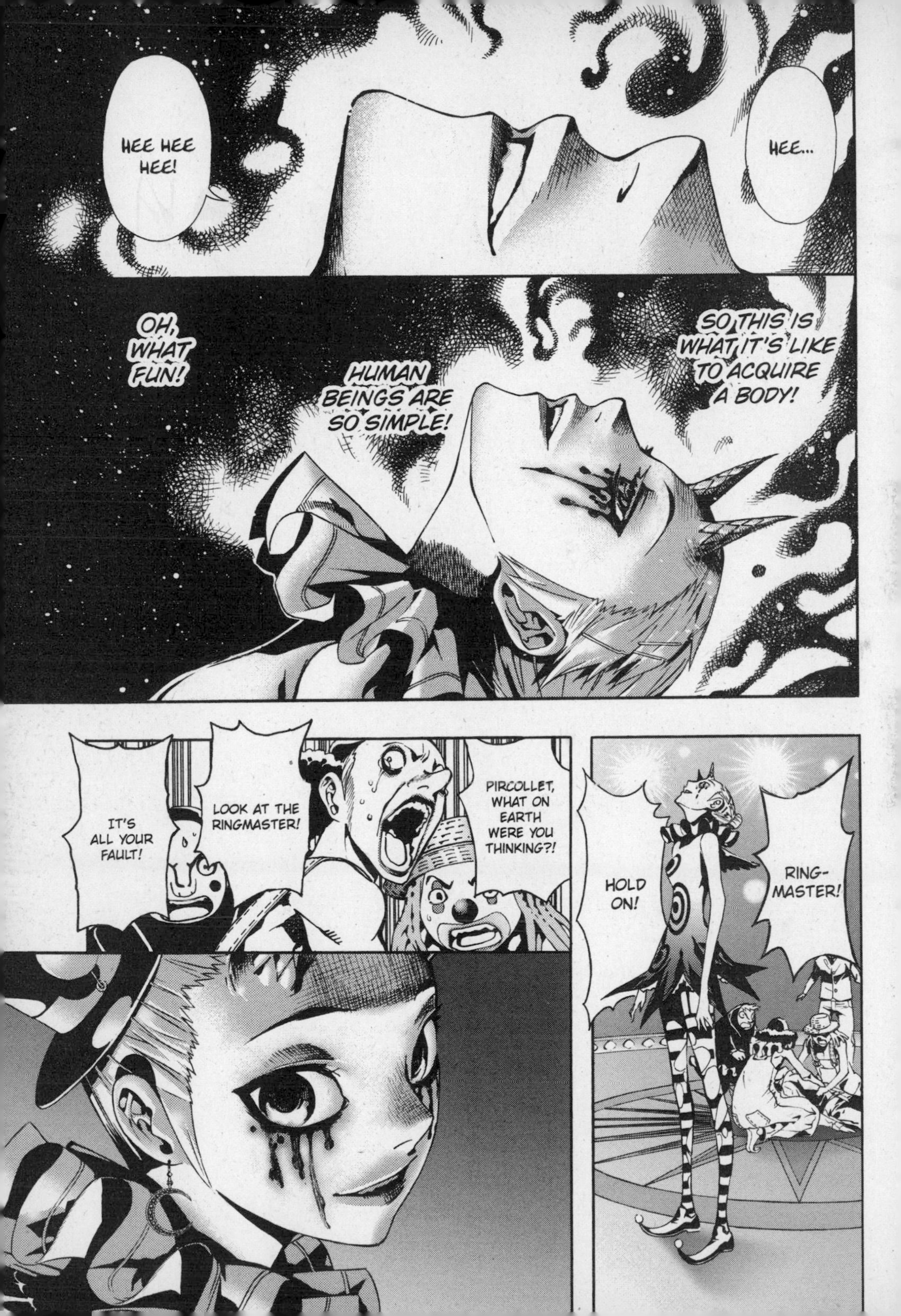
HEE...
HEE HEE HEE!
SO THIS IS WHAT IT'S LIKE TO ACQUIRE A BODY!
HUMAN BEINGS ARE SO SIMPLE!
OH, WHAT FUN!
RING-MASTER!
HOLD ON!
PIRCOLLET, WHAT ON EARTH WERE YOU THINKING?!
LOOK AT THE RINGMASTER!
IT'S ALL YOUR FAULT!

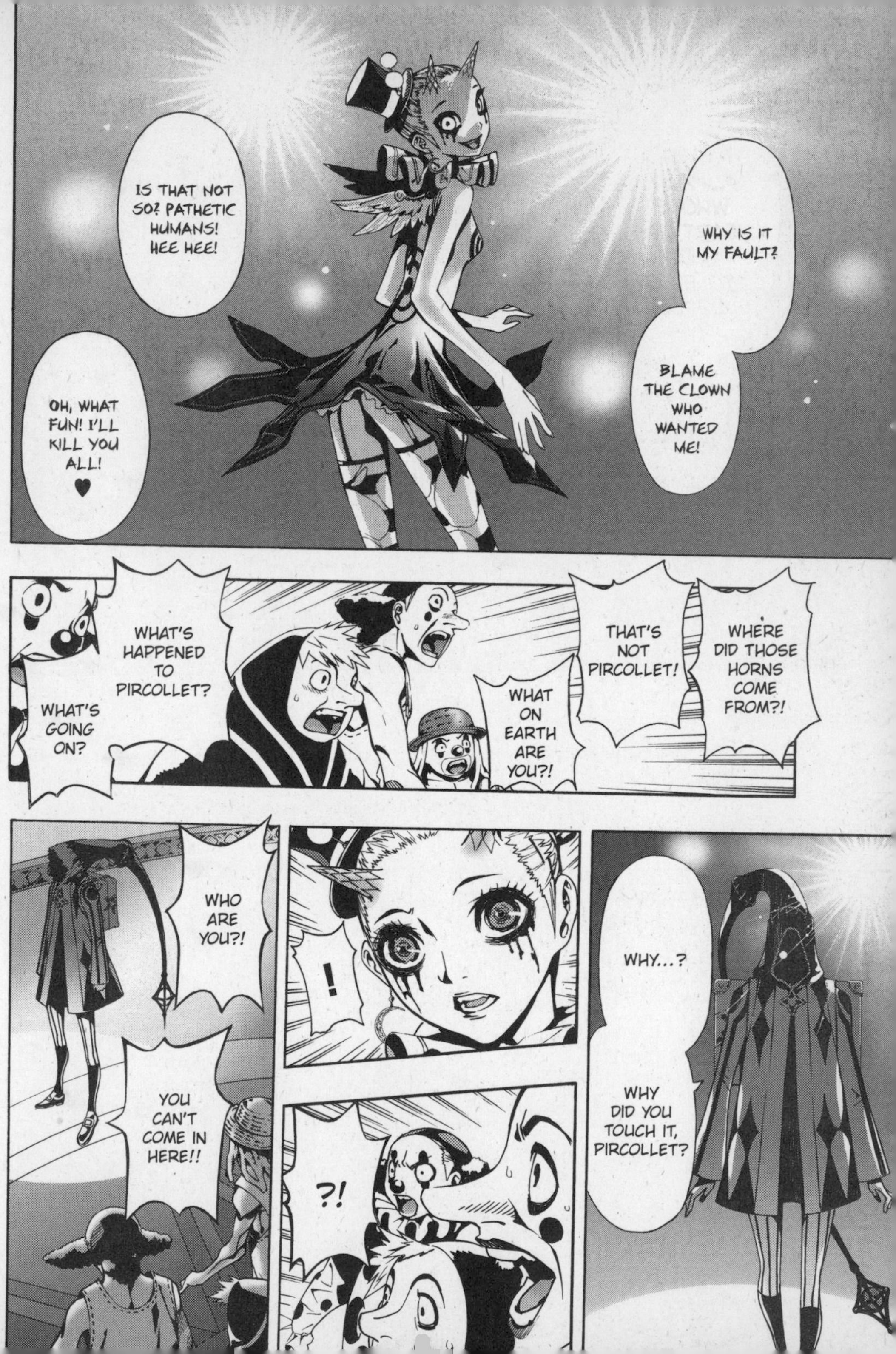
WHY IS IT MY FAULT?
BLAME THE CLOWN WHO WANTED ME!
IS THAT NOT SO? PATHETIC HUMANS! HEE HEE!
OH, WHAT FUN! I'LL KILL YOU ALL! ♥
WHERE DID THOSE HORNS COME FROM?!
THAT'S NOT PIRCOLLET!
WHAT ON EARTH ARE YOU?!
WHAT'S HAPPENED TO PIRCOLLET?
WHAT'S GOING ON?
WHY...?
WHY DID YOU TOUCH IT, PIRCOLLET?
!
?!
WHO ARE YOU?!
YOU CAN'T COME IN HERE!!

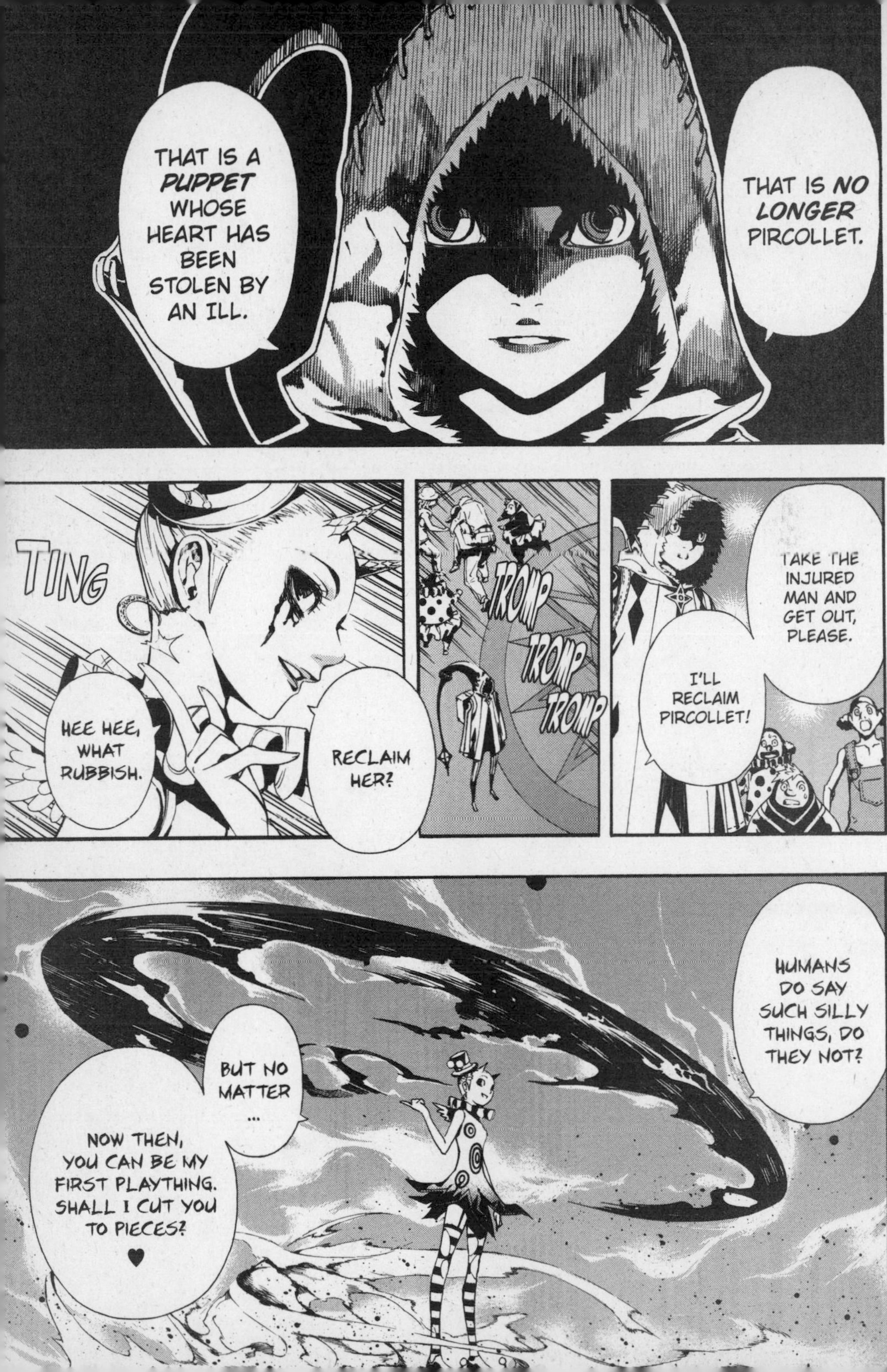
THAT IS NO LONGER PIRCOLLET.
THAT IS A PUPPET WHOSE HEART HAS BEEN STOLEN BY AN ILL.
TAKE THE INJURED MAN AND GET OUT, PLEASE.
I'LL RECLAIM PIRCOLLET!
TROMP TROMP TROMP
TING
RECLAIM HER?
HEE HEE, WHAT RUBBISH.
HUMANS DO SAY SUCH SILLY THINGS, DO THEY NOT?
BUT NO MATTER...
NOW THEN, YOU CAN BE MY FIRST PLAYTHING. SHALL I CUT YOU TO PIECES? ♥

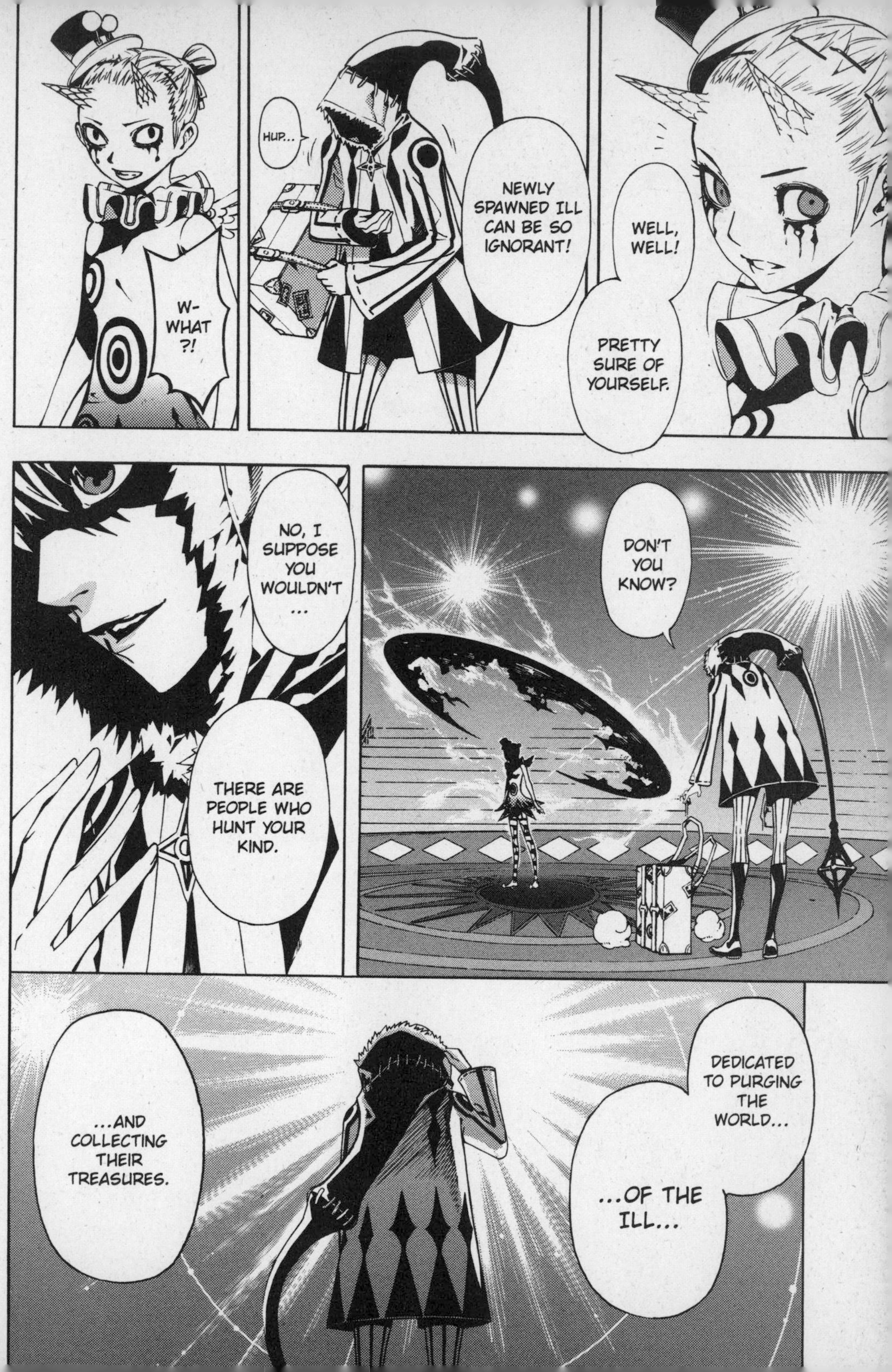
WELL, WELL!
PRETTY SURE OF YOURSELF.
HUP...
NEWLY SPAWNED ILL CAN BE SO IGNORANT!
W-WHAT?!
DON'T YOU KNOW?
NO, I SUPPOSE YOU WOULDN'T...
THERE ARE PEOPLE WHO HUNT YOUR KIND.
DEDICATED TO PURGING THE WORLD...
...OF THE ILL...
...AND COLLECTING THEIR TREASURES.

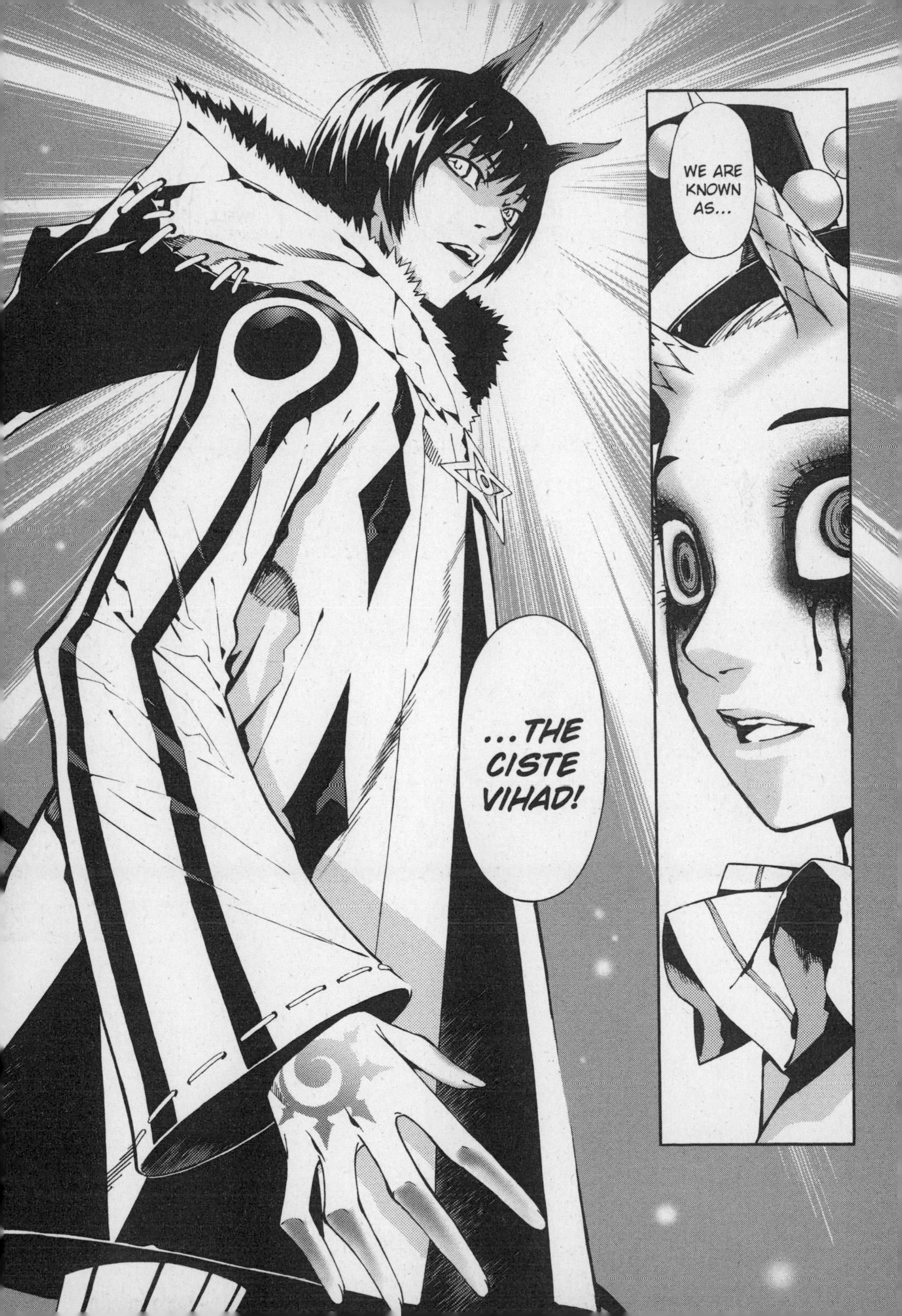
WE ARE KNOWN AS...
...THE CISTE VIHAD!

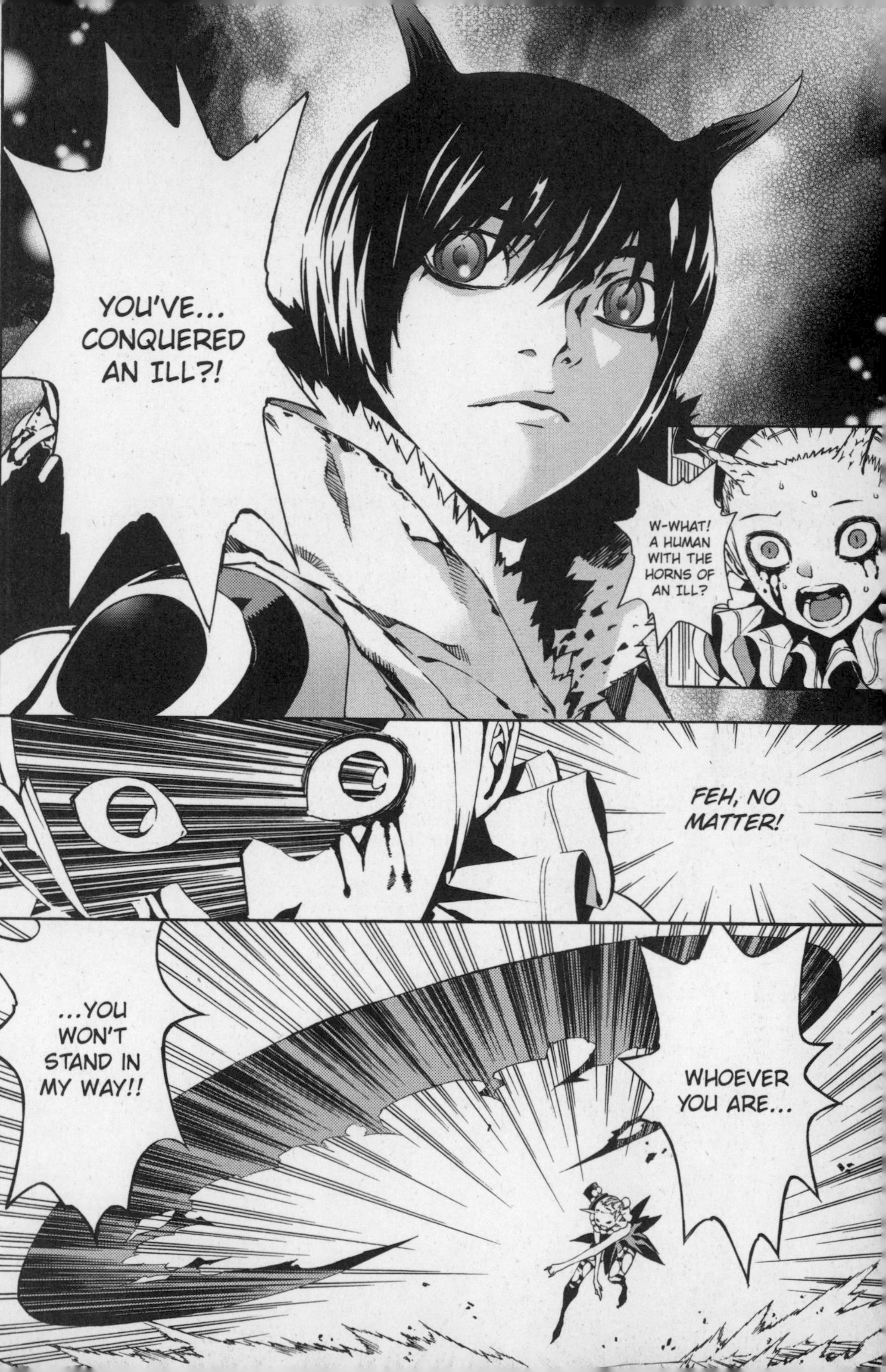
W-WHAT! A HUMAN WITH THE HORNS OF AN ILL?
YOU'VE... CONQUERED AN ILL?!
FEH, NO MATTER!
WHOEVER YOU ARE...
...YOU WON'T STAND IN MY WAY!!

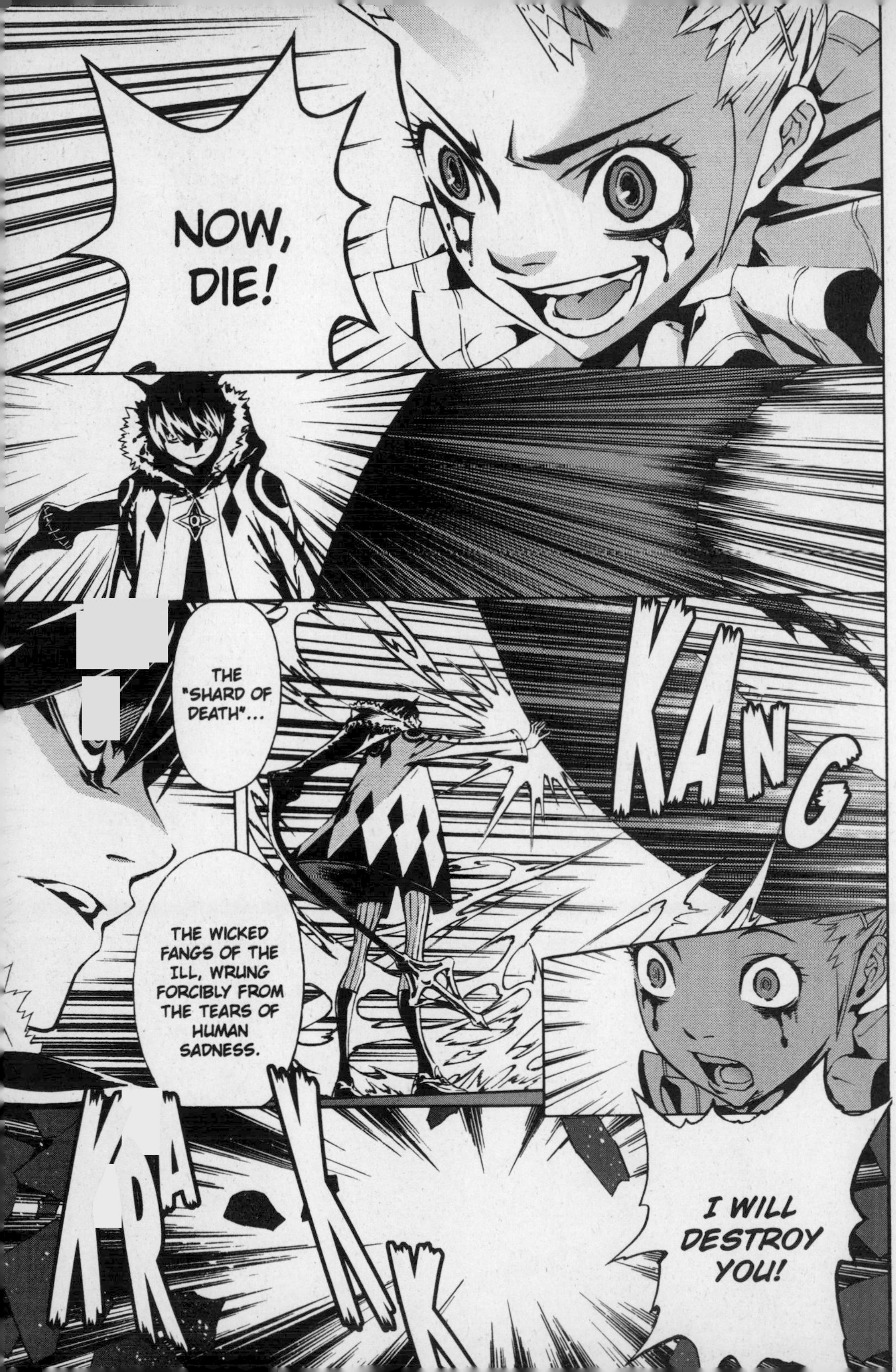
NOW, DIE!
KANG
THE "SHARD OF DEATH"...
THE WICKED FANGS OF THE ILL, WRUNG FORCIBLY FROM THE TEARS OF HUMAN SADNESS.
I WILL DESTROY YOU!

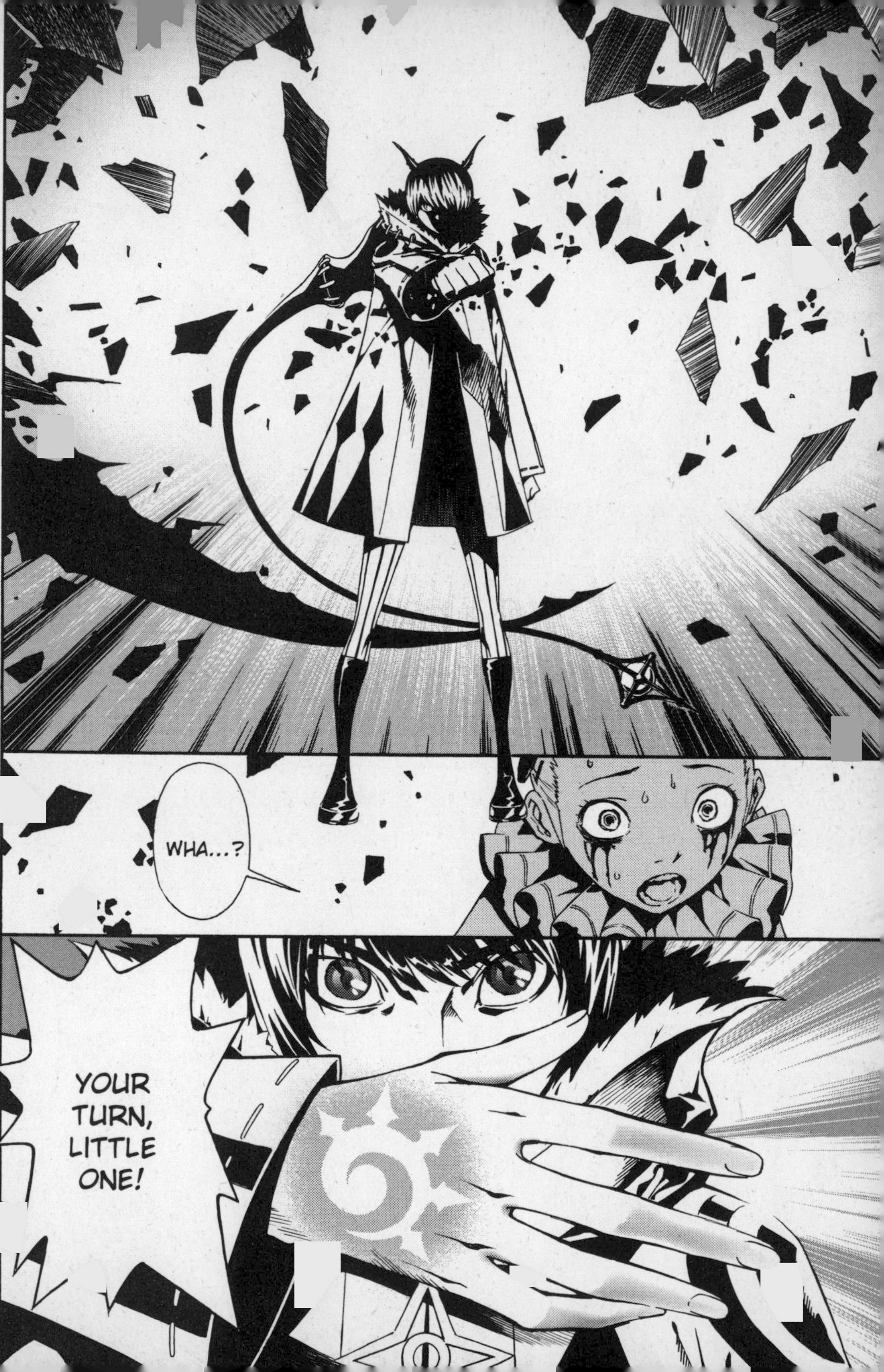
WHA...?
YOUR TURN, LITTLE ONE!

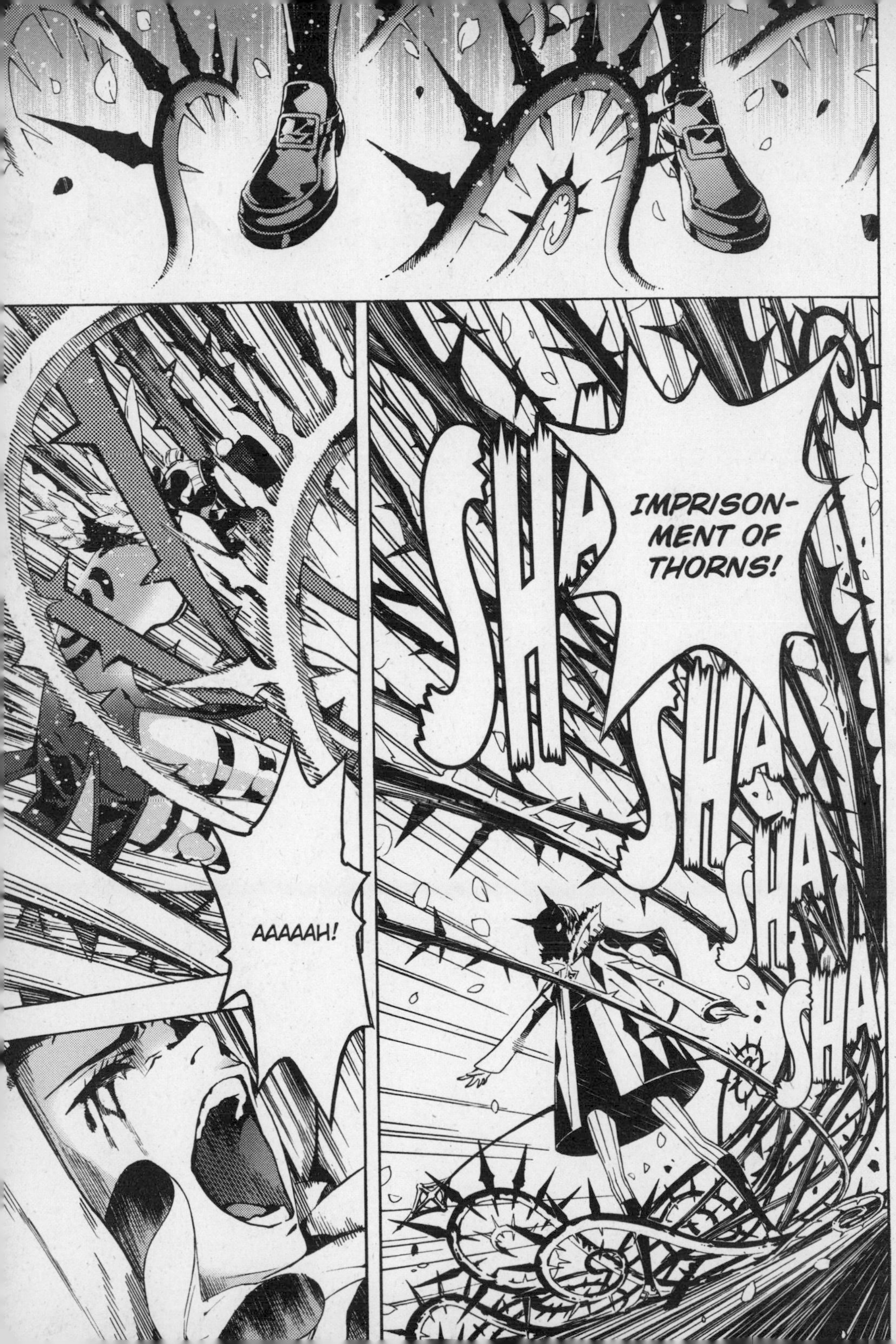
IMPRISONMENT OF THORNS!
SHASHASHASHA
AAAAAH!

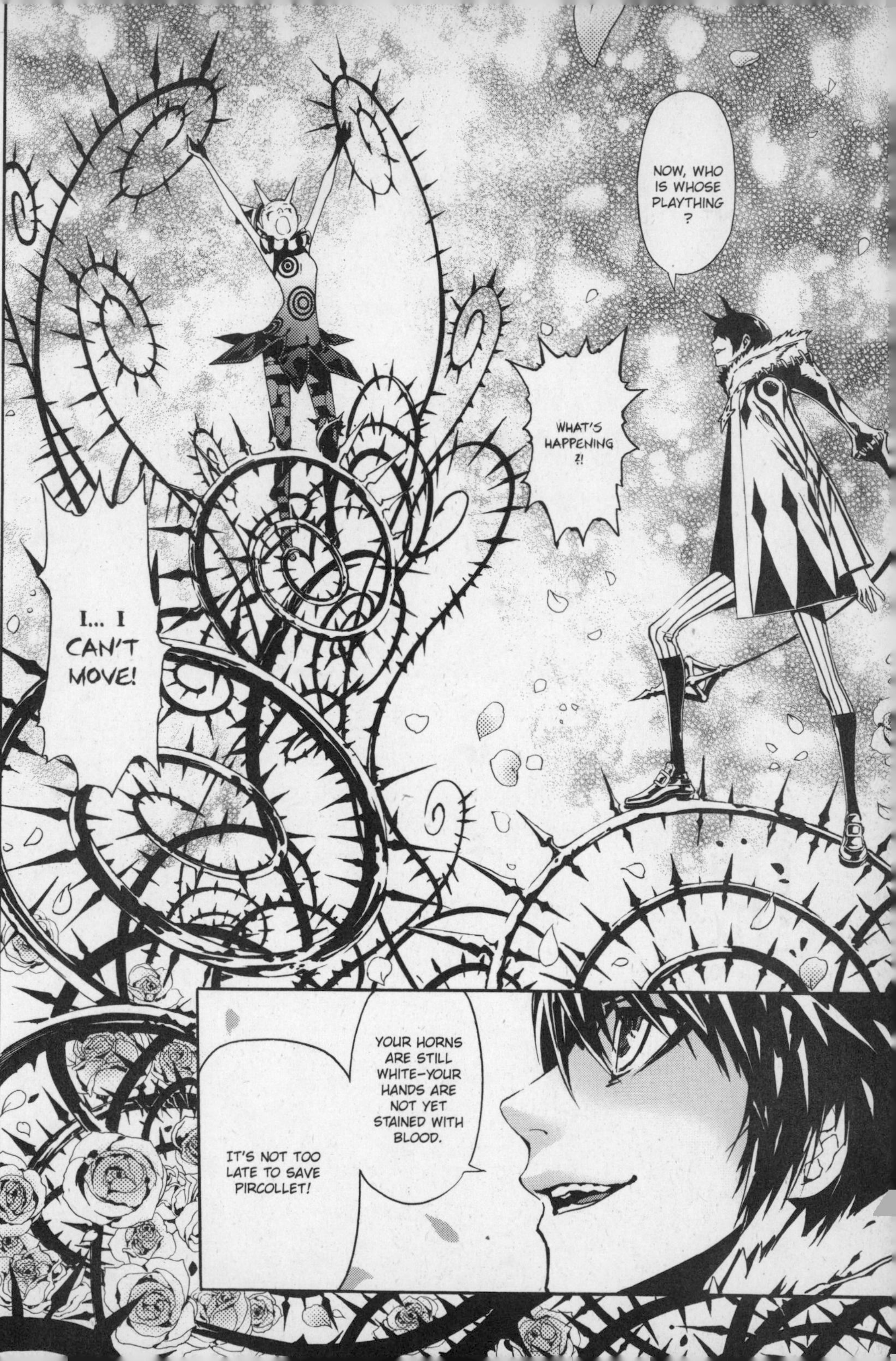
NOW, WHO IS WHOSE PLAYTHING?
WHAT'S HAPPENING?!
I... I CAN'T MOVE!
YOUR HORNS ARE STILL WHITE—YOUR HANDS ARE NOT YET STAINED WITH BLOOD.
IT'S NOT TOO LATE TO SAVE PIRCOLLET!

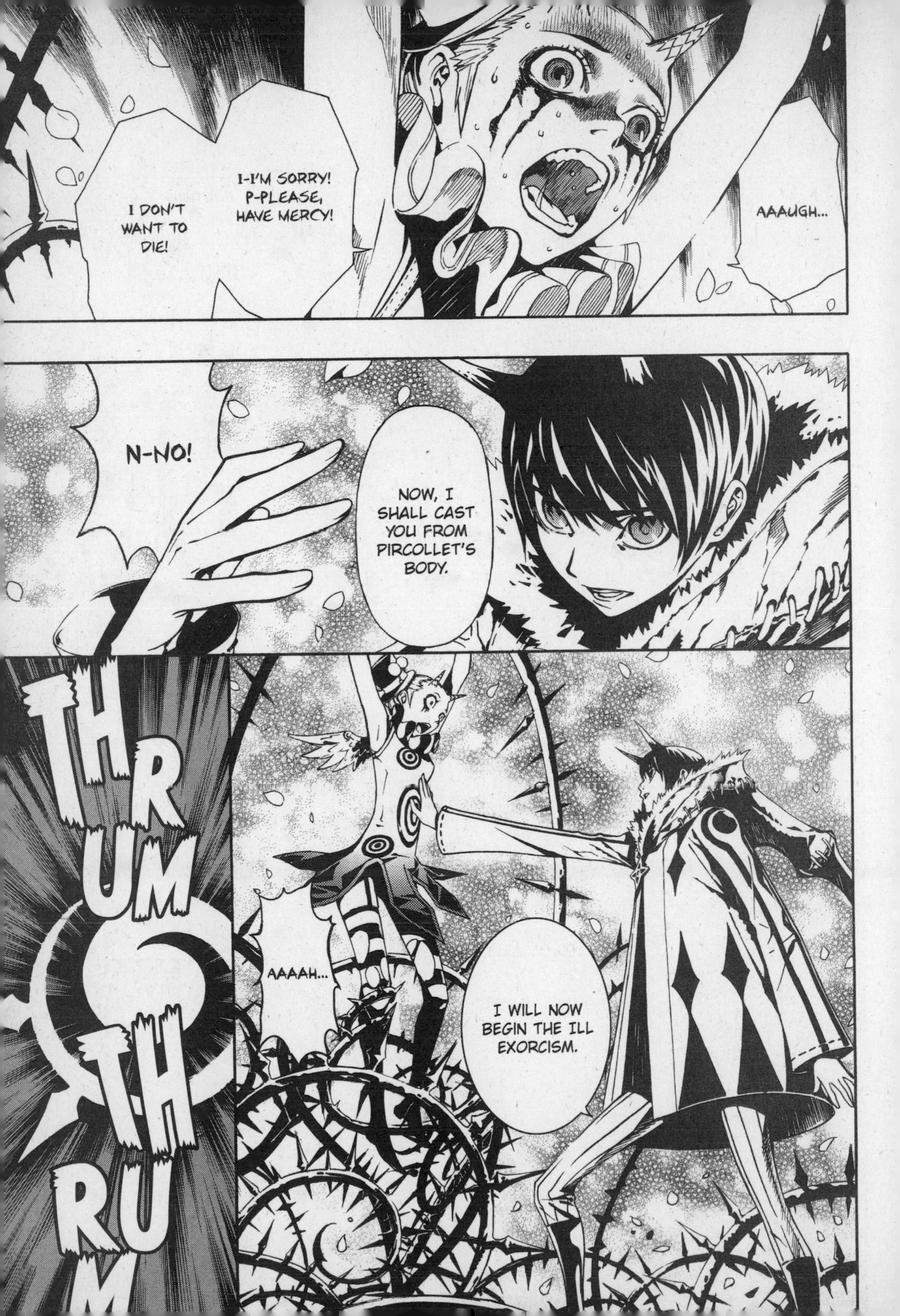
AAAUGH...
I-I'M SORRY! P-PLEASE, HAVE MERCY!
I DON'T WANT TO DIE!
NOW, I SHALL CAST YOU FROM PIRCOLLET'S BODY.
N-NO!
I WILL NOW BEGIN THE ILL EXORCISM.
AAAAH...
THRUM THRUM

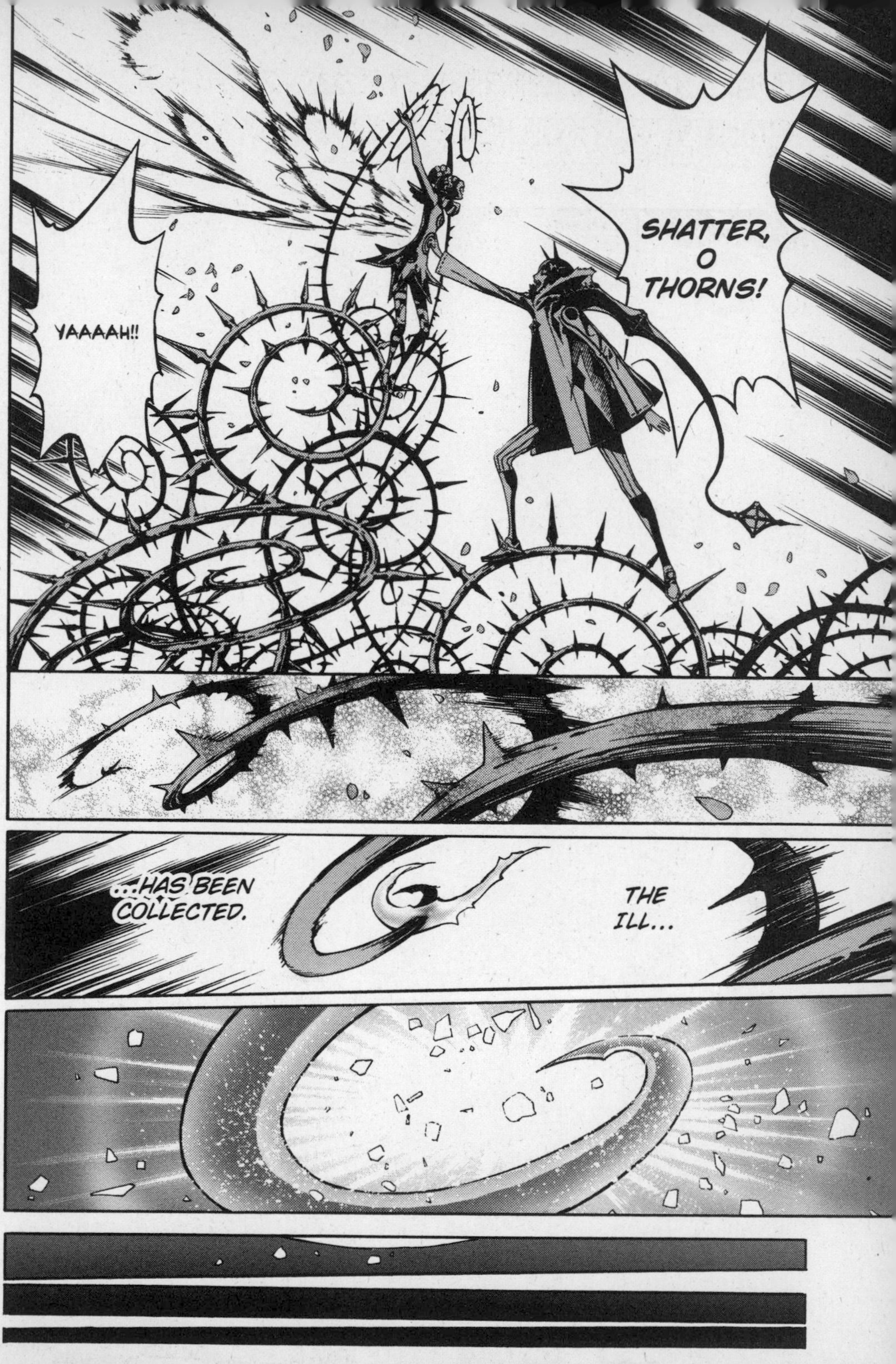
SHATTER, O THORNS!
YAAAAH!!
THE ILL...
...HAS BEEN COLLECTED.

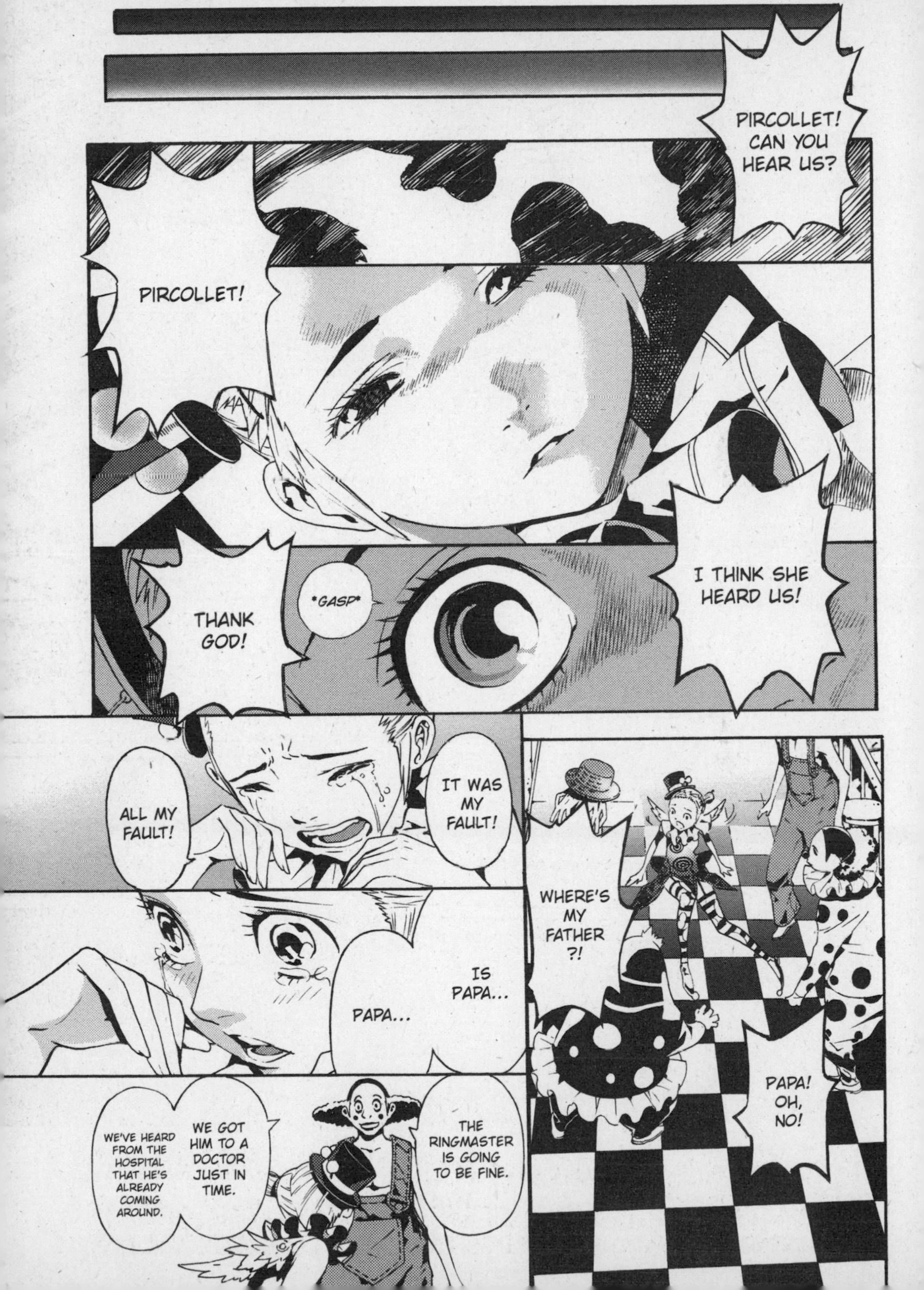
PIRCOLLET! CAN YOU HEAR US?
PIRCOLLET!
I THINK SHE HEARD US!
GASP
THANK GOD!
WHERE'S MY FATHER ?!
PAPA! OH, NO!
IT WAS MY FAULT!
ALL MY FAULT!
IS PAPA...
PAPA...
THE RINGMASTER IS GOING TO BE FINE.
WE GOT HIM TO A DOCTOR JUST IN TIME.
WE'VE HEARD FROM THE HOSPITAL THAT HE'S ALREADY COMING AROUND.

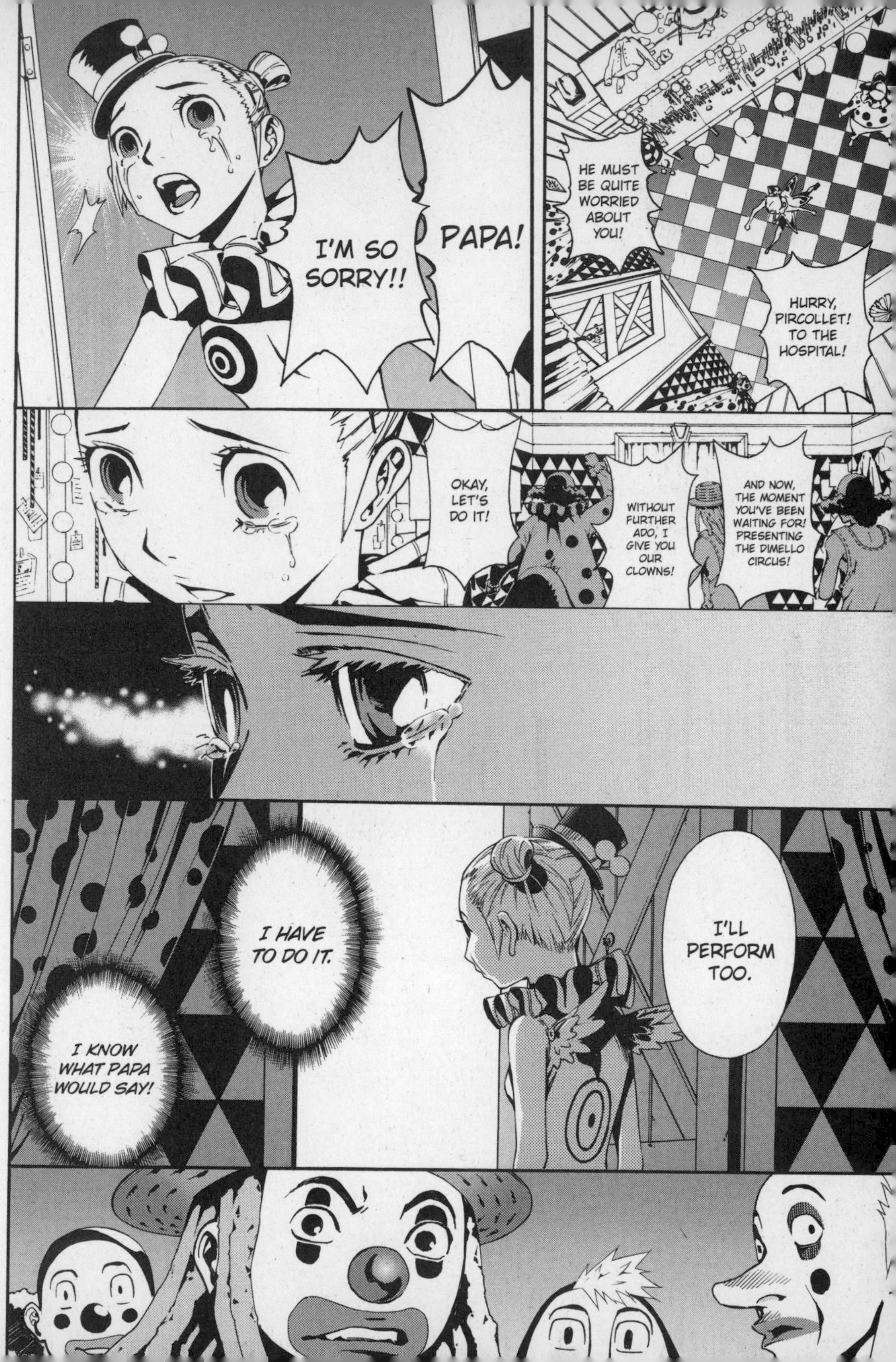
HE MUST BE QUITE WORRIED ABOUT YOU!
HURRY, PIRCOLLET! TO THE HOSPITAL!
PAPA!
I'M SO SORRY!!
AND NOW, THE MOMENT YOU'VE BEEN WAITING FOR! PRESENTING THE DIMELLO CIRCUS!
WITHOUT FURTHER ADO, I GIVE YOU OUR CLOWNS!
OKAY, LET'S DO IT!
I'LL PERFORM TOO.
I HAVE TO DO IT.
I KNOW WHAT PAPA WOULD SAY!

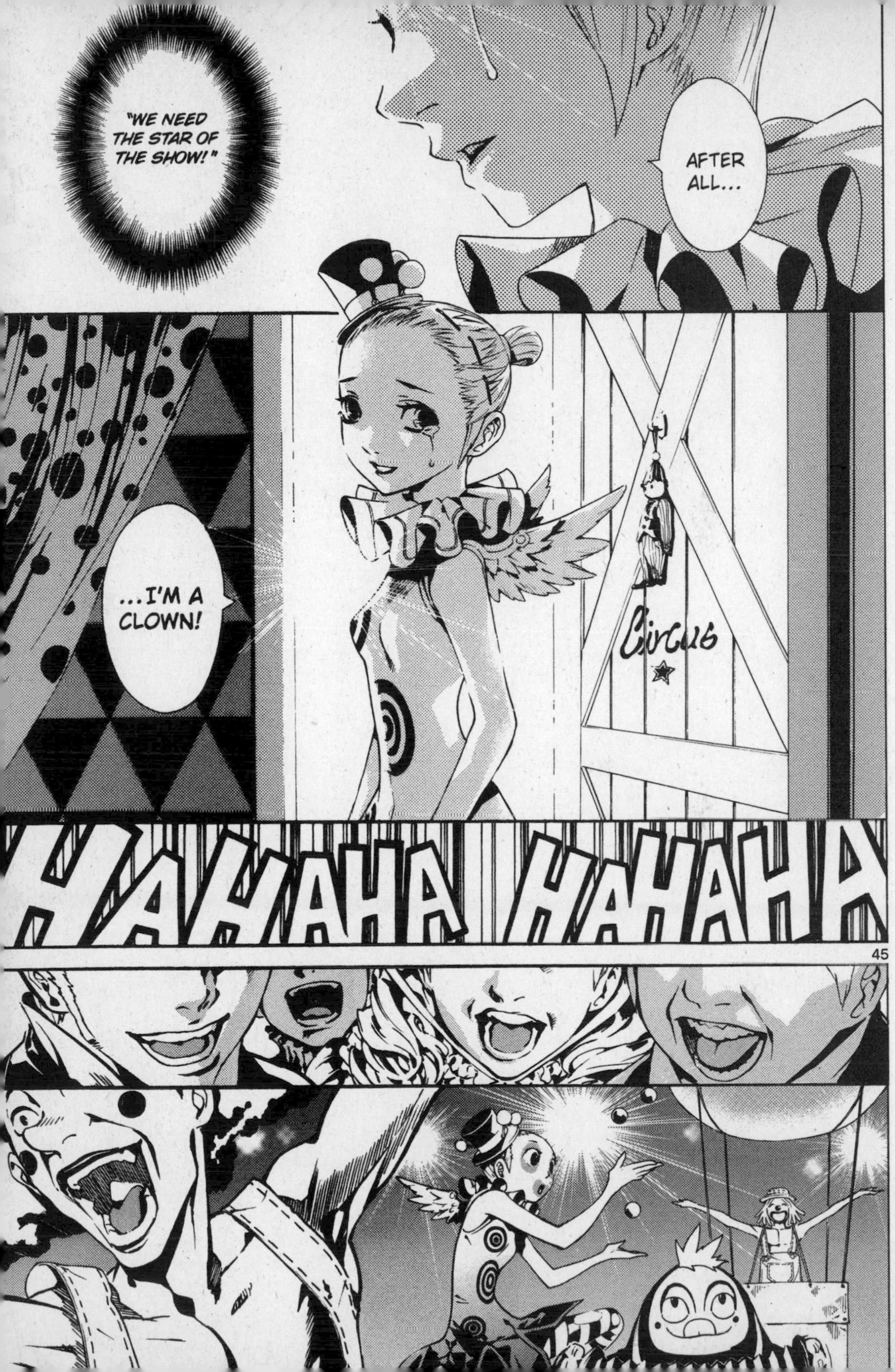
AFTER ALL...
"WE NEED THE STAR OF THE SHOW!"
...I'M A CLOWN!
Circus
HAHAHA HAHAHA

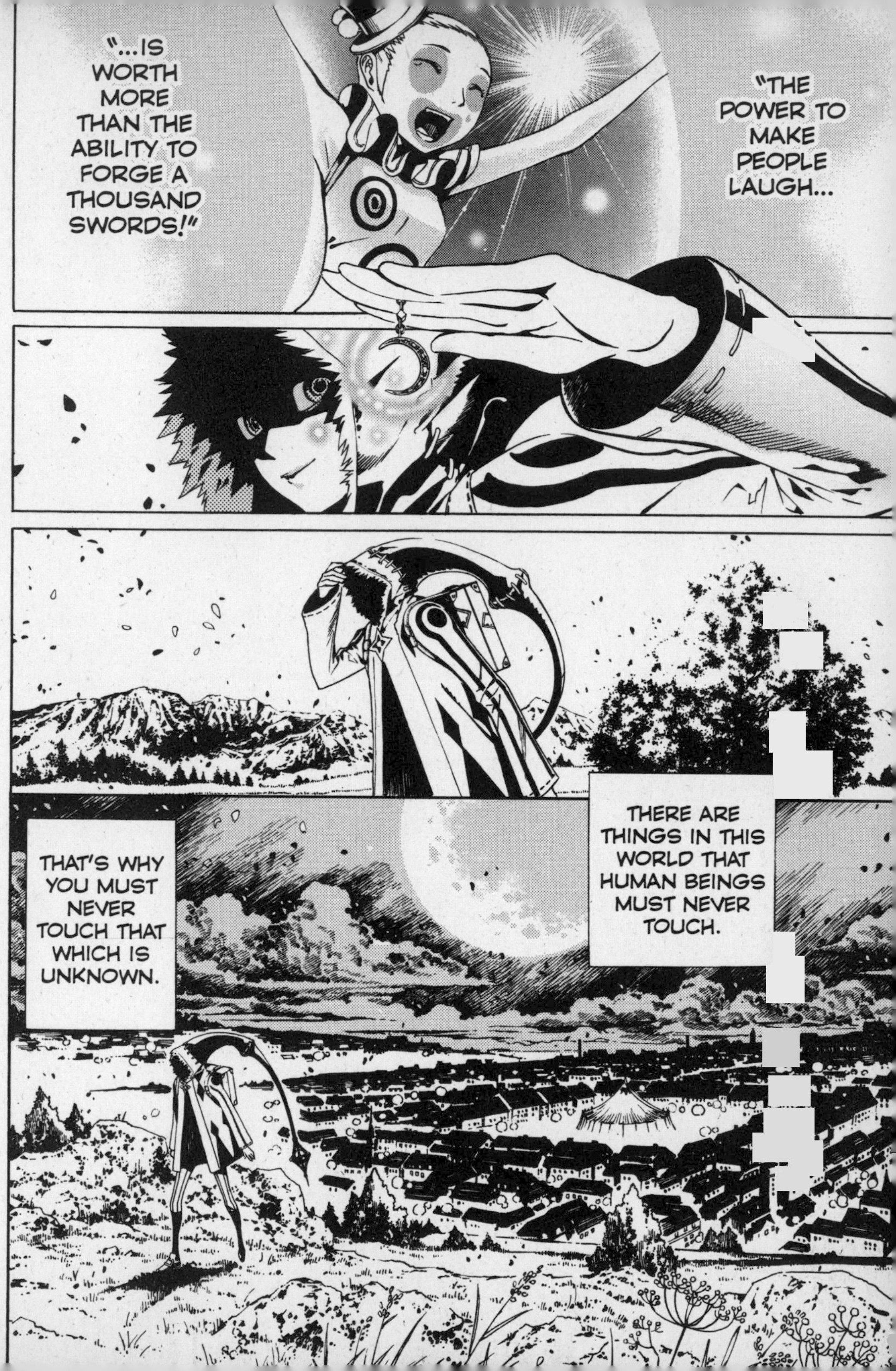
"THE POWER TO MAKE PEOPLE LAUGH...
"...IS WORTH MORE THAN THE ABILITY TO FORGE A THOUSAND SWORDS!"
THERE ARE THINGS IN THIS WORLD THAT HUMAN BEINGS MUST NEVER TOUCH.
THAT'S WHY YOU MUST NEVER TOUCH THAT WHICH IS UNKNOWN.

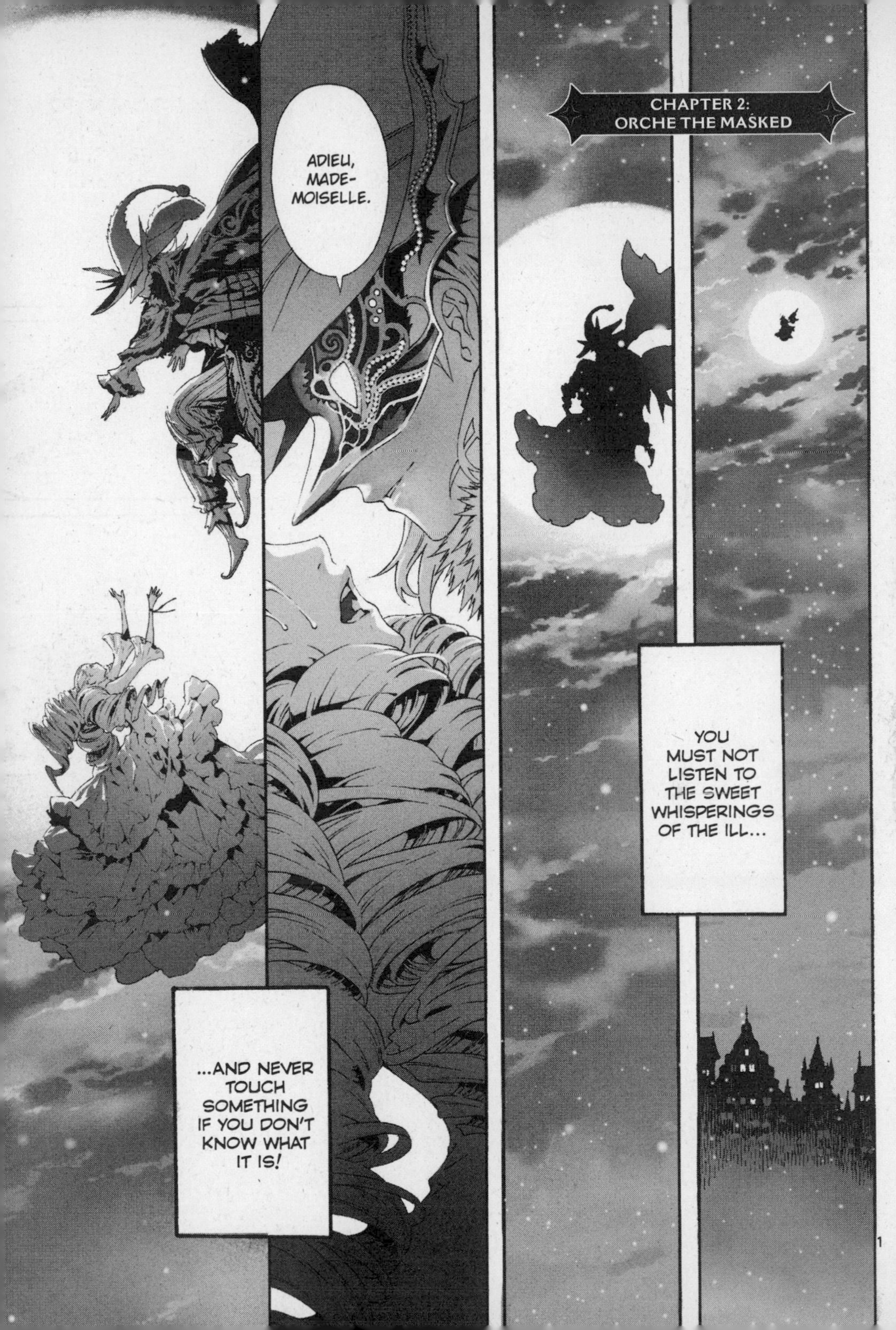
CHAPTER 2:
ORCHE THE MASKED
YOU MUST NOT LISTEN TO THE SWEET WHISPERINGS OF THE ILL...
ADIEU, MADE-MOISELLE.
...AND NEVER TOUCH SOMETHING IF YOU DON'T KNOW WHAT IT IS!

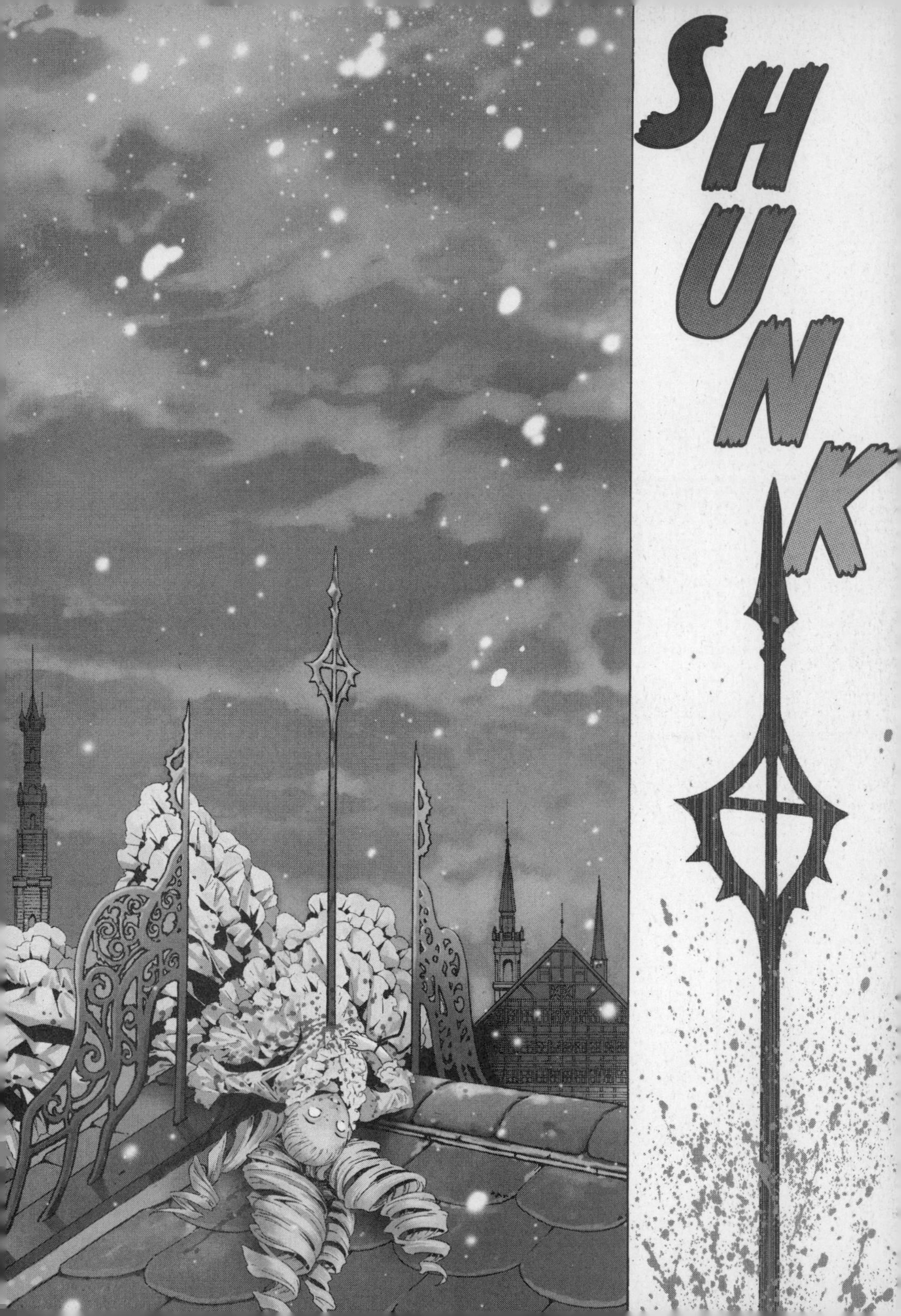
SHUNK

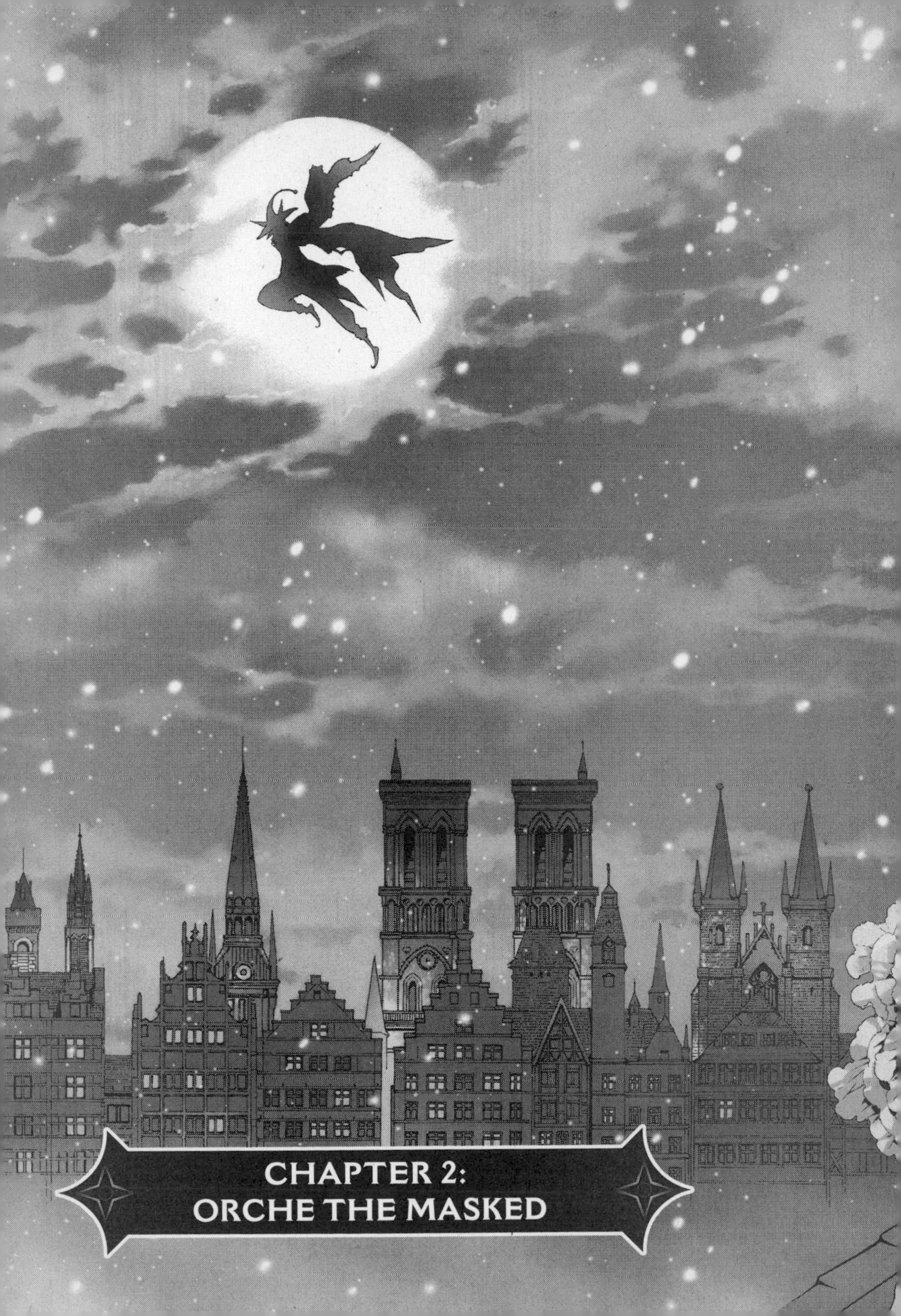
CHAPTER 2:
ORCHE THE MASKED

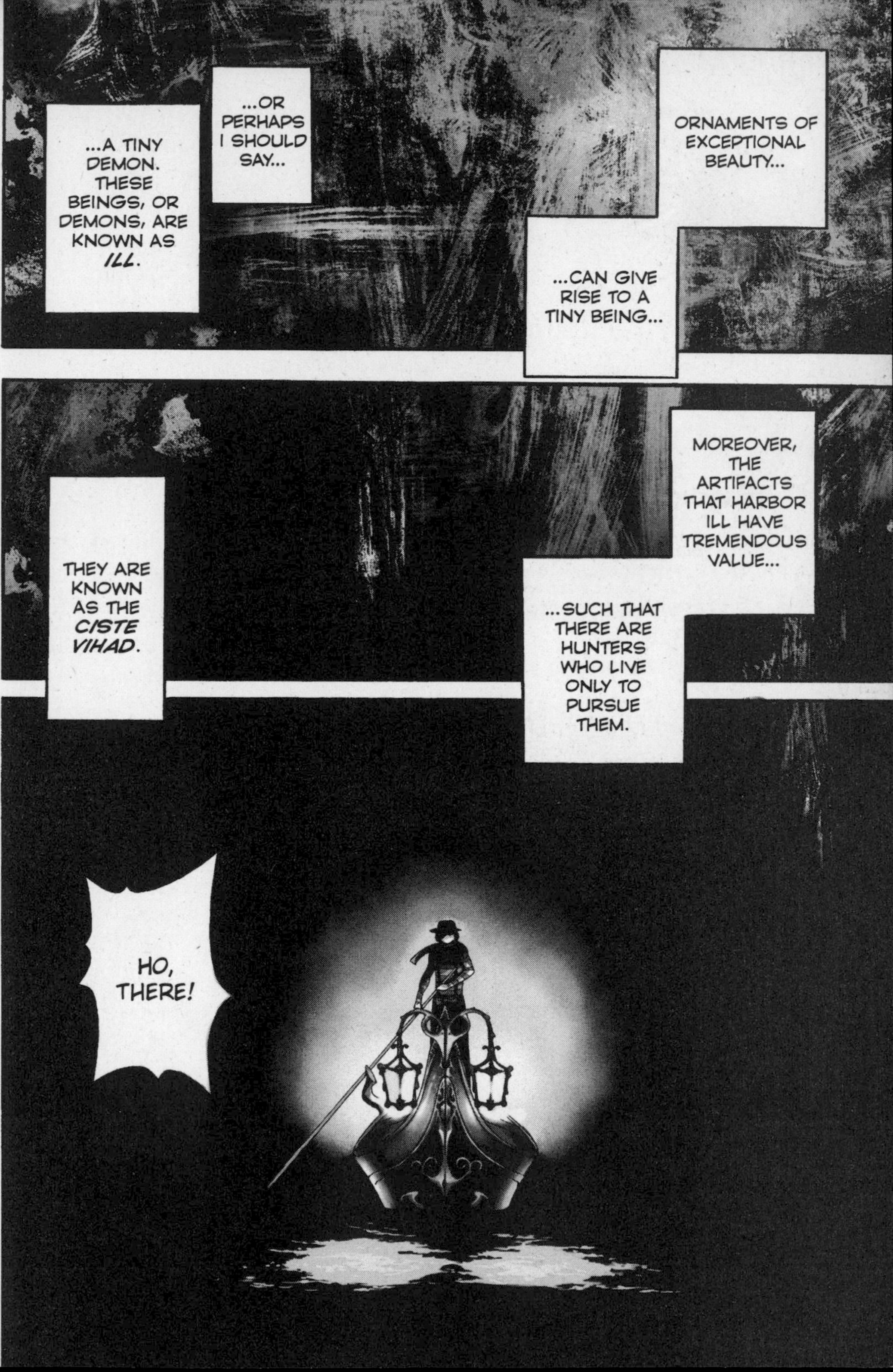
ORNAMENTS OF EXCEPTIONAL BEAUTY...
...CAN GIVE RISE TO A TINY BEING...
...OR PERHAPS I SHOULD SAY...
...A TINY DEMON. THESE BEINGS, OR DEMONS, ARE KNOWN AS *ILL*.
MOREOVER, THE ARTIFACTS THAT HARBOR ILL HAVE TREMENDOUS VALUE...
...SUCH THAT THERE ARE HUNTERS WHO LIVE ONLY TO PURSUE THEM.
THEY ARE KNOWN AS THE *CISTE VIHAD*.
HO, THERE!

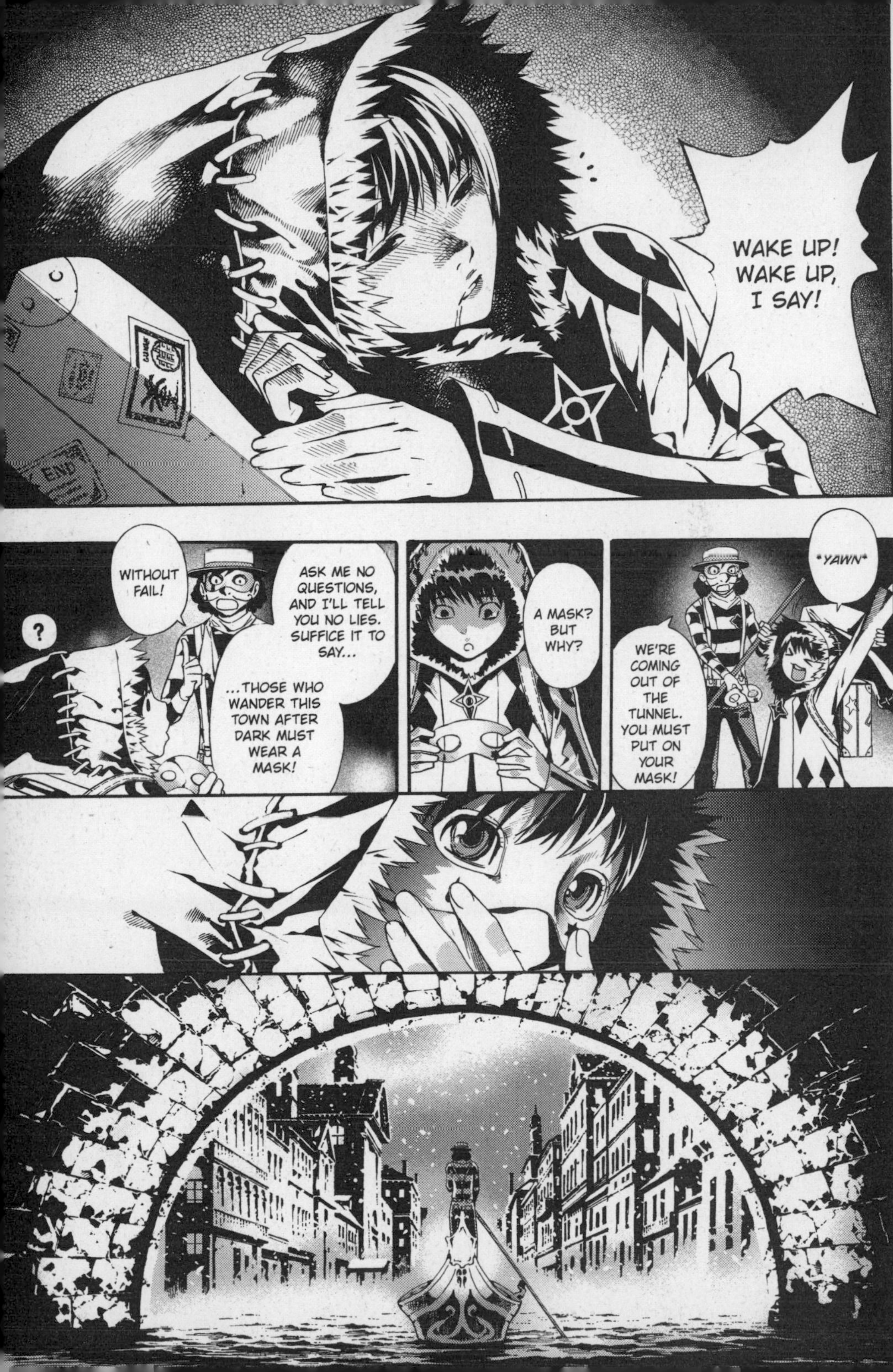
WAKE UP! WAKE UP, I SAY!
YAWN
WE'RE COMING OUT OF THE TUNNEL. YOU MUST PUT ON YOUR MASK!
A MASK? BUT WHY?
ASK ME NO QUESTIONS, AND I'LL TELL YOU NO LIES. SUFFICE IT TO SAY...
...THOSE WHO WANDER THIS TOWN AFTER DARK MUST WEAR A MASK!
WITHOUT FAIL!
?

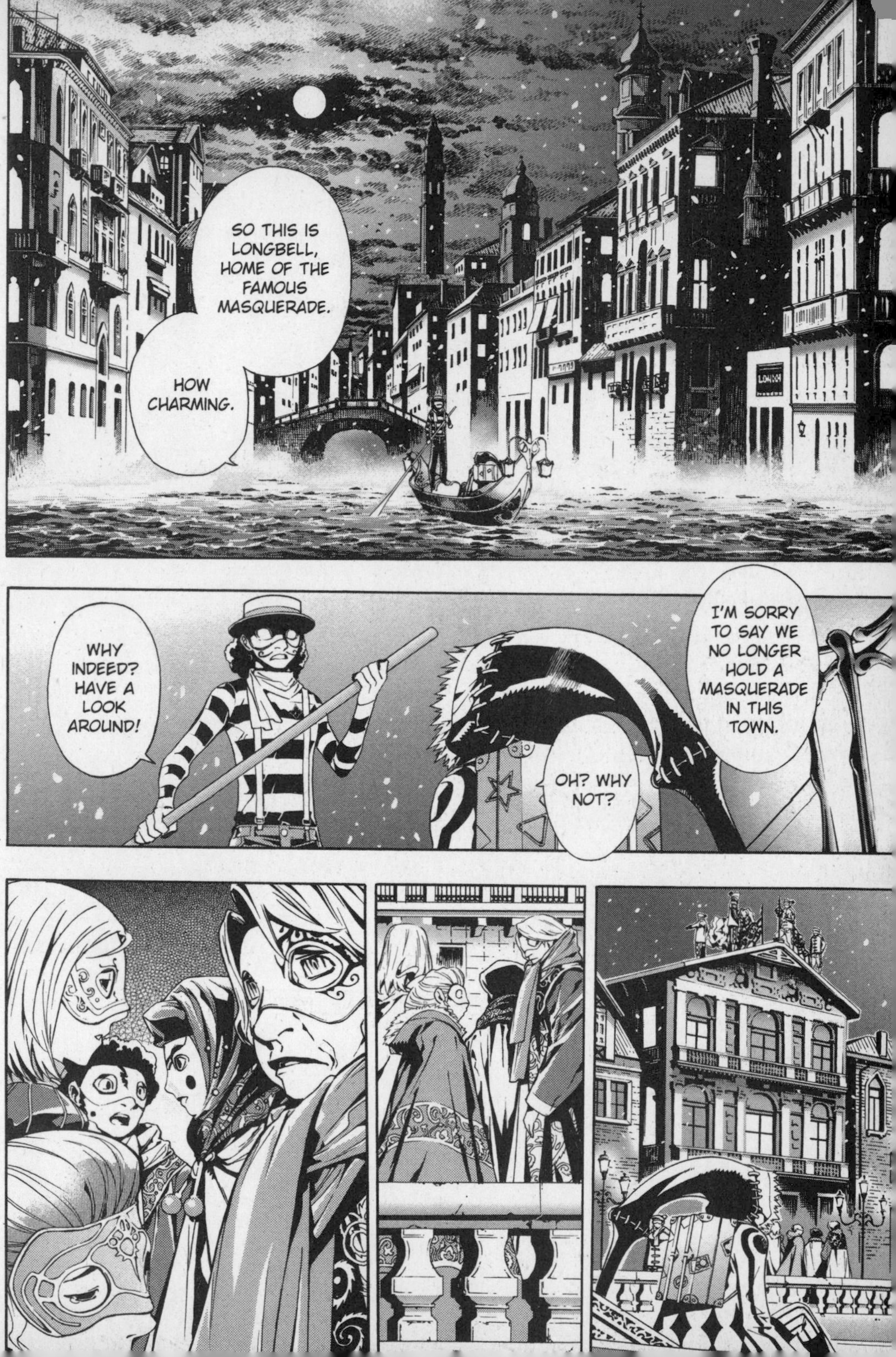
SO THIS IS LONGBELL, HOME OF THE FAMOUS MASQUERADE.
HOW CHARMING.
I'M SORRY TO SAY WE NO LONGER HOLD A MASQUERADE IN THIS TOWN.
OH? WHY NOT?
WHY INDEED? HAVE A LOOK AROUND!

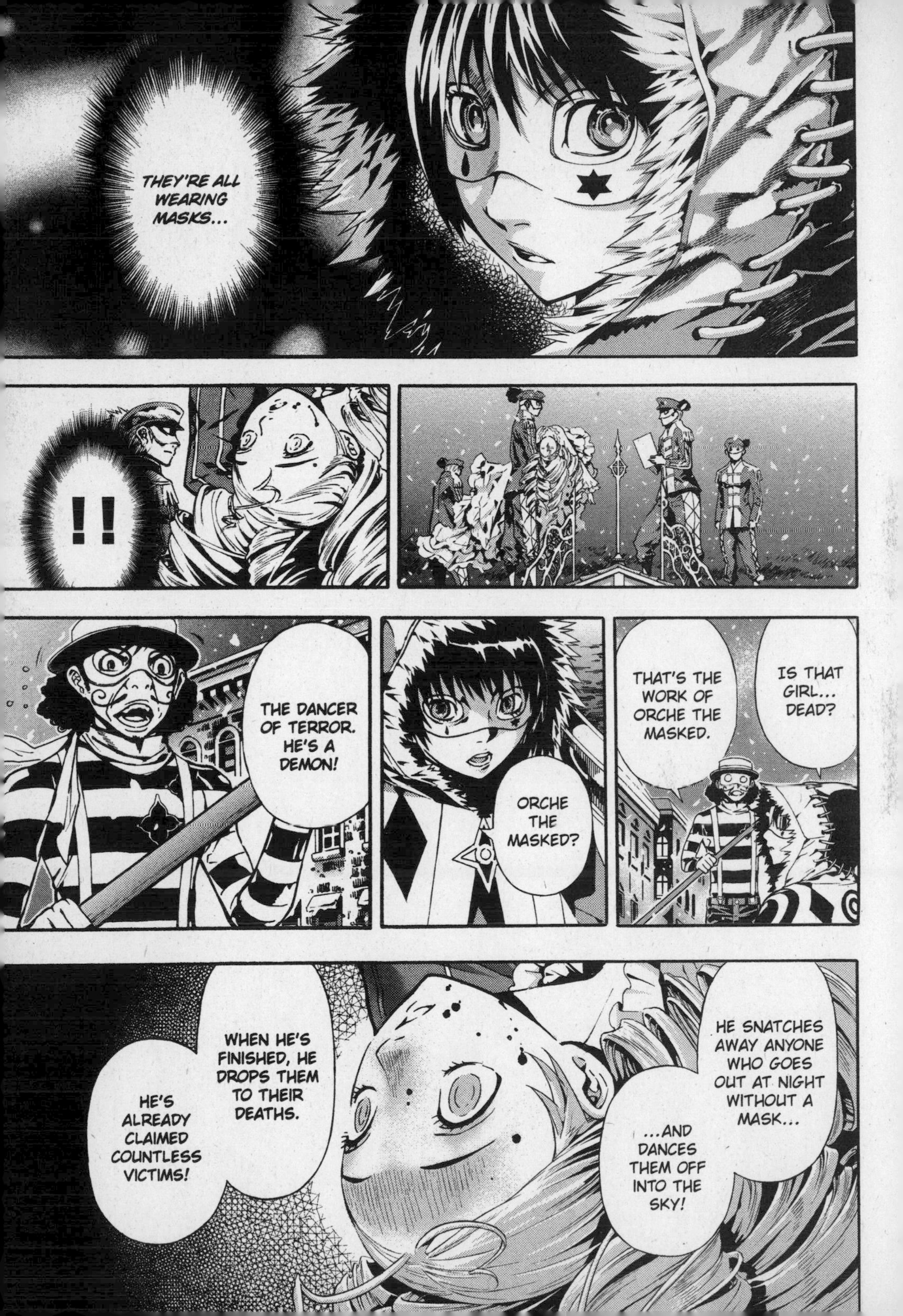
THEY'RE ALL WEARING MASKS...
!!
IS THAT GIRL... DEAD?
THAT'S THE WORK OF ORCHE THE MASKED.
ORCHE THE MASKED?
THE DANCER OF TERROR. HE'S A DEMON!
HE SNATCHES AWAY ANYONE WHO GOES OUT AT NIGHT WITHOUT A MASK...
...AND DANCES THEM OFF INTO THE SKY!
WHEN HE'S FINISHED, HE DROPS THEM TO THEIR DEATHS.
HE'S ALREADY CLAIMED COUNTLESS VICTIMS!

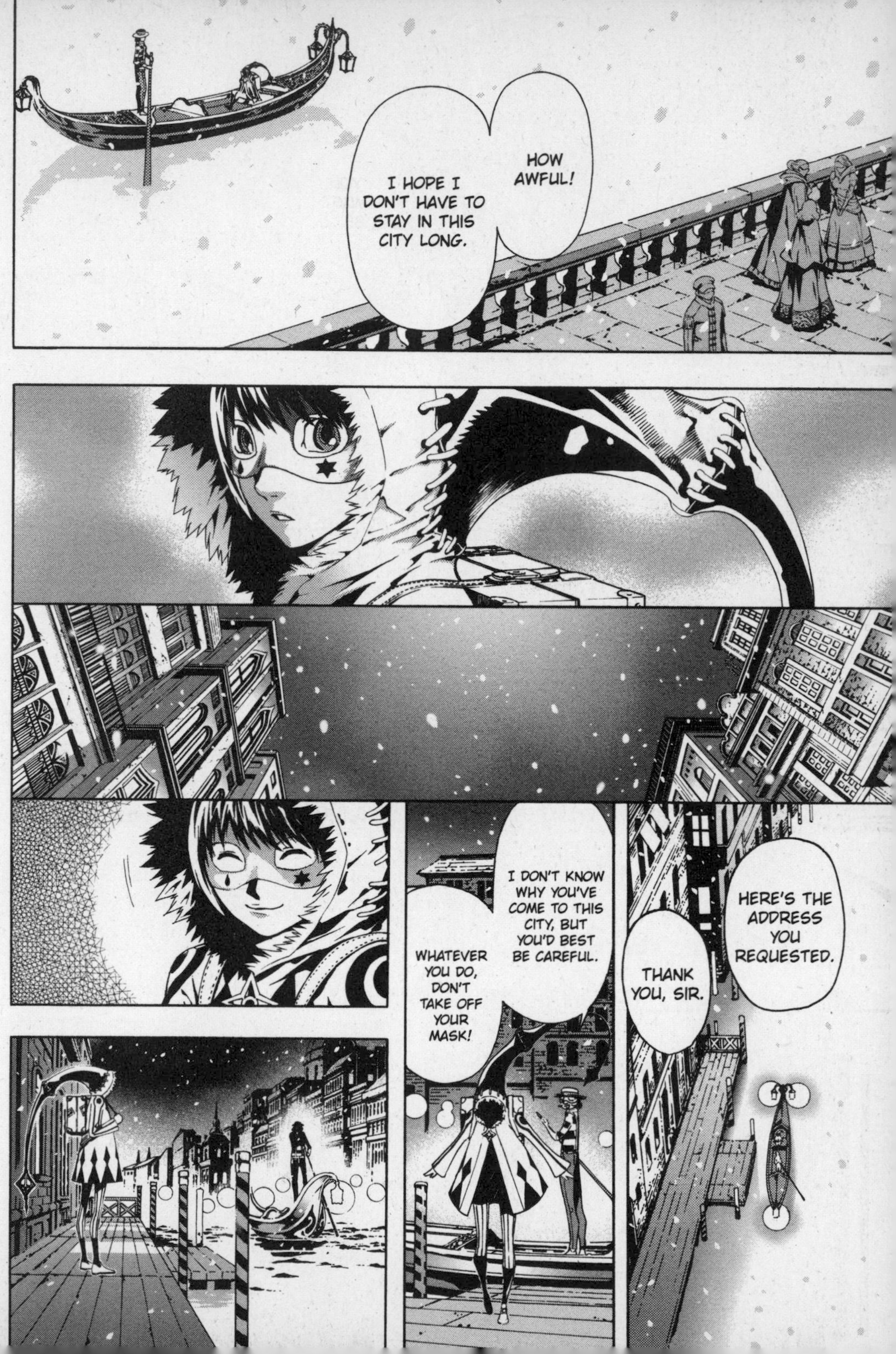
HOW AWFUL!
I HOPE I DON'T HAVE TO STAY IN THIS CITY LONG.
HERE'S THE ADDRESS YOU REQUESTED.
THANK YOU, SIR.
I DON'T KNOW WHY YOU'VE COME TO THIS CITY, BUT YOU'D BEST BE CAREFUL.
WHATEVER YOU DO, DON'T TAKE OFF YOUR MASK!

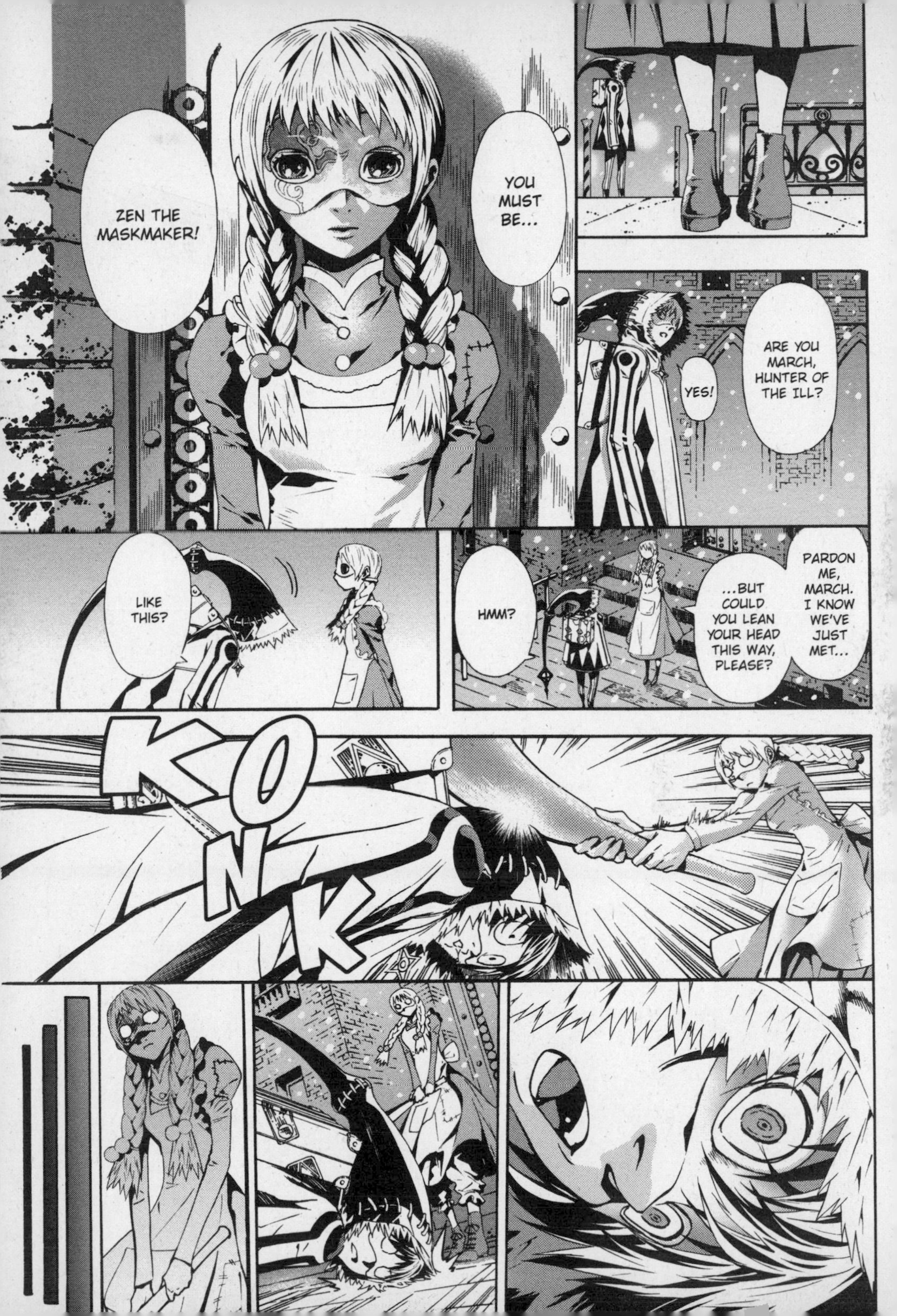
ARE YOU MARCH, HUNTER OF THE ILL?
YES!
YOU MUST BE...
ZEN THE MASKMAKER!
PARDON ME, MARCH. I KNOW WE'VE JUST MET...
...BUT COULD YOU LEAN YOUR HEAD THIS WAY, PLEASE?
HMM?
LIKE THIS?
KONK

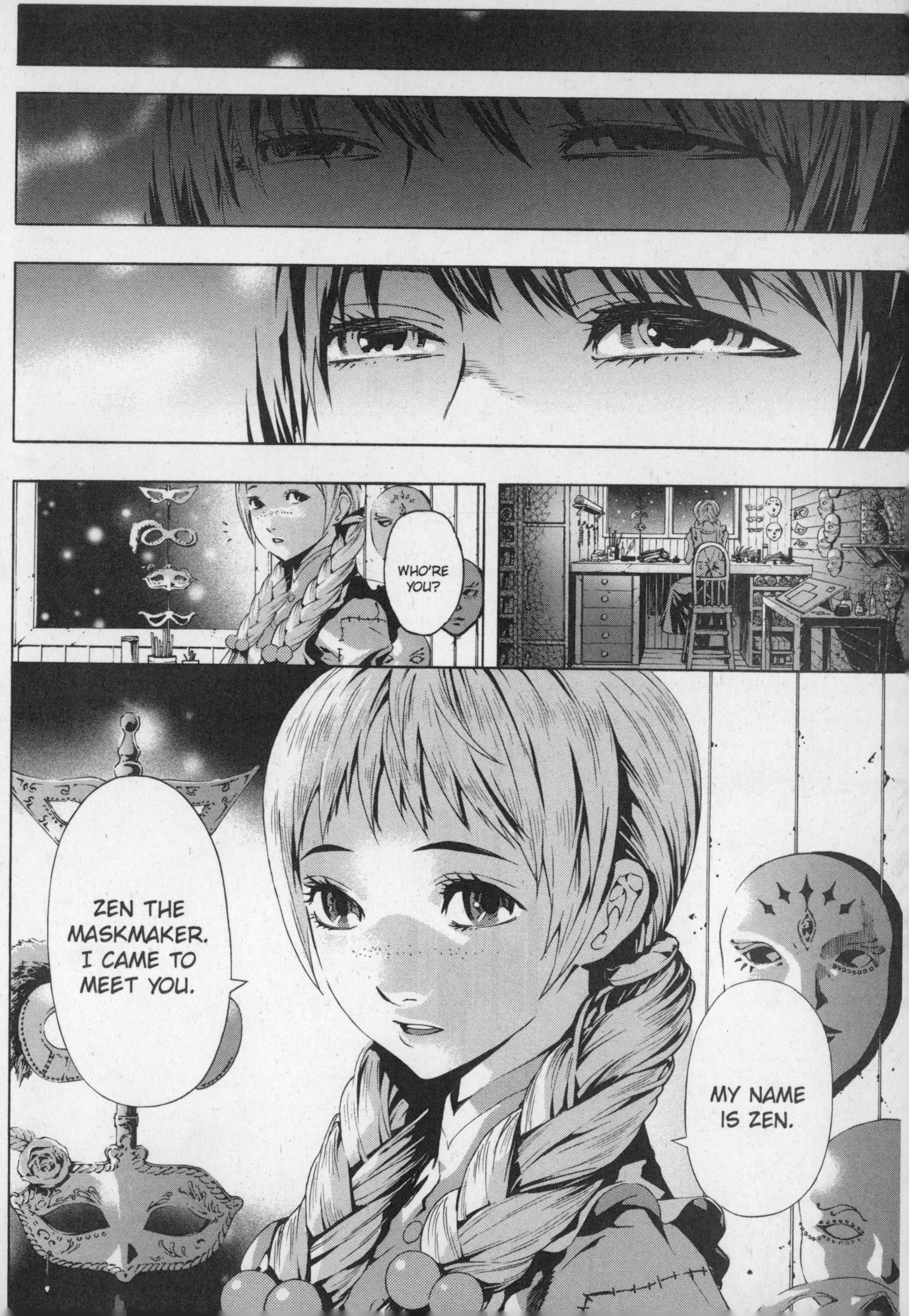
WHO'RE YOU?
MY NAME IS ZEN.
ZEN THE MASKMAKER. I CAME TO MEET YOU.

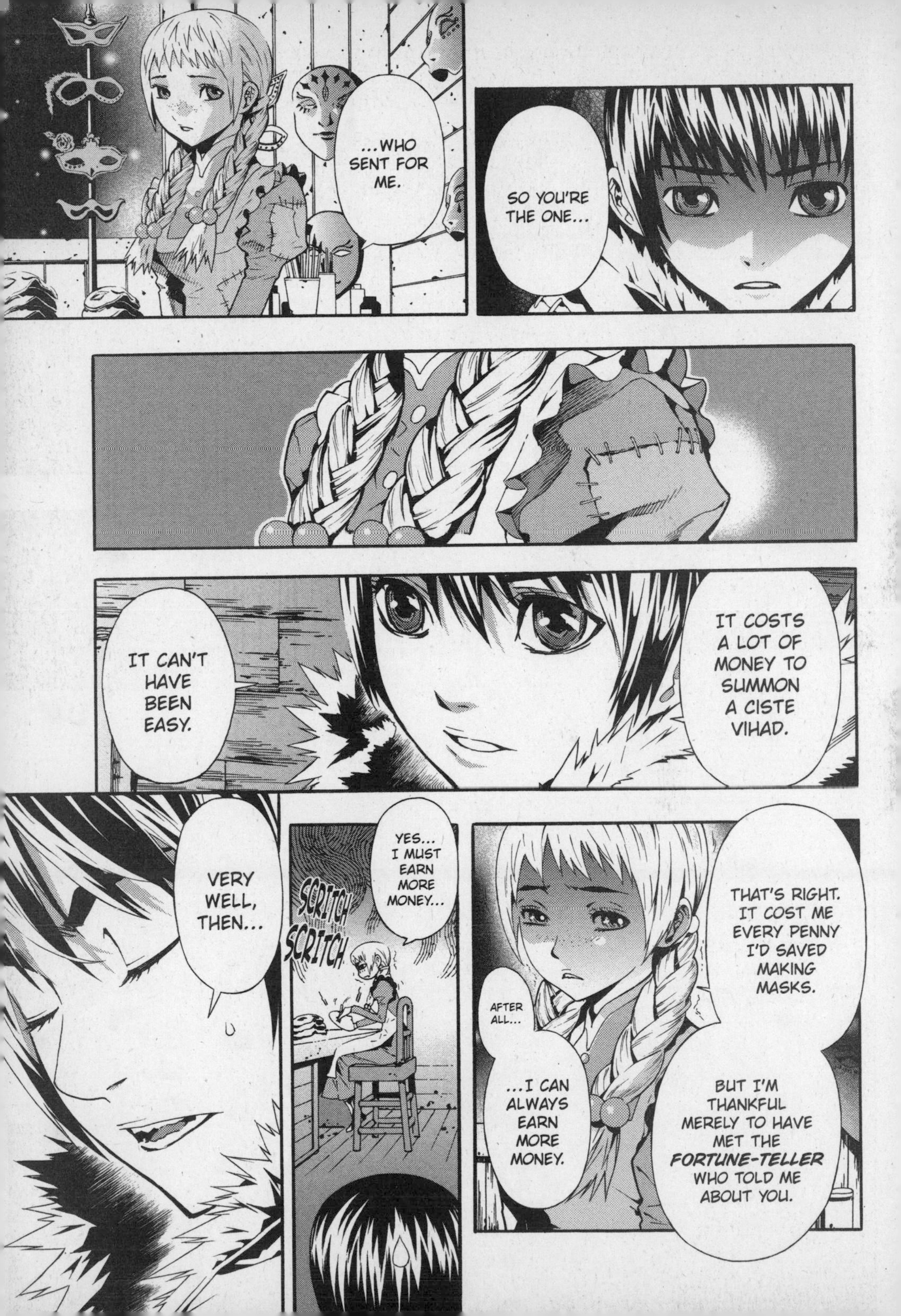
SO YOU'RE THE ONE...
...WHO SENT FOR ME.
IT COSTS A LOT OF MONEY TO SUMMON A CISTE VIHAD.
IT CAN'T HAVE BEEN EASY.
THAT'S RIGHT. IT COST ME EVERY PENNY I'D SAVED MAKING MASKS.
BUT I'M THANKFUL MERELY TO HAVE MET THE FORTUNE-TELLER WHO TOLD ME ABOUT YOU.
AFTER ALL...
...I CAN ALWAYS EARN MORE MONEY.
YES... I MUST EARN MORE MONEY...
SCRITCH
SCRITCH
VERY WELL, THEN...

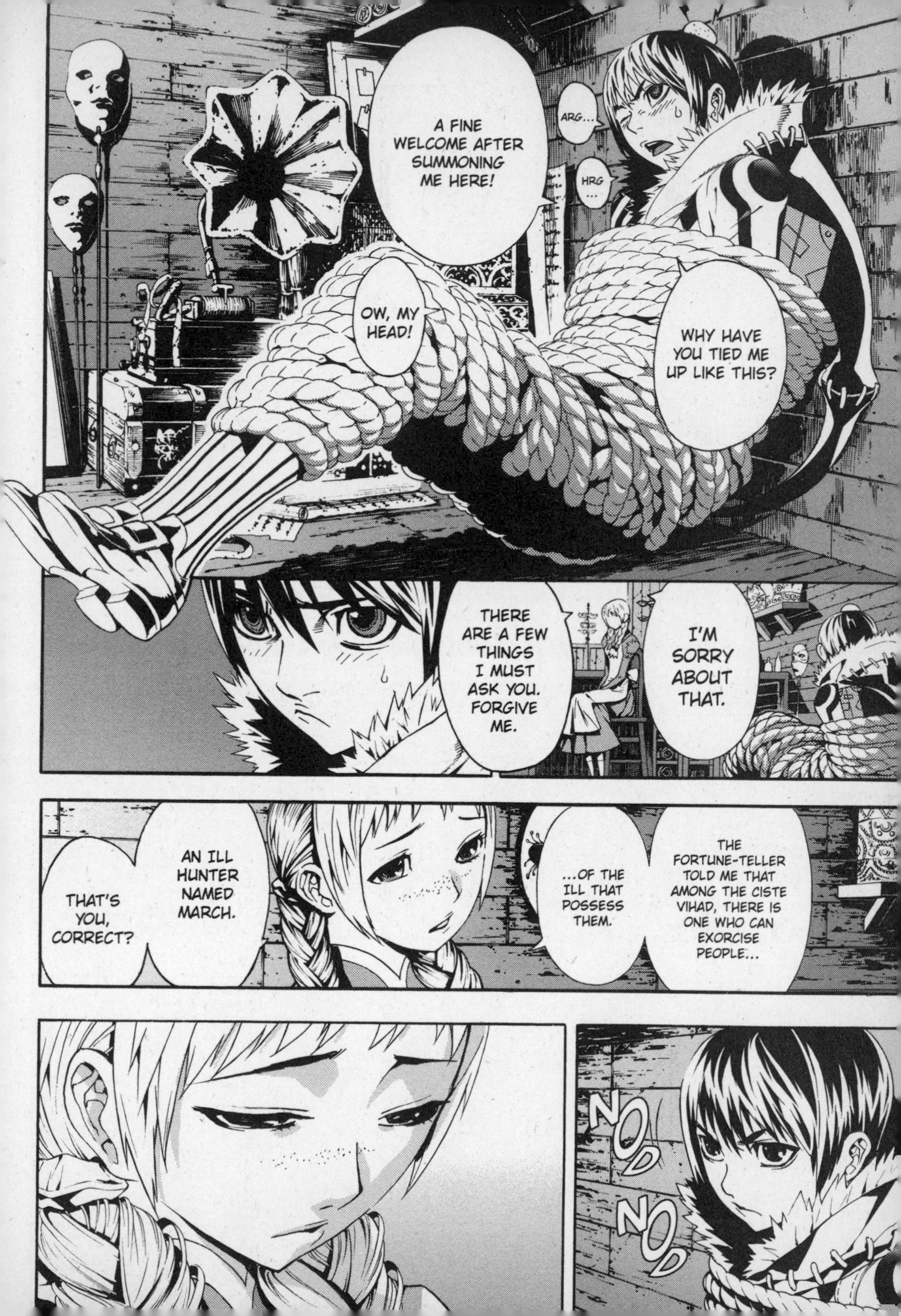
ARG...
HRG...
A FINE WELCOME AFTER SUMMONING ME HERE!
WHY HAVE YOU TIED ME UP LIKE THIS?
OW, MY HEAD!
I'M SORRY ABOUT THAT.
THERE ARE A FEW THINGS I MUST ASK YOU. FORGIVE ME.
THE FORTUNE-TELLER TOLD ME THAT AMONG THE CISTE VIHAD, THERE IS ONE WHO CAN EXORCISE PEOPLE...
...OF THE ILL THAT POSSESS THEM.
AN ILL HUNTER NAMED MARCH.
THAT'S YOU, CORRECT?
NOD
NOD

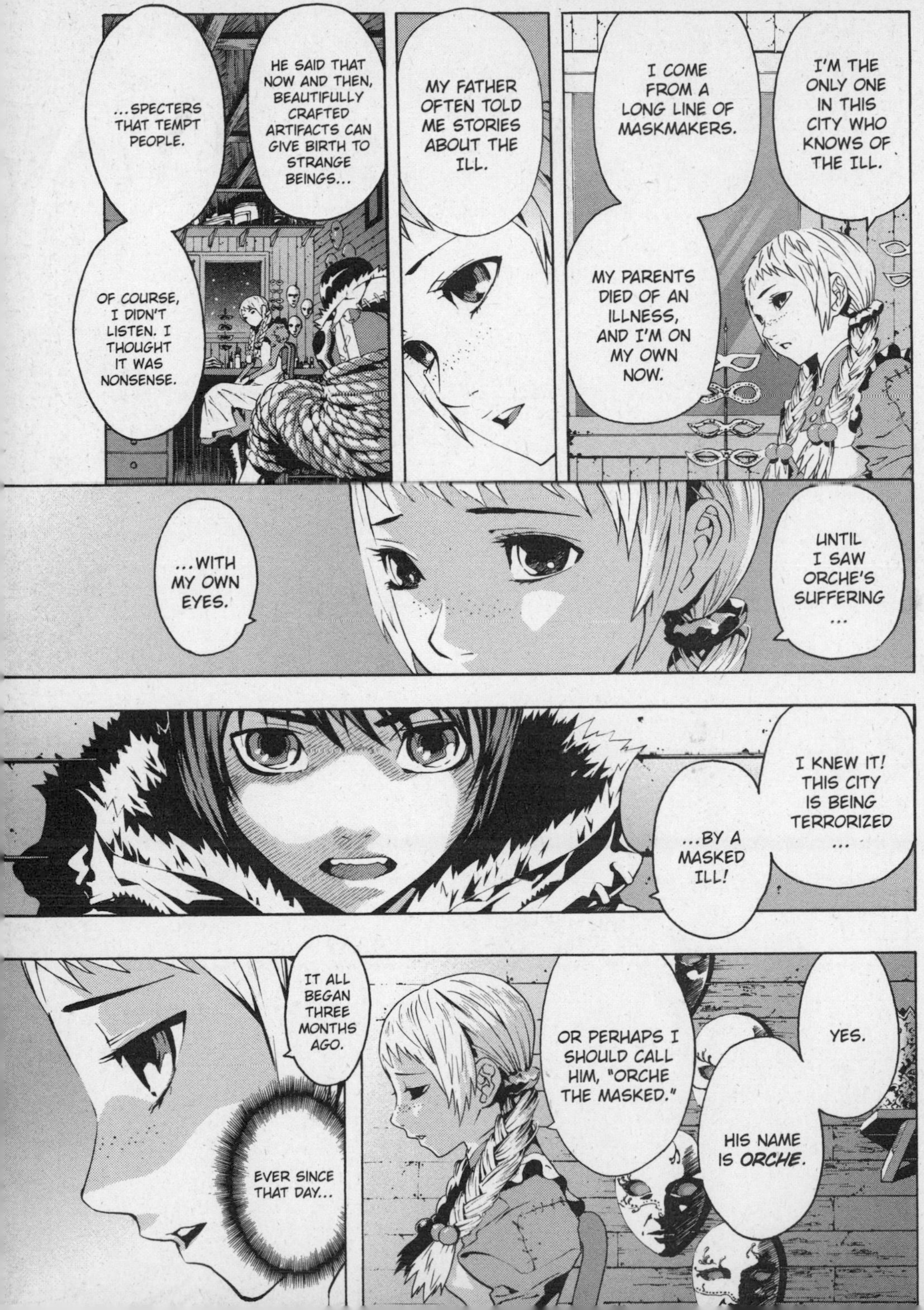
I'M THE ONLY ONE IN THIS CITY WHO KNOWS OF THE ILL.
I COME FROM A LONG LINE OF MASKMAKERS.
MY PARENTS DIED OF AN ILLNESS, AND I'M ON MY OWN NOW.
MY FATHER OFTEN TOLD ME STORIES ABOUT THE ILL.
HE SAID THAT NOW AND THEN, BEAUTIFULLY CRAFTED ARTIFACTS CAN GIVE BIRTH TO STRANGE BEINGS...
...SPECTERS THAT TEMPT PEOPLE.
OF COURSE, I DIDN'T LISTEN. I THOUGHT IT WAS NONSENSE.
UNTIL I SAW ORCHE'S SUFFERING...
...WITH MY OWN EYES.
I KNEW IT! THIS CITY IS BEING TERRORIZED...
...BY A MASKED ILL!
YES.
HIS NAME IS *ORCHE*.
OR PERHAPS I SHOULD CALL HIM, "ORCHE THE MASKED."
IT ALL BEGAN THREE MONTHS AGO.
EVER SINCE THAT DAY...

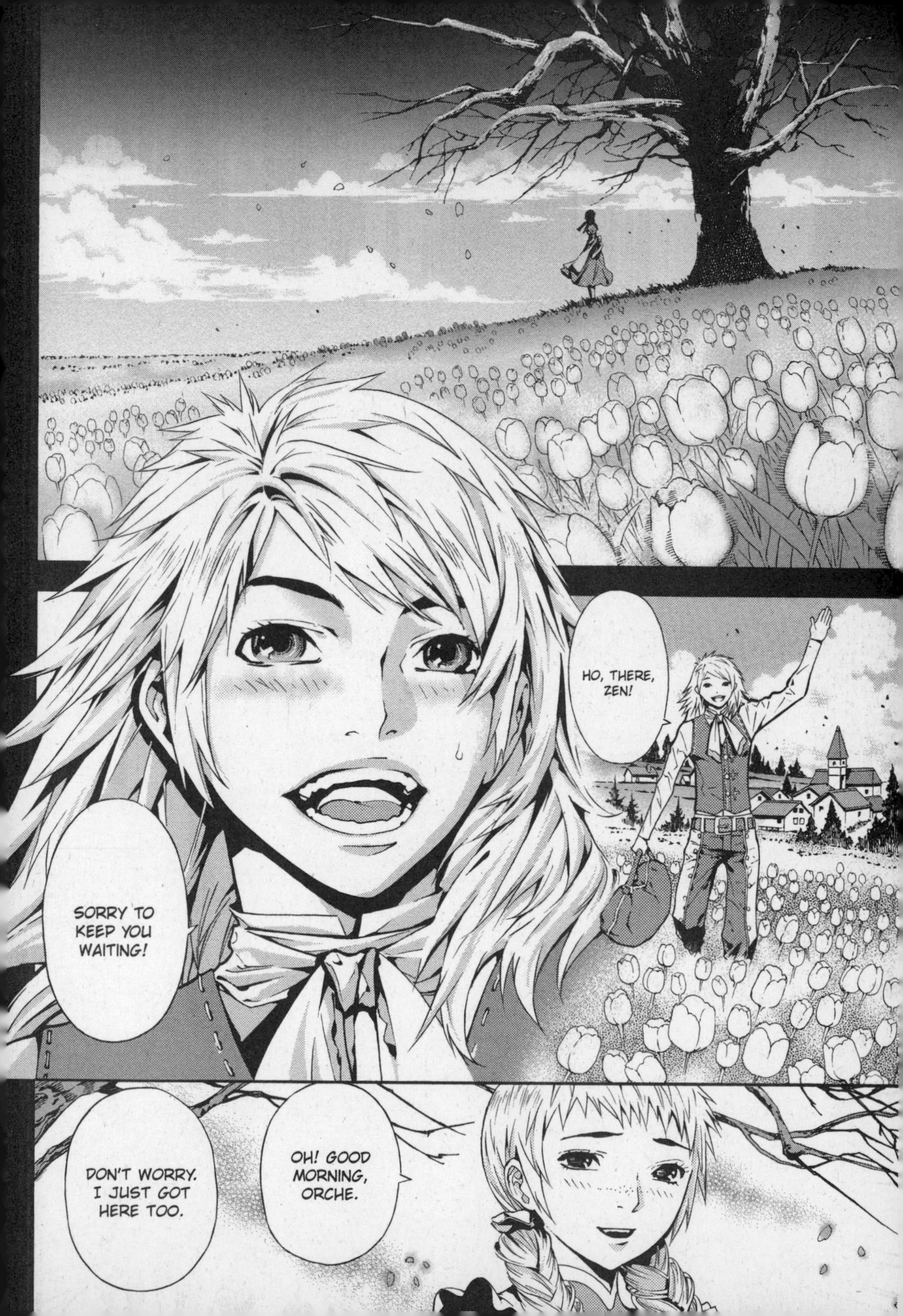

HO, THERE, ZEN!
SORRY TO KEEP YOU WAITING!
OH! GOOD MORNING, ORCHE.
DON'T WORRY. I JUST GOT HERE TOO.

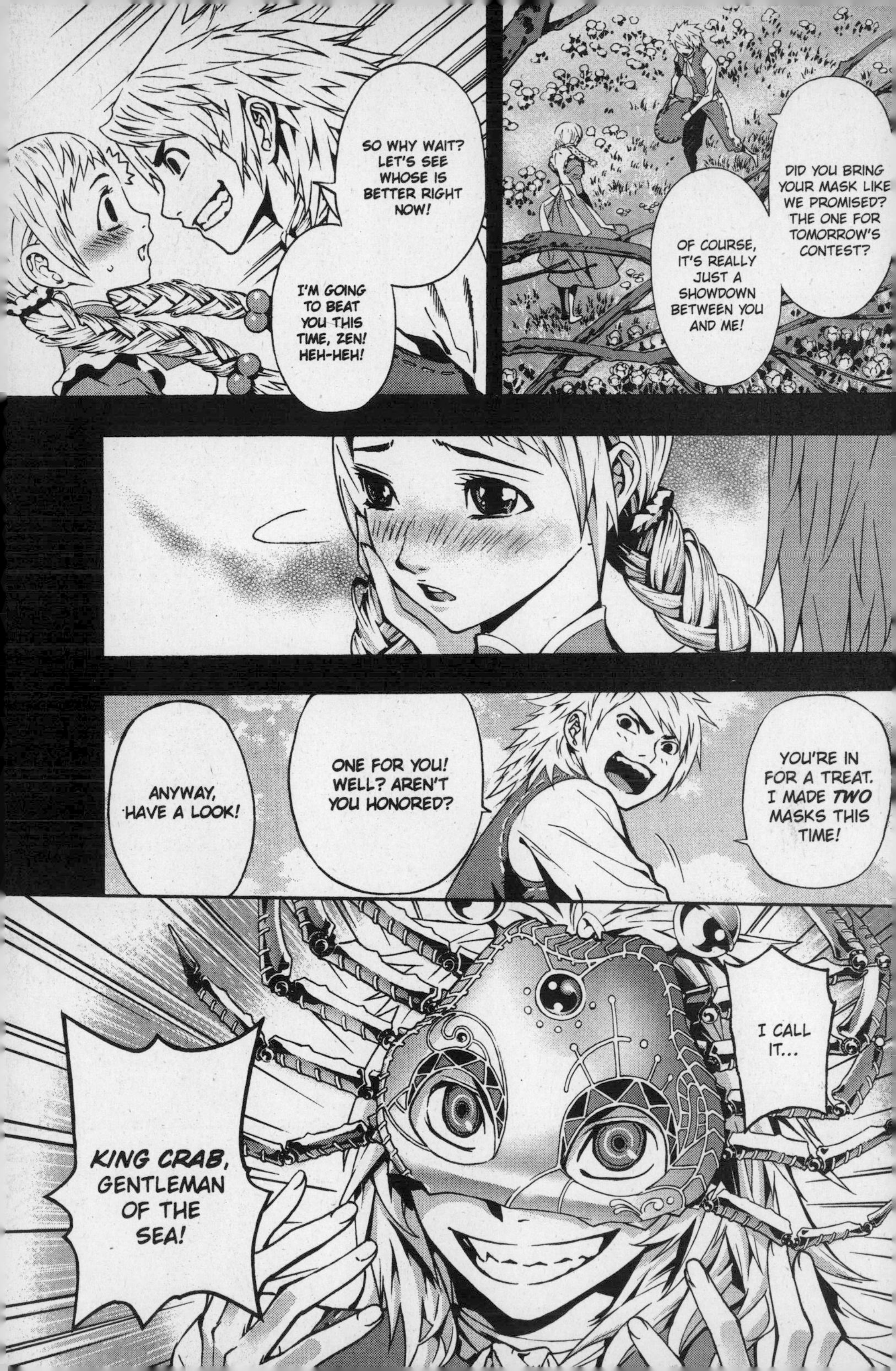
DID YOU BRING YOUR MASK LIKE WE PROMISED? THE ONE FOR TOMORROW'S CONTEST?
OF COURSE, IT'S REALLY JUST A SHOWDOWN BETWEEN YOU AND ME!
SO WHY WAIT? LET'S SEE WHOSE IS BETTER RIGHT NOW!
I'M GOING TO BEAT YOU THIS TIME, ZEN! HEH-HEH!
YOU'RE IN FOR A TREAT. I MADE *TWO* MASKS THIS TIME!
ONE FOR YOU! WELL? AREN'T YOU HONORED?
ANYWAY, HAVE A LOOK!
I CALL IT...
KING CRAB, GENTLEMAN OF THE SEA!

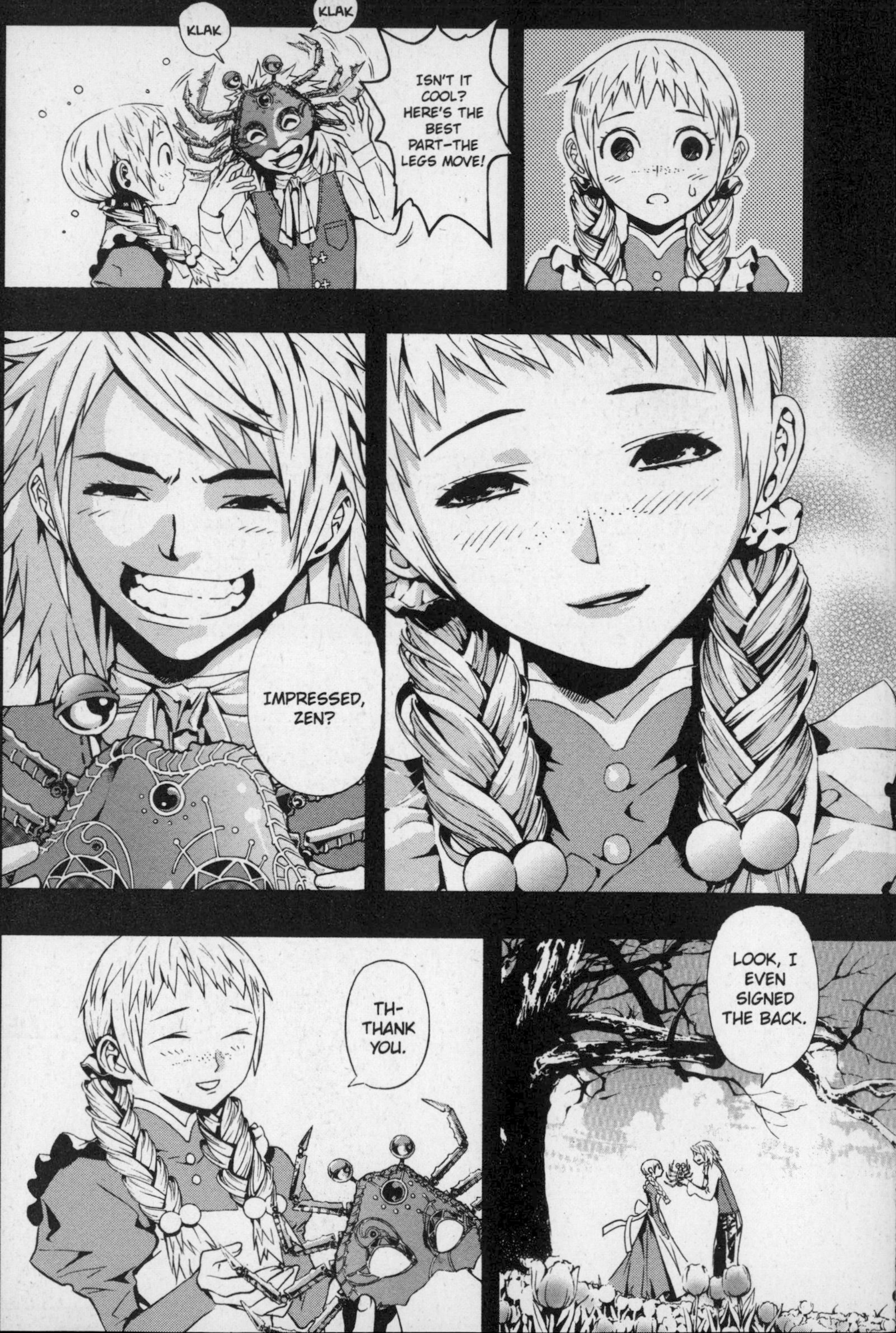
KLAK
KLAK
ISN'T IT COOL? HERE'S THE BEST PART—THE LEGS MOVE!
IMPRESSED, ZEN?
LOOK, I EVEN SIGNED THE BACK.
TH- THANK YOU.

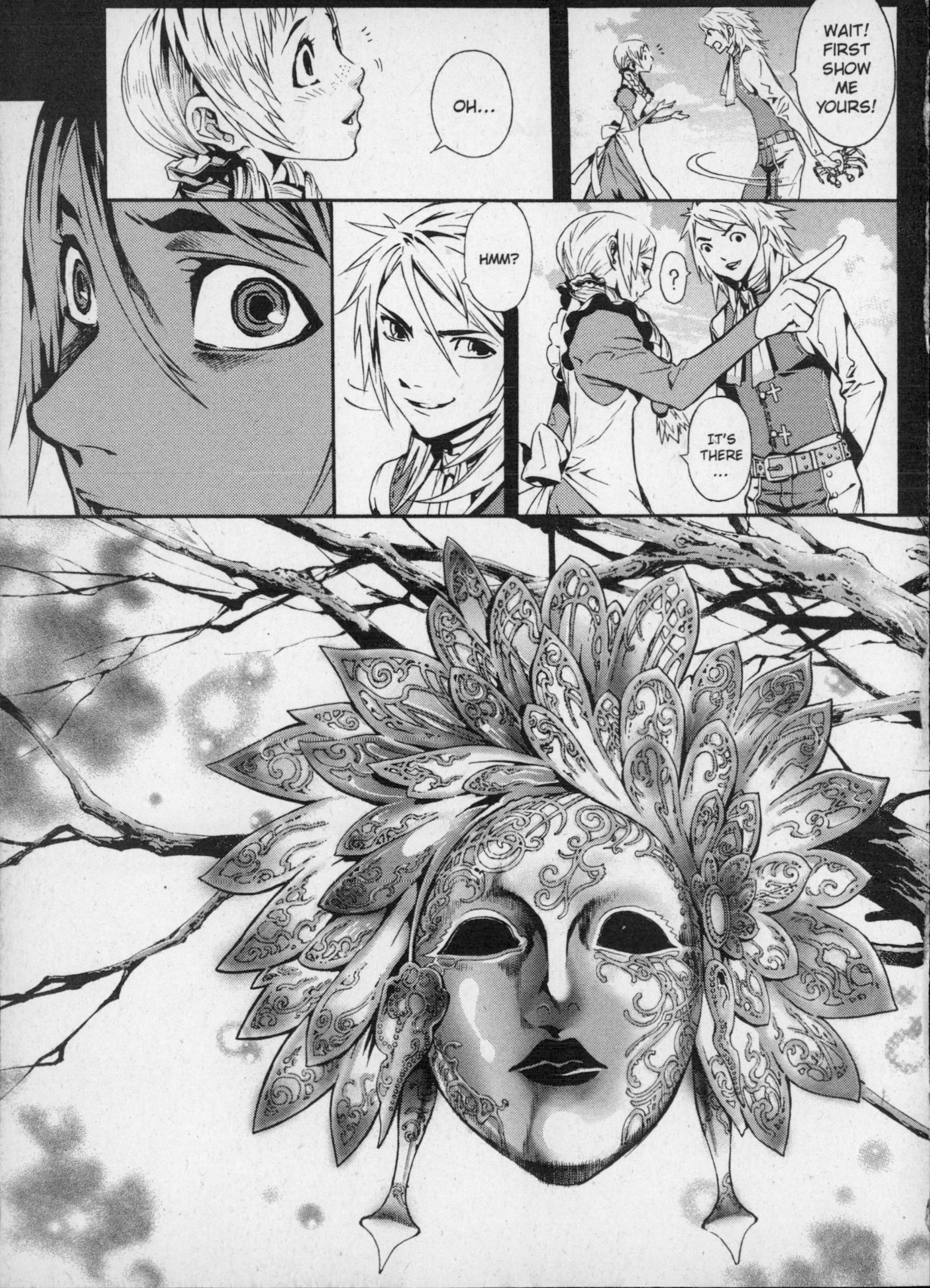
WAIT! FIRST SHOW ME YOURS!
OH...
?
IT'S THERE ...
HMM?

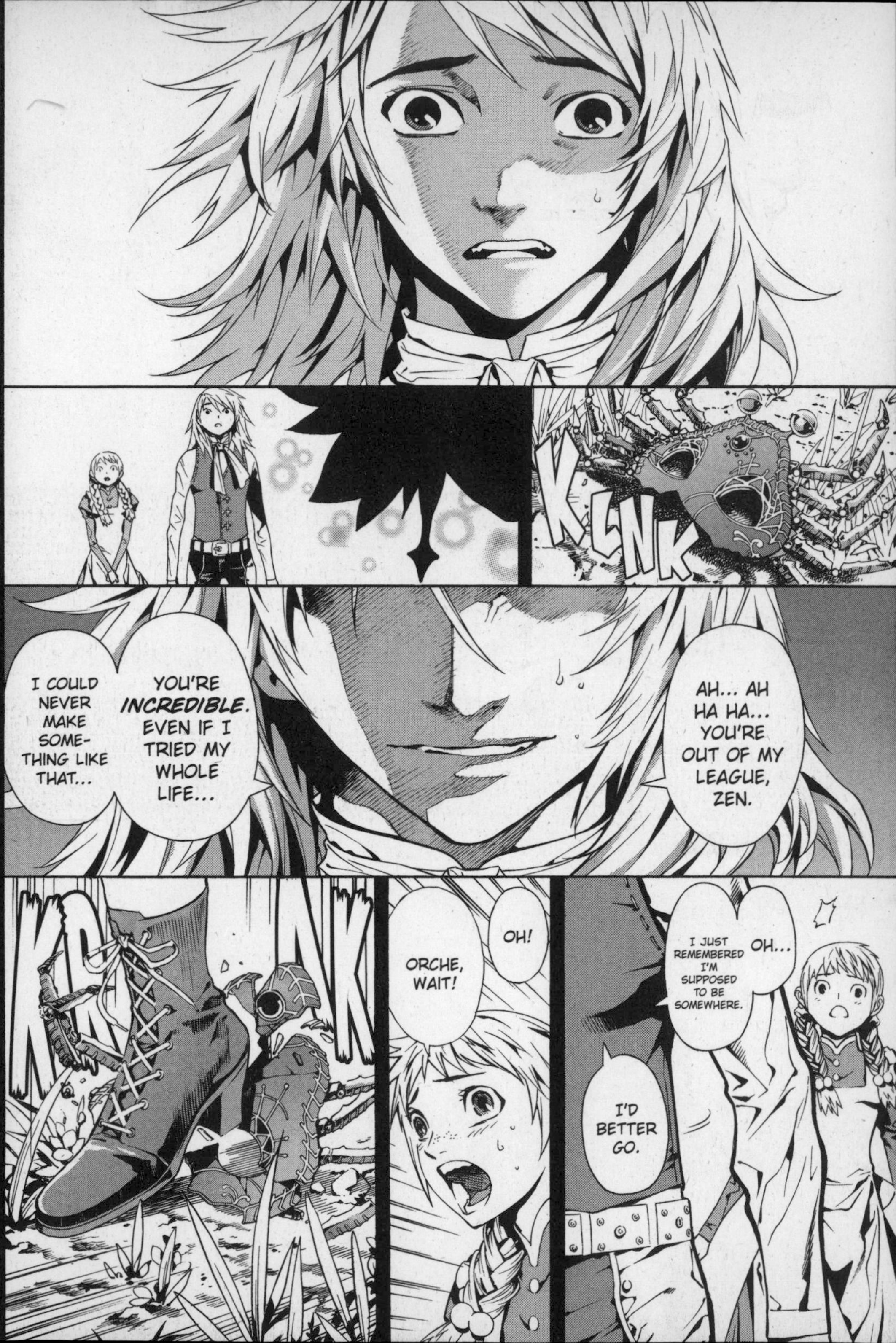
AH... AH HA HA... YOU'RE OUT OF MY LEAGUE, ZEN.
YOU'RE *INCREDIBLE*. EVEN IF I TRIED MY WHOLE LIFE...
I COULD NEVER MAKE SOME-THING LIKE THAT...
OH...
I JUST REMEMBERED I'M SUPPOSED TO BE SOMEWHERE.
I'D BETTER GO.
OH!
ORCHE, WAIT!

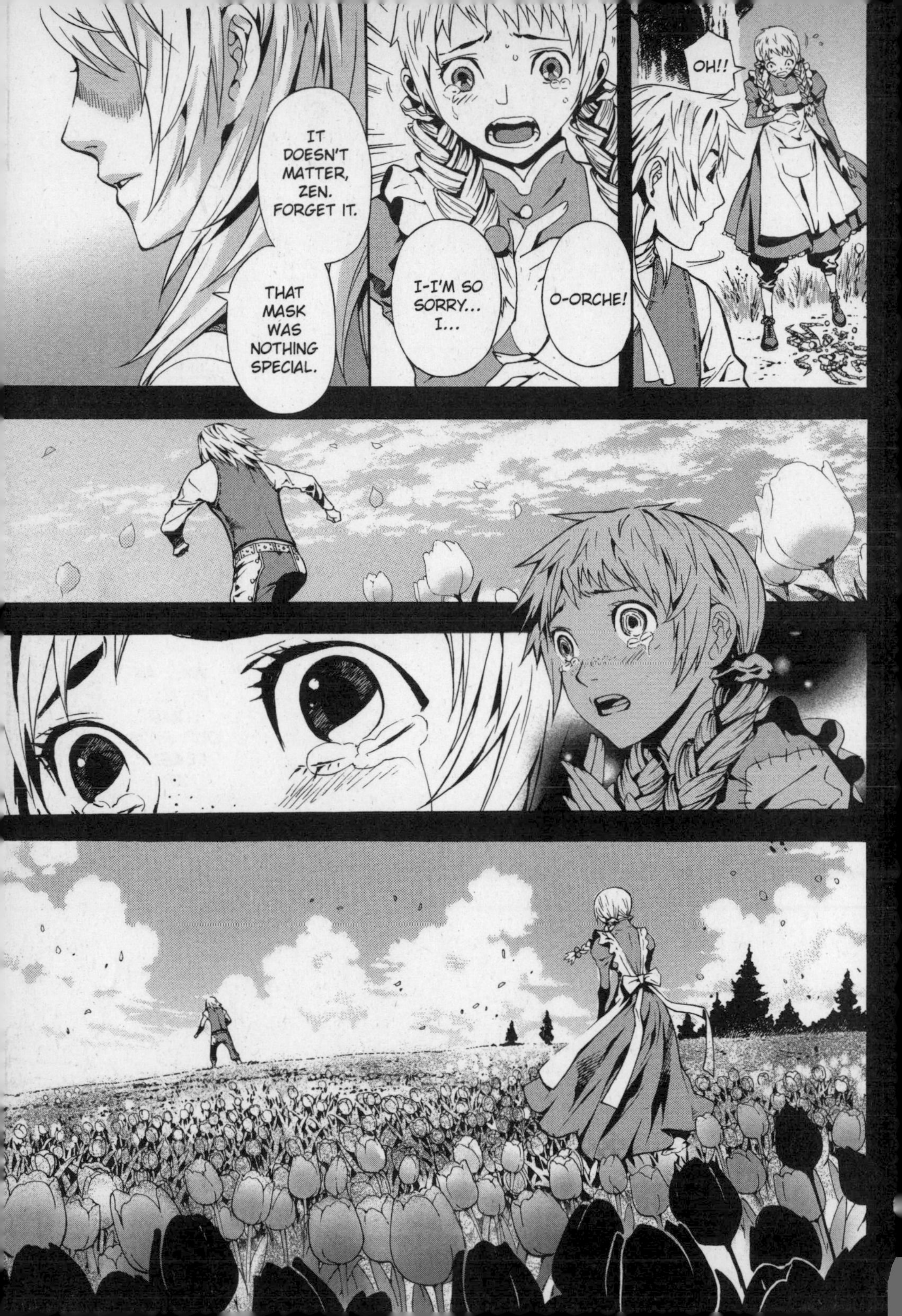
OH!!
O-ORCHE!
I-I'M SO SORRY... I...
IT DOESN'T MATTER, ZEN. FORGET IT.
THAT MASK WAS NOTHING SPECIAL.

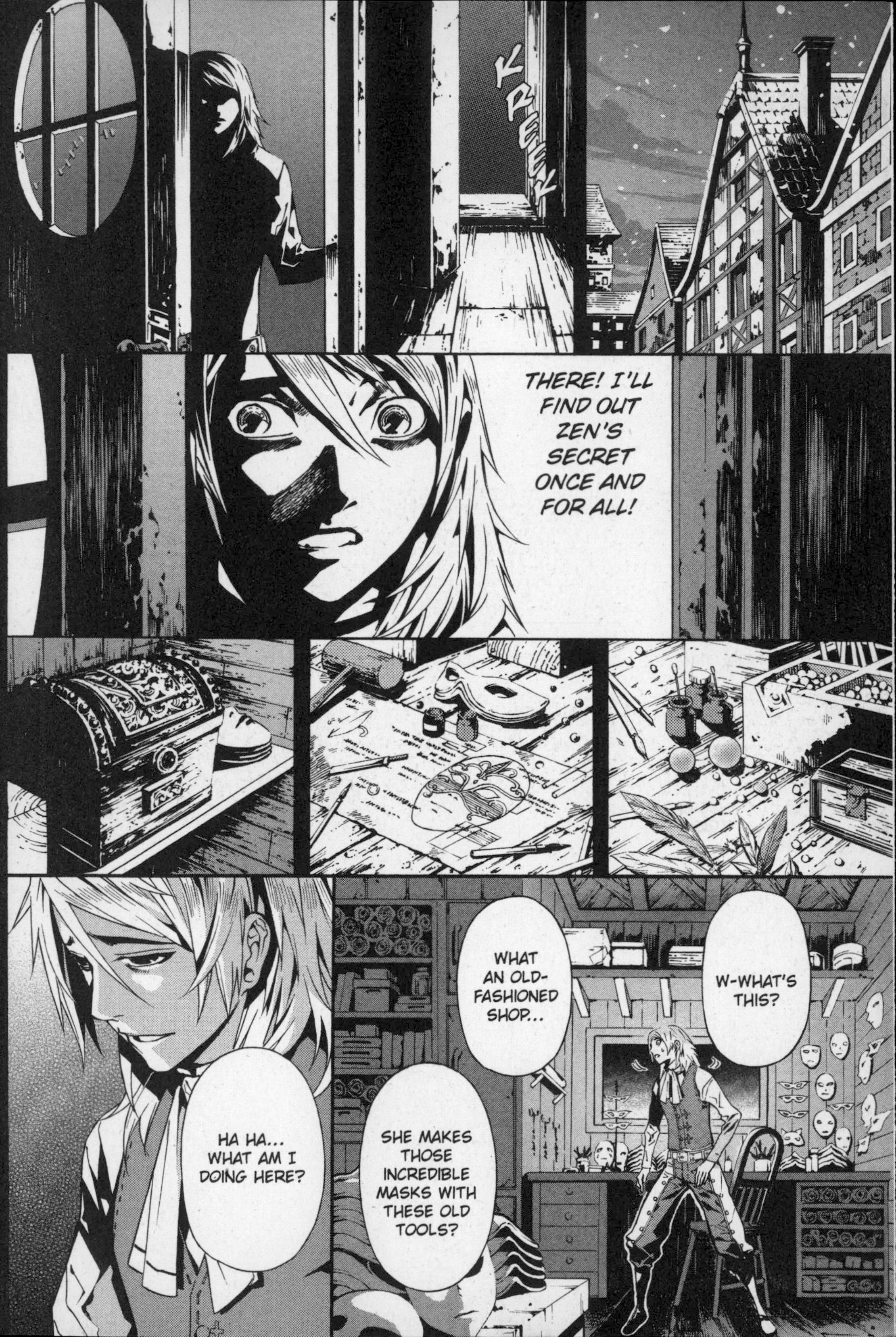
KREEK
THERE! I'LL FIND OUT ZEN'S SECRET ONCE AND FOR ALL!
W-WHAT'S THIS?
WHAT AN OLD-FASHIONED SHOP...
SHE MAKES THOSE INCREDIBLE MASKS WITH THESE OLD TOOLS?
HA HA... WHAT AM I DOING HERE?

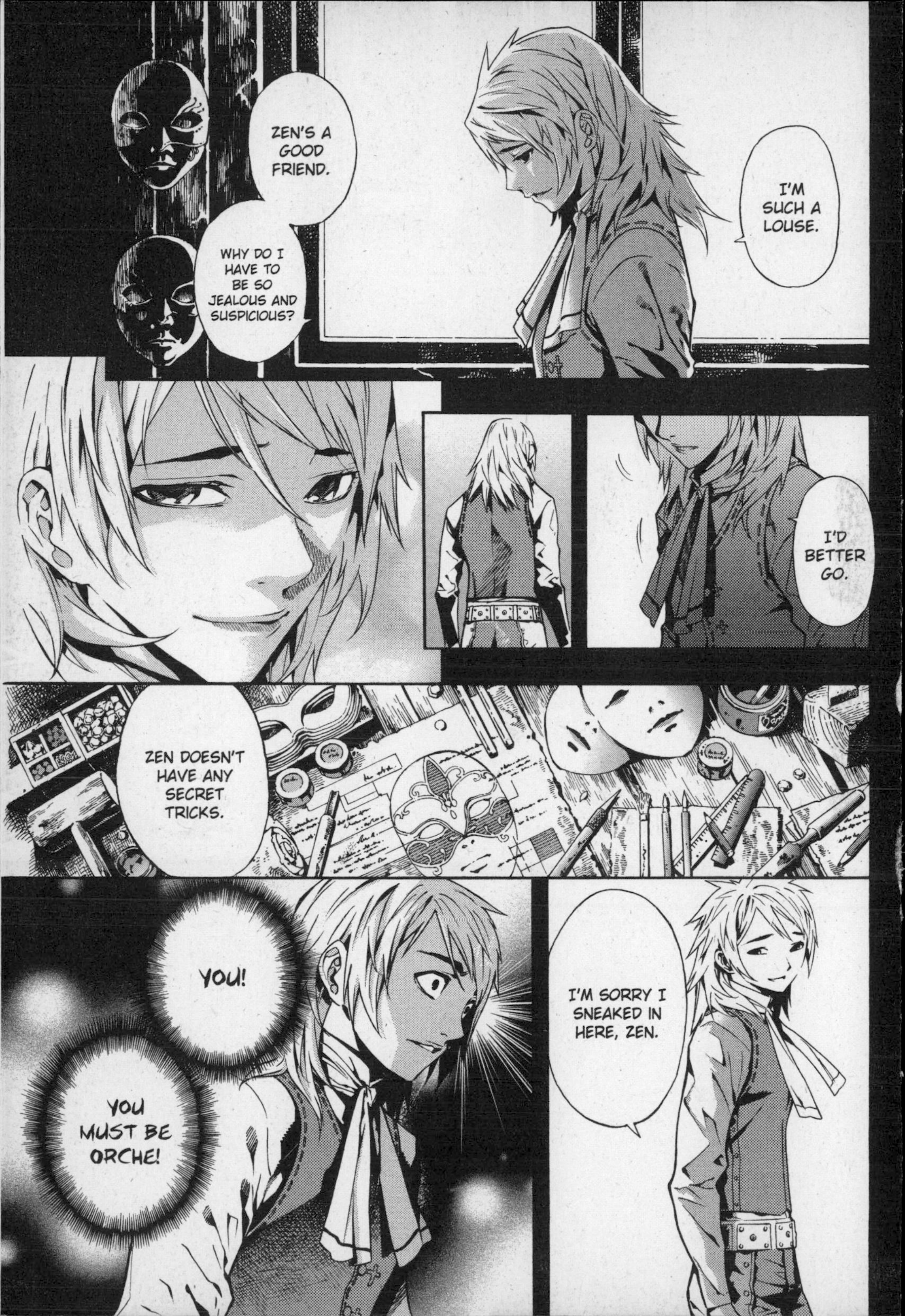
I'M SUCH A LOUSE.
ZEN'S A GOOD FRIEND.
WHY DO I HAVE TO BE SO JEALOUS AND SUSPICIOUS?
I'D BETTER GO.
ZEN DOESN'T HAVE ANY SECRET TRICKS.
I'M SORRY I SNEAKED IN HERE, ZEN.
YOU!
YOU MUST BE ORCHE!

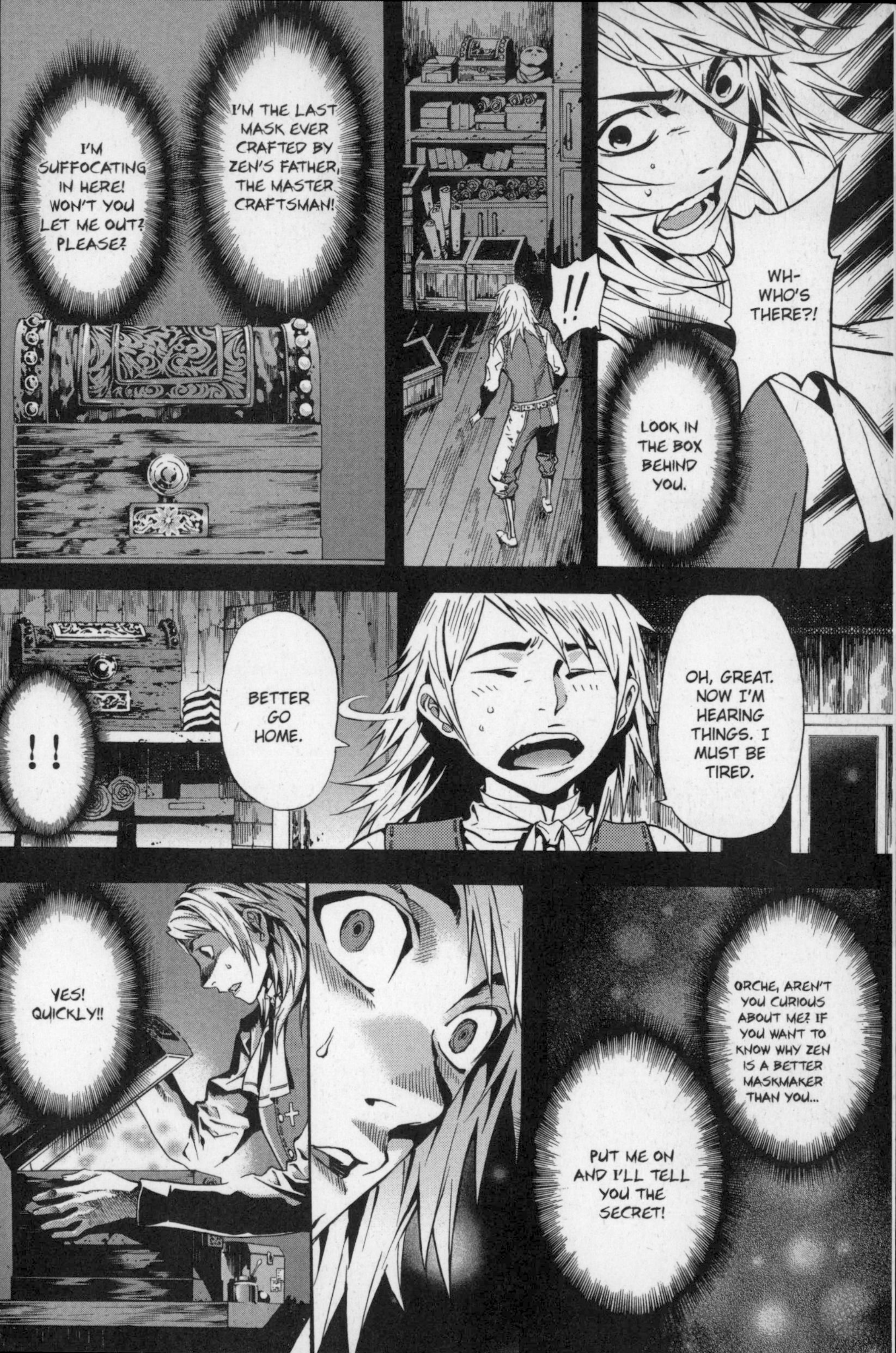
!!
WH- WHO'S THERE?!
LOOK IN THE BOX BEHIND YOU.
I'M THE LAST MASK EVER CRAFTED BY ZEN'S FATHER, THE MASTER CRAFTSMAN!
I'M SUFFOCATING IN HERE! WON'T YOU LET ME OUT? PLEASE?
OH, GREAT. NOW I'M HEARING THINGS. I MUST BE TIRED.
BETTER GO HOME.
!!
ORCHE, AREN'T YOU CURIOUS ABOUT ME? IF YOU WANT TO KNOW WHY ZEN IS A BETTER MASKMAKER THAN YOU...
PUT ME ON AND I'LL TELL YOU THE SECRET!
YES! QUICKLY!!

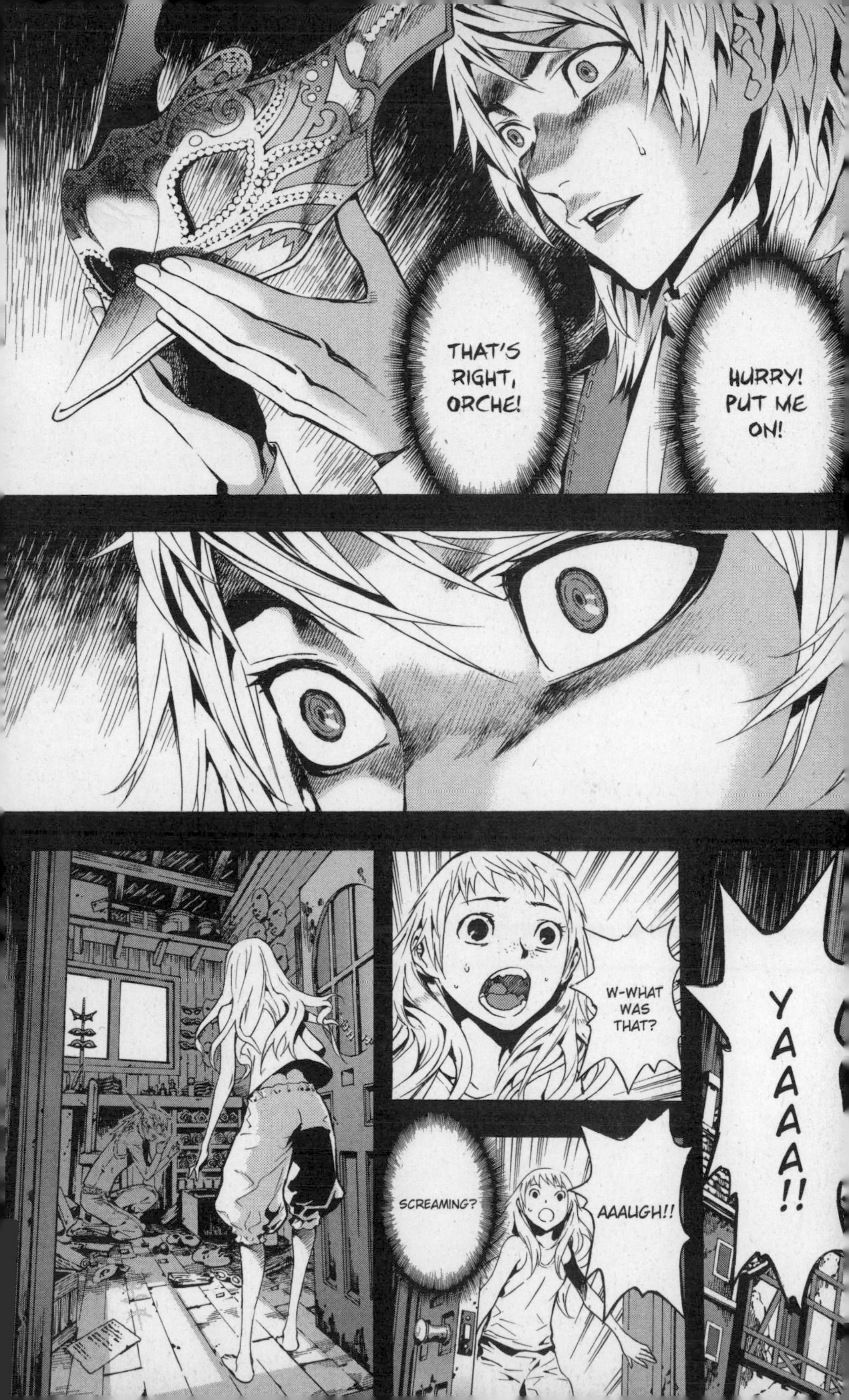
HURRY! PUT ME ON!
THAT'S RIGHT, ORCHE!
YAAAA!!
W-WHAT WAS THAT?
AAAUGH!!
SCREAMING?

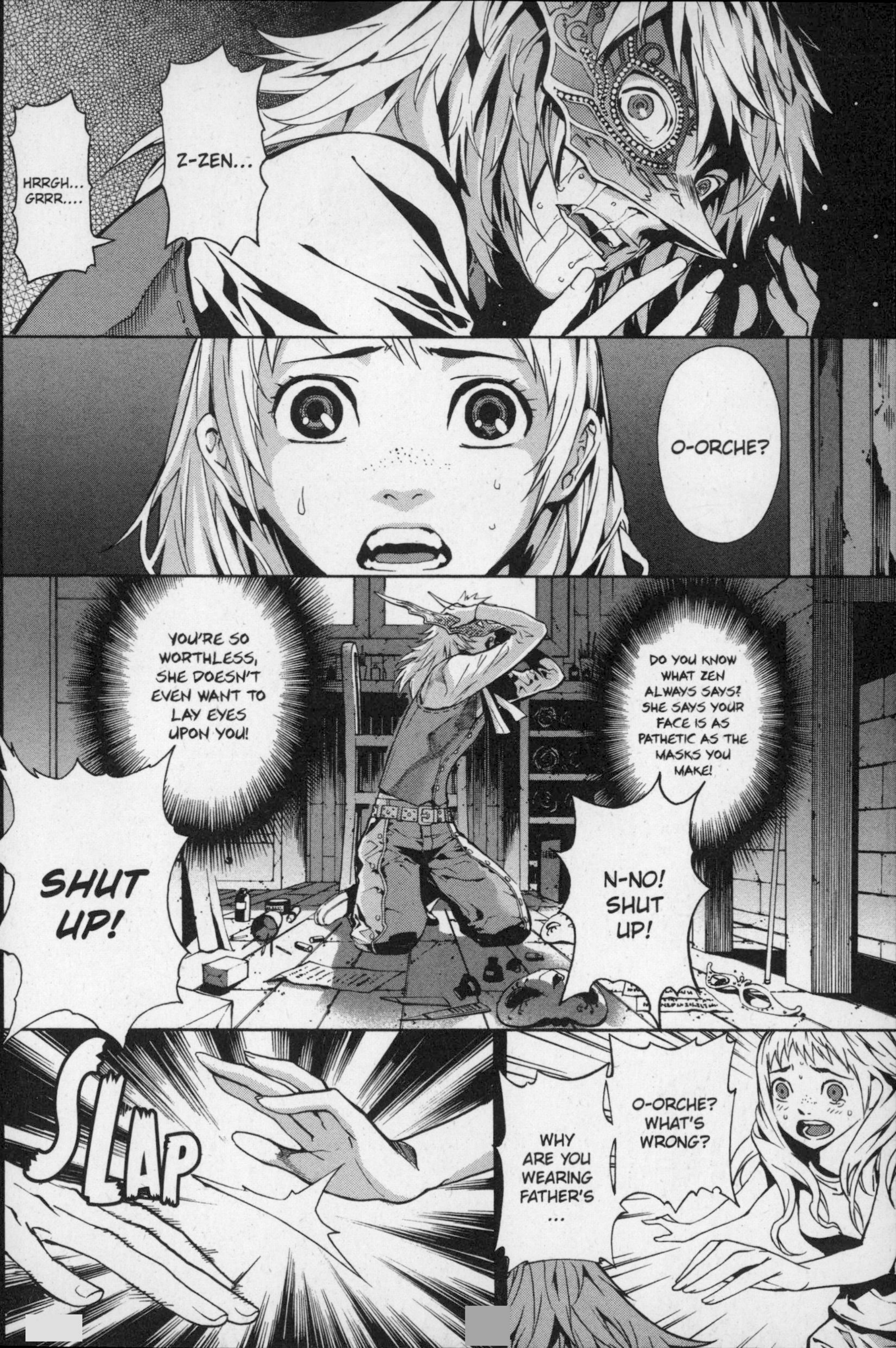
Z-ZEN...
HRRGH... GRRR....
O-ORCHE?
DO YOU KNOW WHAT ZEN ALWAYS SAYS? SHE SAYS YOUR FACE IS AS PATHETIC AS THE MASKS YOU MAKE!
YOU'RE SO WORTHLESS, SHE DOESN'T EVEN WANT TO LAY EYES UPON YOU!
N-NO! SHUT UP!
SHUT UP!
O-ORCHE? WHAT'S WRONG?
WHY ARE YOU WEARING FATHER'S ...
SLAP

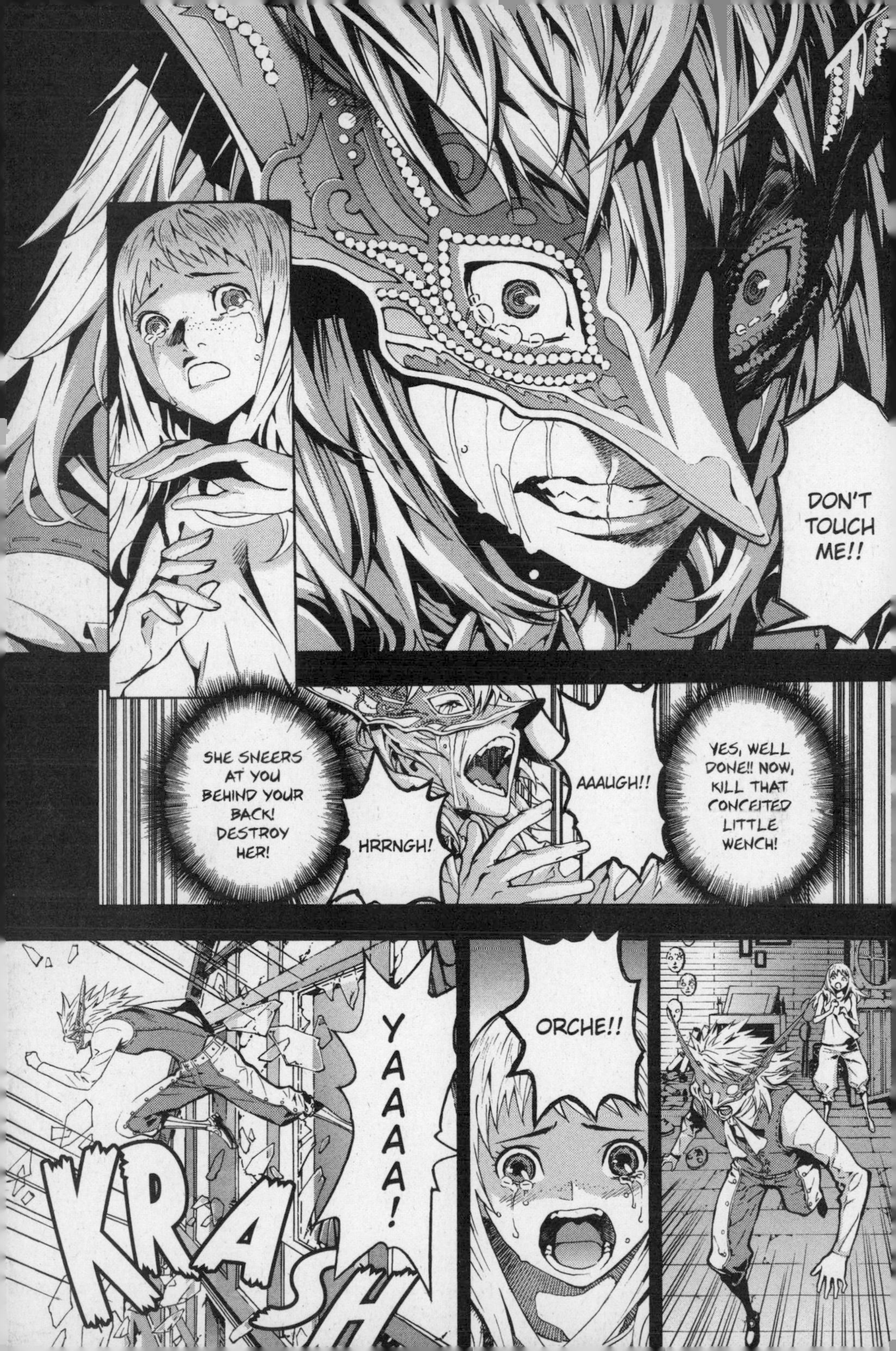
DON'T TOUCH ME!!
YES, WELL DONE!! NOW, KILL THAT CONCEITED LITTLE WENCH!
AAAUGH!!
HRRNGH!
SHE SNEERS AT YOU BEHIND YOUR BACK! DESTROY HER!
ORCHE!!
YAAAAA!
KRASH

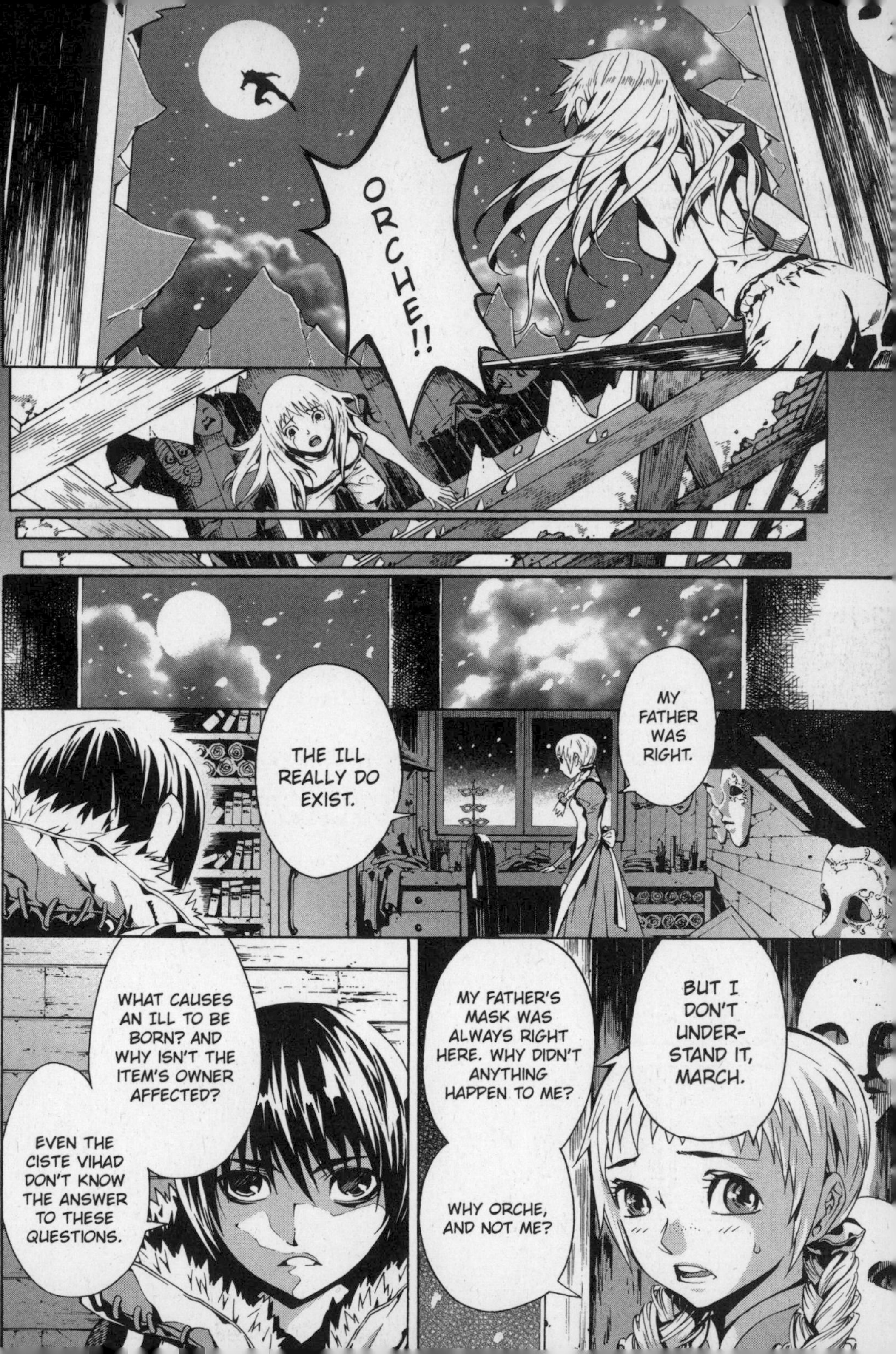
ORCHE!!
MY FATHER WAS RIGHT.
THE ILL REALLY DO EXIST.
BUT I DON'T UNDER-STAND IT, MARCH.
MY FATHER'S MASK WAS ALWAYS RIGHT HERE. WHY DIDN'T ANYTHING HAPPEN TO ME?
WHY ORCHE, AND NOT ME?
WHAT CAUSES AN ILL TO BE BORN? AND WHY ISN'T THE ITEM'S OWNER AFFECTED?
EVEN THE CISTE VIHAD DON'T KNOW THE ANSWER TO THESE QUESTIONS.

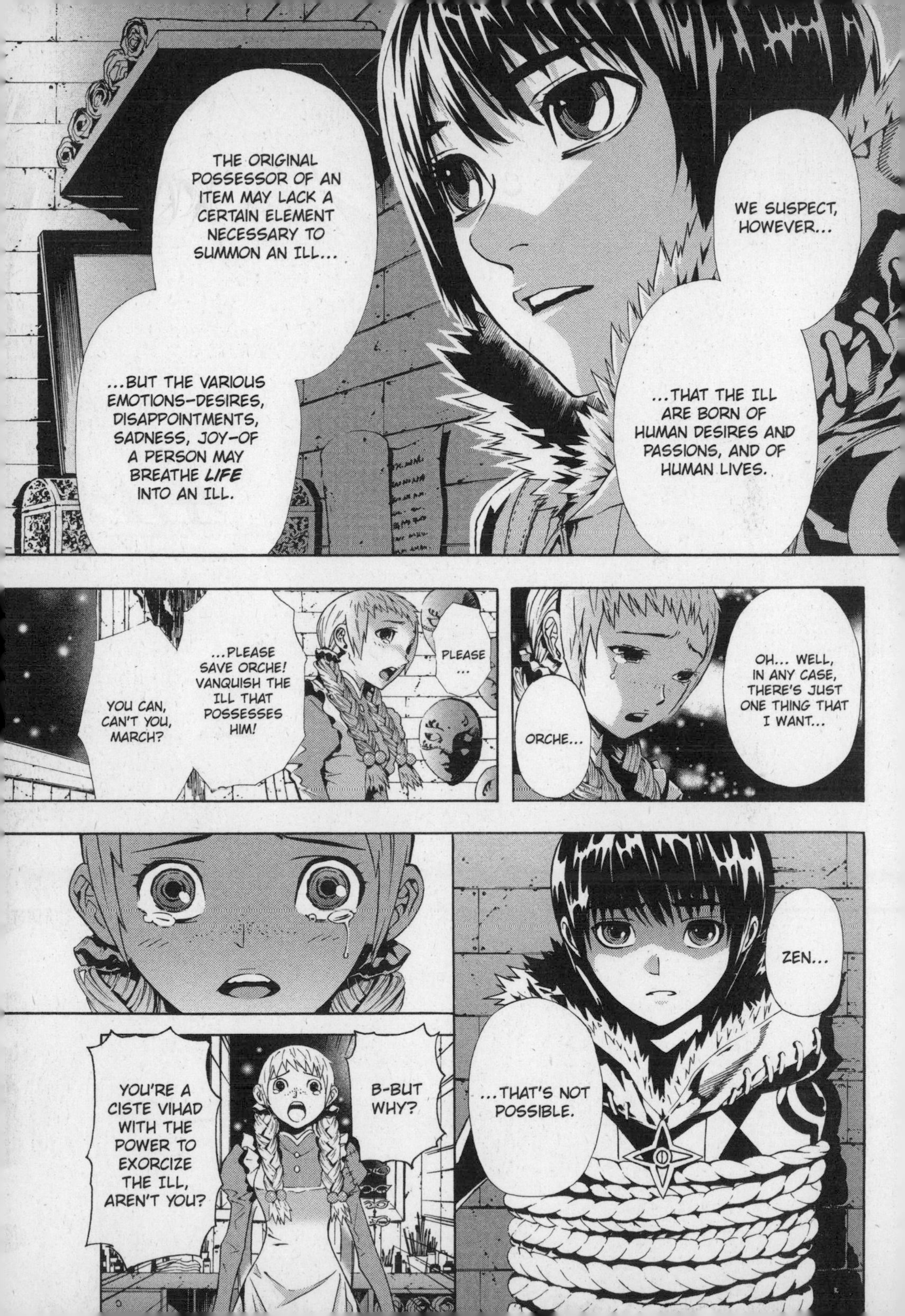
WE SUSPECT, HOWEVER...
...THAT THE ILL ARE BORN OF HUMAN DESIRES AND PASSIONS, AND OF HUMAN LIVES.
THE ORIGINAL POSSESSOR OF AN ITEM MAY LACK A CERTAIN ELEMENT NECESSARY TO SUMMON AN ILL...
...BUT THE VARIOUS EMOTIONS–DESIRES, DISAPPOINTMENTS, SADNESS, JOY–OF A PERSON MAY BREATHE ***LIFE*** INTO AN ILL.
OH... WELL, IN ANY CASE, THERE'S JUST ONE THING THAT I WANT...
ORCHE...
PLEASE ...
...PLEASE SAVE ORCHE! VANQUISH THE ILL THAT POSSESSES HIM!
YOU CAN, CAN'T YOU, MARCH?
ZEN...
...THAT'S NOT POSSIBLE.
B-BUT WHY?
YOU'RE A CISTE VIHAD WITH THE POWER TO EXORCIZE THE ILL, AREN'T YOU?

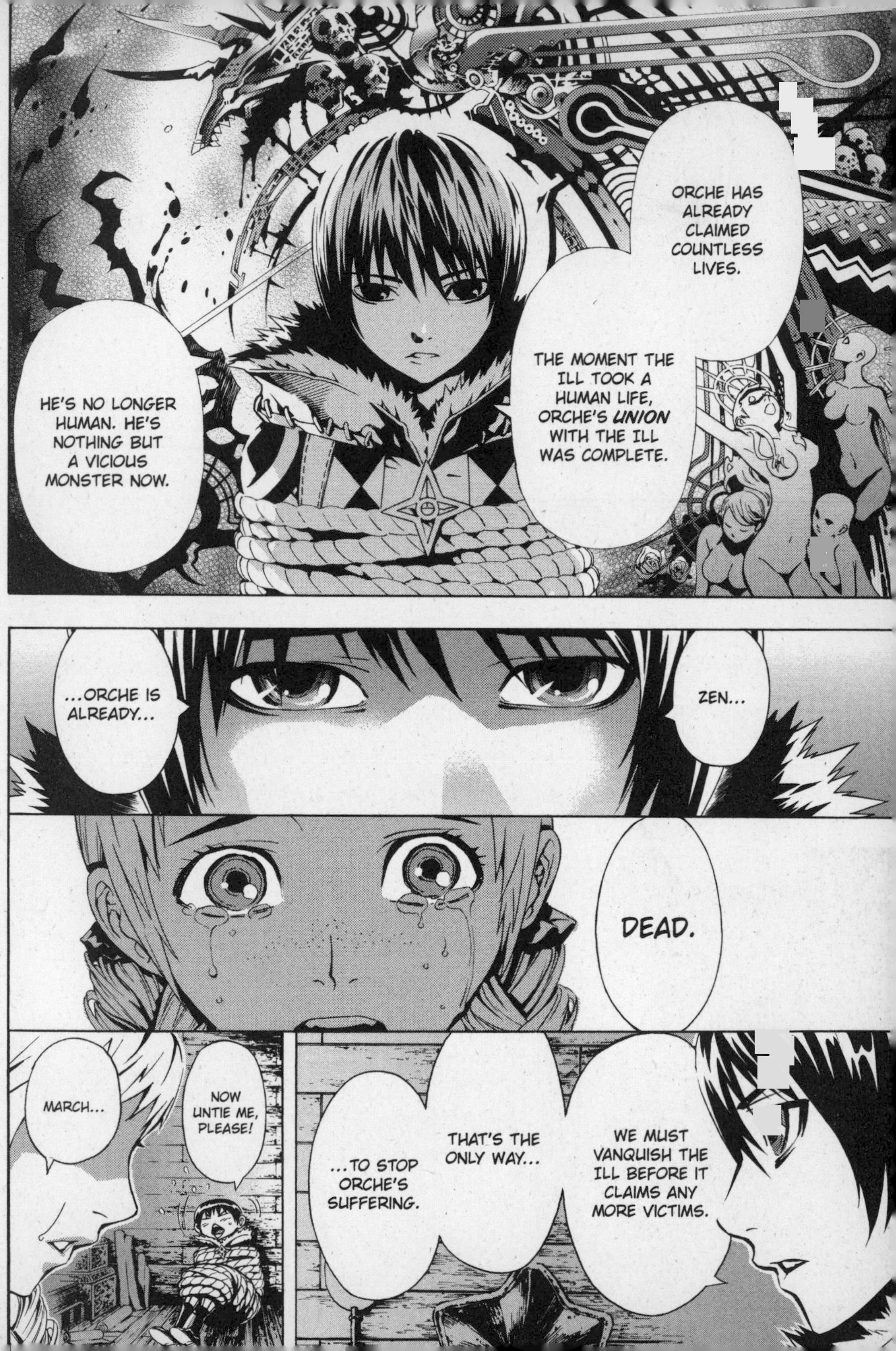
ORCHE HAS ALREADY CLAIMED COUNTLESS LIVES.
THE MOMENT THE ILL TOOK A HUMAN LIFE, ORCHE'S *UNION* WITH THE ILL WAS COMPLETE.
HE'S NO LONGER HUMAN. HE'S NOTHING BUT A VICIOUS MONSTER NOW.
ZEN...
...ORCHE IS ALREADY...
DEAD.
WE MUST VANQUISH THE ILL BEFORE IT CLAIMS ANY MORE VICTIMS.
THAT'S THE ONLY WAY...
...TO STOP ORCHE'S SUFFERING.
NOW UNTIE ME, PLEASE!
MARCH...

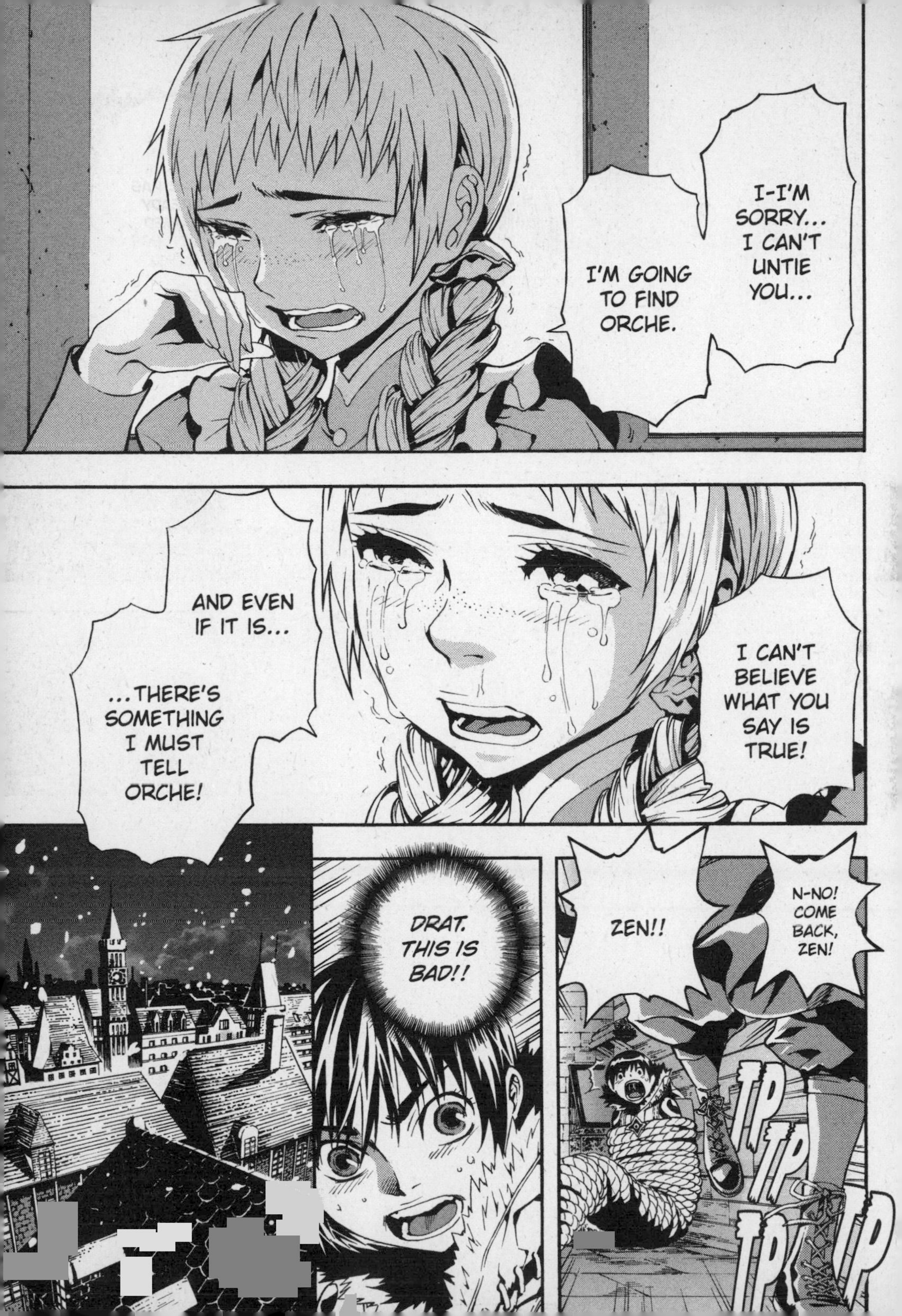
I-I'M SORRY... I CAN'T UNTIE YOU...
I'M GOING TO FIND ORCHE.
I CAN'T BELIEVE WHAT YOU SAY IS TRUE!
AND EVEN IF IT IS...
...THERE'S SOMETHING I MUST TELL ORCHE!
N-NO! COME BACK, ZEN!
ZEN!!
TP TP TP TP
DRAT. THIS IS BAD!!

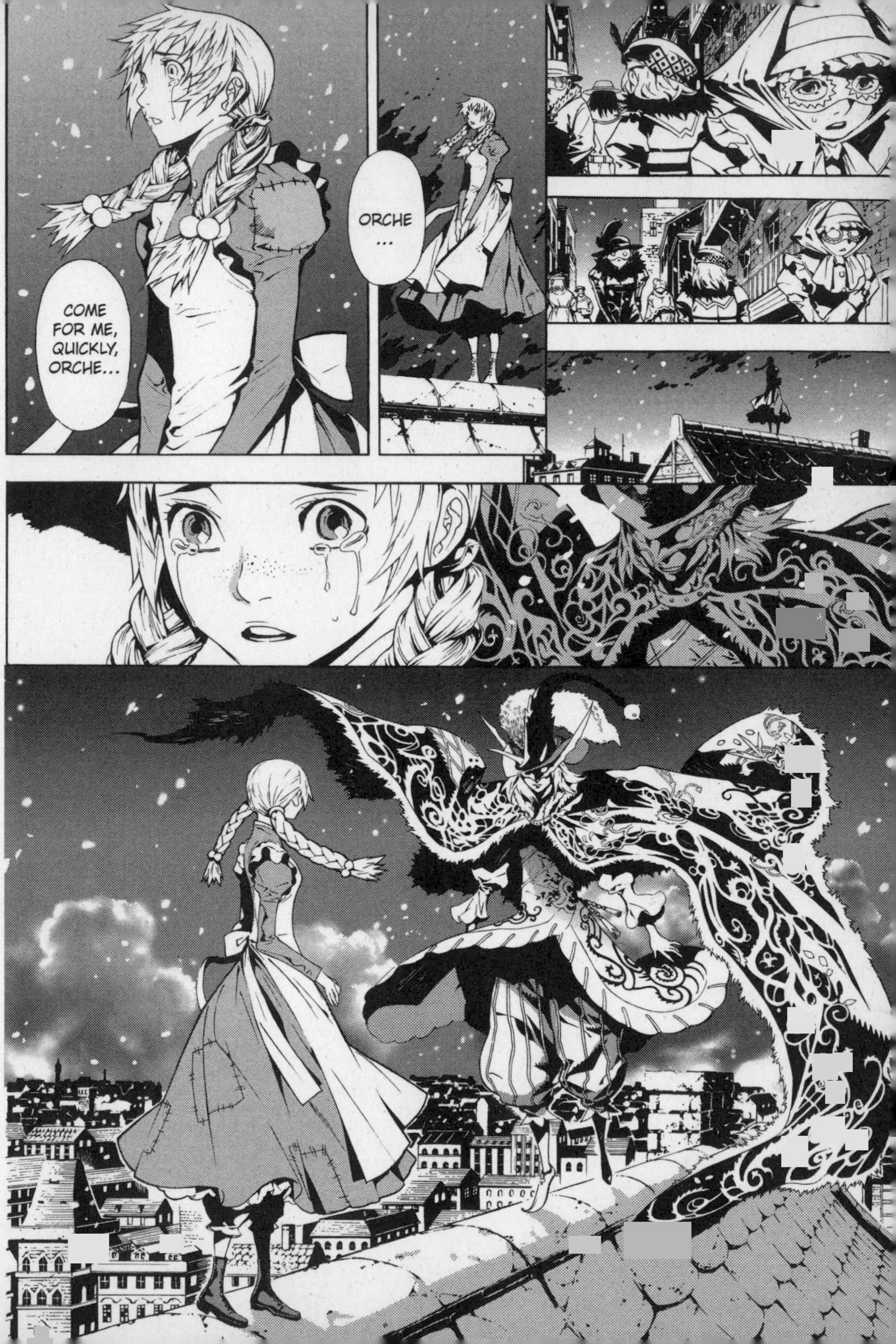
ORCHE ...
COME FOR ME, QUICKLY, ORCHE...

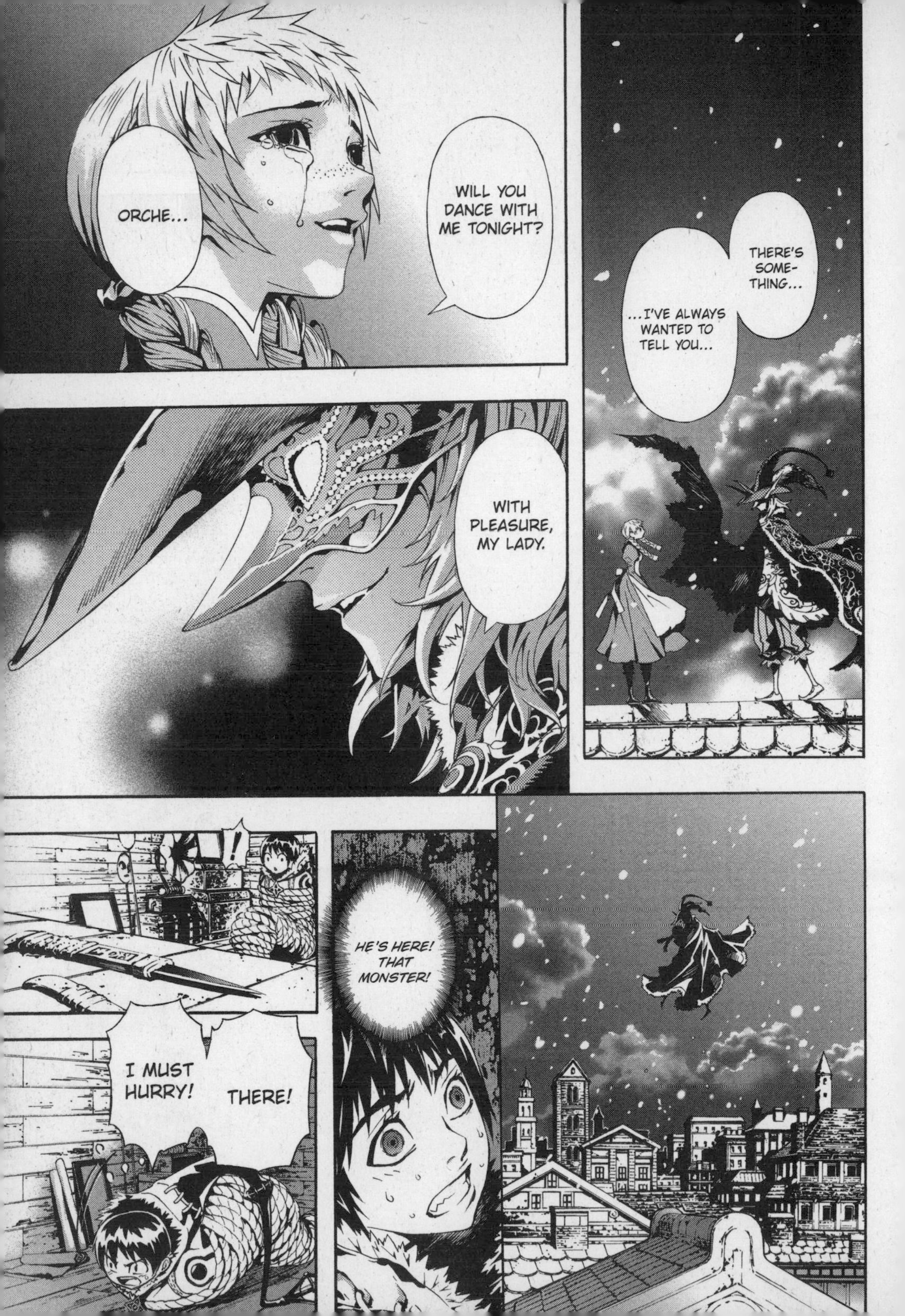
THERE'S SOME-THING...
...I'VE ALWAYS WANTED TO TELL YOU...
WILL YOU DANCE WITH ME TONIGHT?
ORCHE...
WITH PLEASURE, MY LADY.
HE'S HERE! THAT MONSTER!
!
THERE!
I MUST HURRY!

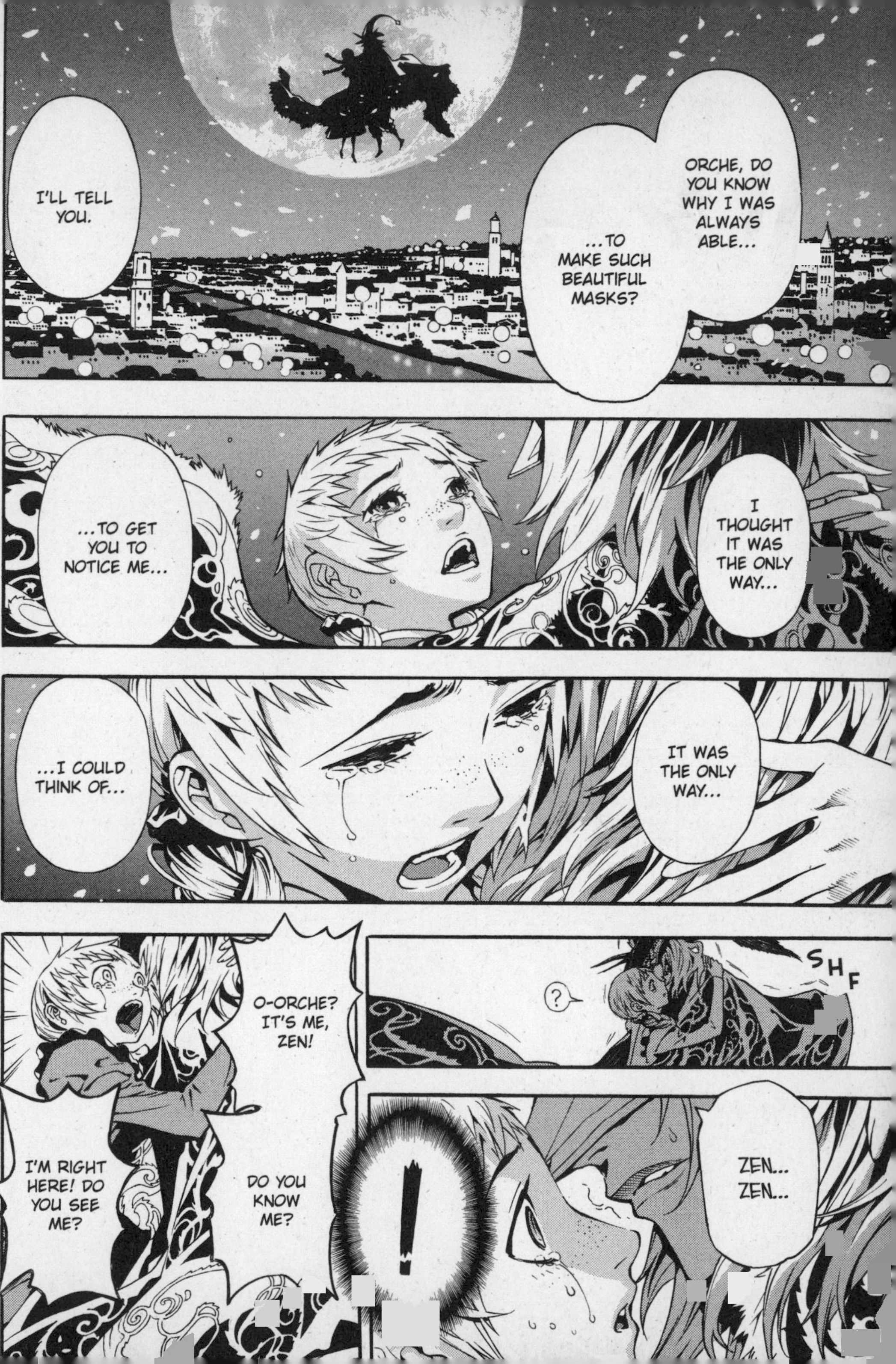
ORCHE, DO YOU KNOW WHY I WAS ALWAYS ABLE...
...TO MAKE SUCH BEAUTIFUL MASKS?
I'LL TELL YOU.
I THOUGHT IT WAS THE ONLY WAY...
...TO GET YOU TO NOTICE ME...
IT WAS THE ONLY WAY...
...I COULD THINK OF...
SHF
?
O-ORCHE? IT'S ME, ZEN!
ZEN... ZEN...
!
DO YOU KNOW ME?
I'M RIGHT HERE! DO YOU SEE ME?

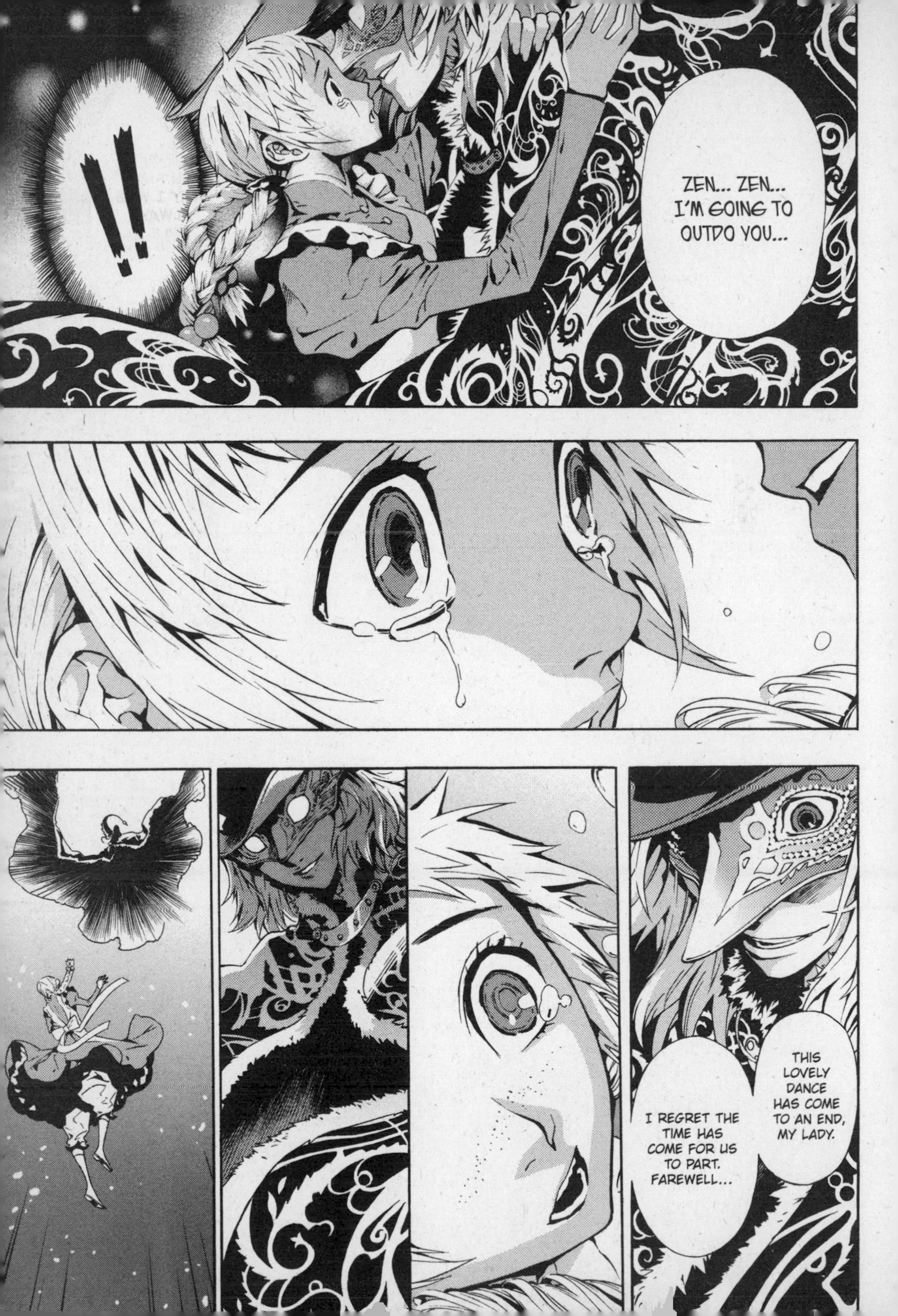
ZEN... ZEN... I'M GOING TO OUTDO YOU...
!!
THIS LOVELY DANCE HAS COME TO AN END, MY LADY.
I REGRET THE TIME HAS COME FOR US TO PART. FAREWELL...

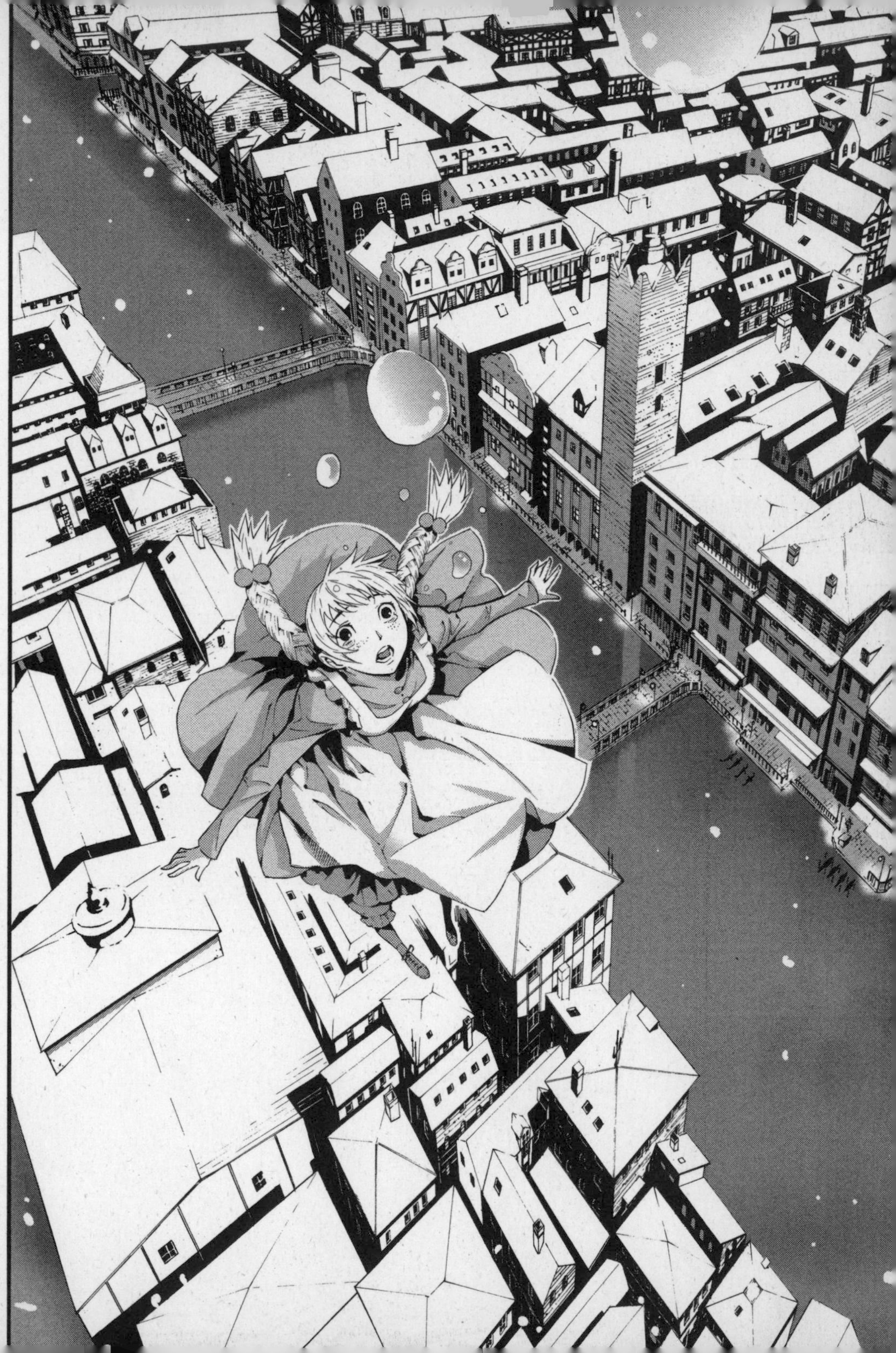

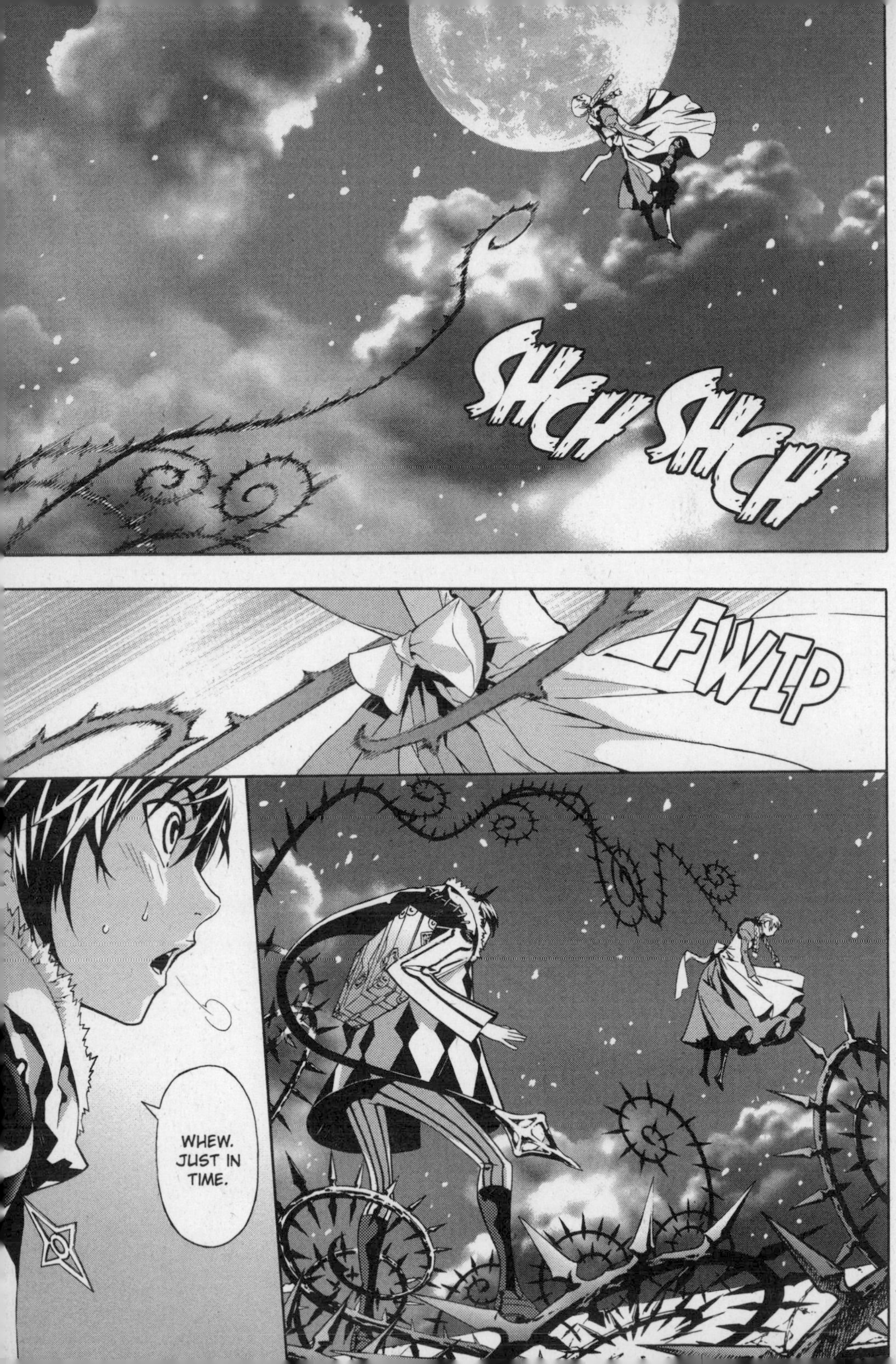
SHCH SHCH
FWIP
WHEW. JUST IN TIME.

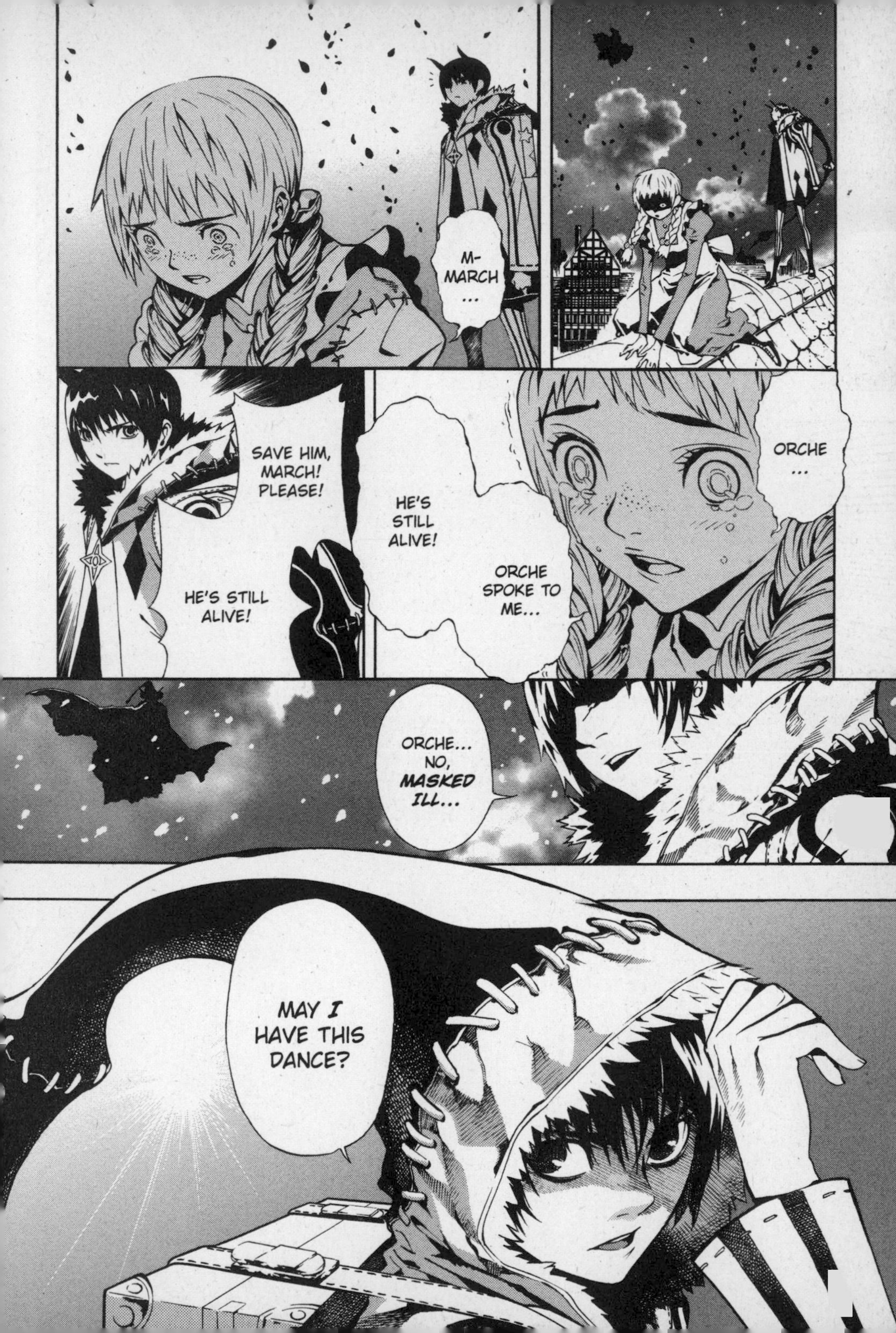
M-MARCH...
ORCHE...
HE'S STILL ALIVE!
ORCHE SPOKE TO ME...
SAVE HIM, MARCH! PLEASE!
HE'S STILL ALIVE!
ORCHE... NO, *MASKED ILL*...
MAY *I* HAVE THIS DANCE?

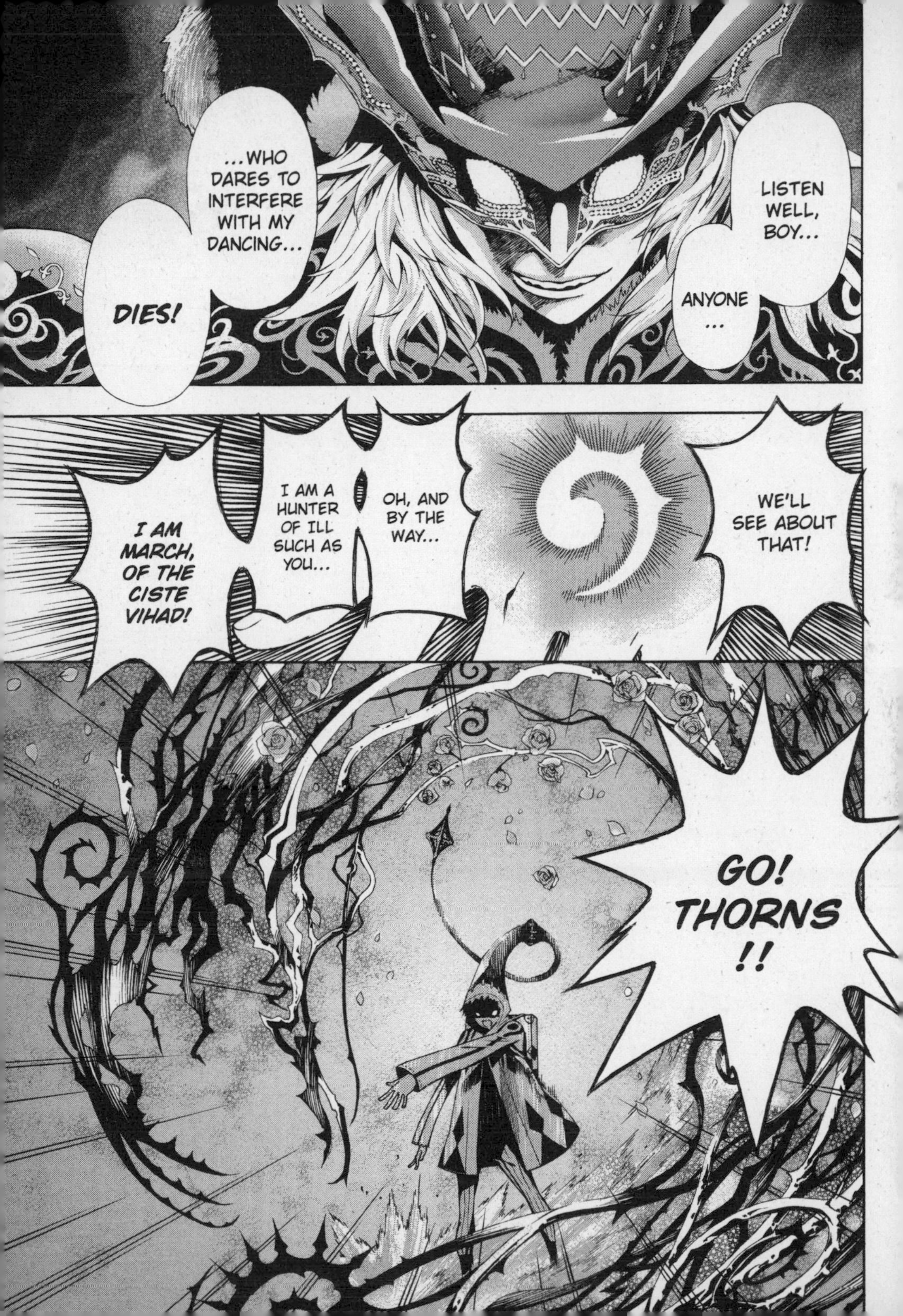
LISTEN WELL, BOY...
ANYONE ...
...WHO DARES TO INTERFERE WITH MY DANCING...
DIES!
WE'LL SEE ABOUT THAT!
OH, AND BY THE WAY...
I AM A HUNTER OF ILL SUCH AS YOU...
I AM MARCH, OF THE CISTE VIHAD!
GO! THORNS !!

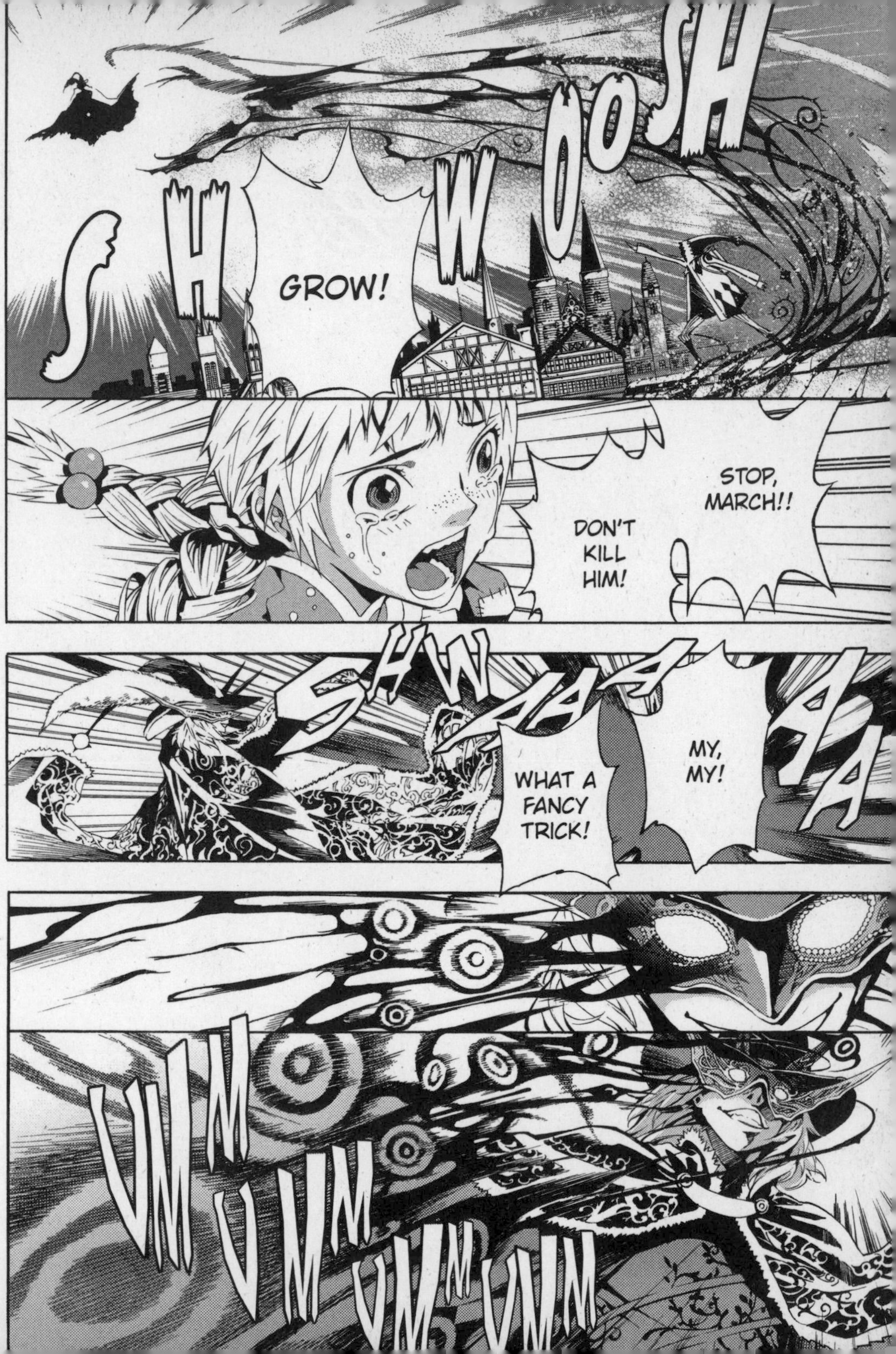
SHWOOSH
GROW!
STOP, MARCH!!
DON'T KILL HIM!
SHWAAAAA
MY, MY!
WHAT A FANCY TRICK!
VMMVMMVMMVMM

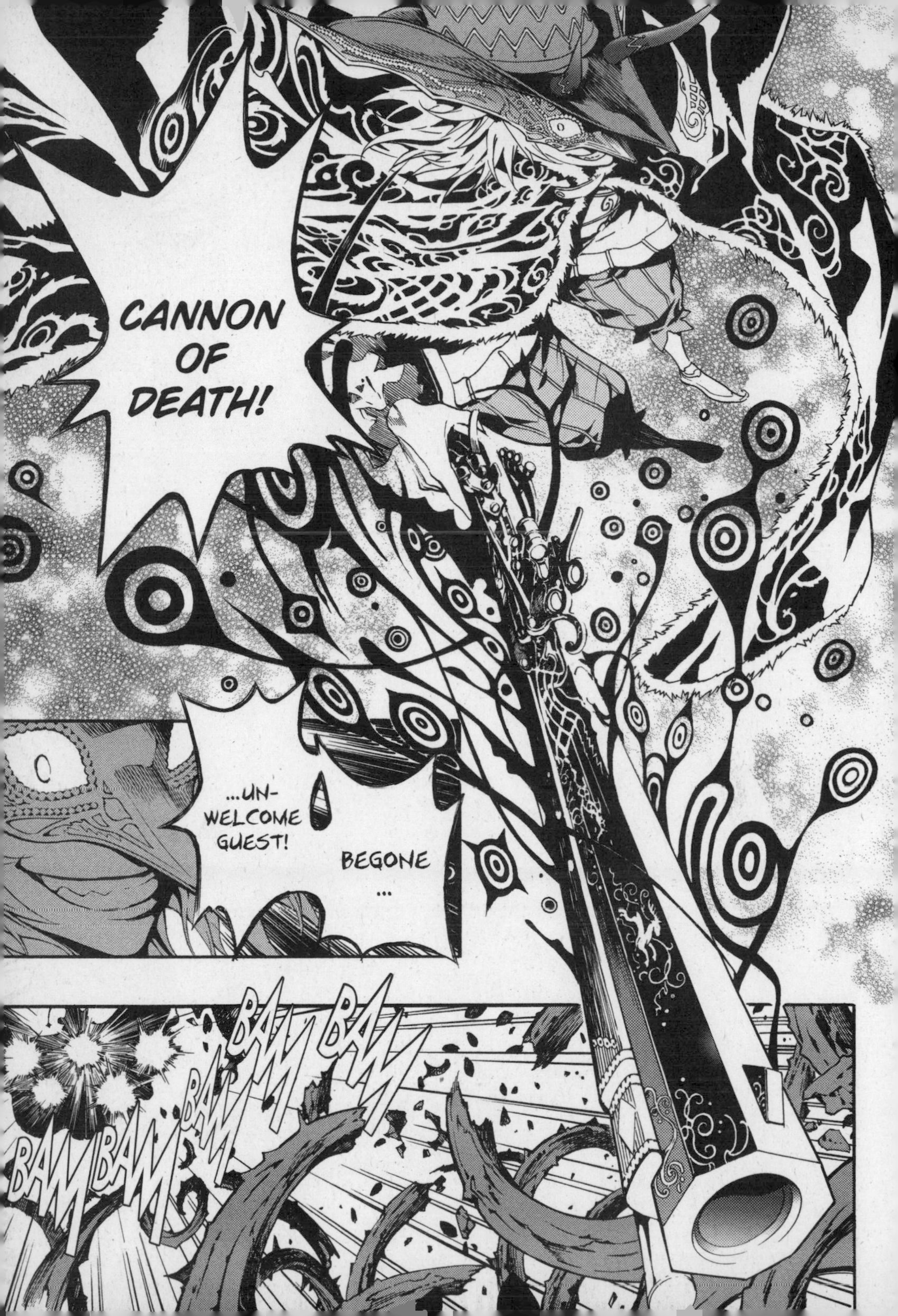
CANNON OF DEATH!
BEGONE ...
...UN-WELCOME GUEST!
BAM BAM BAM BAM BAM BAM

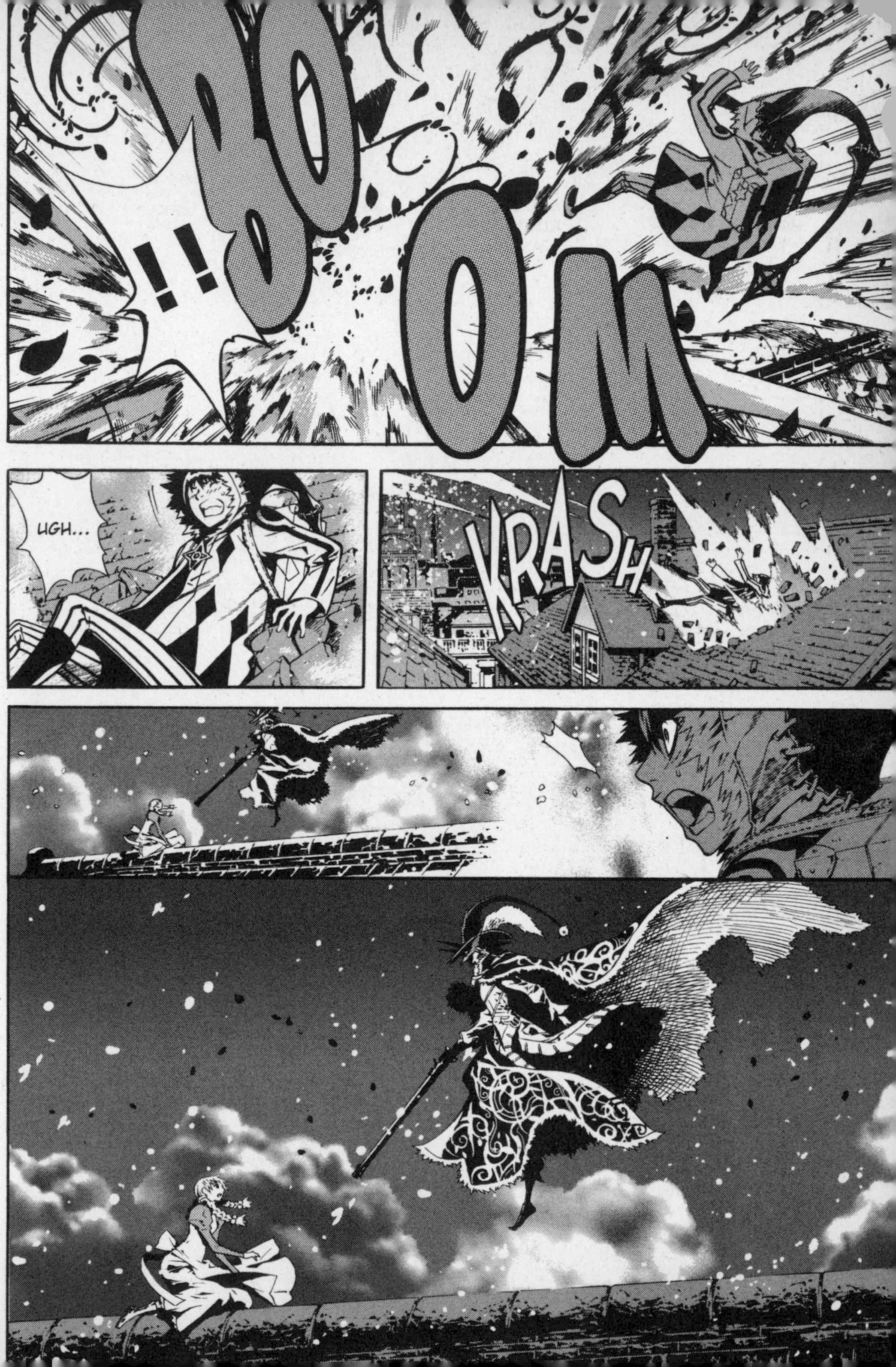
BOOOM
!!
KRASH
UGH...

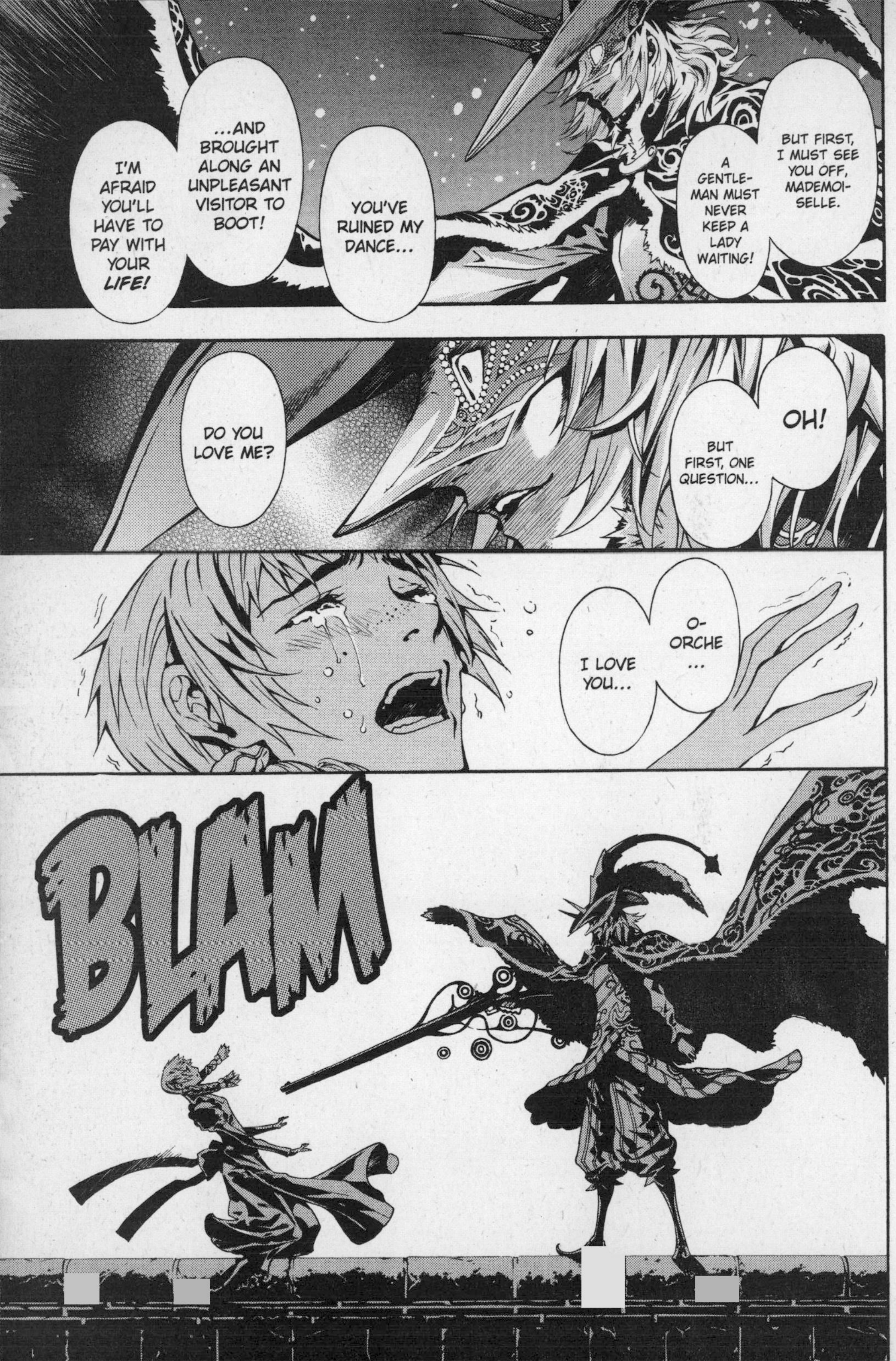
BUT FIRST, I MUST SEE YOU OFF, MADEMOISELLE.
A GENTLEMAN MUST NEVER KEEP A LADY WAITING!
YOU'VE RUINED MY DANCE...
...AND BROUGHT ALONG AN UNPLEASANT VISITOR TO BOOT!
I'M AFRAID YOU'LL HAVE TO PAY WITH YOUR *LIFE!*
OH!
BUT FIRST, ONE QUESTION...
DO YOU LOVE ME?
O-ORCHE...
I LOVE YOU...
BLAM

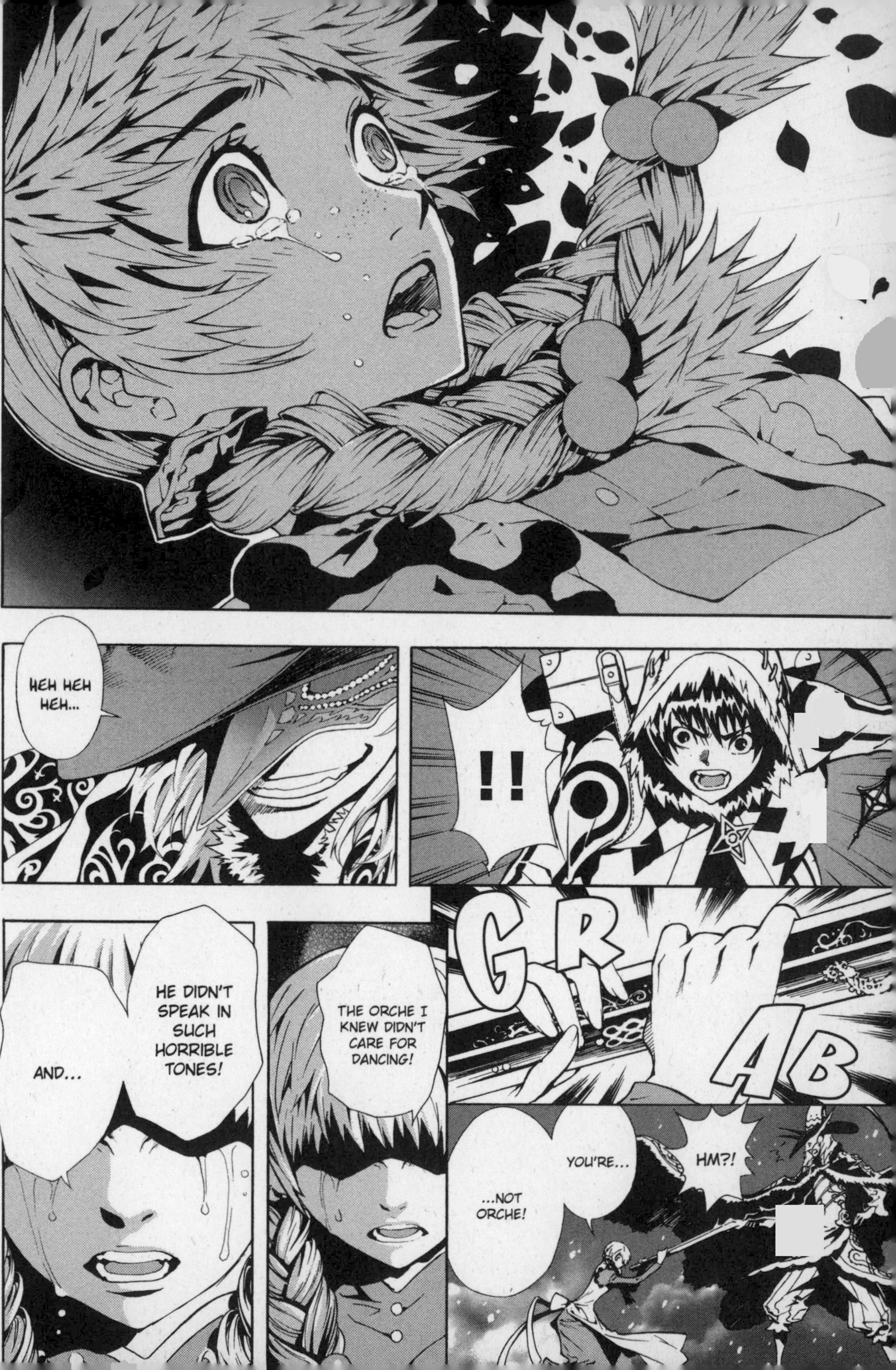
!!
HEH HEH HEH...
GRAB
HM?!
YOU'RE...
...NOT ORCHE!
THE ORCHE I KNEW DIDN'T CARE FOR DANCING!
AND...
HE DIDN'T SPEAK IN SUCH HORRIBLE TONES!

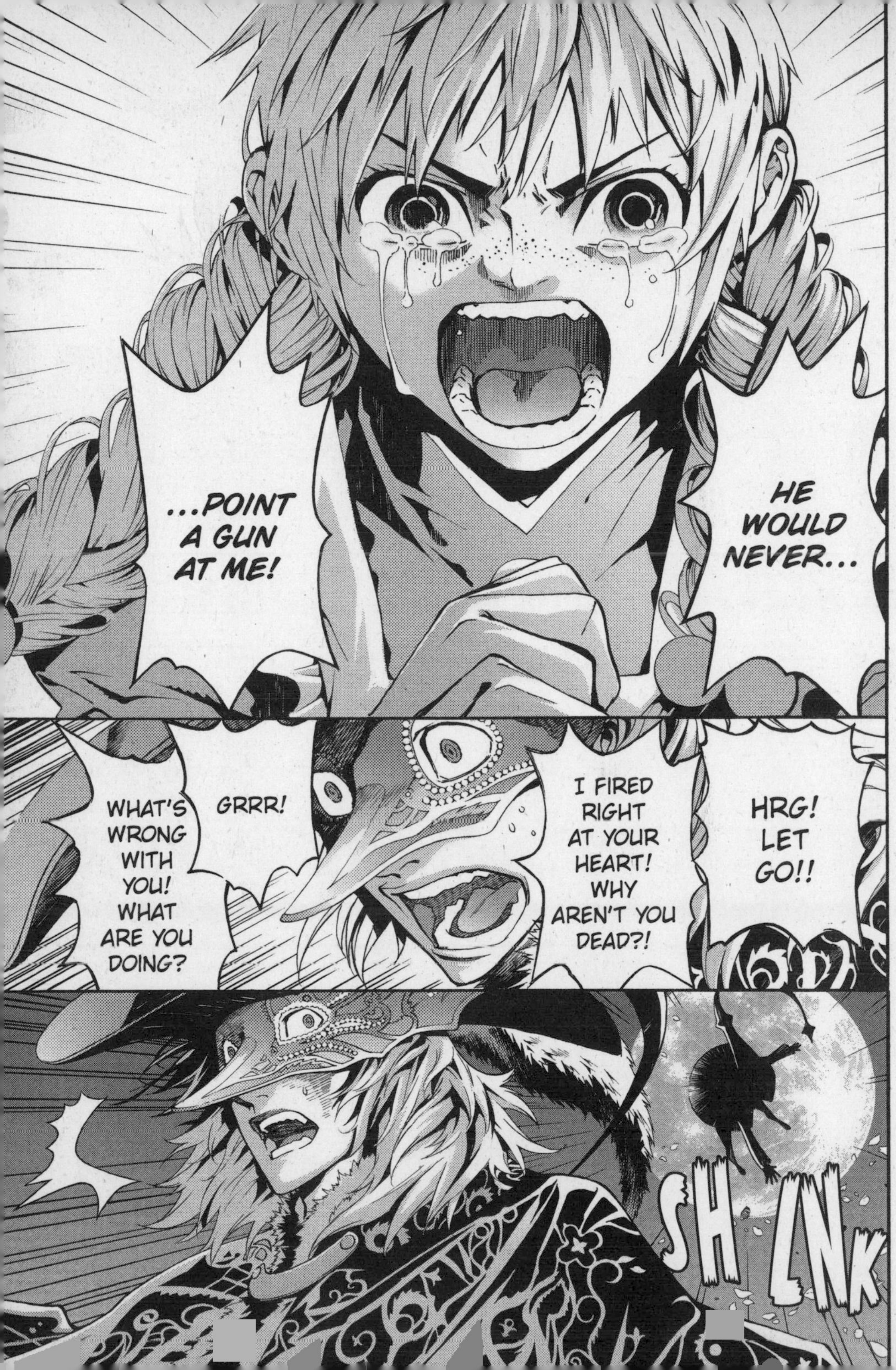
HE WOULD NEVER...
...POINT A GUN AT ME!
HRG! LET GO!!
I FIRED RIGHT AT YOUR HEART! WHY AREN'T YOU DEAD?!
GRRR!
WHAT'S WRONG WITH YOU! WHAT ARE YOU DOING?
SHINK

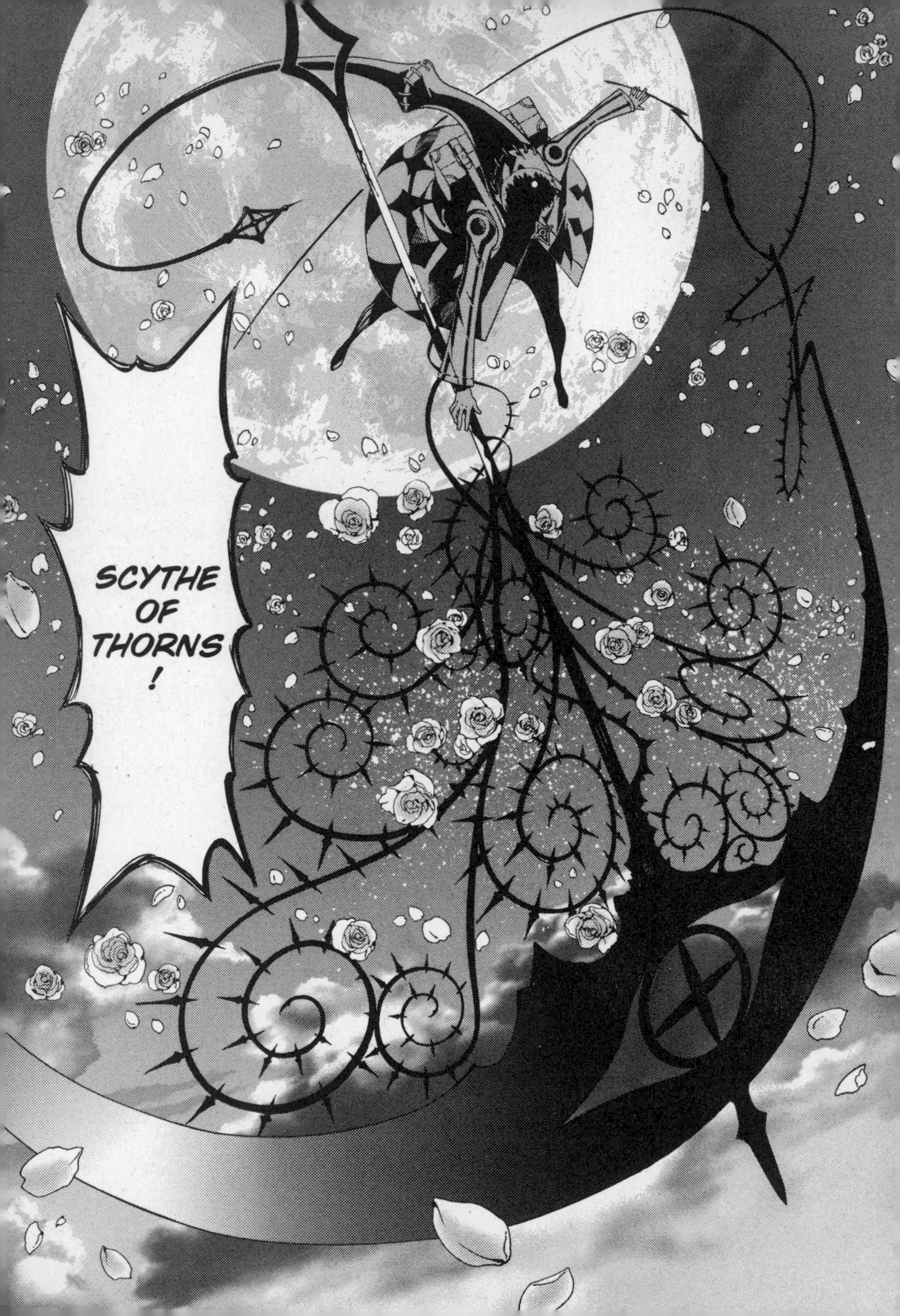
SCYTHE OF THORNS !

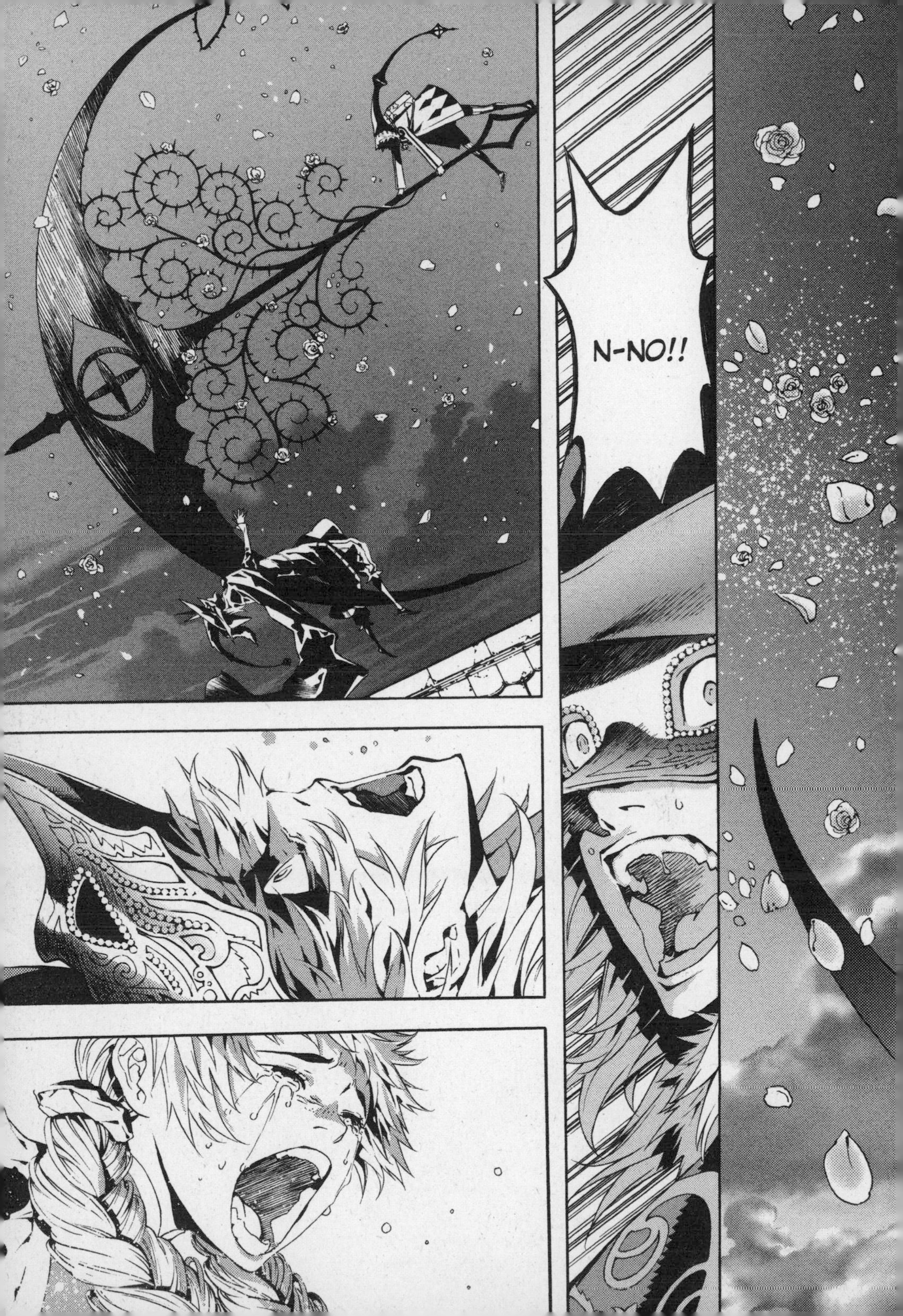
N-NO!!

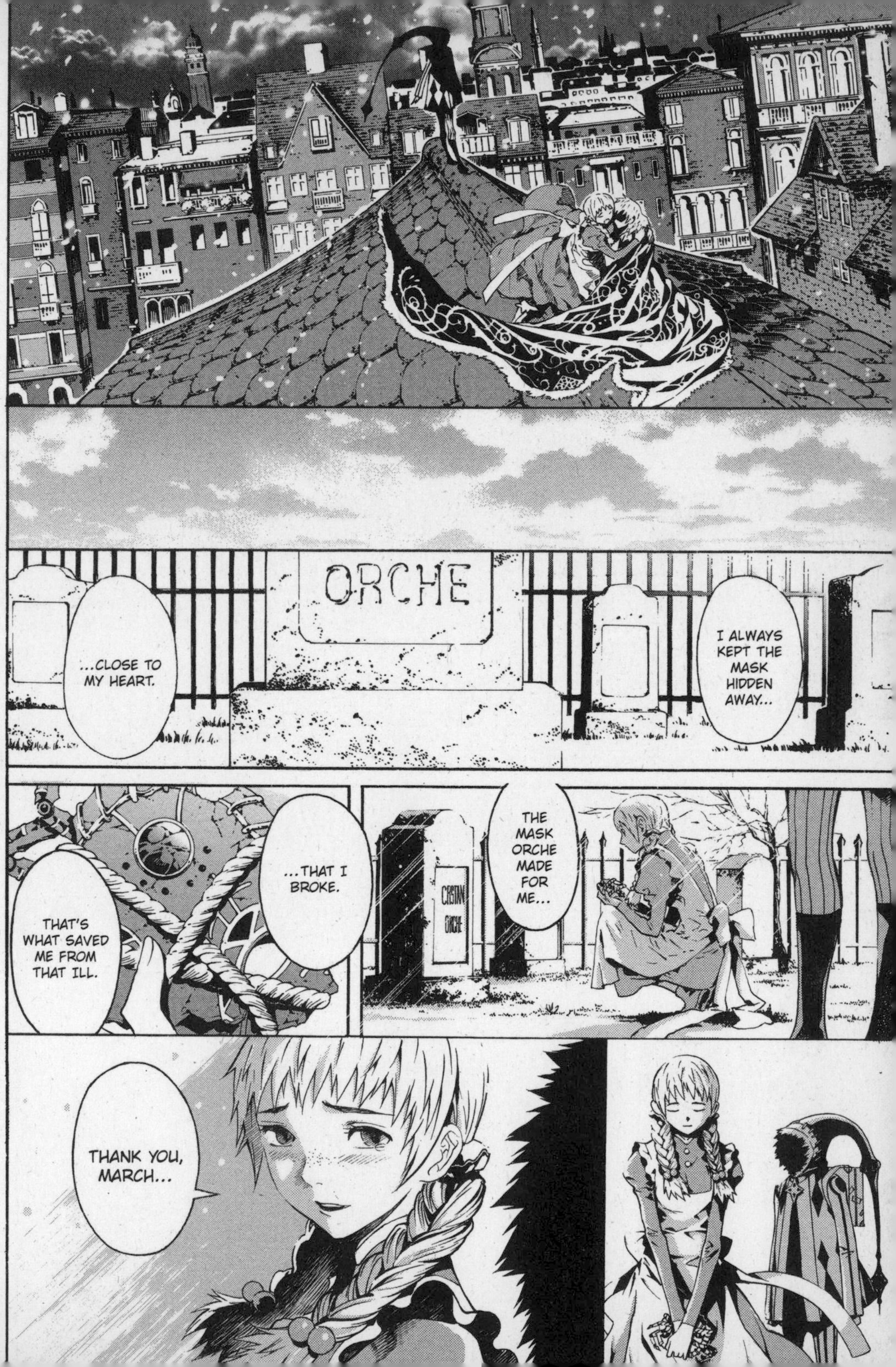
ORCHE
I ALWAYS KEPT THE MASK HIDDEN AWAY...
...CLOSE TO MY HEART.
THE MASK ORCHE MADE FOR ME...
...THAT I BROKE.
THAT'S WHAT SAVED ME FROM THAT ILL.
THANK YOU, MARCH...

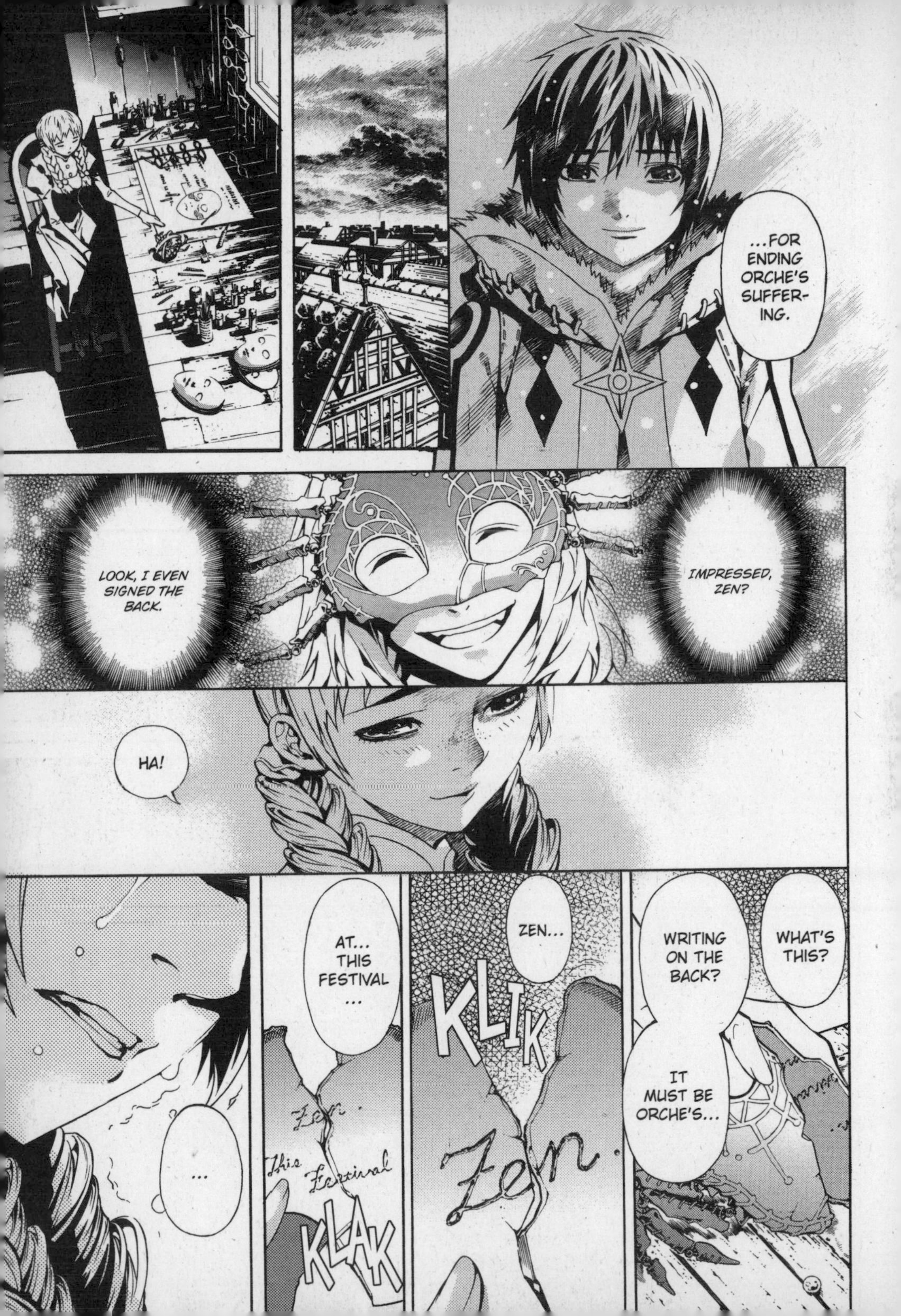
...FOR ENDING ORCHE'S SUFFER-ING.
IMPRESSED, ZEN?
LOOK, I EVEN SIGNED THE BACK.
HA!
WHAT'S THIS?
WRITING ON THE BACK?
IT MUST BE ORCHE'S...
ZEN...
KLIK
Zen
AT... THIS FESTIVAL ...
Zen
This Festival
KLAK
...

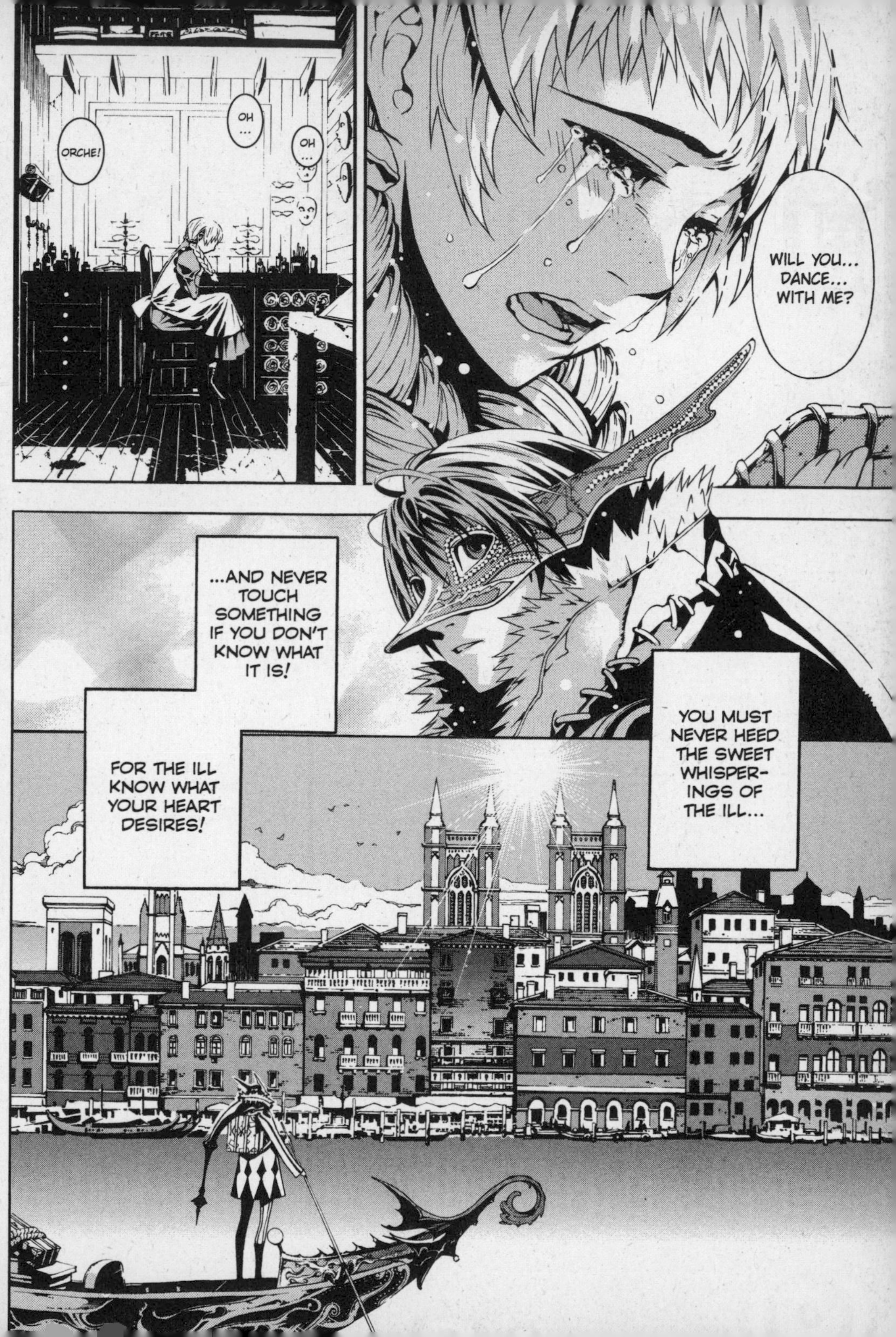
WILL YOU... DANCE... WITH ME?
OH ...
OH ...
ORCHE!
YOU MUST NEVER HEED THE SWEET WHISPER-INGS OF THE ILL...
...AND NEVER TOUCH SOMETHING IF YOU DON'T KNOW WHAT IT IS!
FOR THE ILL KNOW WHAT YOUR HEART DESIRES!

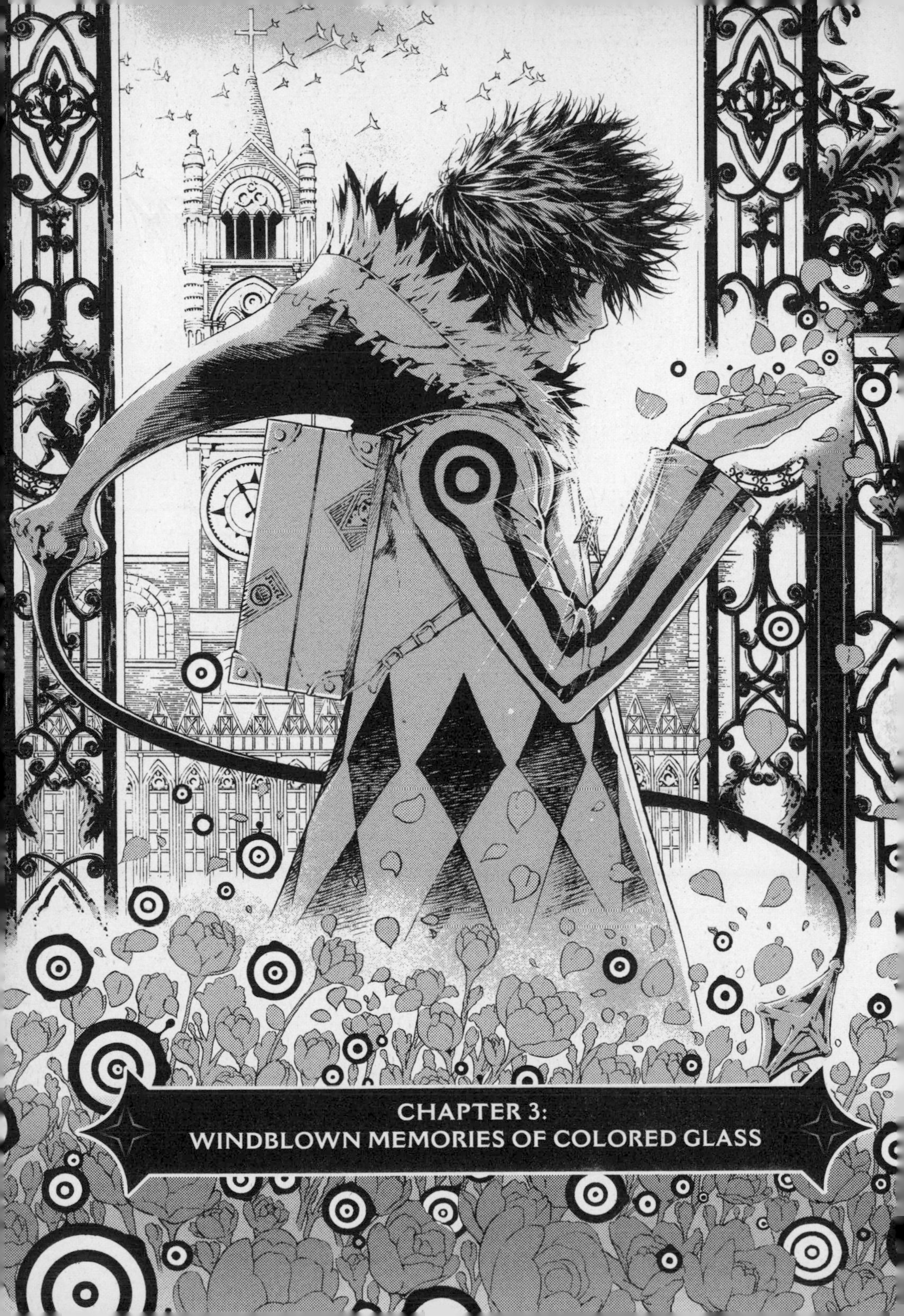
CHAPTER 3:
WINDBLOWN MEMORIES OF COLORED GLASS

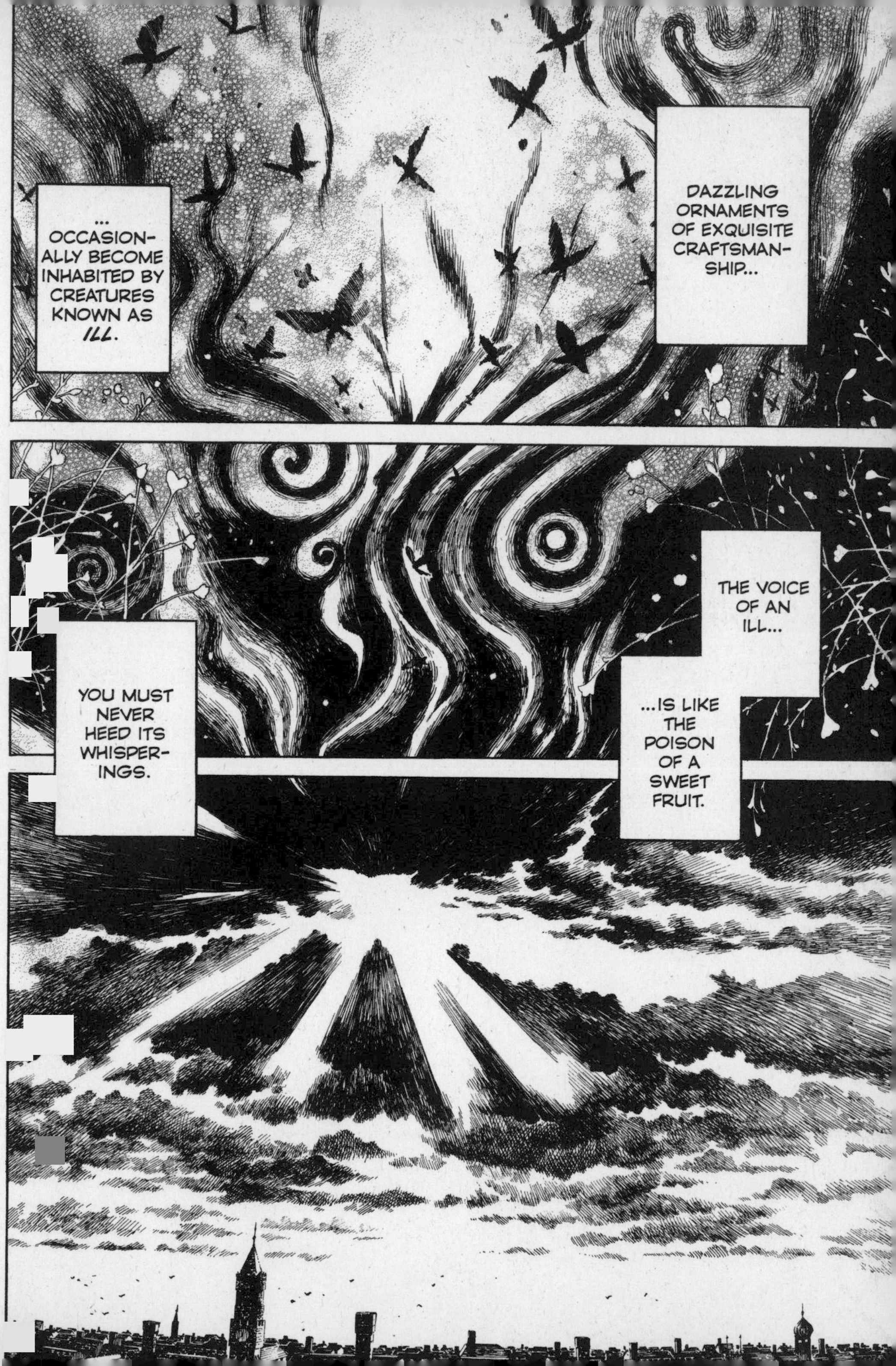
DAZZLING ORNAMENTS OF EXQUISITE CRAFTSMANSHIP...
...OCCASIONALLY BECOME INHABITED BY CREATURES KNOWN AS *ILL*.
THE VOICE OF AN ILL...
...IS LIKE THE POISON OF A SWEET FRUIT.
YOU MUST NEVER HEED ITS WHISPERINGS.

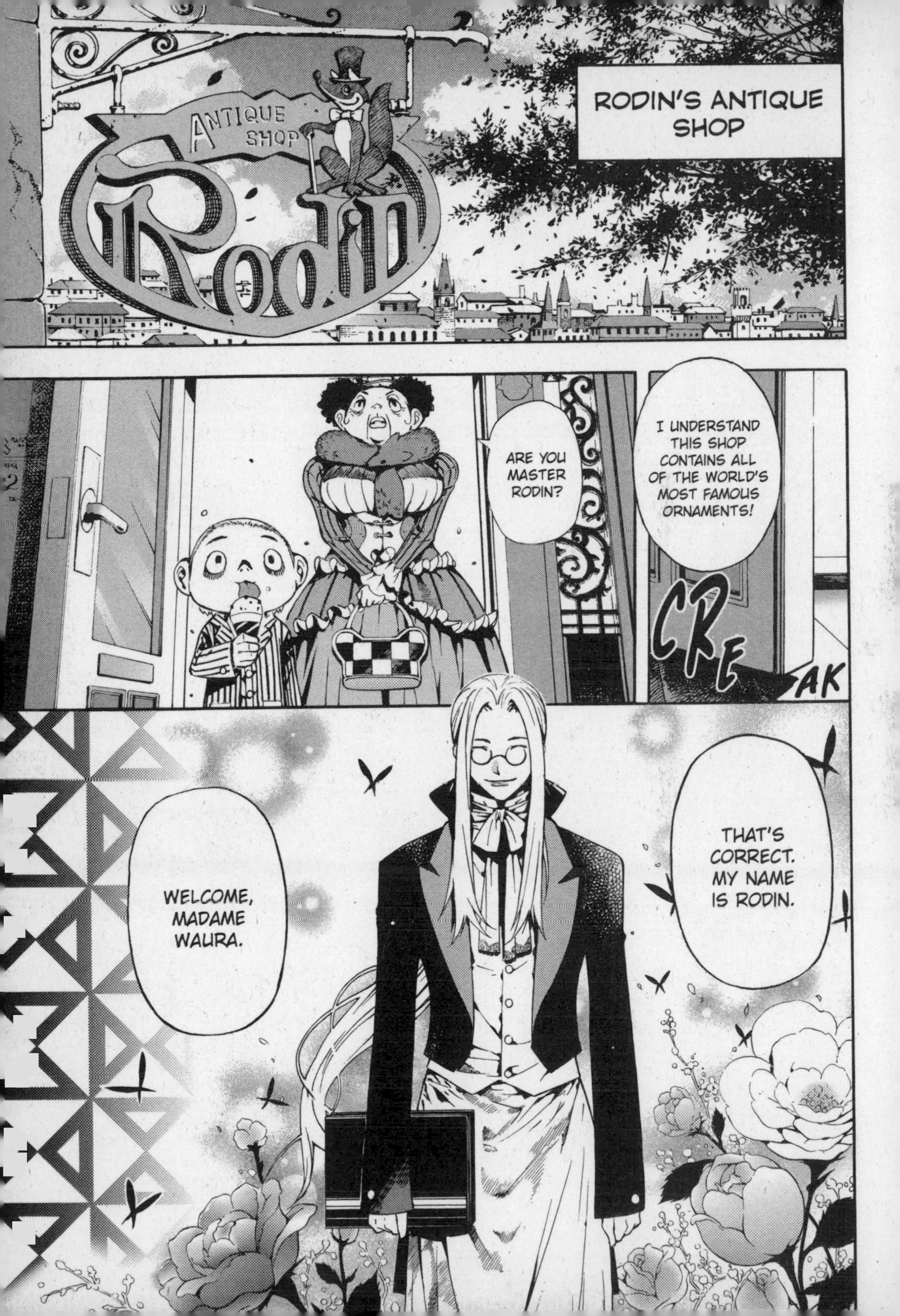
RODIN'S ANTIQUE SHOP
ANTIQUE SHOP
Rodin
I UNDERSTAND THIS SHOP CONTAINS ALL OF THE WORLD'S MOST FAMOUS ORNAMENTS!
CREAK
ARE YOU MASTER RODIN?
THAT'S CORRECT. MY NAME IS RODIN.
WELCOME, MADAME WAURA.

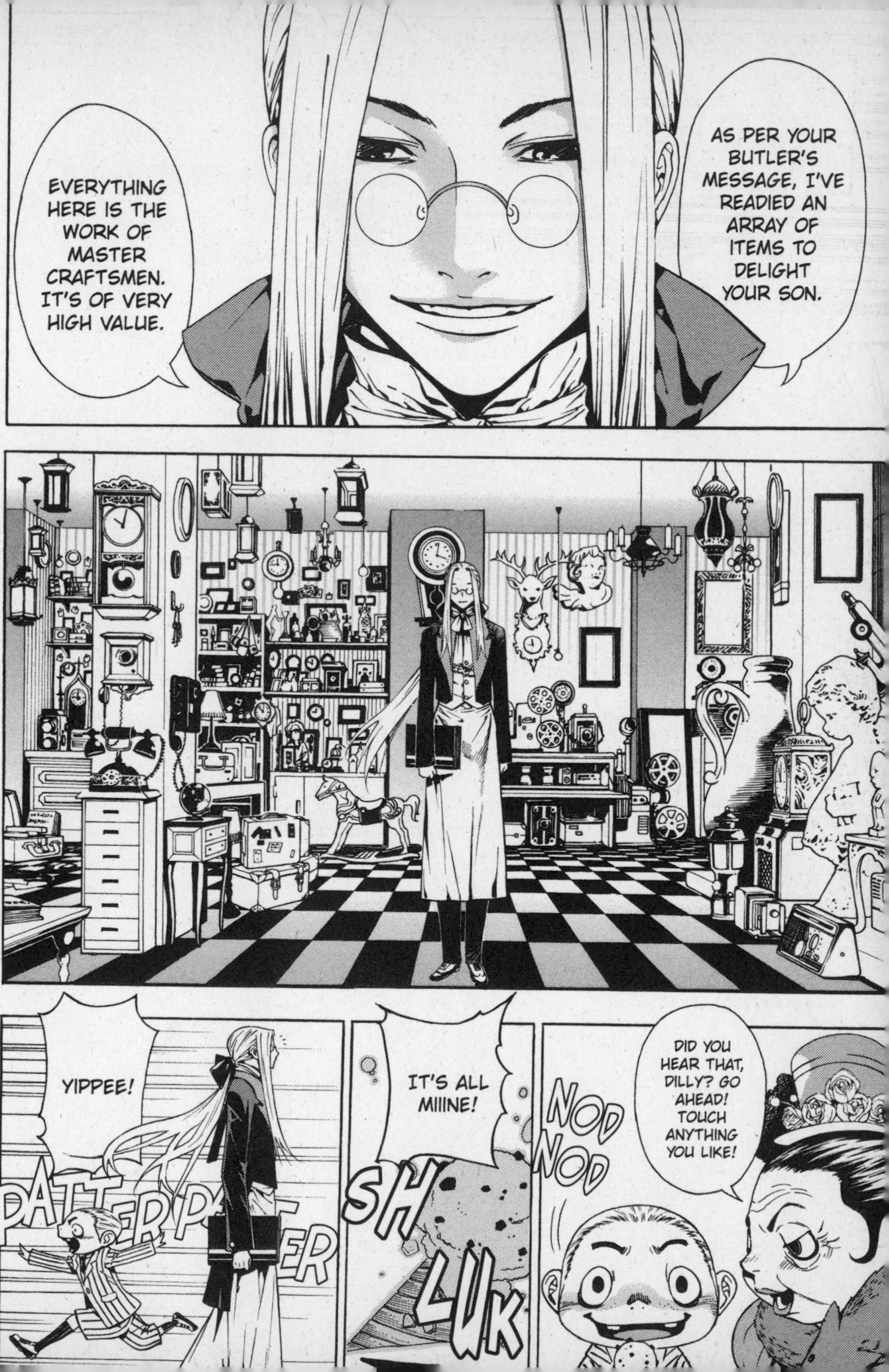
AS PER YOUR BUTLER'S MESSAGE, I'VE READIED AN ARRAY OF ITEMS TO DELIGHT YOUR SON.
EVERYTHING HERE IS THE WORK OF MASTER CRAFTSMEN. IT'S OF VERY HIGH VALUE.
DID YOU HEAR THAT, DILLY? GO AHEAD! TOUCH ANYTHING YOU LIKE!
NOD NOD
IT'S ALL MIIINE!
SHLUK
YIPPEE!
PATTER PATTER

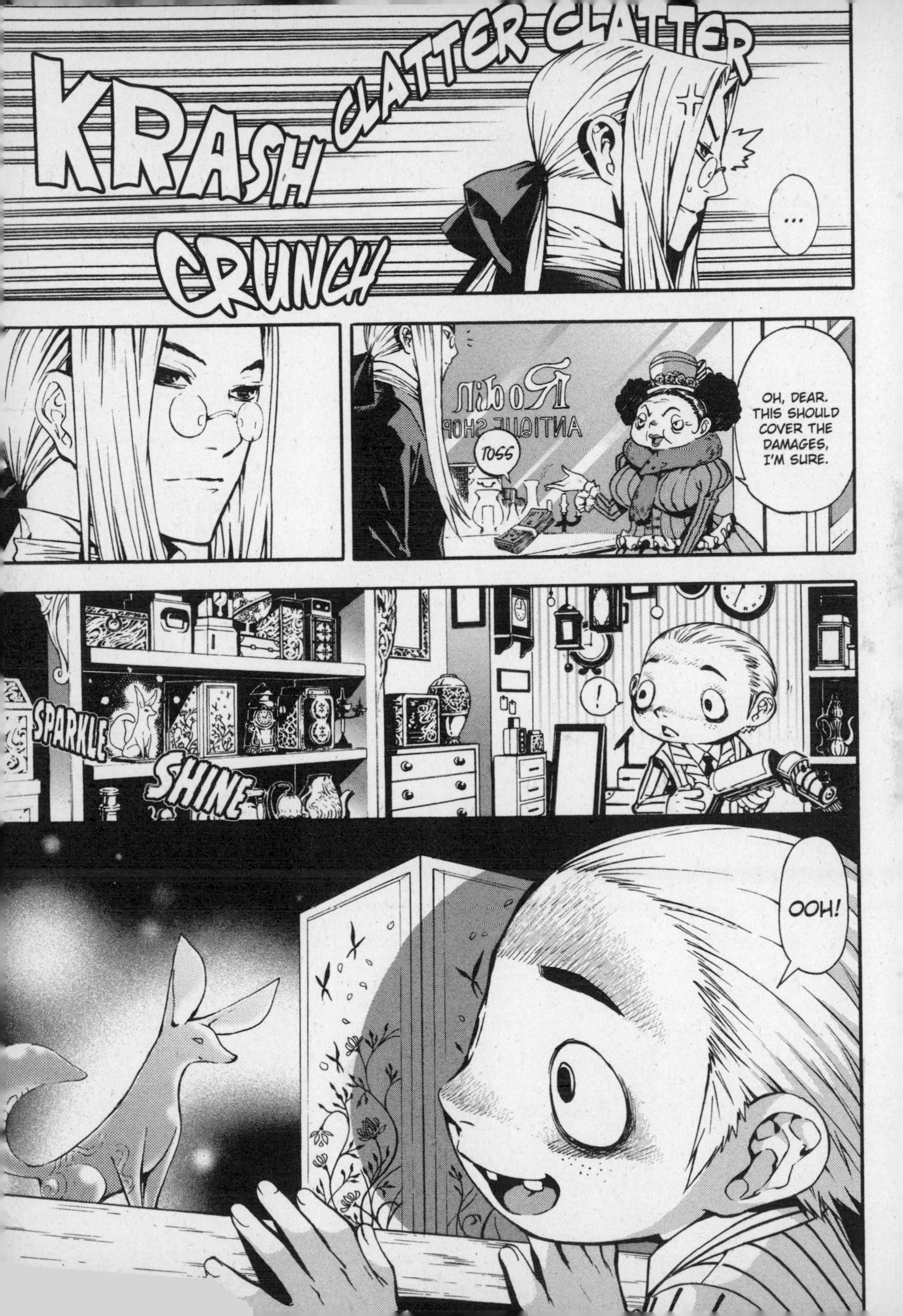
...
CLATTER CLATTER
KRASH
CRUNCH
OH, DEAR. THIS SHOULD COVER THE DAMAGES, I'M SURE.
TOSS
!
SPARKLE
SHINE
OOH!

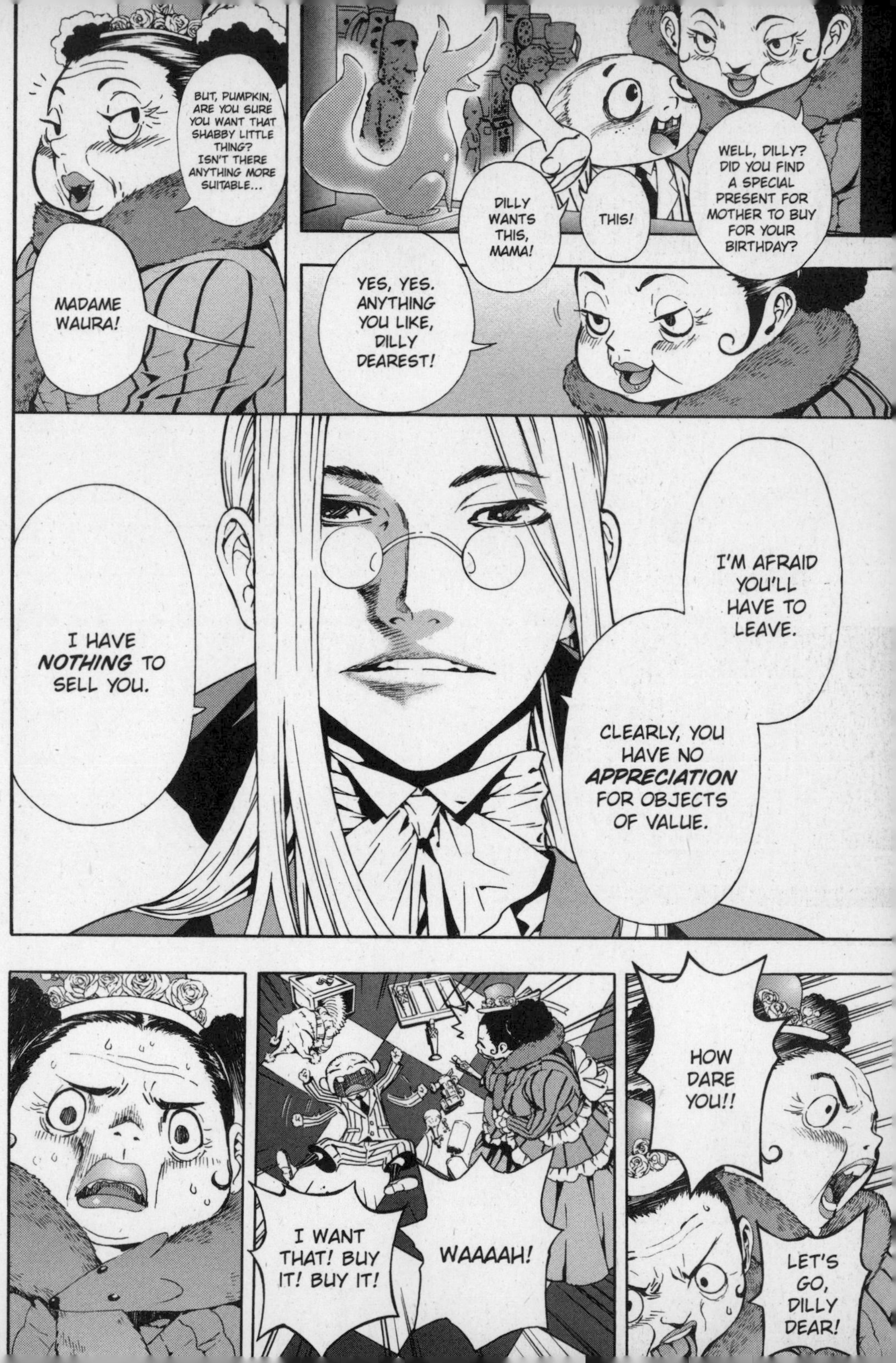
WELL, DILLY? DID YOU FIND A SPECIAL PRESENT FOR MOTHER TO BUY FOR YOUR BIRTHDAY?
THIS!
DILLY WANTS THIS, MAMA!
YES, YES. ANYTHING YOU LIKE, DILLY DEAREST!
BUT, PUMPKIN, ARE YOU SURE YOU WANT THAT SHABBY LITTLE THING? ISN'T THERE ANYTHING MORE SUITABLE...
MADAME WAURA!
I'M AFRAID YOU'LL HAVE TO LEAVE.
CLEARLY, YOU HAVE NO APPRECIATION FOR OBJECTS OF VALUE.
I HAVE NOTHING TO SELL YOU.
HOW DARE YOU!!
LET'S GO, DILLY DEAR!
WAAAAH!
I WANT THAT! BUY IT! BUY IT!

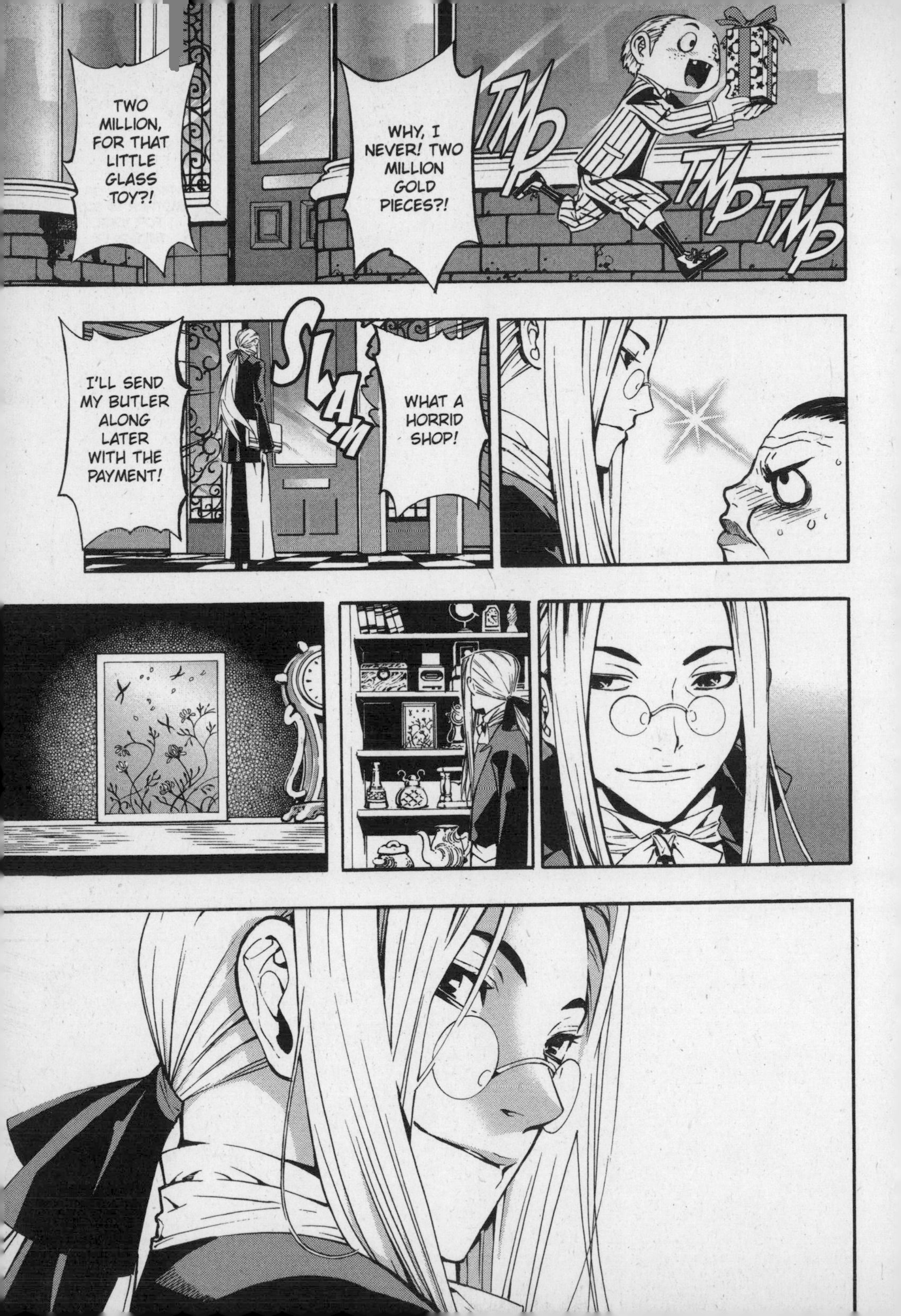
TMP
TMP TMP TMP
WHY, I NEVER! TWO MILLION GOLD PIECES?!
TWO MILLION, FOR THAT LITTLE GLASS TOY?!
WHAT A HORRID SHOP!
SLAM
I'LL SEND MY BUTLER ALONG LATER WITH THE PAYMENT!

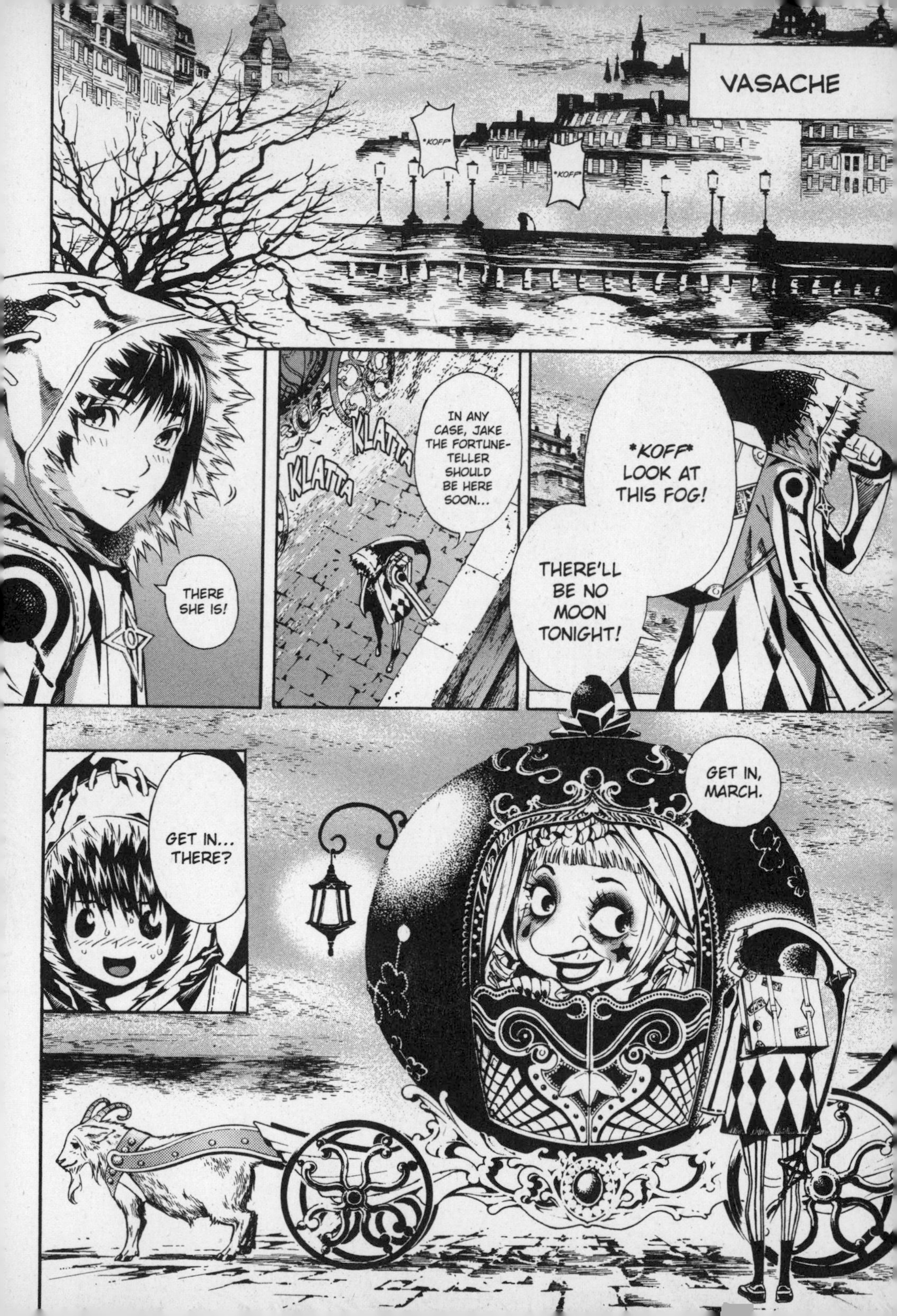
VASACHE
KOFF
KOFF
KOFF LOOK AT THIS FOG!
THERE'LL BE NO MOON TONIGHT!
KLATTA
KLATTA
IN ANY CASE, JAKE THE FORTUNE-TELLER SHOULD BE HERE SOON...
THERE SHE IS!
GET IN, MARCH.
GET IN... THERE?

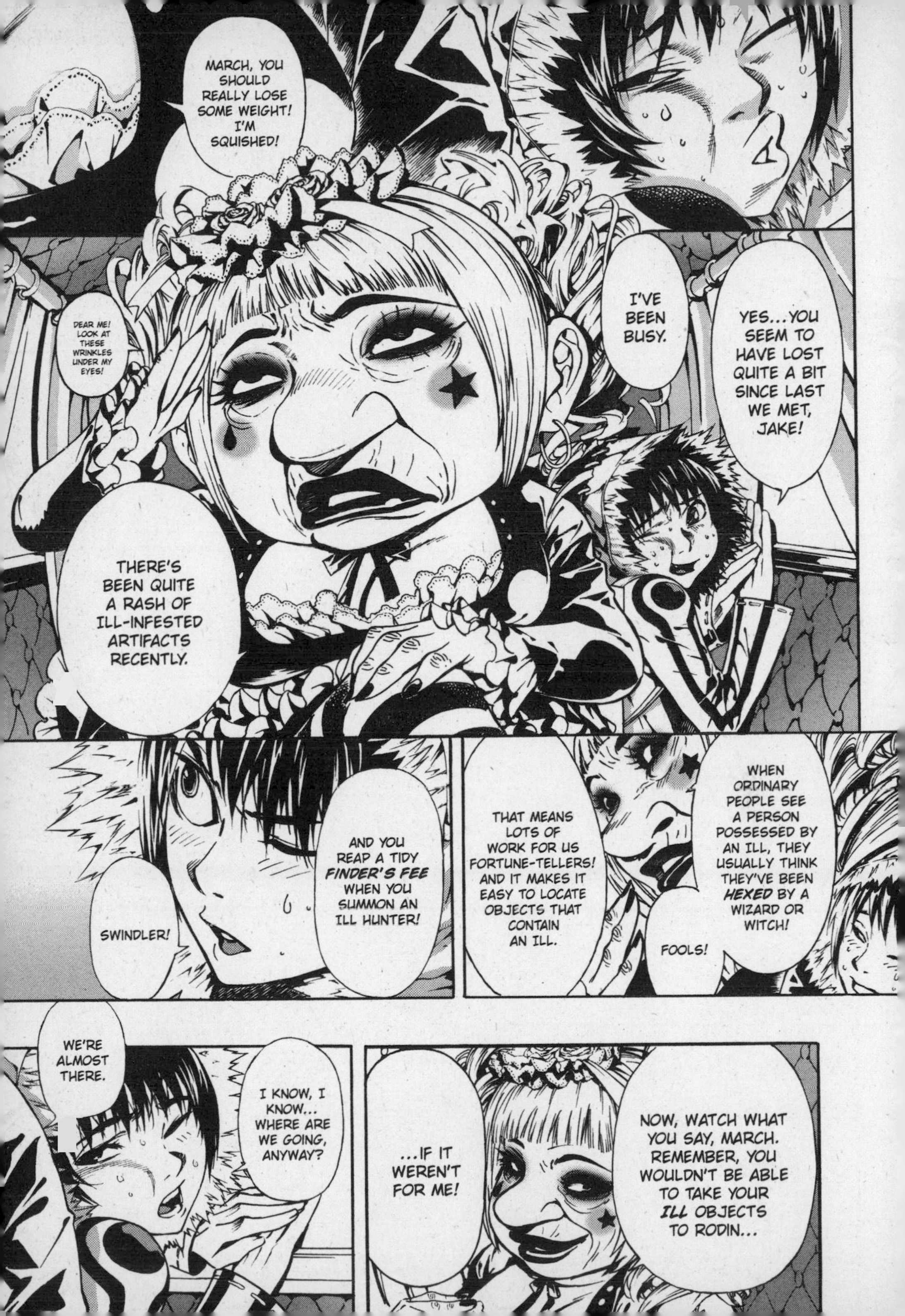
MARCH, YOU SHOULD REALLY LOSE SOME WEIGHT! I'M SQUISHED!
YES...YOU SEEM TO HAVE LOST QUITE A BIT SINCE LAST WE MET, JAKE!
I'VE BEEN BUSY.
DEAR ME! LOOK AT THESE WRINKLES UNDER MY EYES!
THERE'S BEEN QUITE A RASH OF ILL-INFESTED ARTIFACTS RECENTLY.
WHEN ORDINARY PEOPLE SEE A PERSON POSSESSED BY AN ILL, THEY USUALLY THINK THEY'VE BEEN *HEXED* BY A WIZARD OR WITCH!
FOOLS!
THAT MEANS LOTS OF WORK FOR US FORTUNE-TELLERS! AND IT MAKES IT EASY TO LOCATE OBJECTS THAT CONTAIN AN ILL.
AND YOU REAP A TIDY *FINDER'S FEE* WHEN YOU SUMMON AN ILL HUNTER!
SWINDLER!
NOW, WATCH WHAT YOU SAY, MARCH. REMEMBER, YOU WOULDN'T BE ABLE TO TAKE YOUR *ILL* OBJECTS TO RODIN...
...IF IT WEREN'T FOR ME!
I KNOW, I KNOW... WHERE ARE WE GOING, ANYWAY?
WE'RE ALMOST THERE.

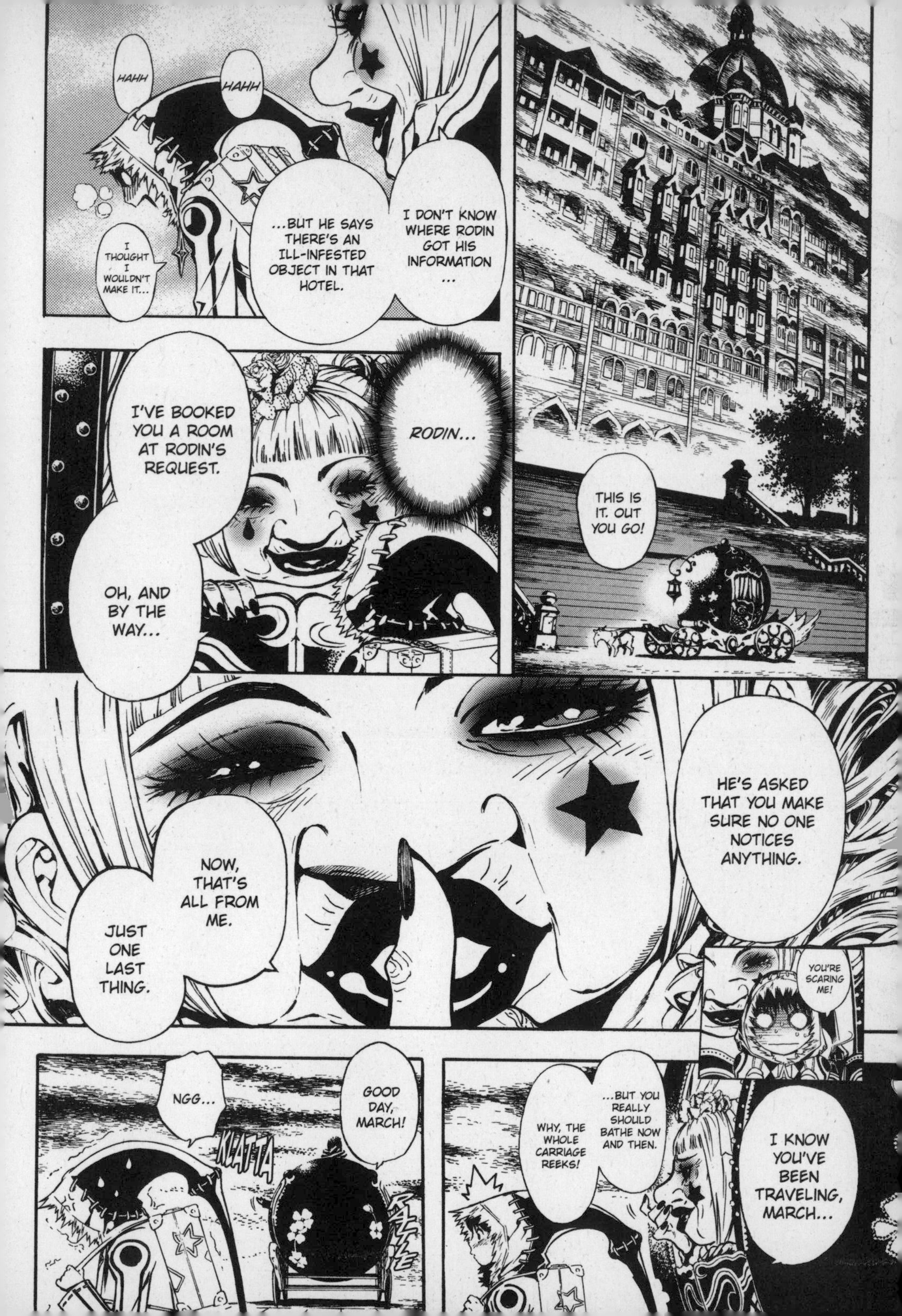
THIS IS IT. OUT YOU GO!
I DON'T KNOW WHERE RODIN GOT HIS INFORMATION ...
...BUT HE SAYS THERE'S AN ILL-INFESTED OBJECT IN THAT HOTEL.
HAHH
HAHH
I THOUGHT I WOULDN'T MAKE IT...
RODIN...
I'VE BOOKED YOU A ROOM AT RODIN'S REQUEST.
OH, AND BY THE WAY...
HE'S ASKED THAT YOU MAKE SURE NO ONE NOTICES ANYTHING.
NOW, THAT'S ALL FROM ME.
JUST ONE LAST THING.
YOU'RE SCARING ME!
I KNOW YOU'VE BEEN TRAVELING, MARCH...
...BUT YOU REALLY SHOULD BATHE NOW AND THEN.
WHY, THE WHOLE CARRIAGE REEKS!
GOOD DAY, MARCH!
KATTA
RATTLE
NGG...

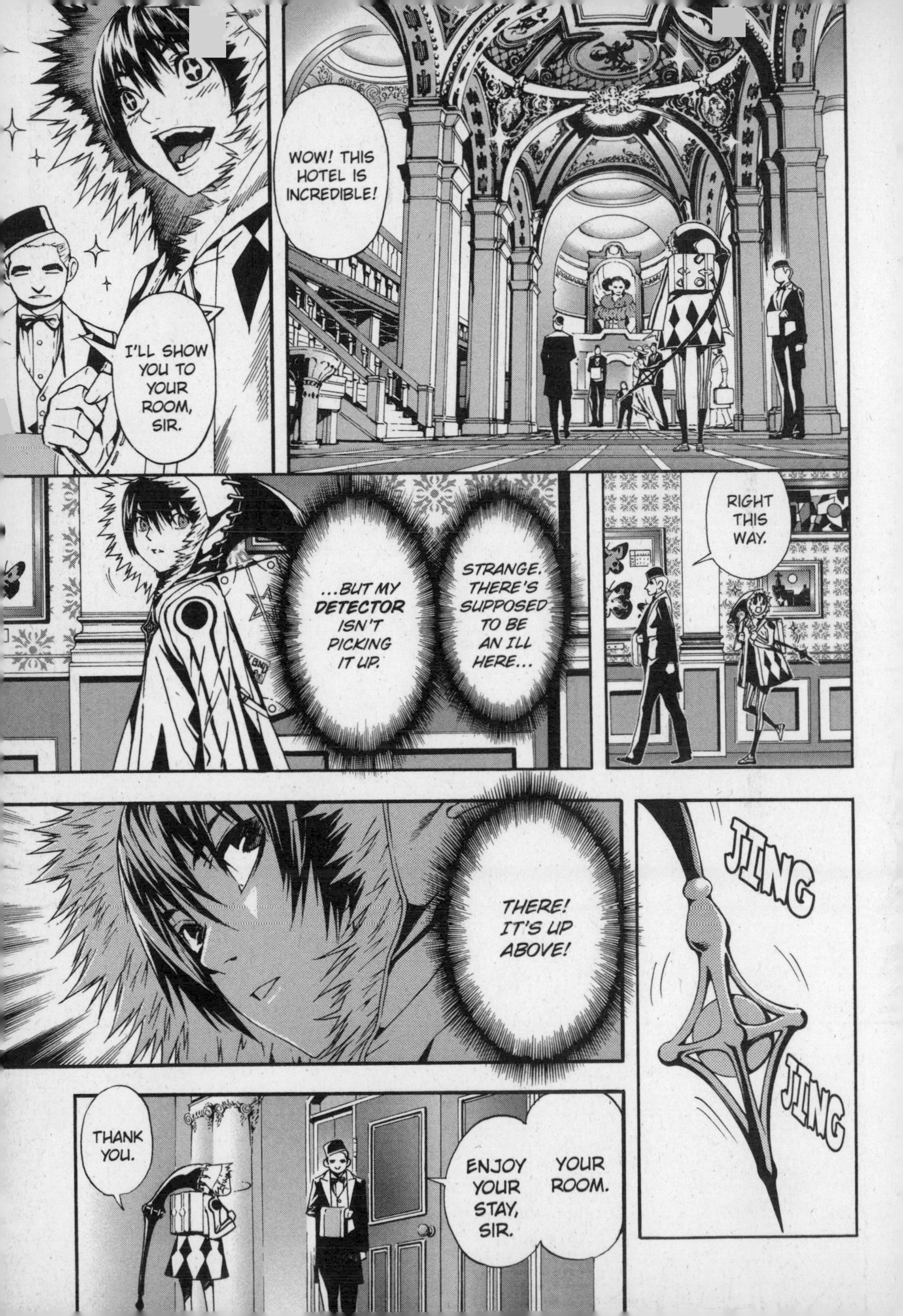
WOW! THIS HOTEL IS INCREDIBLE!
I'LL SHOW YOU TO YOUR ROOM, SIR.
RIGHT THIS WAY.
STRANGE. THERE'S SUPPOSED TO BE AN ILL HERE...
...BUT MY DETECTOR ISN'T PICKING IT UP.
JING
JING
THERE! IT'S UP ABOVE!
YOUR ROOM.
ENJOY YOUR STAY, SIR.
THANK YOU.

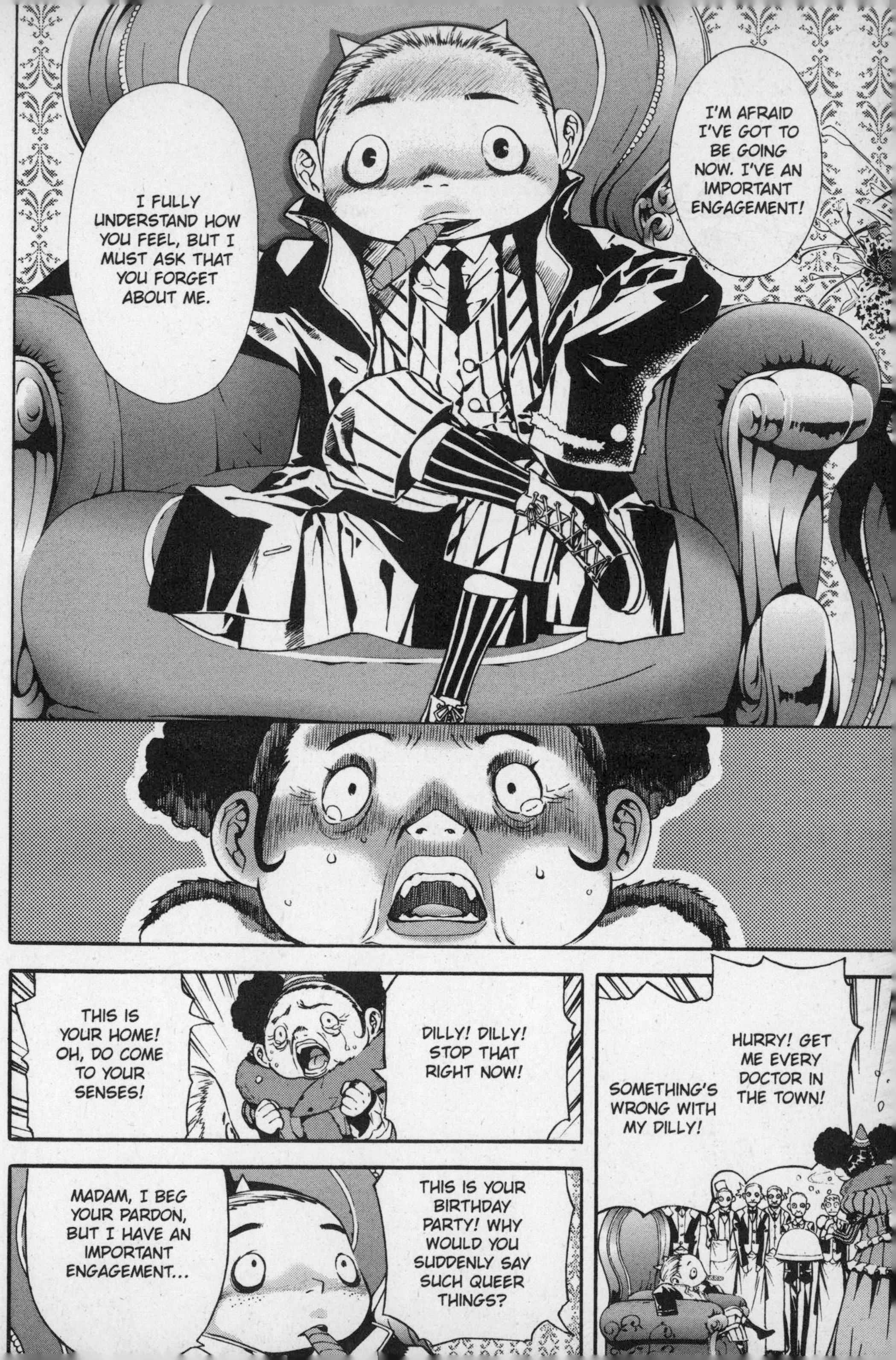
I'M AFRAID I'VE GOT TO BE GOING NOW. I'VE AN IMPORTANT ENGAGEMENT!
I FULLY UNDERSTAND HOW YOU FEEL, BUT I MUST ASK THAT YOU FORGET ABOUT ME.
HURRY! GET ME EVERY DOCTOR IN THE TOWN!
SOMETHING'S WRONG WITH MY DILLY!
DILLY! DILLY! STOP THAT RIGHT NOW!
THIS IS YOUR HOME! OH, DO COME TO YOUR SENSES!
THIS IS YOUR BIRTHDAY PARTY! WHY WOULD YOU SUDDENLY SAY SUCH QUEER THINGS?
MADAM, I BEG YOUR PARDON, BUT I HAVE AN IMPORTANT ENGAGEMENT...

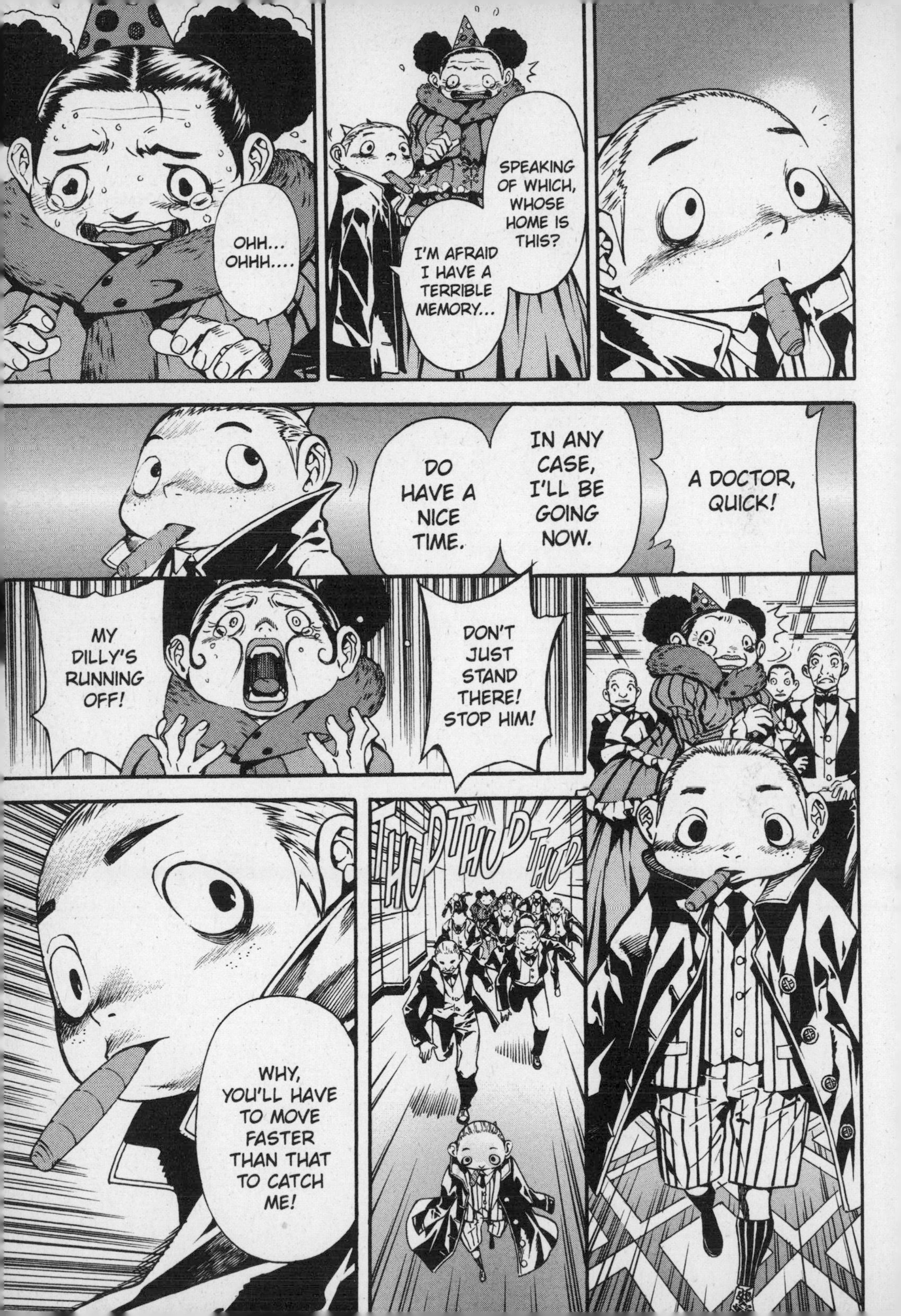
SPEAKING OF WHICH, WHOSE HOME IS THIS?
I'M AFRAID I HAVE A TERRIBLE MEMORY...
OHH... OHHH....
A DOCTOR, QUICK!
IN ANY CASE, I'LL BE GOING NOW.
DO HAVE A NICE TIME.
DON'T JUST STAND THERE! STOP HIM!
MY DILLY'S RUNNING OFF!
THUD THUD THUD
WHY, YOU'LL HAVE TO MOVE FASTER THAN THAT TO CATCH ME!

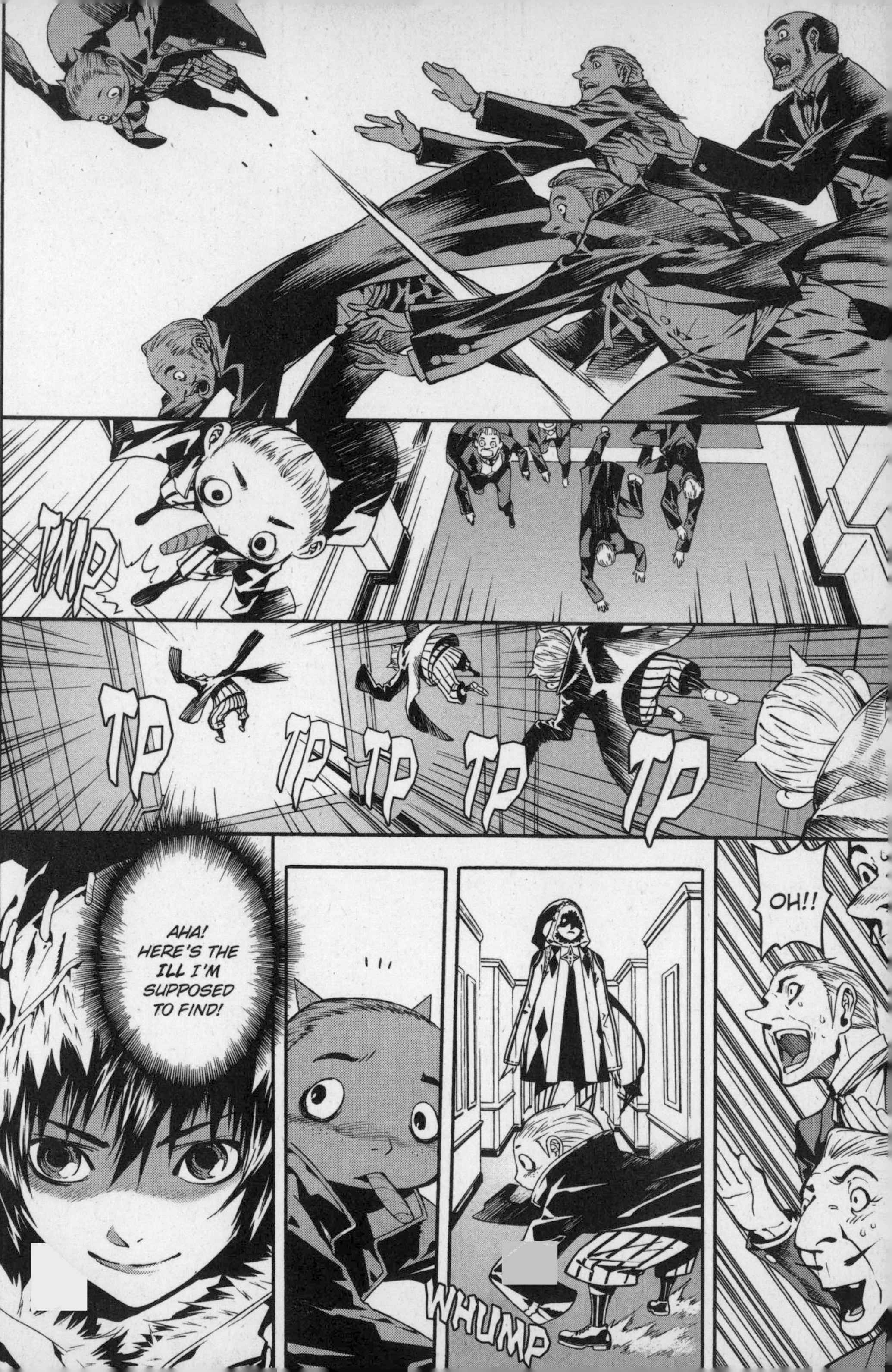
TMP
TP
TP
TP
TP
TP
OH!!
WHUMP
AHA! HERE'S THE ILL I'M SUPPOSED TO FIND!

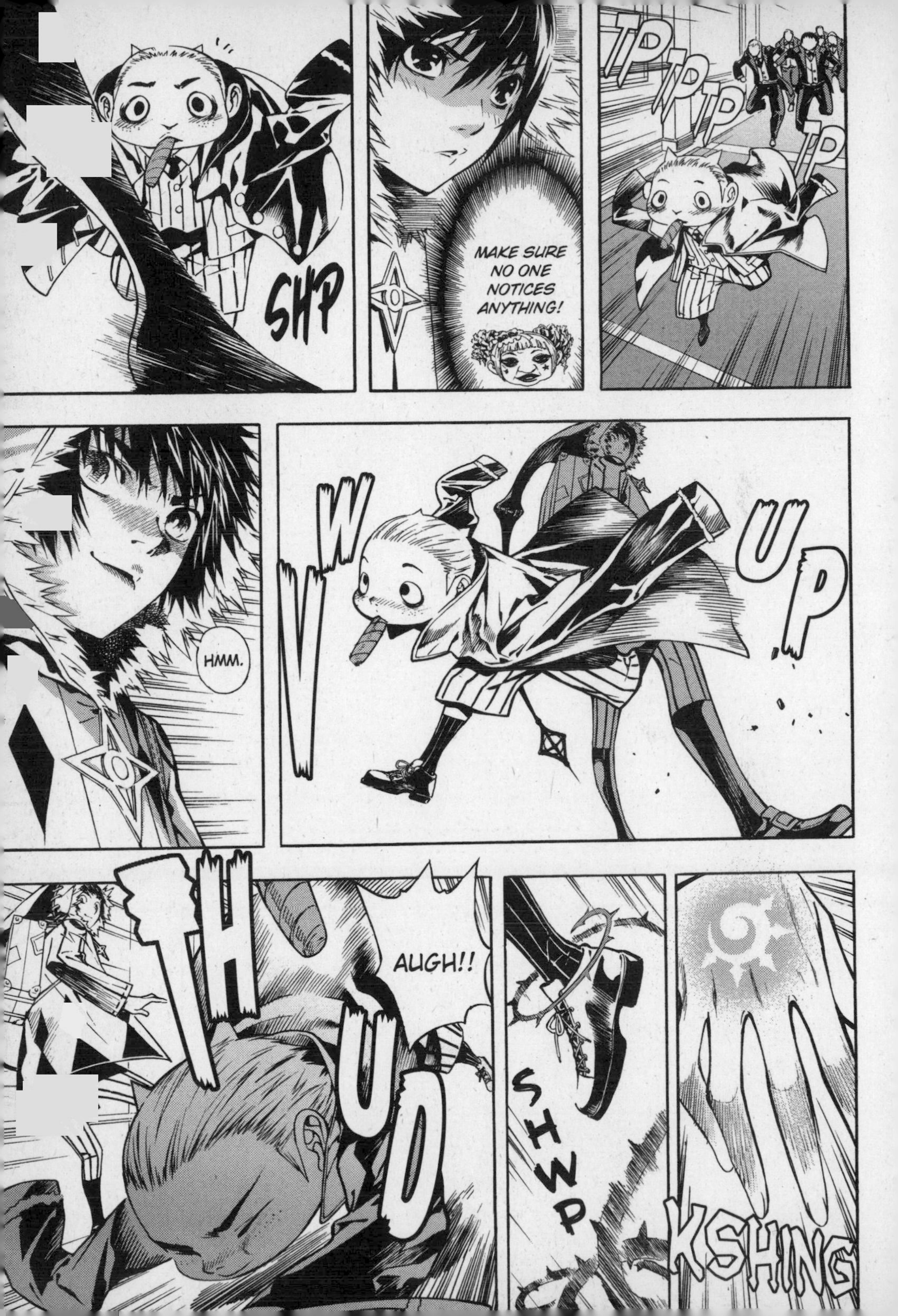
TP TP TP TP TP
MAKE SURE NO ONE NOTICES ANYTHING!
SHP
VWUP
HMM.
KSHING
SHWP
AUGH!!
THUD

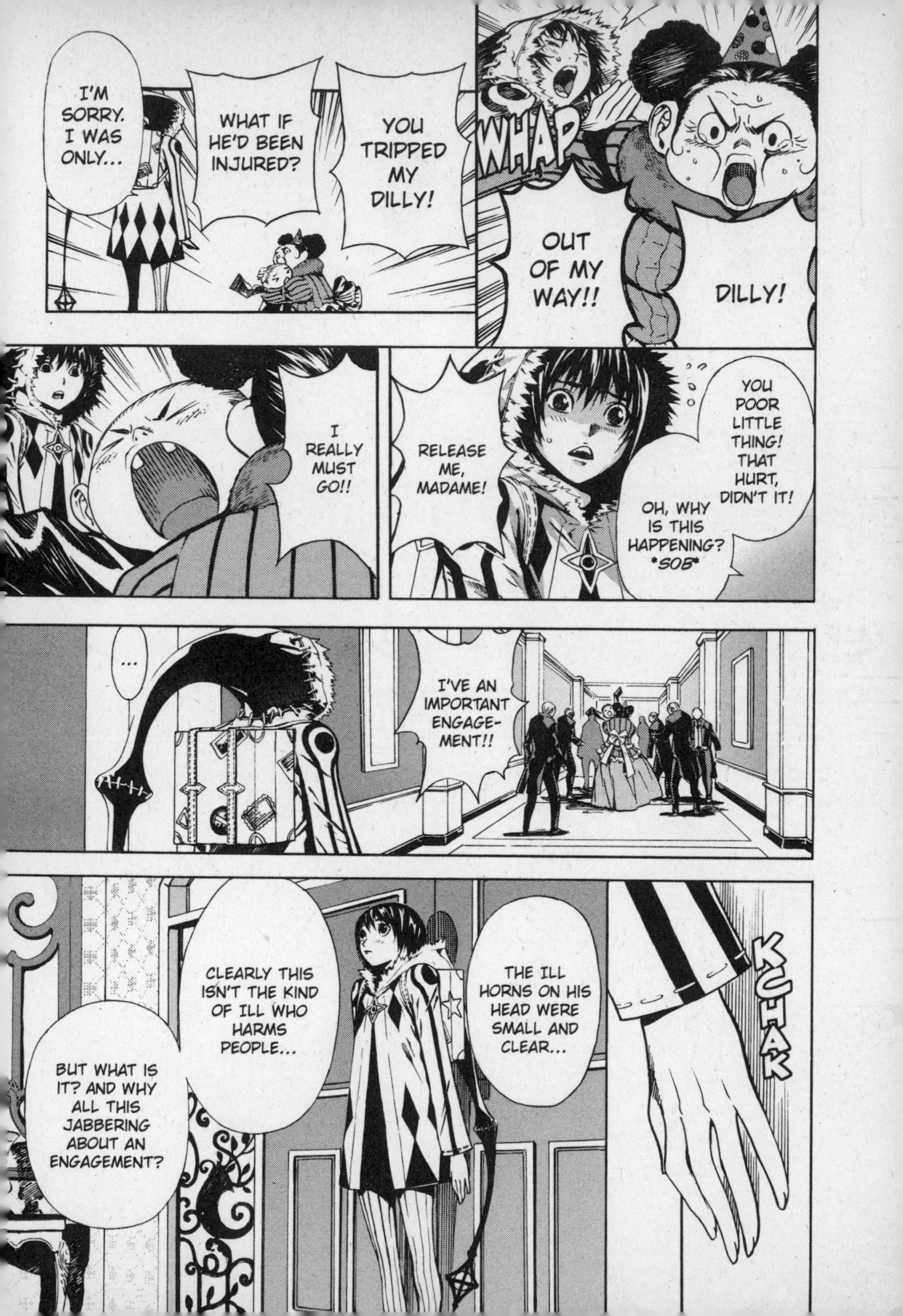
WHAP
DILLY!
OUT OF MY WAY!!
YOU TRIPPED MY DILLY!
WHAT IF HE'D BEEN INJURED?
I'M SORRY. I WAS ONLY...
YOU POOR LITTLE THING! THAT HURT, DIDN'T IT!
OH, WHY IS THIS HAPPENING? *SOB*
RELEASE ME, MADAME!
I REALLY MUST GO!!
I'VE AN IMPORTANT ENGAGE-MENT!!
...
KCHAK
THE ILL HORNS ON HIS HEAD WERE SMALL AND CLEAR...
CLEARLY THIS ISN'T THE KIND OF ILL WHO HARMS PEOPLE...
BUT WHAT IS IT? AND WHY ALL THIS JABBERING ABOUT AN ENGAGEMENT?

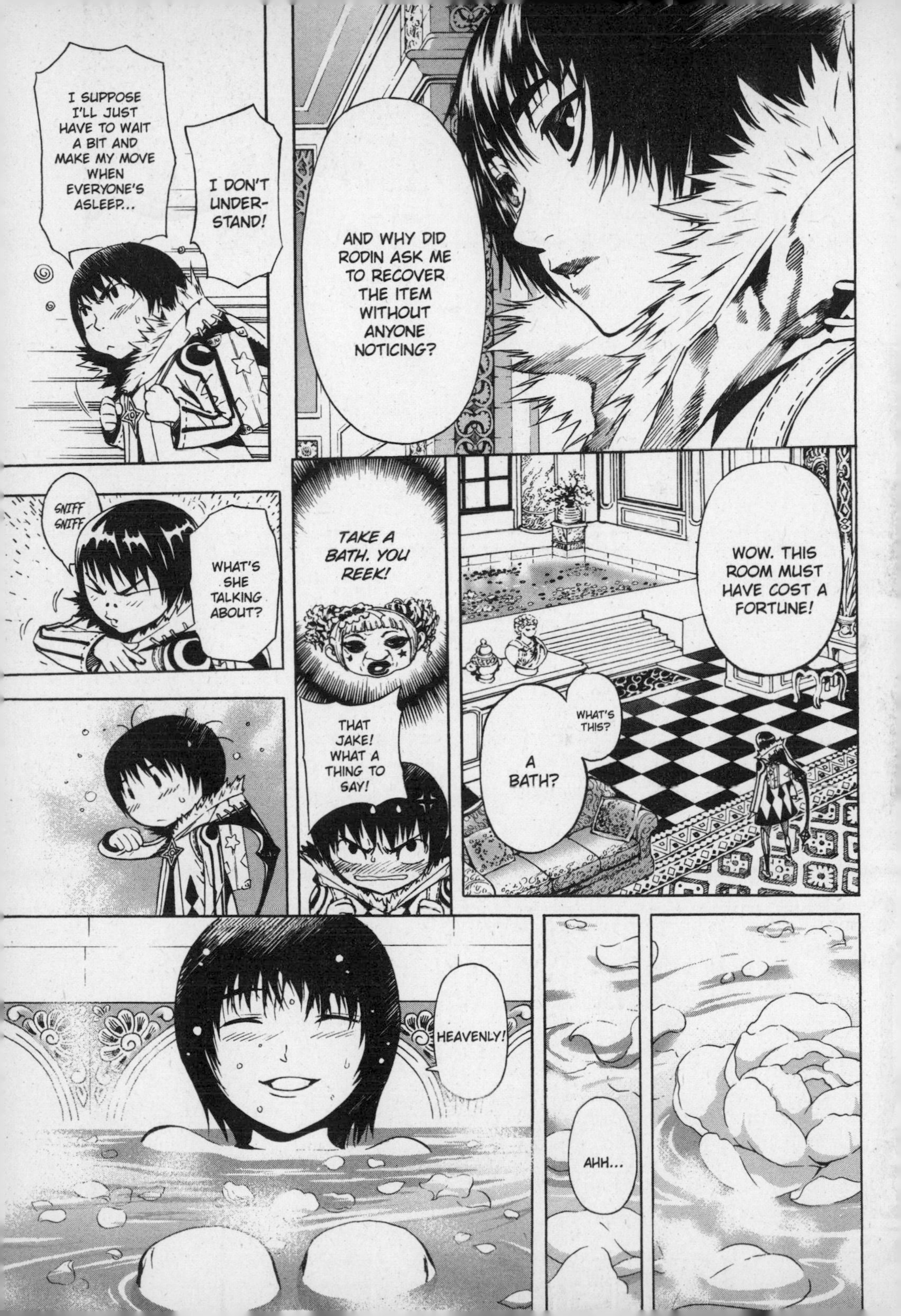
AND WHY DID RODIN ASK ME TO RECOVER THE ITEM WITHOUT ANYONE NOTICING?
I DON'T UNDER-STAND!
I SUPPOSE I'LL JUST HAVE TO WAIT A BIT AND MAKE MY MOVE WHEN EVERYONE'S ASLEEP...
WOW. THIS ROOM MUST HAVE COST A FORTUNE!
WHAT'S THIS?
A BATH?
TAKE A BATH. YOU REEK!
THAT JAKE! WHAT A THING TO SAY!
SNIFF SNIFF
WHAT'S SHE TALKING ABOUT?
AHH...
HEAVENLY!

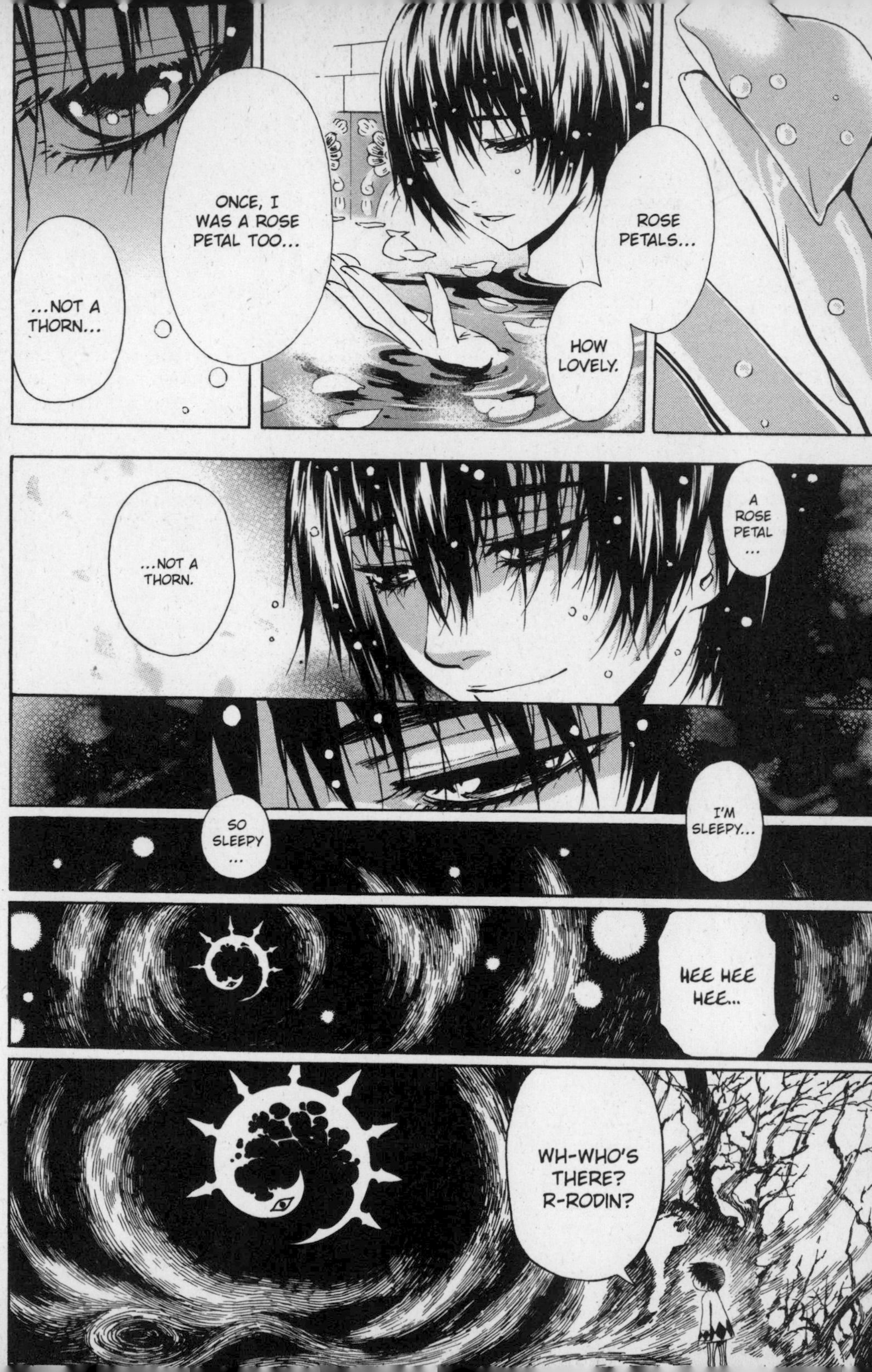
ROSE PETALS...
HOW LOVELY.
ONCE, I WAS A ROSE PETAL TOO...
...NOT A THORN...
A ROSE PETAL...
...NOT A THORN.
I'M SLEEPY...
SO SLEEPY...
HEE HEE HEE...
WH-WHO'S THERE? R-RODIN?

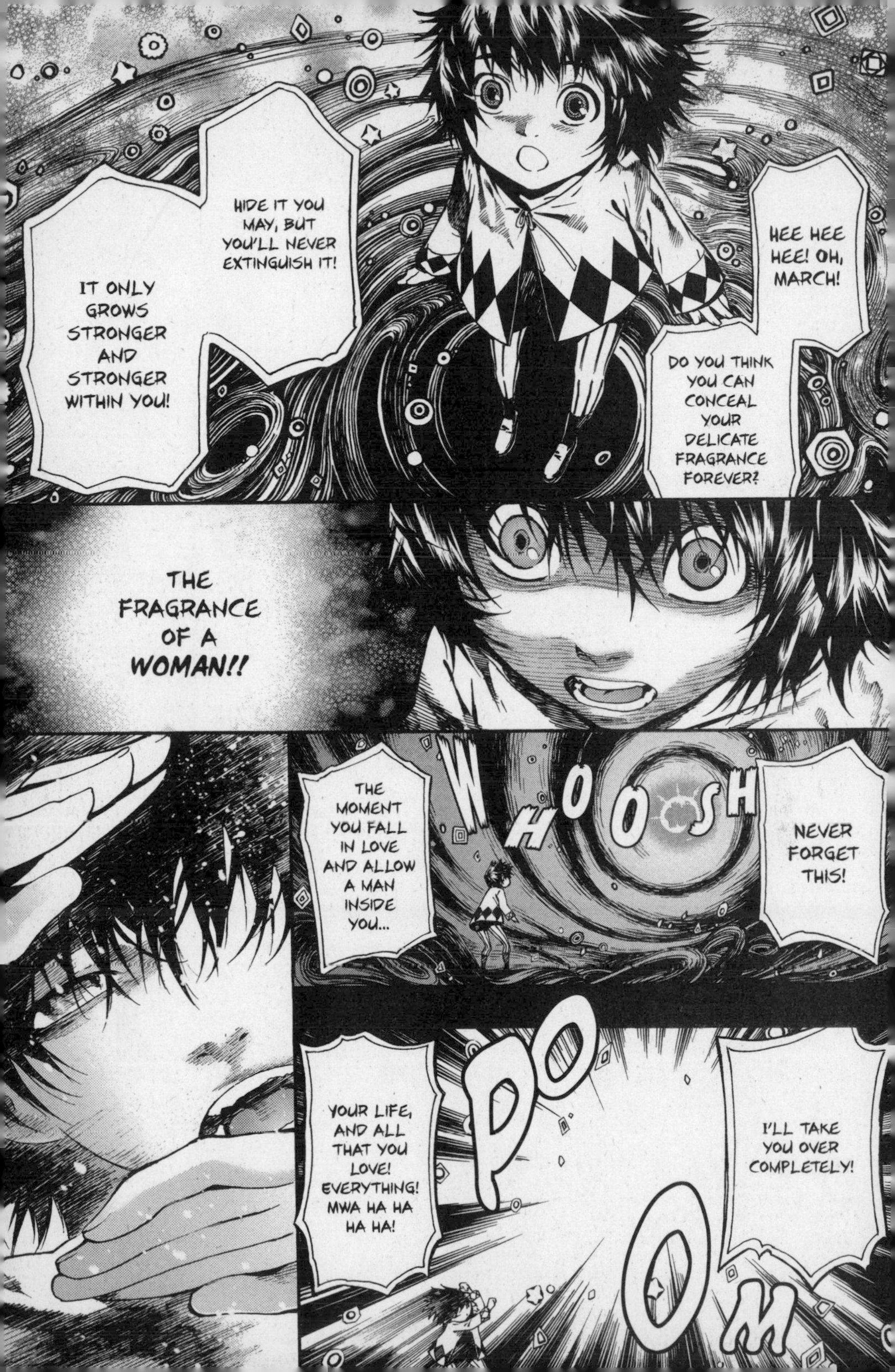
HEE HEE HEE! OH, MARCH!
DO YOU THINK YOU CAN CONCEAL YOUR DELICATE FRAGRANCE FOREVER?
HIDE IT YOU MAY, BUT YOU'LL NEVER EXTINGUISH IT!
IT ONLY GROWS STRONGER AND STRONGER WITHIN YOU!
THE FRAGRANCE OF A WOMAN!!
NEVER FORGET THIS!
WHOOSH
THE MOMENT YOU FALL IN LOVE AND ALLOW A MAN INSIDE YOU...
I'LL TAKE YOU OVER COMPLETELY!
POOM
YOUR LIFE, AND ALL THAT YOU LOVE! EVERYTHING! MWA HA HA HA HA!

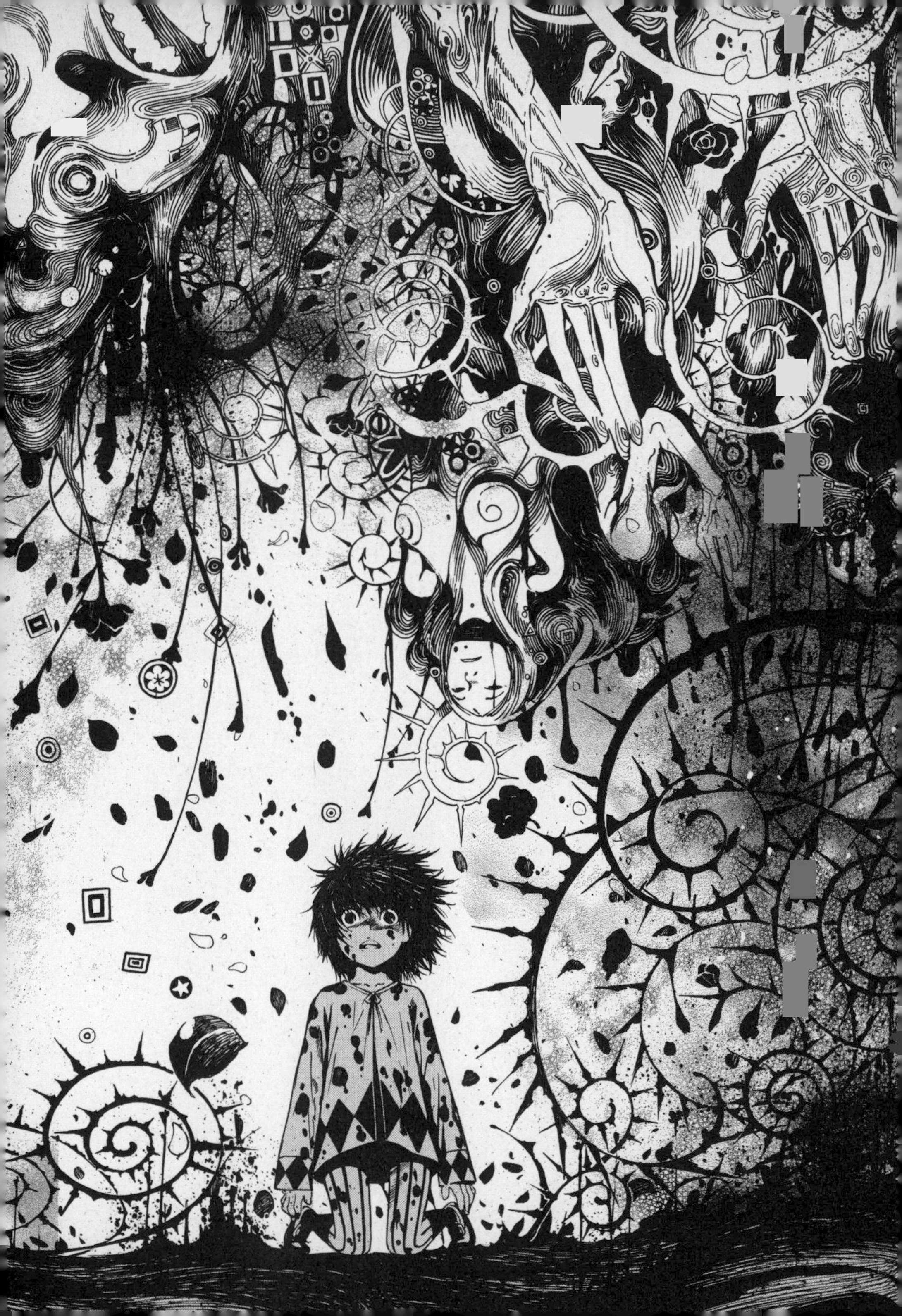

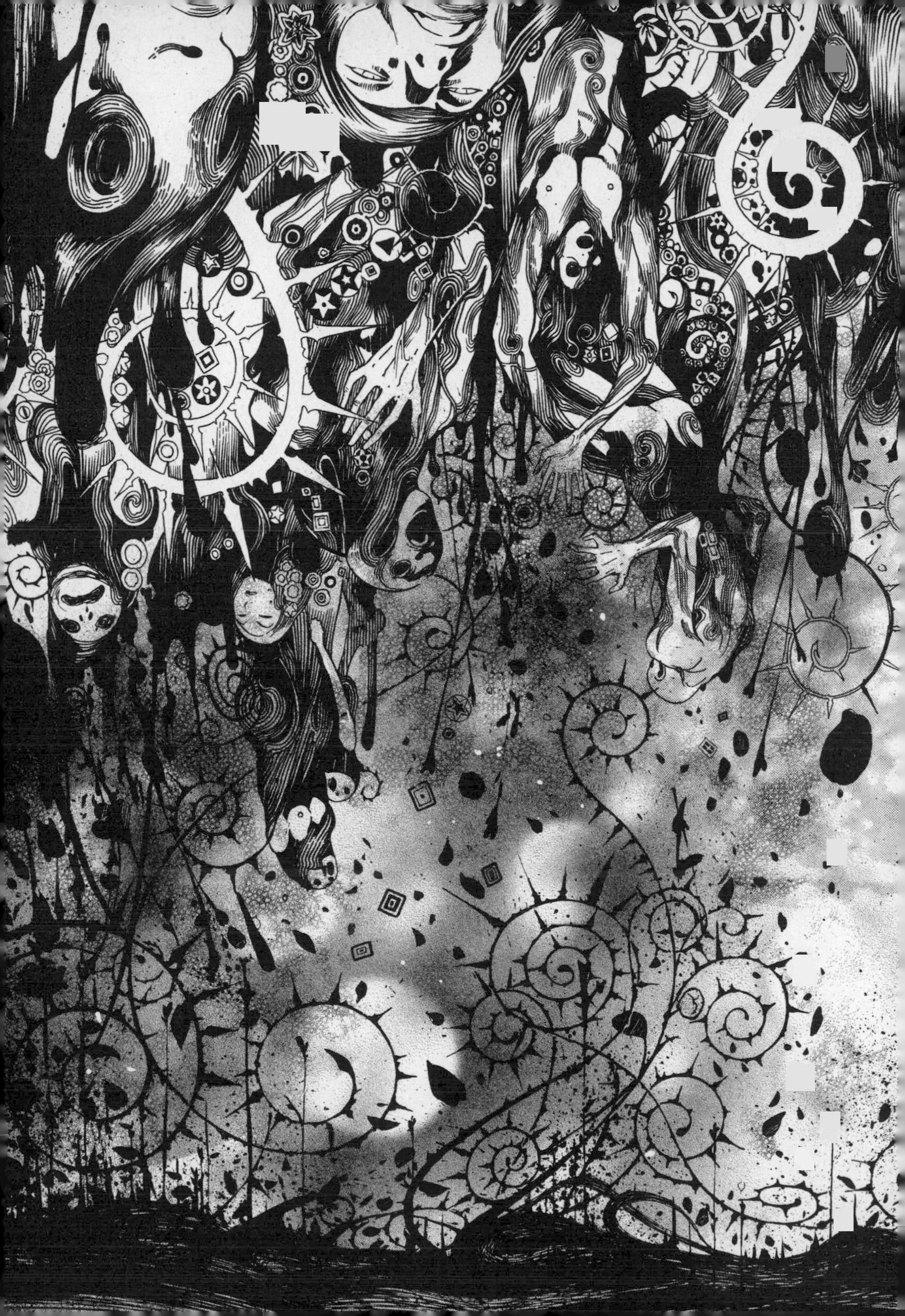

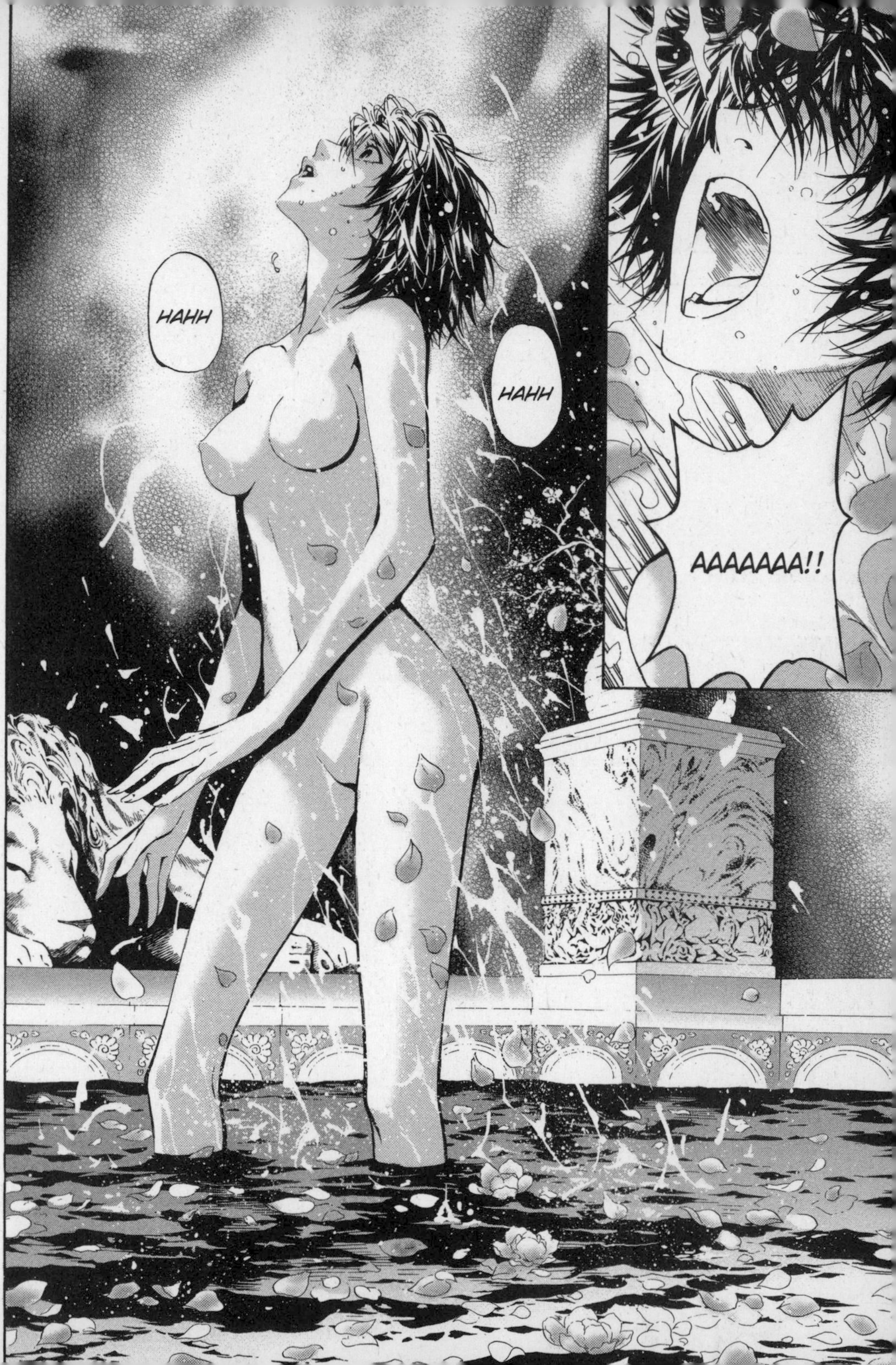
AAAAAAA!!
HAHH
HAHH

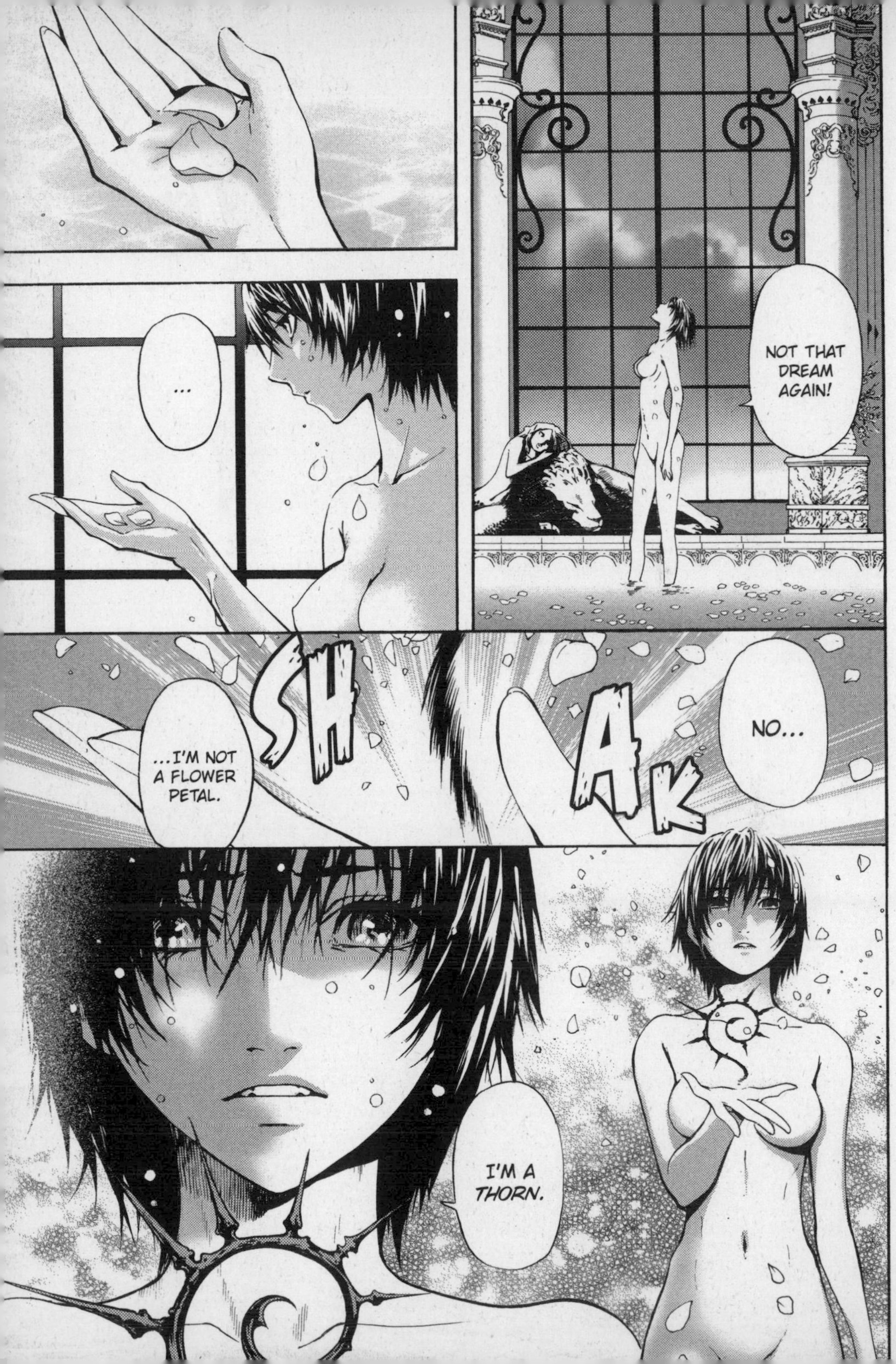
NOT THAT DREAM AGAIN!
...
NO...
SHAK
...I'M NOT A FLOWER PETAL.
I'M A THORN.

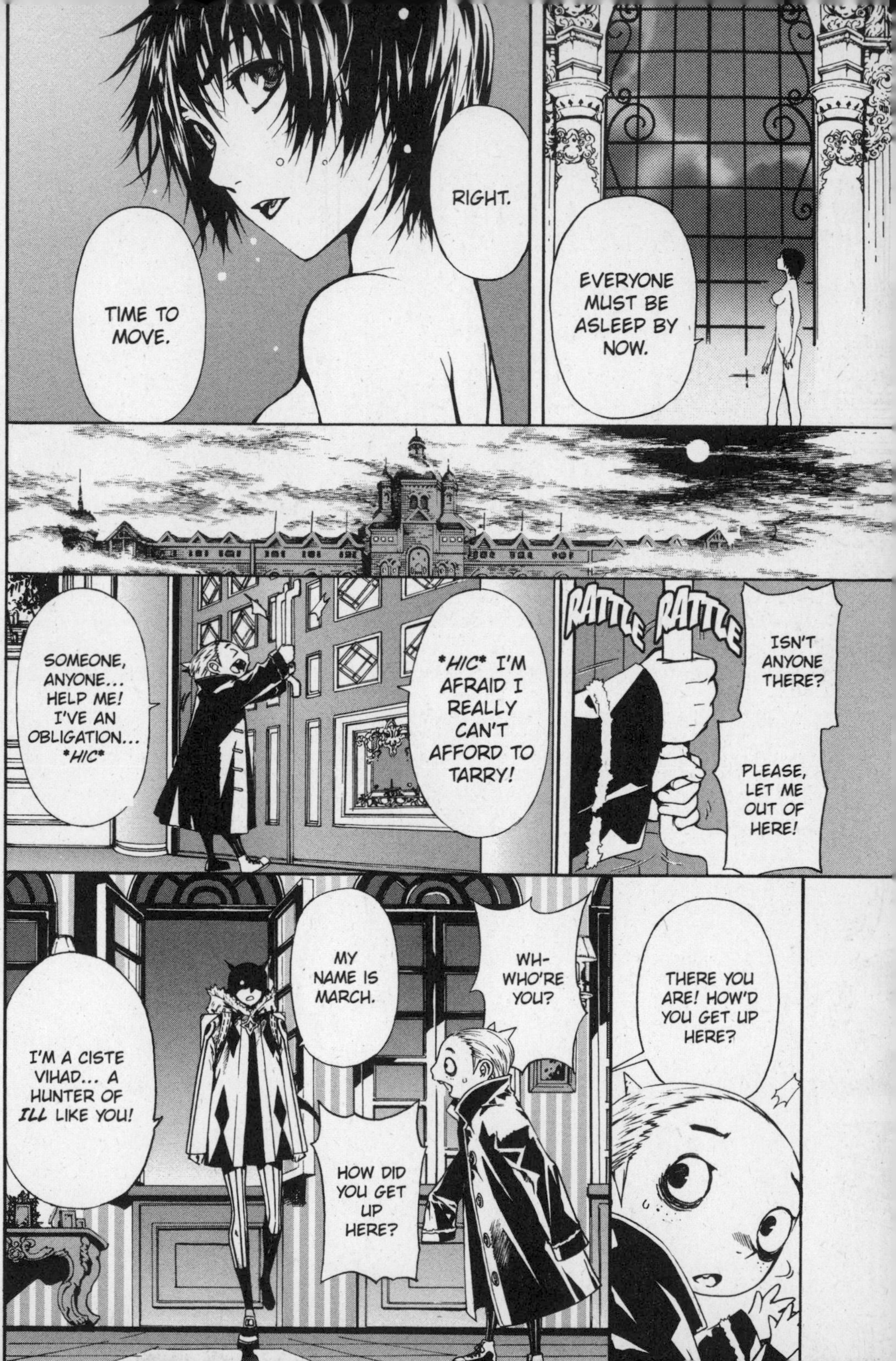
EVERYONE MUST BE ASLEEP BY NOW.
RIGHT.
TIME TO MOVE.
RATTLE RATTLE
ISN'T ANYONE THERE?
PLEASE, LET ME OUT OF HERE!
HIC I'M AFRAID I REALLY CAN'T AFFORD TO TARRY!
SOMEONE, ANYONE... HELP ME! I'VE AN OBLIGATION... *HIC*
THERE YOU ARE! HOW'D YOU GET UP HERE?
WH-WHO'RE YOU?
MY NAME IS MARCH.
HOW DID YOU GET UP HERE?
I'M A CISTE VIHAD... A HUNTER OF ILL LIKE YOU!

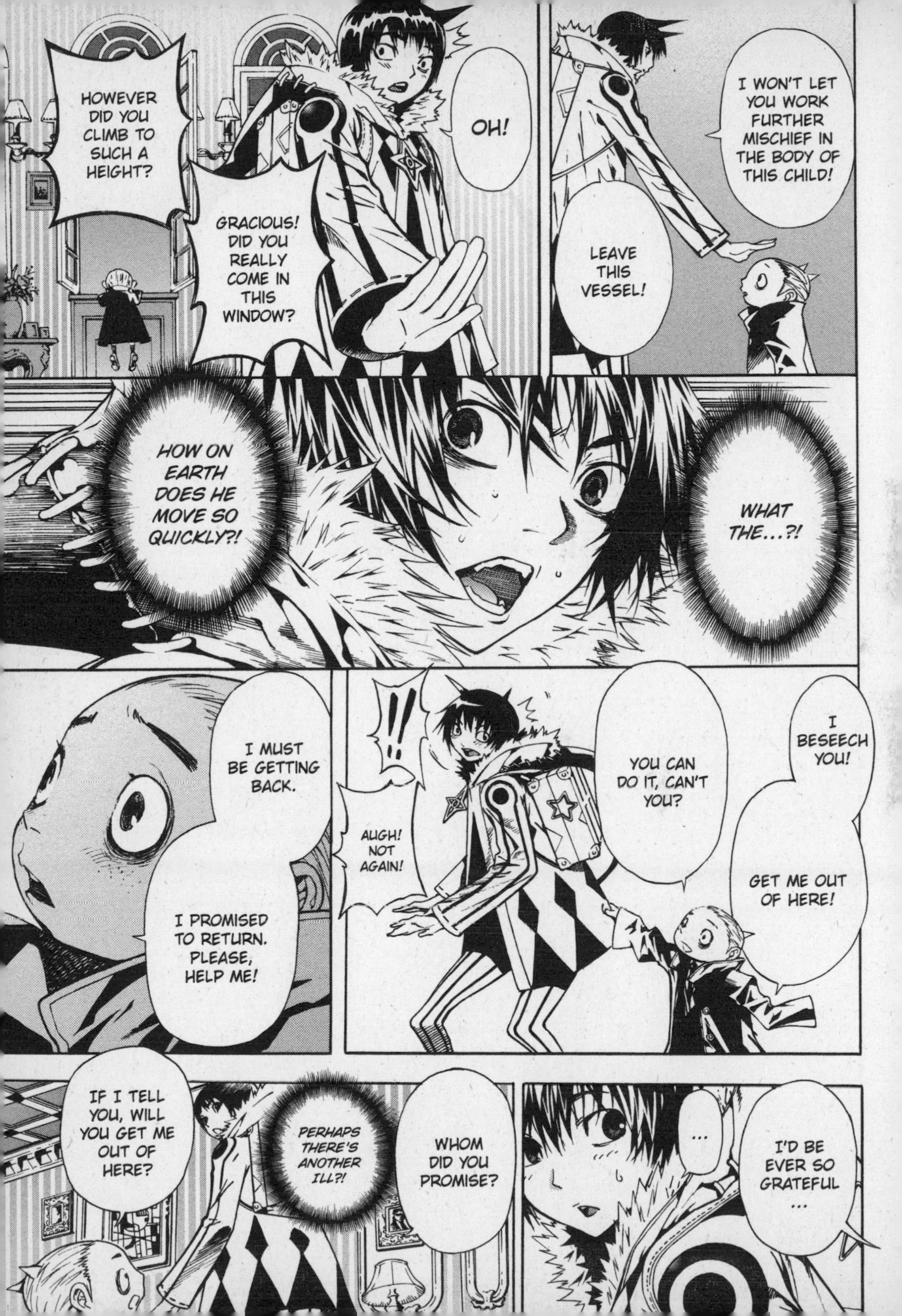
I WON'T LET YOU WORK FURTHER MISCHIEF IN THE BODY OF THIS CHILD!
LEAVE THIS VESSEL!
OH!
HOWEVER DID YOU CLIMB TO SUCH A HEIGHT?
GRACIOUS! DID YOU REALLY COME IN THIS WINDOW?
WHAT THE...?!
HOW ON EARTH DOES HE MOVE SO QUICKLY?!
I BESEECH YOU!
YOU CAN DO IT, CAN'T YOU?
GET ME OUT OF HERE!
!!
AUGH! NOT AGAIN!
I MUST BE GETTING BACK.
I PROMISED TO RETURN. PLEASE, HELP ME!
...
I'D BE EVER SO GRATEFUL ...
WHOM DID YOU PROMISE?
PERHAPS THERE'S ANOTHER ILL?!
IF I TELL YOU, WILL YOU GET ME OUT OF HERE?

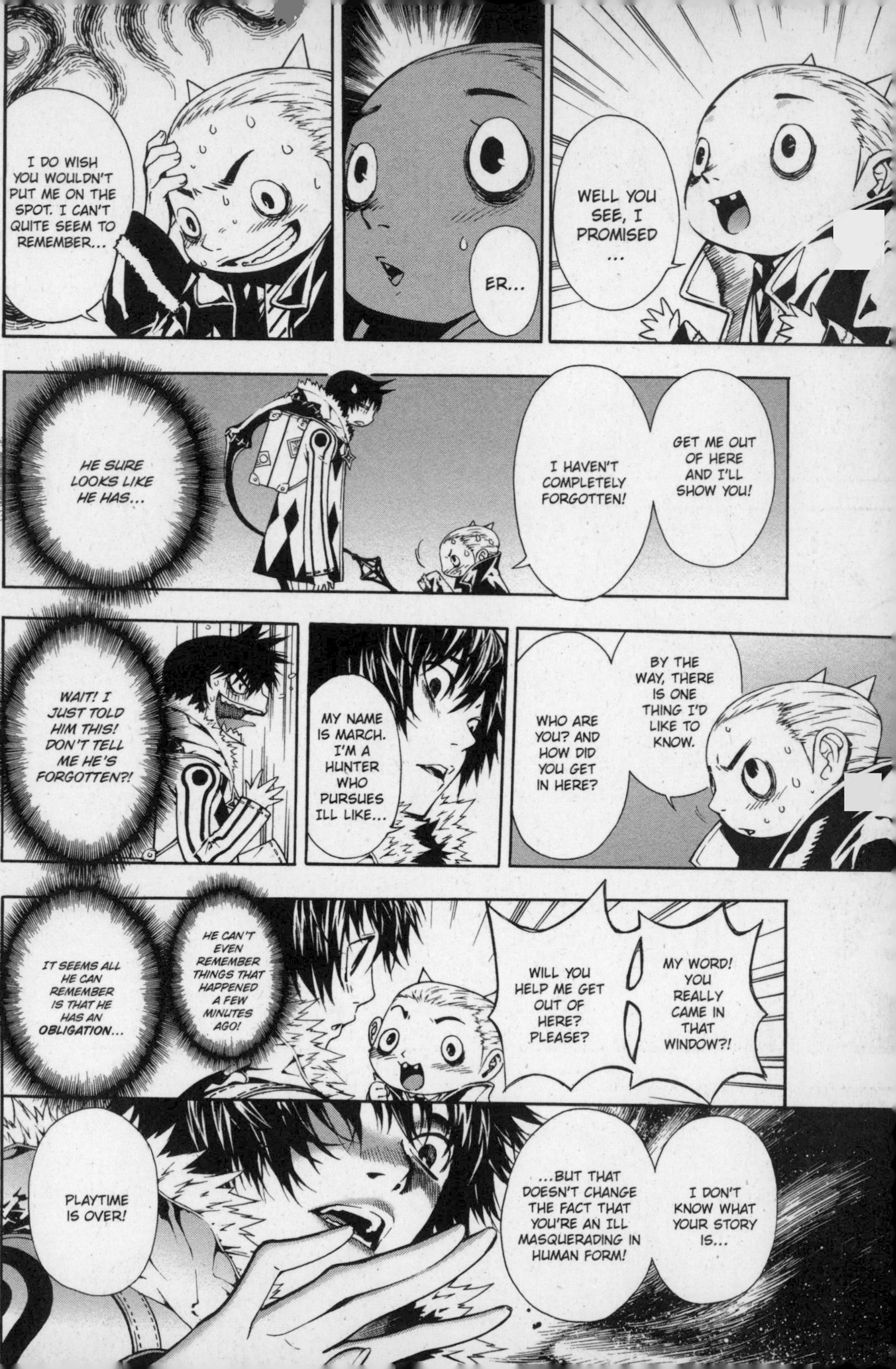
WELL YOU SEE, I PROMISED ...
ER...
I DO WISH YOU WOULDN'T PUT ME ON THE SPOT. I CAN'T QUITE SEEM TO REMEMBER...
GET ME OUT OF HERE AND I'LL SHOW YOU!
I HAVEN'T COMPLETELY FORGOTTEN!
HE SURE LOOKS LIKE HE HAS...
BY THE WAY, THERE IS ONE THING I'D LIKE TO KNOW.
WHO ARE YOU? AND HOW DID YOU GET IN HERE?
MY NAME IS MARCH. I'M A HUNTER WHO PURSUES ILL LIKE...
WAIT! I JUST TOLD HIM THIS! DON'T TELL ME HE'S FORGOTTEN?!
MY WORD! YOU REALLY CAME IN THAT WINDOW?!
WILL YOU HELP ME GET OUT OF HERE? PLEASE?
HE CAN'T EVEN REMEMBER THINGS THAT HAPPENED A FEW MINUTES AGO!
IT SEEMS ALL HE CAN REMEMBER IS THAT HE HAS AN OBLIGATION...
I DON'T KNOW WHAT YOUR STORY IS...
...BUT THAT DOESN'T CHANGE THE FACT THAT YOU'RE AN ILL MASQUERADING IN HUMAN FORM!
PLAYTIME IS OVER!

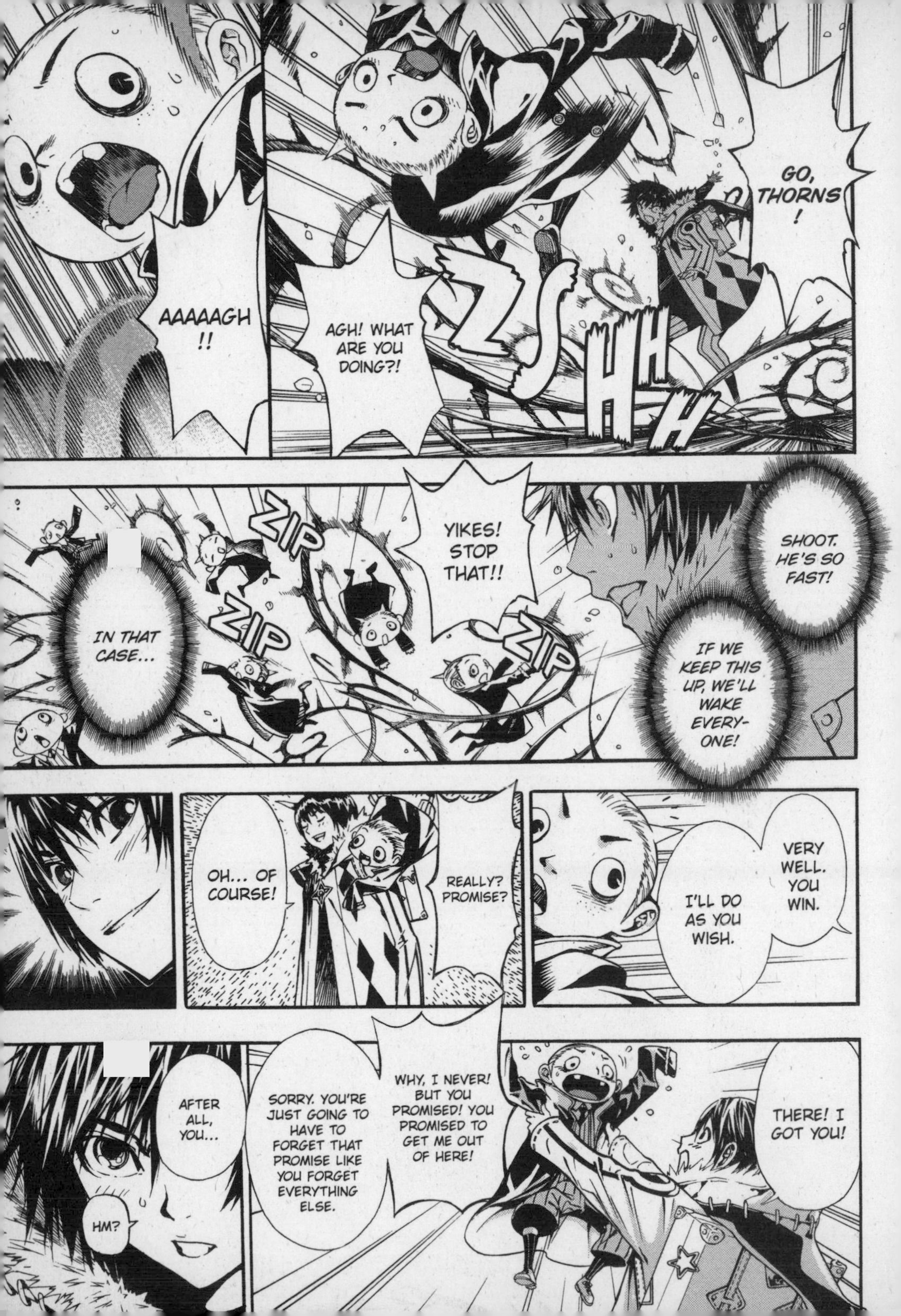
GO, THORNS!
AGH! WHAT ARE YOU DOING?!
ZUSHHH
AAAAAGH!!
SHOOT. HE'S SO FAST!
IF WE KEEP THIS UP, WE'LL WAKE EVERYONE!
YIKES! STOP THAT!!
ZIP
ZIP
ZIP
IN THAT CASE...
VERY WELL. YOU WIN.
I'LL DO AS YOU WISH.
REALLY? PROMISE?
OH... OF COURSE!
THERE! I GOT YOU!
WHY, I NEVER! BUT YOU PROMISED! YOU PROMISED TO GET ME OUT OF HERE!
SORRY. YOU'RE JUST GOING TO HAVE TO FORGET THAT PROMISE LIKE YOU FORGET EVERYTHING ELSE.
AFTER ALL, YOU...
HM?

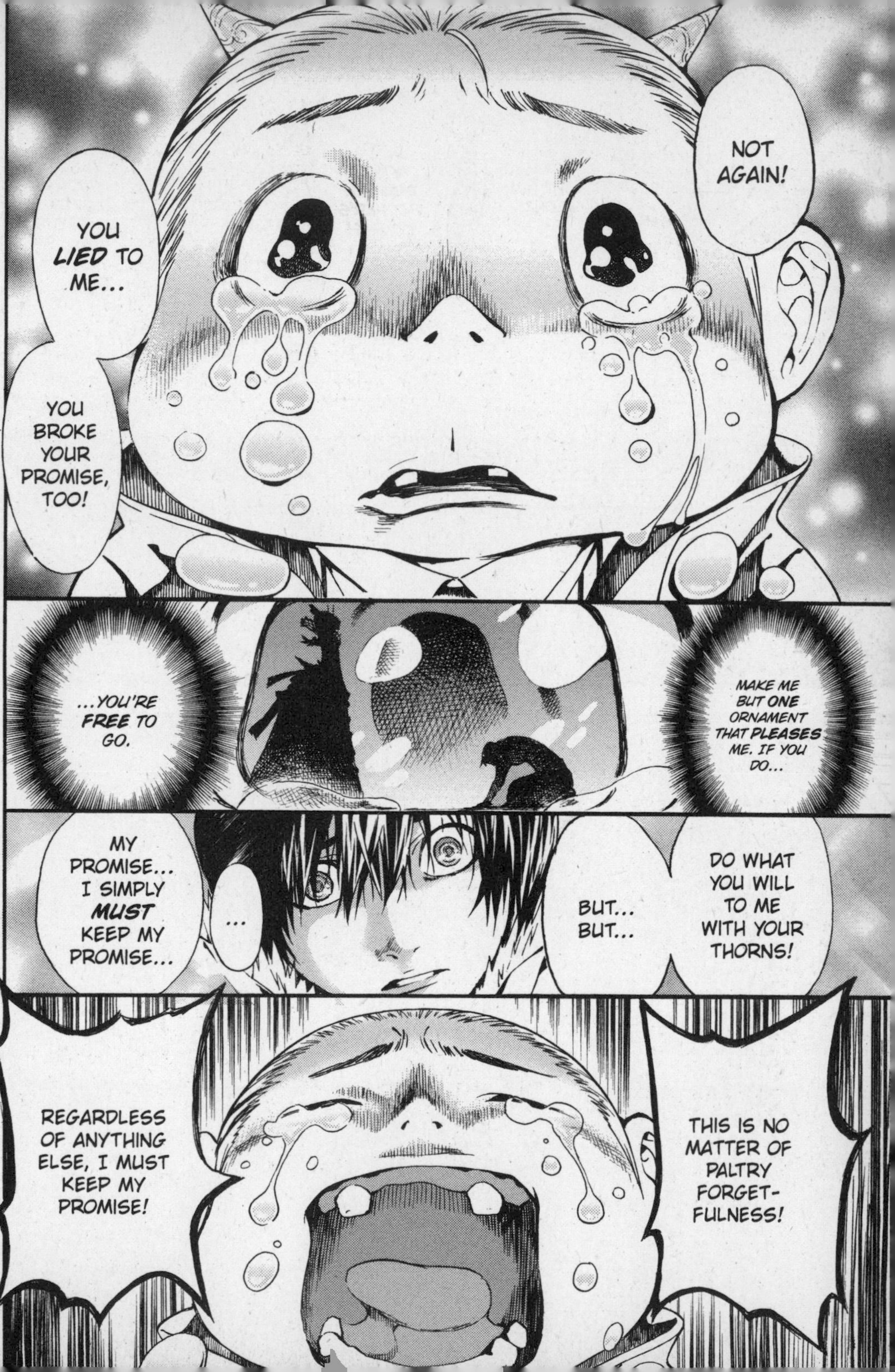
NOT AGAIN!
YOU LIED TO ME...
YOU BROKE YOUR PROMISE, TOO!
MAKE ME BUT ONE ORNAMENT THAT PLEASES ME. IF YOU DO...
...YOU'RE FREE TO GO.
DO WHAT YOU WILL TO ME WITH YOUR THORNS!
BUT... BUT...
...
MY PROMISE... I SIMPLY MUST KEEP MY PROMISE...
THIS IS NO MATTER OF PALTRY FORGET-FULNESS!
REGARDLESS OF ANYTHING ELSE, I MUST KEEP MY PROMISE!

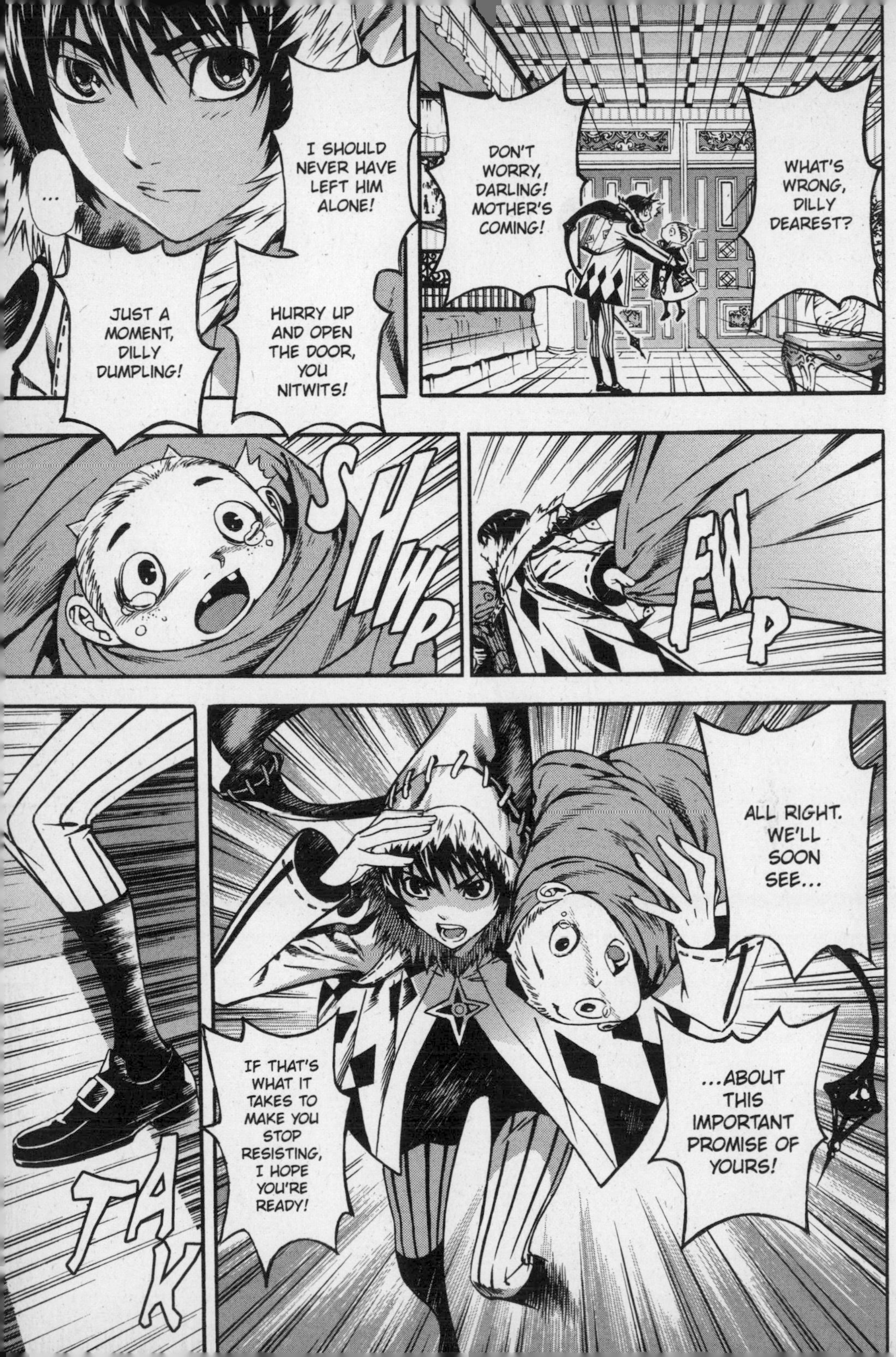
WHAT'S WRONG, DILLY DEAREST?
DON'T WORRY, DARLING! MOTHER'S COMING!
I SHOULD NEVER HAVE LEFT HIM ALONE!
...
HURRY UP AND OPEN THE DOOR, YOU NITWITS!
JUST A MOMENT, DILLY DUMPLING!
FWP
SHWIP
ALL RIGHT. WE'LL SOON SEE...
...ABOUT THIS IMPORTANT PROMISE OF YOURS!
IF THAT'S WHAT IT TAKES TO MAKE YOU STOP RESISTING, I HOPE YOU'RE READY!
TAK

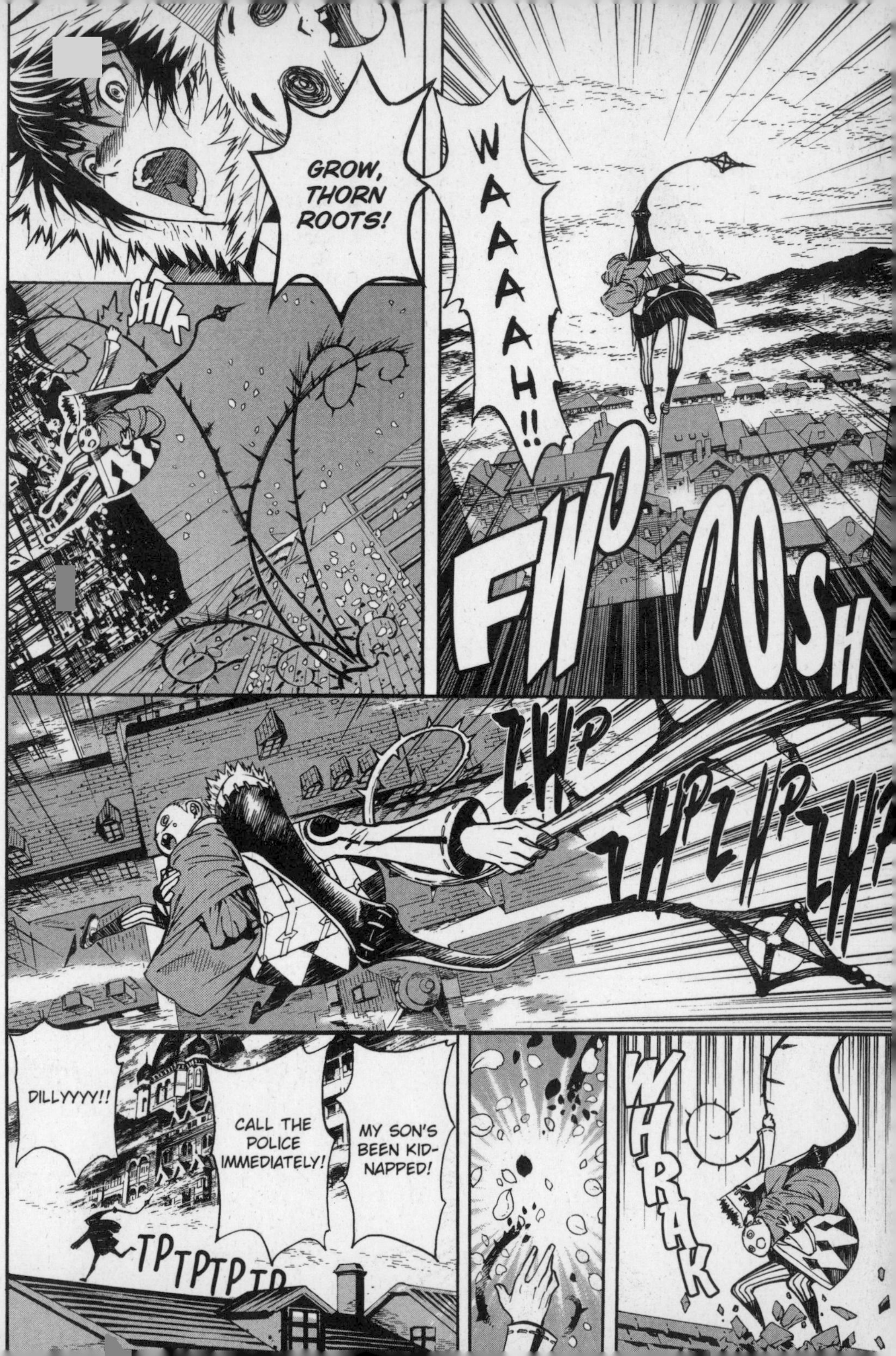
WAAAAH!!
FWOOOSH
GROW, THORN ROOTS!
SHIK
ZHP ZHPZHPZHP
WHRAK
DILLYYYY!!
CALL THE POLICE IMMEDIATELY!
MY SON'S BEEN KID-NAPPED!
TPTPTPTP

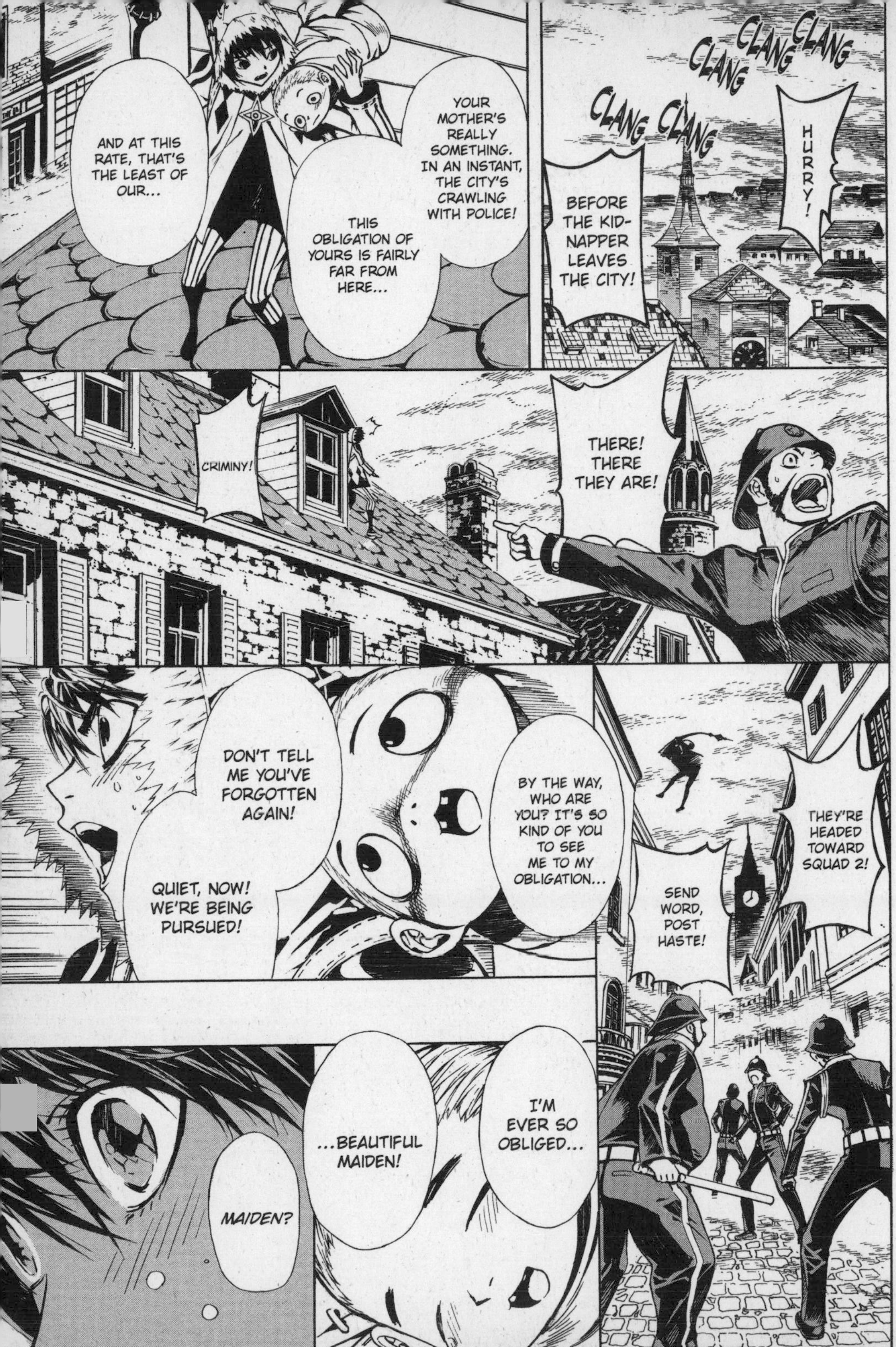
CLANG CLANG
CLANG CLANG
CLANG CLANG
HURRY!
BEFORE THE KID-NAPPER LEAVES THE CITY!
YOUR MOTHER'S REALLY SOMETHING. IN AN INSTANT, THE CITY'S CRAWLING WITH POLICE!
THIS OBLIGATION OF YOURS IS FAIRLY FAR FROM HERE...
AND AT THIS RATE, THAT'S THE LEAST OF OUR...
THERE! THERE THEY ARE!
CRIMINY!
THEY'RE HEADED TOWARD SQUAD 2!
SEND WORD, POST HASTE!
BY THE WAY, WHO ARE YOU? IT'S SO KIND OF YOU TO SEE ME TO MY OBLIGATION...
DON'T TELL ME YOU'VE FORGOTTEN AGAIN!
QUIET, NOW! WE'RE BEING PURSUED!
I'M EVER SO OBLIGED...
...BEAUTIFUL MAIDEN!
MAIDEN?

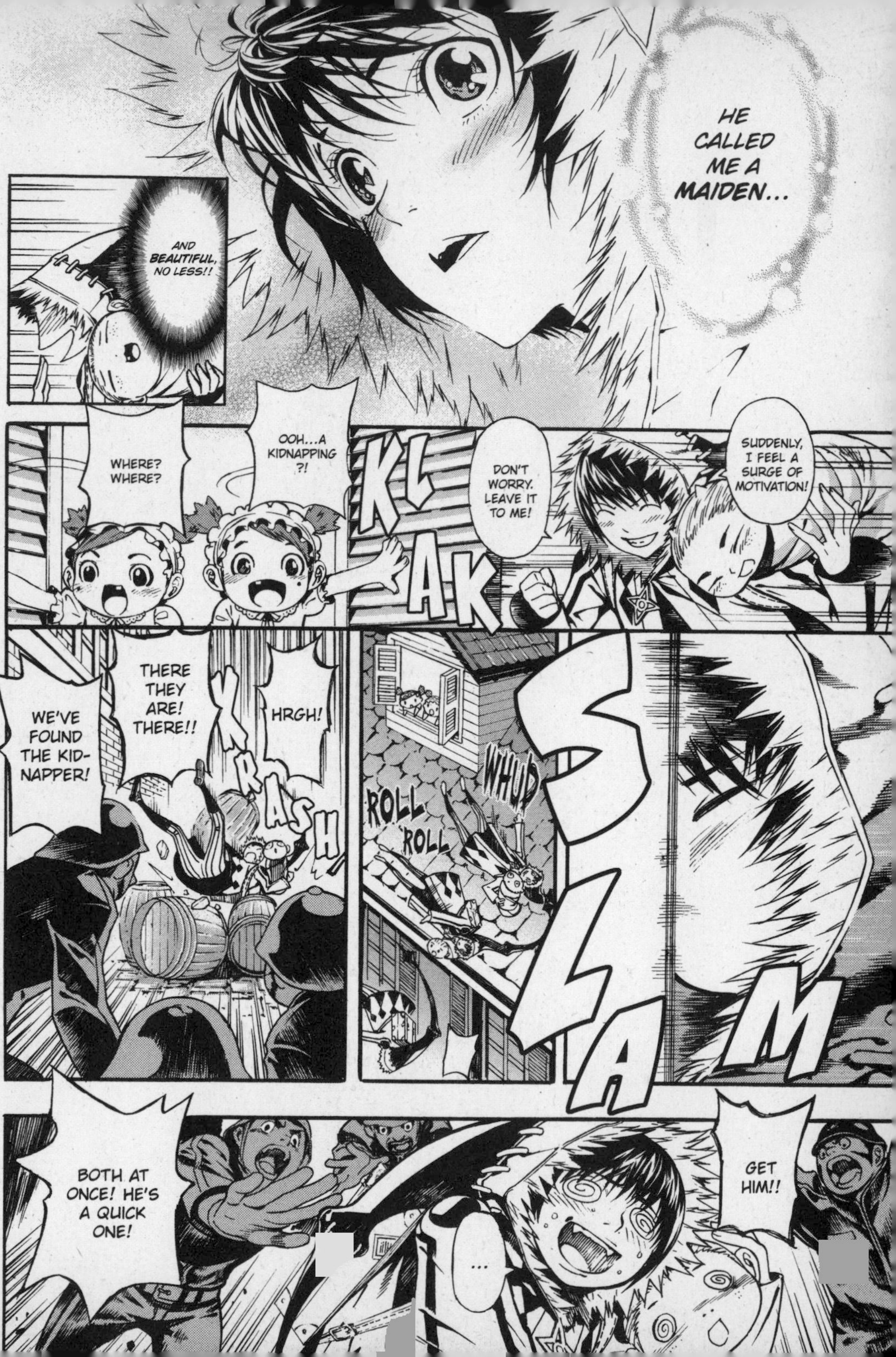
HE CALLED ME A MAIDEN...
AND BEAUTIFUL, NO LESS!!
SUDDENLY, I FEEL A SURGE OF MOTIVATION!
DON'T WORRY. LEAVE IT TO ME!
KLAK
OOH...A KIDNAPPING?!
WHERE? WHERE?
SLAM
WHUD
ROLL ROLL
HRGH!
KRASH
THERE THEY ARE! THERE!!
WE'VE FOUND THE KID-NAPPER!
GET HIM!!
...
BOTH AT ONCE! HE'S A QUICK ONE!

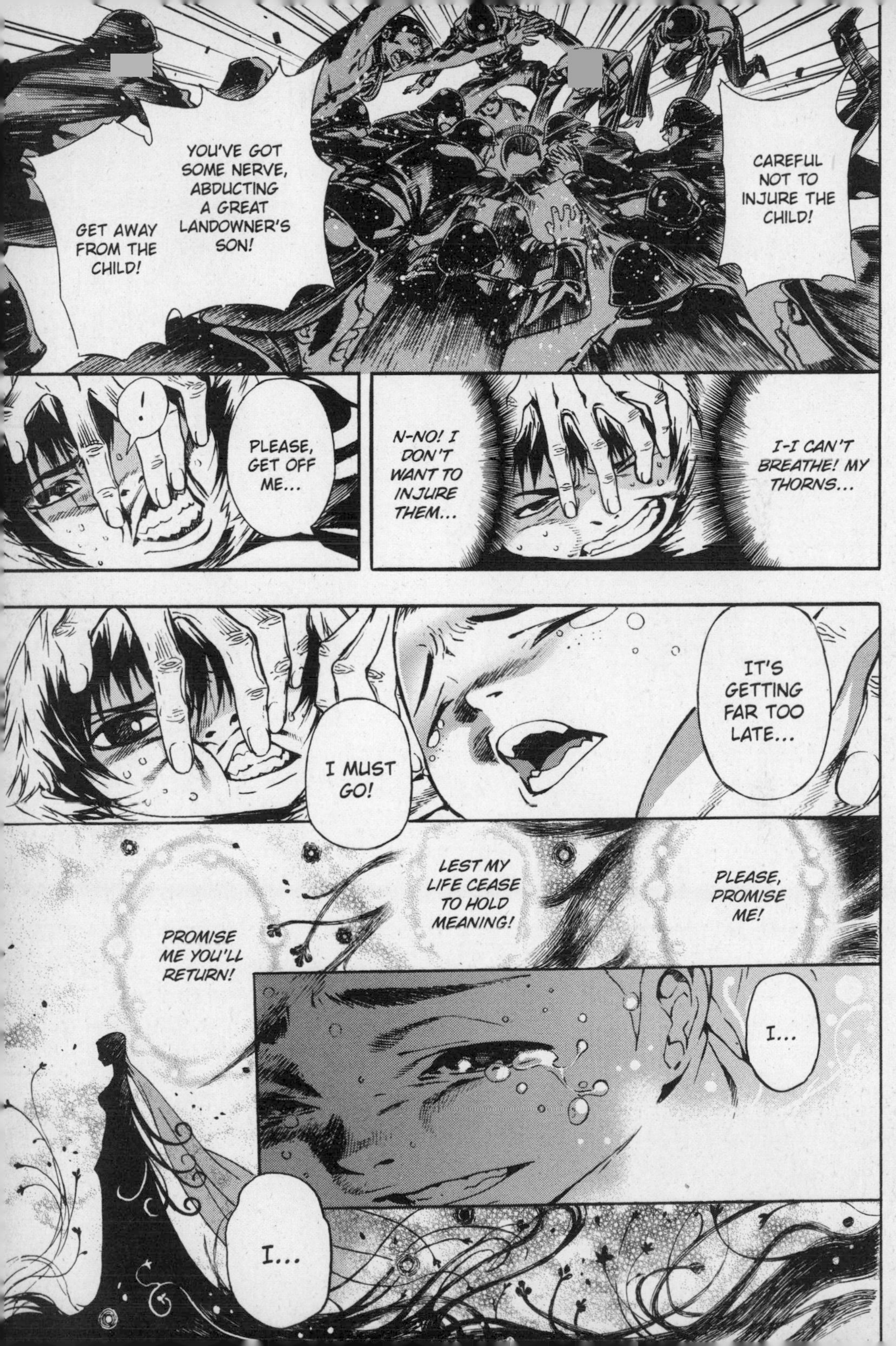
CAREFUL NOT TO INJURE THE CHILD!
YOU'VE GOT SOME NERVE, ABDUCTING A GREAT LANDOWNER'S SON!
GET AWAY FROM THE CHILD!
I-I CAN'T BREATHE! MY THORNS...
N-NO! I DON'T WANT TO INJURE THEM...
!
PLEASE, GET OFF ME...
IT'S GETTING FAR TOO LATE...
I MUST GO!
PLEASE, PROMISE ME!
LEST MY LIFE CEASE TO HOLD MEANING!
PROMISE ME YOU'LL RETURN!
I...
I...

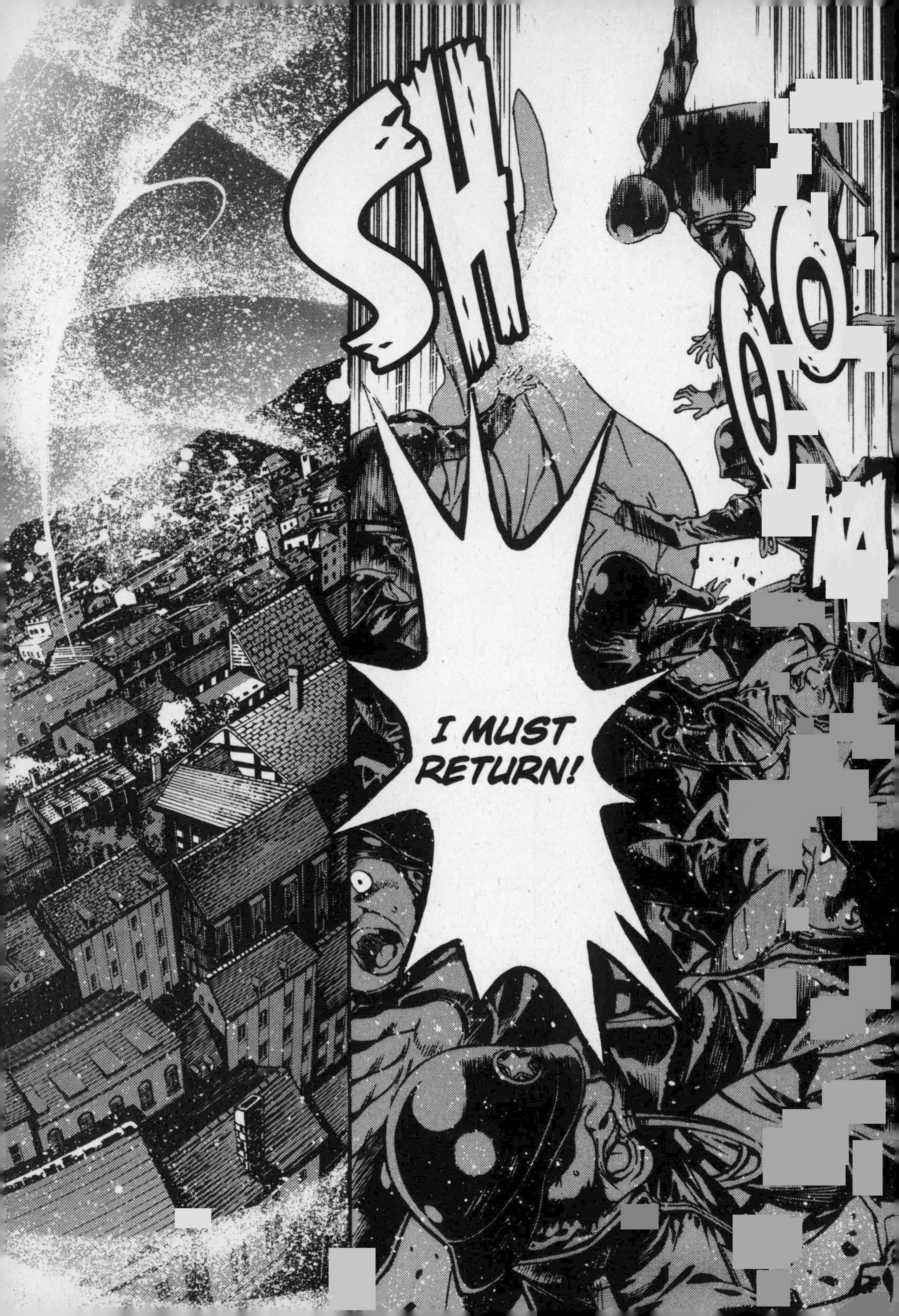
SH
I MUST RETURN!

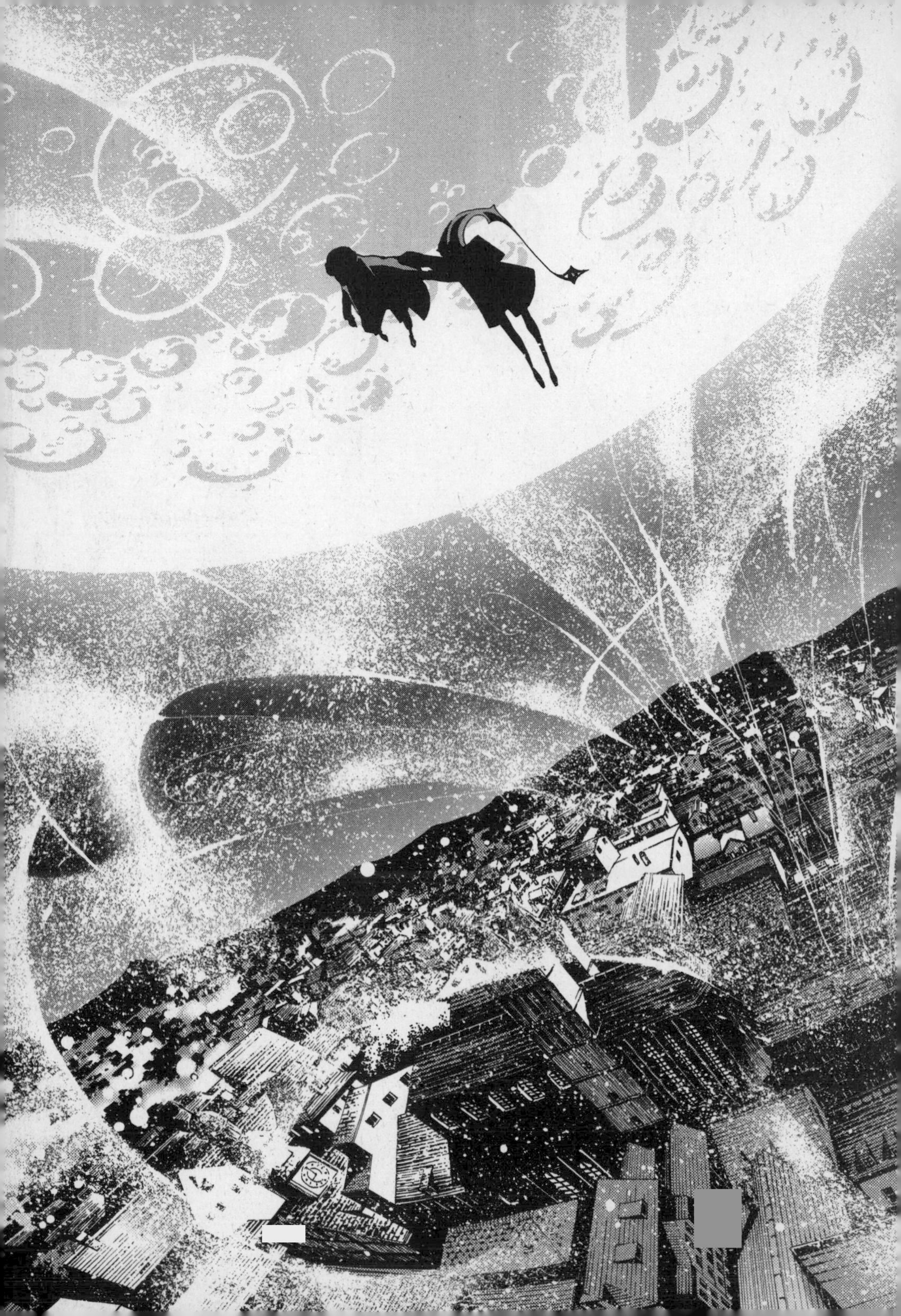

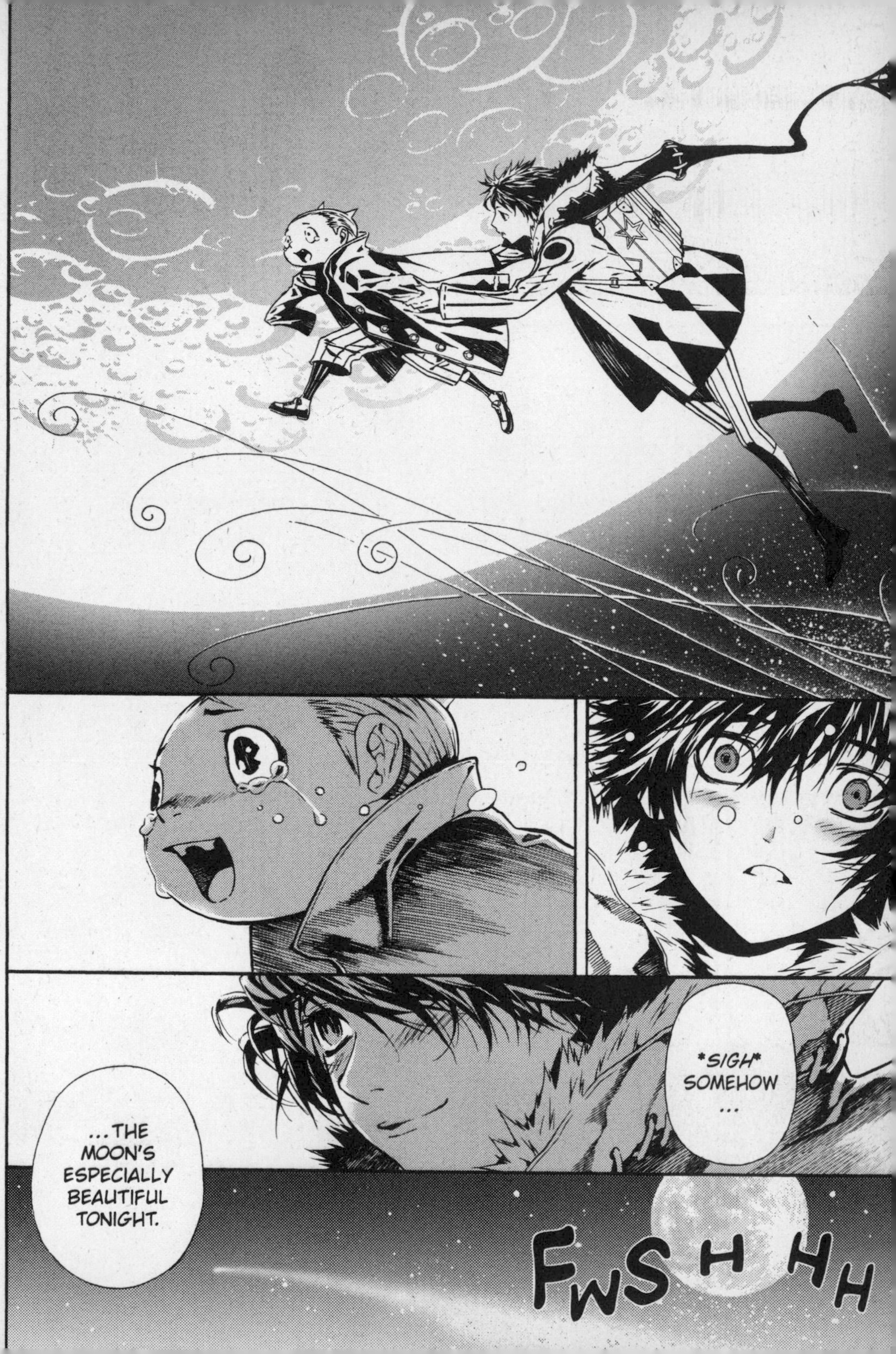
SIGH SOMEHOW ...
...THE MOON'S ESPECIALLY BEAUTIFUL TONIGHT.
FWSHHH

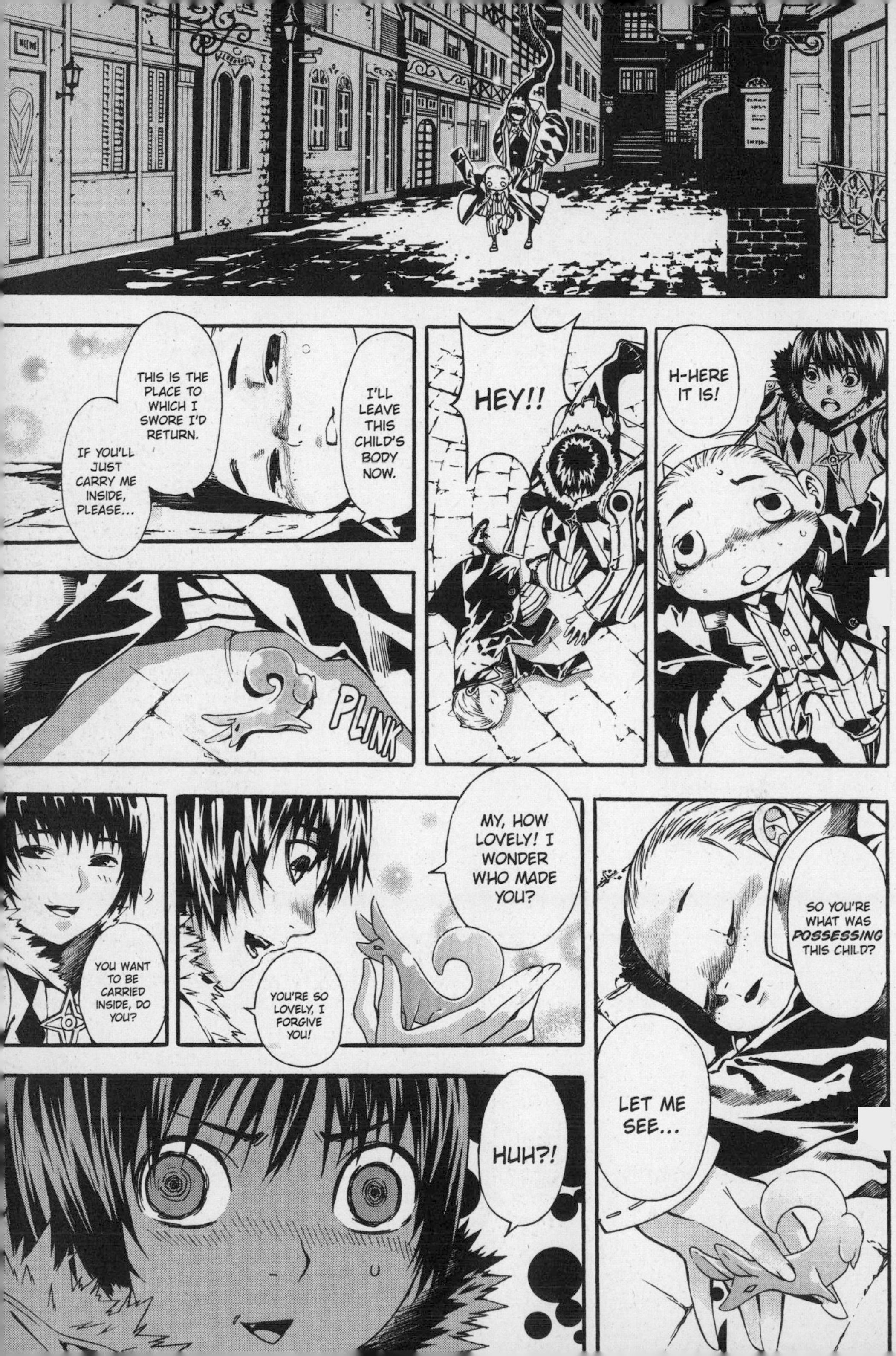
H-HERE IT IS!
HEY!!
I'LL LEAVE THIS CHILD'S BODY NOW.
THIS IS THE PLACE TO WHICH I SWORE I'D RETURN.
IF YOU'LL JUST CARRY ME INSIDE, PLEASE...
PLINK
SO YOU'RE WHAT WAS *POSSESSING* THIS CHILD?
LET ME SEE...
MY, HOW LOVELY! I WONDER WHO MADE YOU?
YOU'RE SO LOVELY, I FORGIVE YOU!
YOU WANT TO BE CARRIED INSIDE, DO YOU?
HUH?!

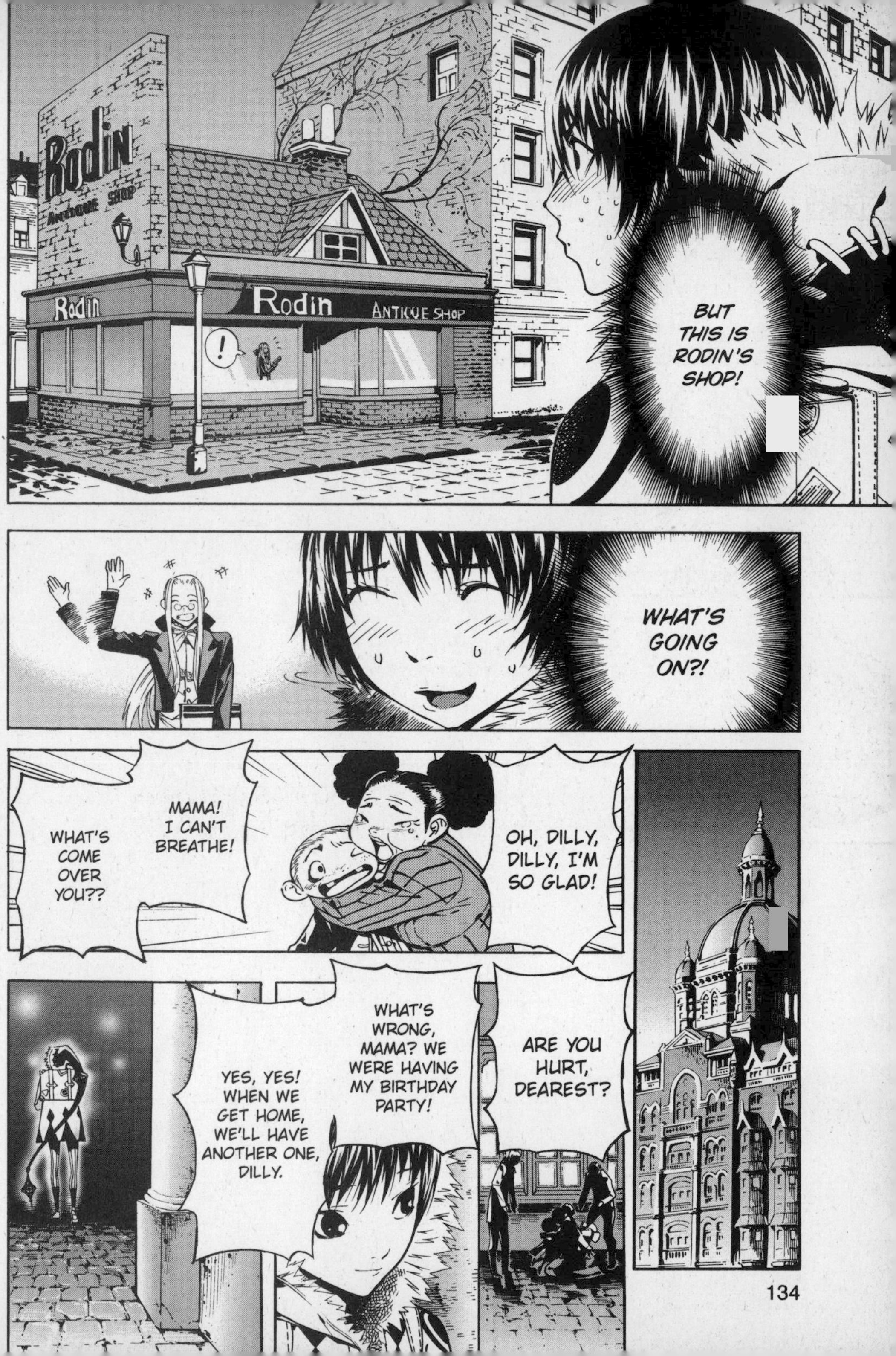
Rodin
Antique SHOP
Rodin
Rodin
ANTIQUE SHOP
!
BUT THIS IS RODIN'S SHOP!
WHAT'S GOING ON?!
OH, DILLY, DILLY, I'M SO GLAD!
MAMA! I CAN'T BREATHE!
WHAT'S COME OVER YOU??
ARE YOU HURT, DEAREST?
WHAT'S WRONG, MAMA? WE WERE HAVING MY BIRTHDAY PARTY!
YES, YES! WHEN WE GET HOME, WE'LL HAVE ANOTHER ONE, DILLY.

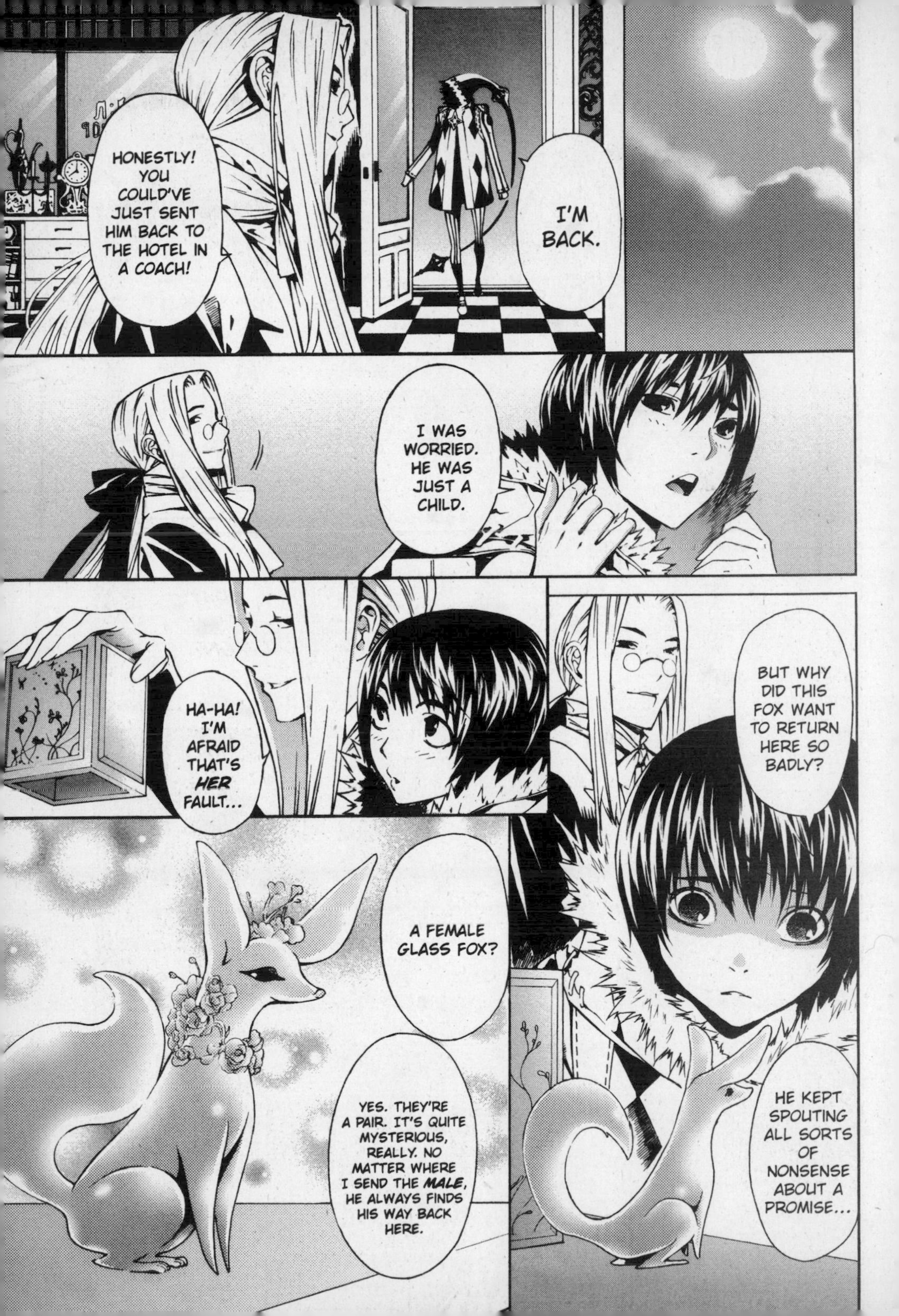
I'M BACK.
HONESTLY! YOU COULD'VE JUST SENT HIM BACK TO THE HOTEL IN A COACH!
I WAS WORRIED. HE WAS JUST A CHILD.
BUT WHY DID THIS FOX WANT TO RETURN HERE SO BADLY?
HE KEPT SPOUTING ALL SORTS OF NONSENSE ABOUT A PROMISE...
HA-HA! I'M AFRAID THAT'S *HER* FAULT...
A FEMALE GLASS FOX?
YES. THEY'RE A PAIR. IT'S QUITE MYSTERIOUS, REALLY. NO MATTER WHERE I SEND THE *MALE*, HE ALWAYS FINDS HIS WAY BACK HERE.

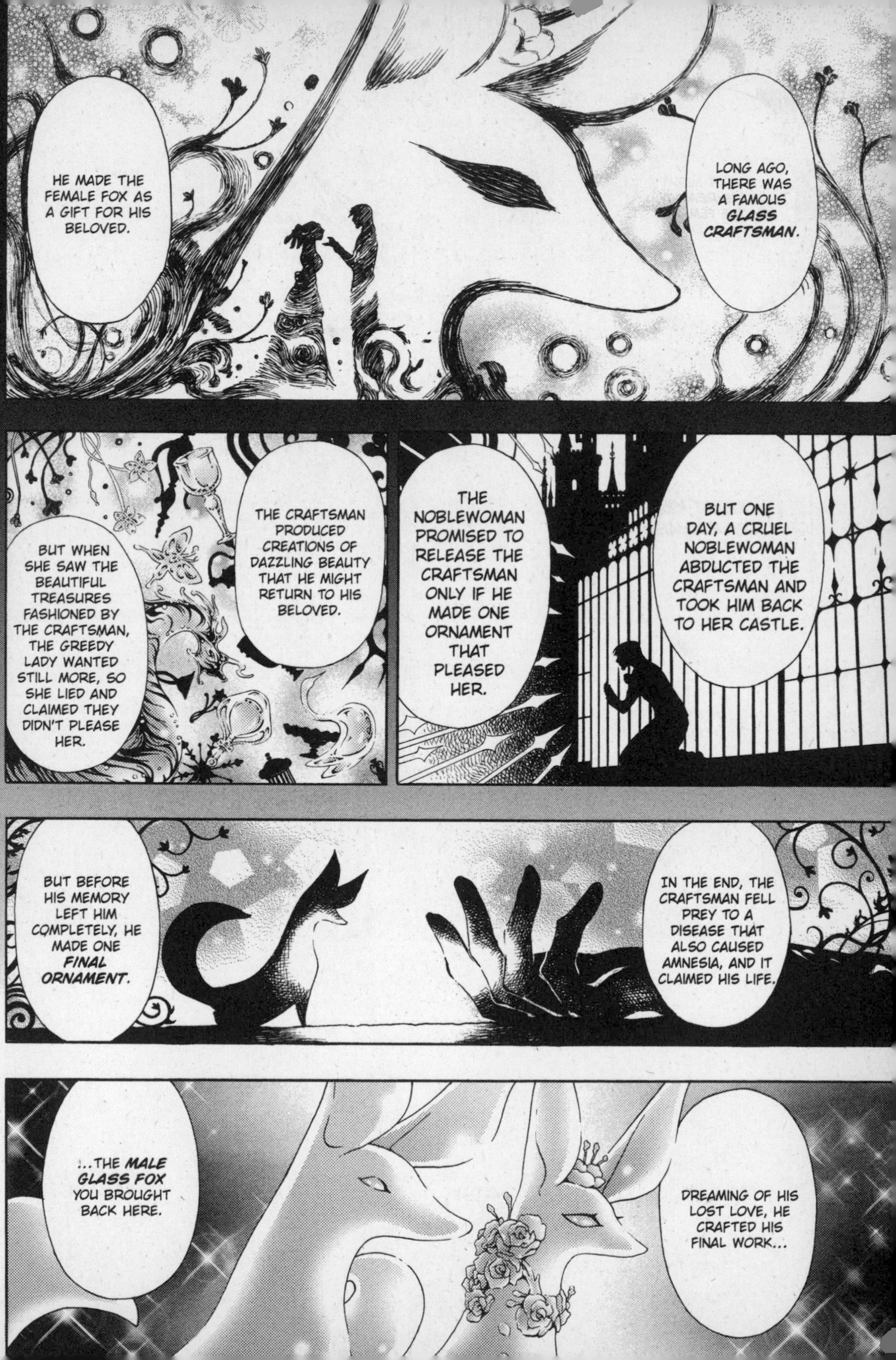
LONG AGO, THERE WAS A FAMOUS **GLASS CRAFTSMAN**.
HE MADE THE FEMALE FOX AS A GIFT FOR HIS BELOVED.
BUT ONE DAY, A CRUEL NOBLEWOMAN ABDUCTED THE CRAFTSMAN AND TOOK HIM BACK TO HER CASTLE.
THE NOBLEWOMAN PROMISED TO RELEASE THE CRAFTSMAN ONLY IF HE MADE ONE ORNAMENT THAT PLEASED HER.
THE CRAFTSMAN PRODUCED CREATIONS OF DAZZLING BEAUTY THAT HE MIGHT RETURN TO HIS BELOVED.
BUT WHEN SHE SAW THE BEAUTIFUL TREASURES FASHIONED BY THE CRAFTSMAN, THE GREEDY LADY WANTED STILL MORE, SO SHE LIED AND CLAIMED THEY DIDN'T PLEASE HER.
IN THE END, THE CRAFTSMAN FELL PREY TO A DISEASE THAT ALSO CAUSED AMNESIA, AND IT CLAIMED HIS LIFE.
BUT BEFORE HIS MEMORY LEFT HIM COMPLETELY, HE MADE ONE ***FINAL ORNAMENT***.
DREAMING OF HIS LOST LOVE, HE CRAFTED HIS FINAL WORK...
...THE ***MALE GLASS FOX*** YOU BROUGHT BACK HERE.

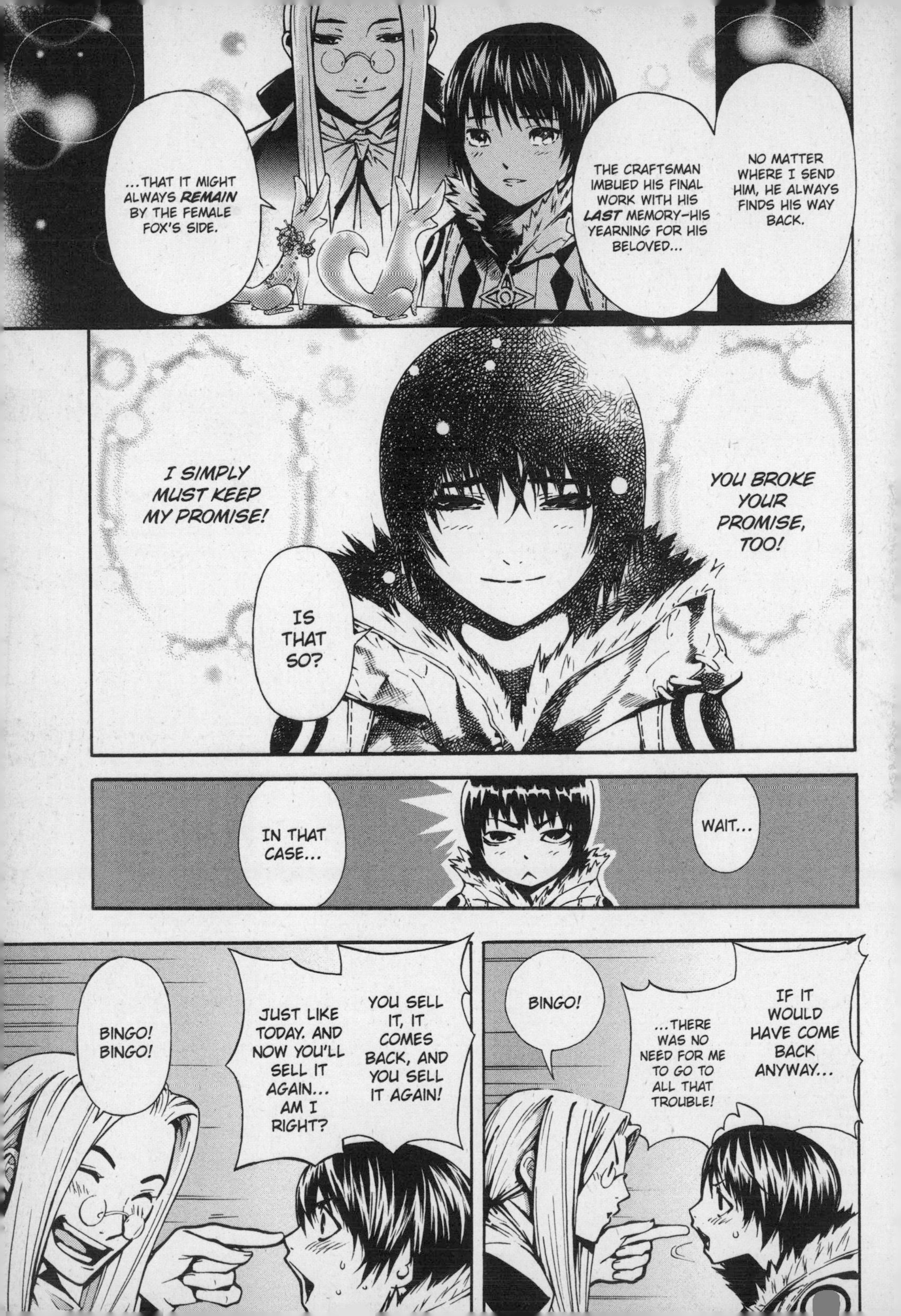
NO MATTER WHERE I SEND HIM, HE ALWAYS FINDS HIS WAY BACK.
THE CRAFTSMAN IMBUED HIS FINAL WORK WITH HIS LAST MEMORY–HIS YEARNING FOR HIS BELOVED...
...THAT IT MIGHT ALWAYS REMAIN BY THE FEMALE FOX'S SIDE.
YOU BROKE YOUR PROMISE, TOO!
I SIMPLY MUST KEEP MY PROMISE!
IS THAT SO?
WAIT...
IN THAT CASE...
IF IT WOULD HAVE COME BACK ANYWAY...
...THERE WAS NO NEED FOR ME TO GO TO ALL THAT TROUBLE!
BINGO!
YOU SELL IT, IT COMES BACK, AND YOU SELL IT AGAIN!
JUST LIKE TODAY. AND NOW YOU'LL SELL IT AGAIN... AM I RIGHT?
BINGO! BINGO!

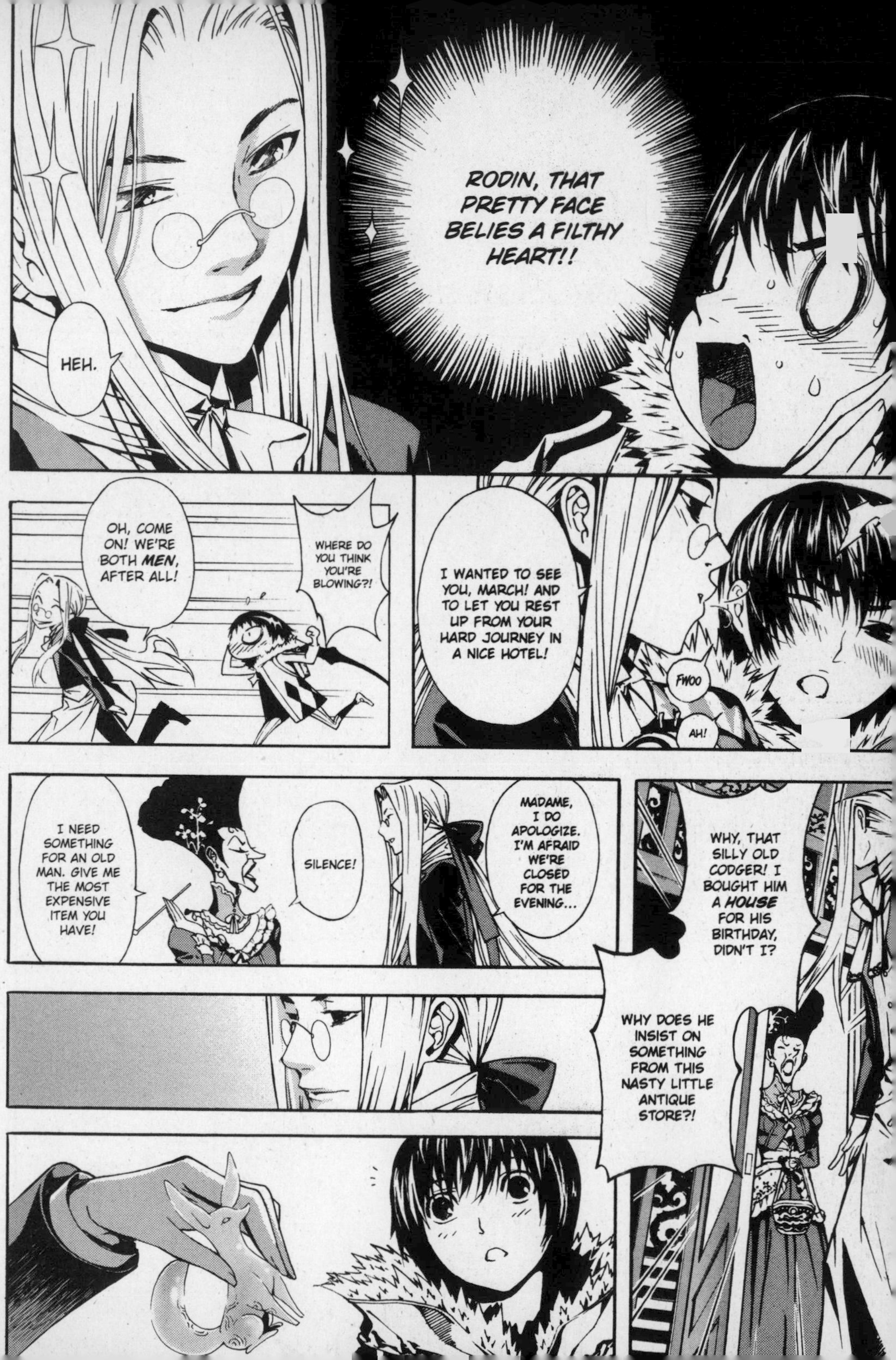
RODIN, THAT PRETTY FACE BELIES A FILTHY HEART!!
HEH.
I WANTED TO SEE YOU, MARCH! AND TO LET YOU REST UP FROM YOUR HARD JOURNEY IN A NICE HOTEL!
FWOO
AH!
WHERE DO YOU THINK YOU'RE BLOWING?!
OH, COME ON! WE'RE BOTH MEN, AFTER ALL!
WHY, THAT SILLY OLD CODGER! I BOUGHT HIM A HOUSE FOR HIS BIRTHDAY, DIDN'T I?
WHY DOES HE INSIST ON SOMETHING FROM THIS NASTY LITTLE ANTIQUE STORE?!
MADAME, I DO APOLOGIZE. I'M AFRAID WE'RE CLOSED FOR THE EVENING...
SILENCE!
I NEED SOMETHING FOR AN OLD MAN. GIVE ME THE MOST EXPENSIVE ITEM YOU HAVE!

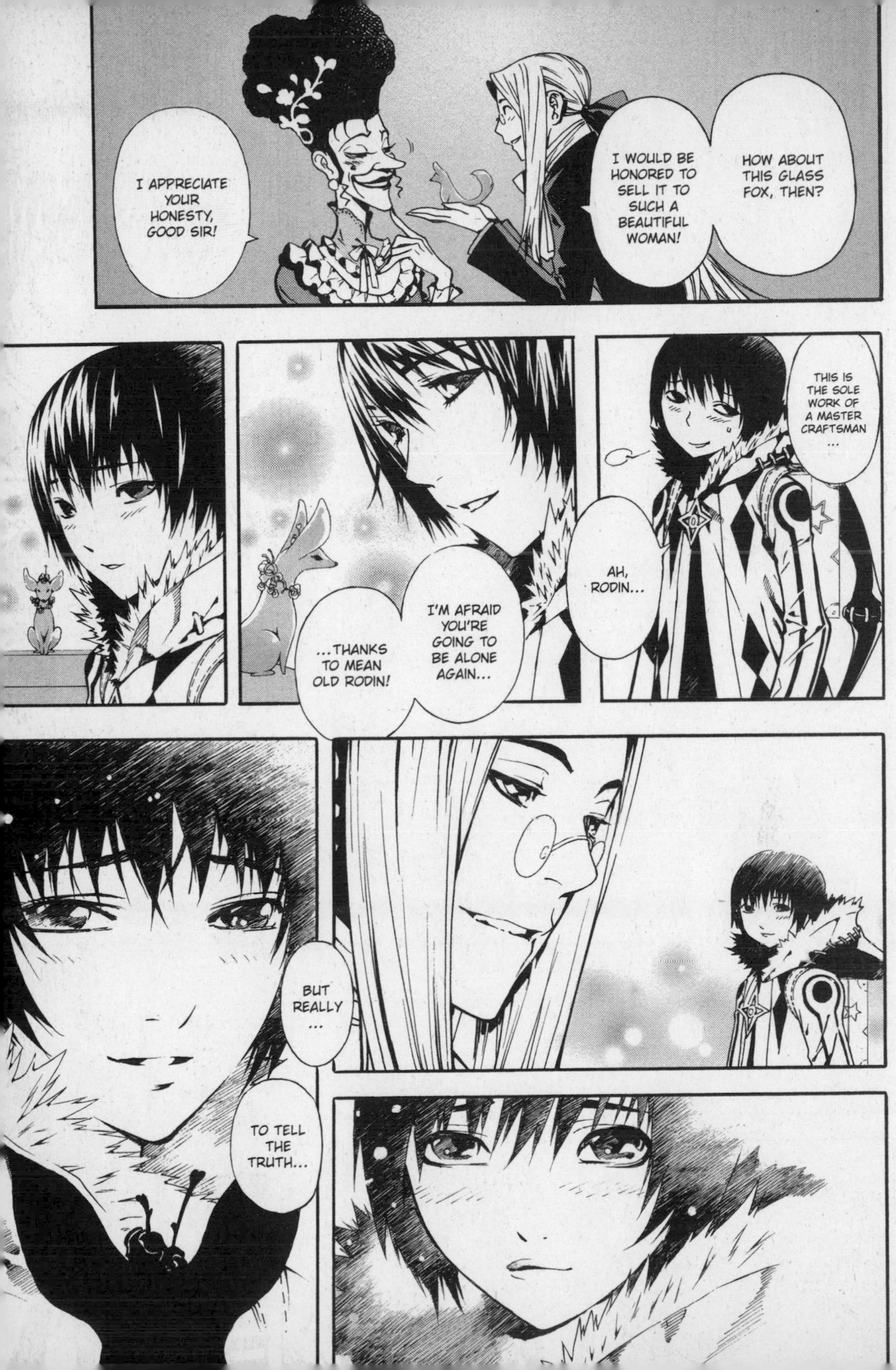
HOW ABOUT THIS GLASS FOX, THEN?
I WOULD BE HONORED TO SELL IT TO SUCH A BEAUTIFUL WOMAN!
I APPRECIATE YOUR HONESTY, GOOD SIR!
THIS IS THE SOLE WORK OF A MASTER CRAFTSMAN ...
AH, RODIN...
I'M AFRAID YOU'RE GOING TO BE ALONE AGAIN...
...THANKS TO MEAN OLD RODIN!
BUT REALLY ...
TO TELL THE TRUTH...

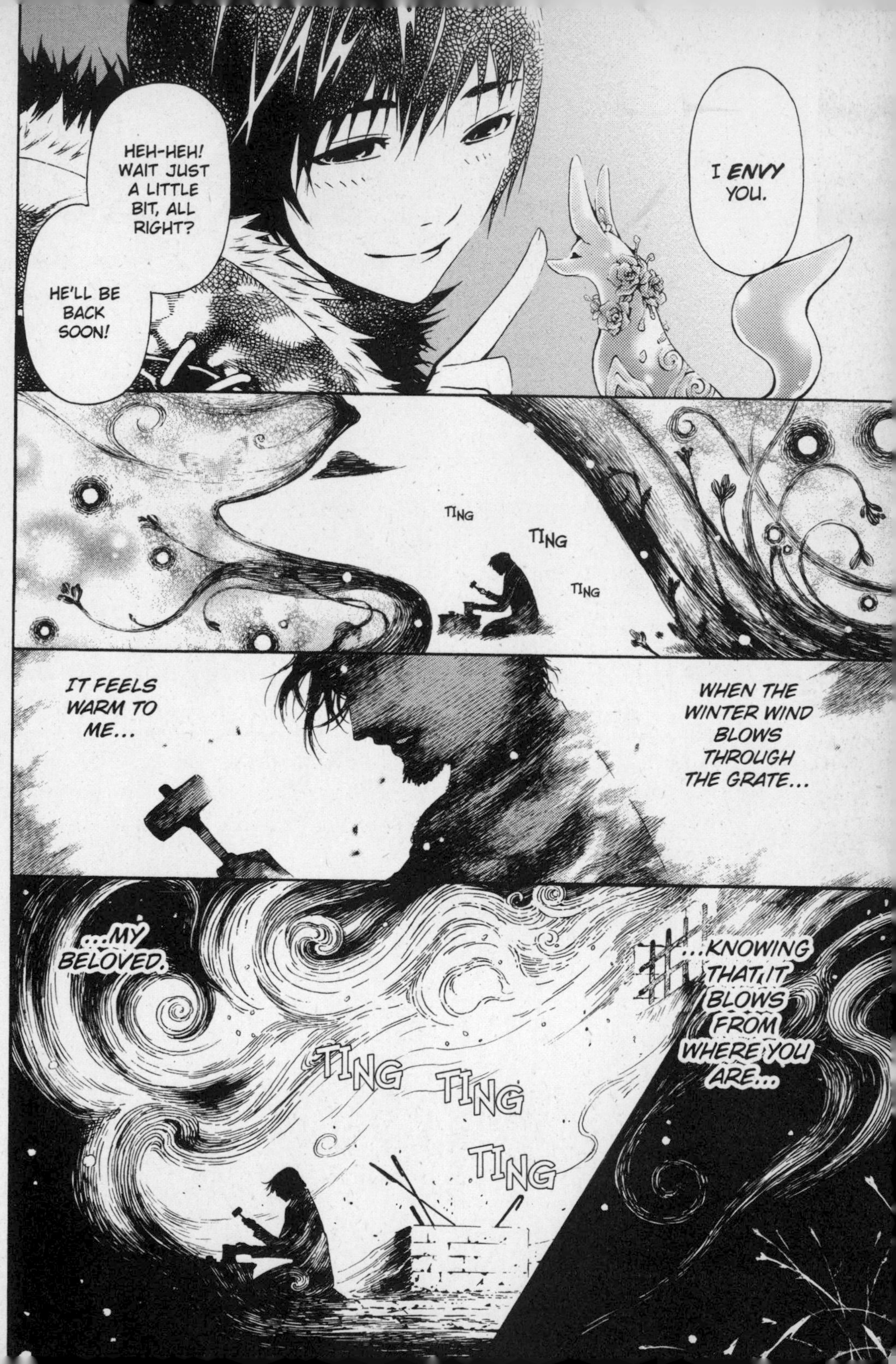
I ENVY YOU.
HEH-HEH! WAIT JUST A LITTLE BIT, ALL RIGHT?
HE'LL BE BACK SOON!
TING
TING
TING
WHEN THE WINTER WIND BLOWS THROUGH THE GRATE...
IT FEELS WARM TO ME...
...KNOWING THAT IT BLOWS FROM WHERE YOU ARE...
...MY BELOVED.
TING
TING
TING

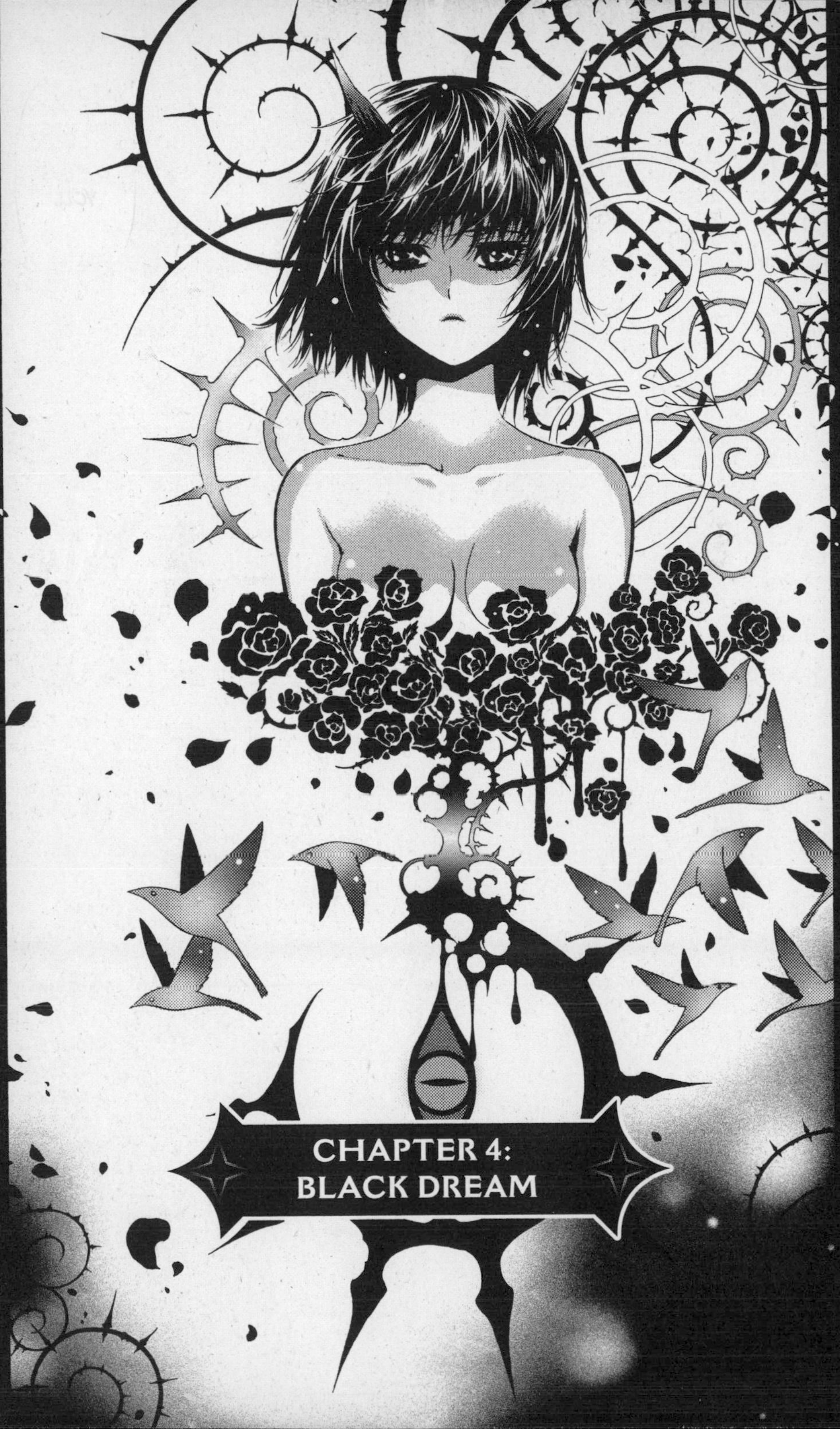
CHAPTER 4:
BLACK DREAM

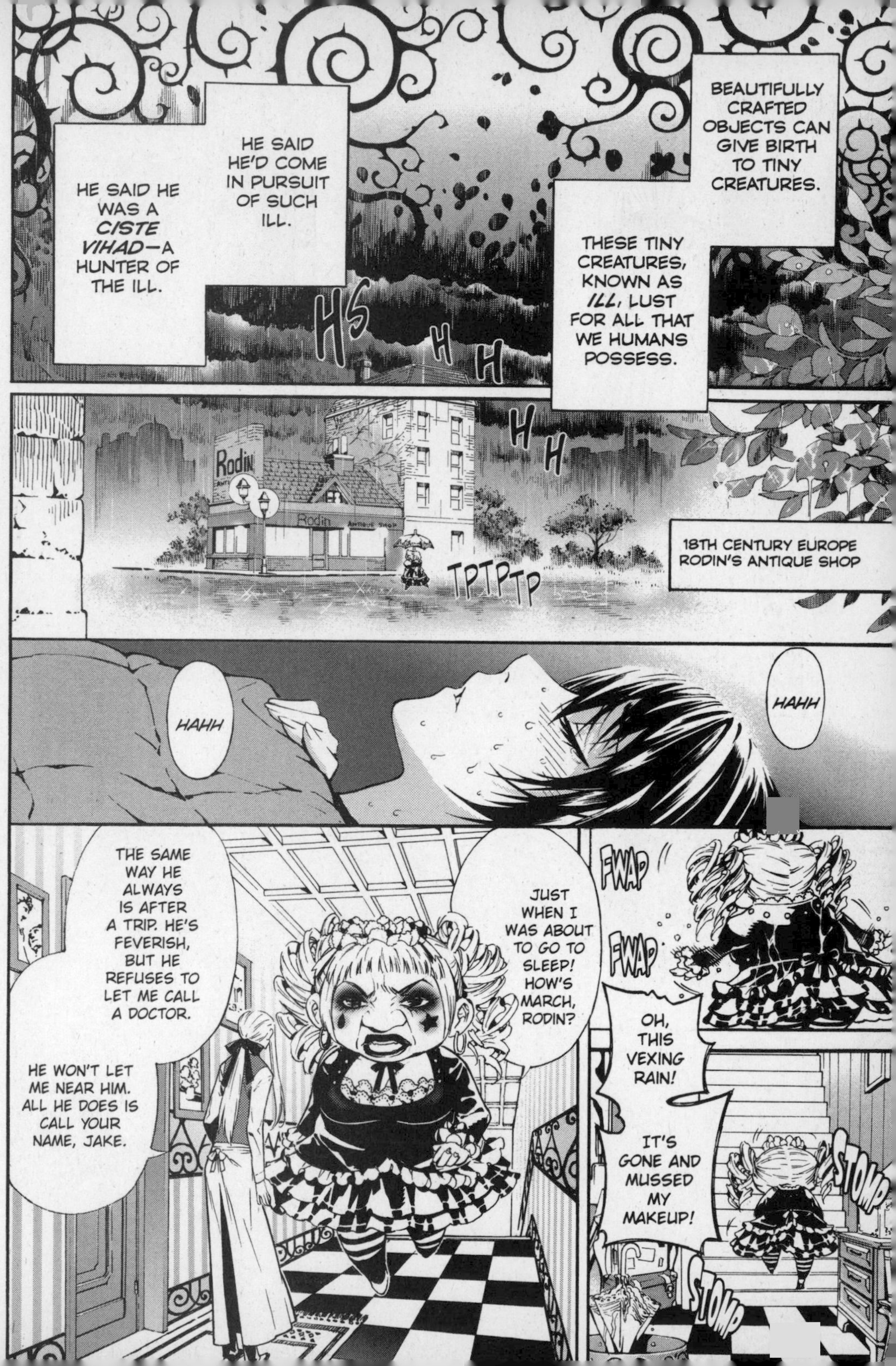
BEAUTIFULLY CRAFTED OBJECTS CAN GIVE BIRTH TO TINY CREATURES.
THESE TINY CREATURES, KNOWN AS ILL, LUST FOR ALL THAT WE HUMANS POSSESS.
HE SAID HE'D COME IN PURSUIT OF SUCH ILL.
HE SAID HE WAS A CISTE VIHAD—A HUNTER OF THE ILL.
HS H H H H
18TH CENTURY EUROPE RODIN'S ANTIQUE SHOP
Rodin
Rodin ANTIQUE SHOP
TPTPTP
HAHH
HAHH
FWAP
FWAP
OH, THIS VEXING RAIN!
IT'S GONE AND MUSSED MY MAKEUP!
STOMP
STOMP
JUST WHEN I WAS ABOUT TO GO TO SLEEP! HOW'S MARCH, RODIN?
THE SAME WAY HE ALWAYS IS AFTER A TRIP. HE'S FEVERISH, BUT HE REFUSES TO LET ME CALL A DOCTOR.
HE WON'T LET ME NEAR HIM. ALL HE DOES IS CALL YOUR NAME, JAKE.

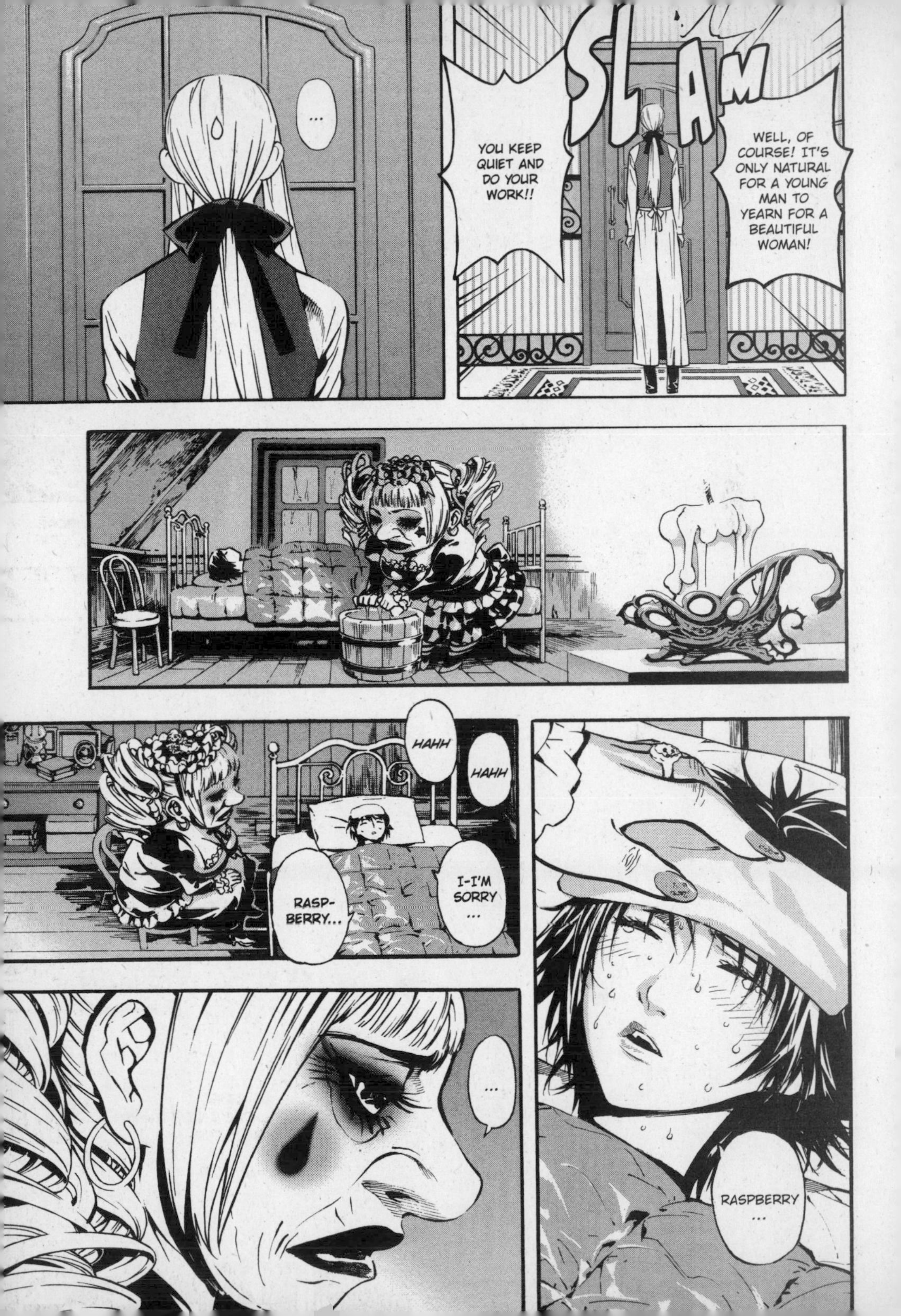
SLAM
WELL, OF COURSE! IT'S ONLY NATURAL FOR A YOUNG MAN TO YEARN FOR A BEAUTIFUL WOMAN!
YOU KEEP QUIET AND DO YOUR WORK!!
...
HAHH
HAHH
I-I'M SORRY ...
RASP-BERRY...
RASPBERRY ...
...

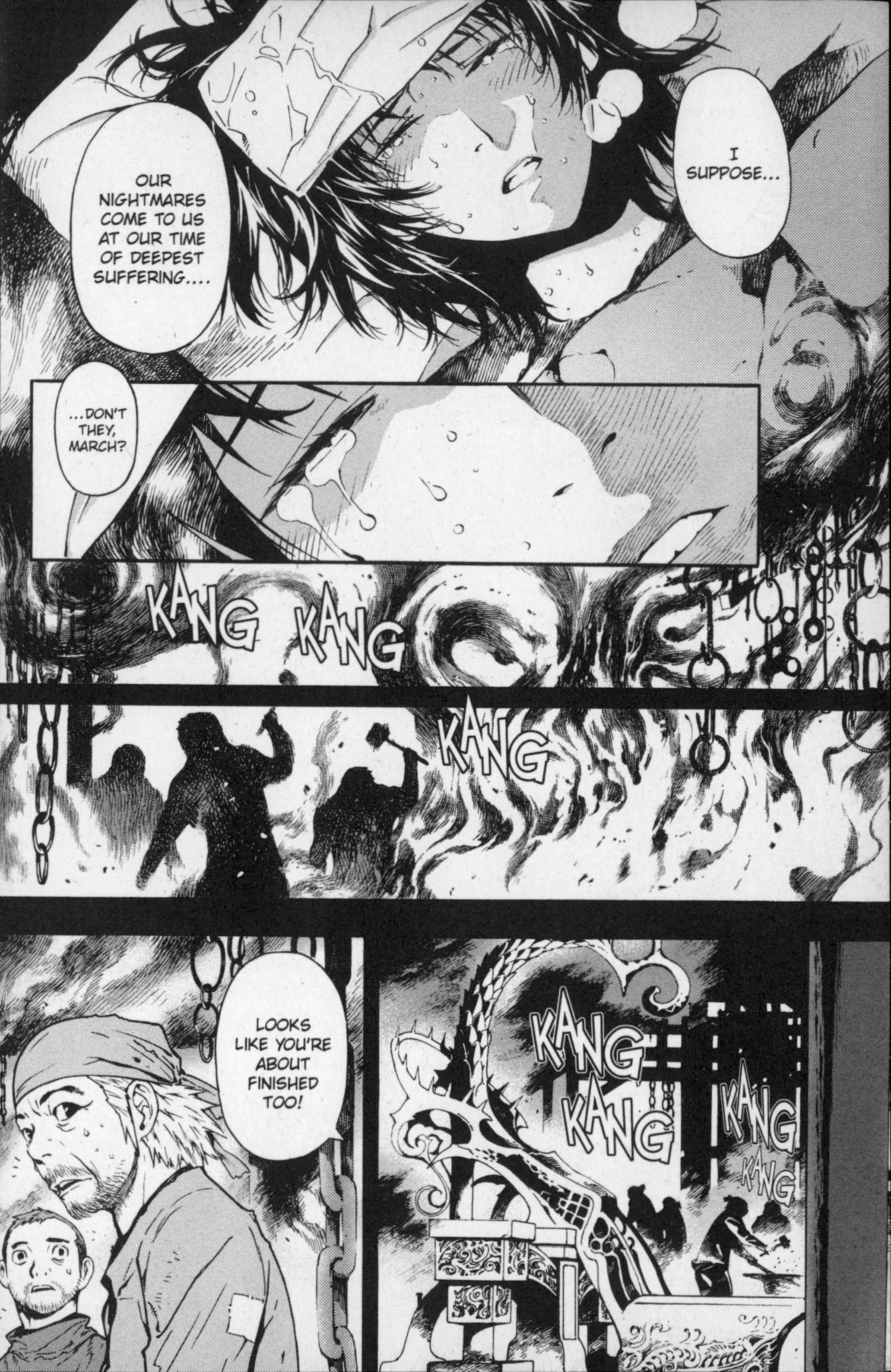
I SUPPOSE...
OUR NIGHTMARES COME TO US AT OUR TIME OF DEEPEST SUFFERING....
...DON'T THEY, MARCH?
KANG KANG
KANG
KANG KANG
KANG KANG
LOOKS LIKE YOU'RE ABOUT FINISHED TOO!

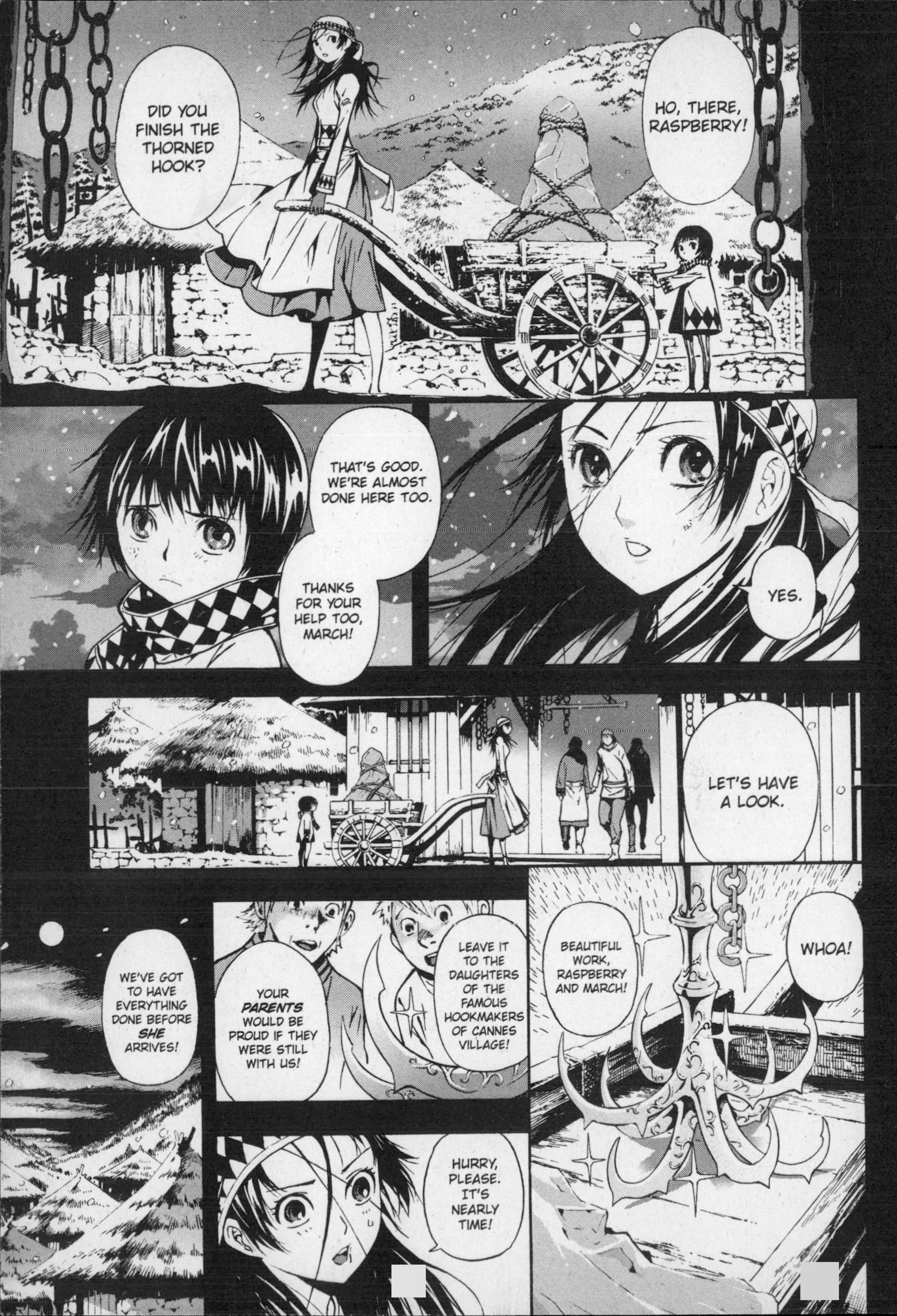
HO, THERE, RASPBERRY!
DID YOU FINISH THE THORNED HOOK?
YES.
THAT'S GOOD. WE'RE ALMOST DONE HERE TOO.
THANKS FOR YOUR HELP TOO, MARCH!
LET'S HAVE A LOOK.
WHOA!
BEAUTIFUL WORK, RASPBERRY AND MARCH!
LEAVE IT TO THE DAUGHTERS OF THE FAMOUS HOOKMAKERS OF CANNES VILLAGE!
YOUR *PARENTS* WOULD BE PROUD IF THEY WERE STILL WITH US!
HURRY, PLEASE. IT'S NEARLY TIME!
WE'VE GOT TO HAVE EVERYTHING DONE BEFORE *SHE* ARRIVES!

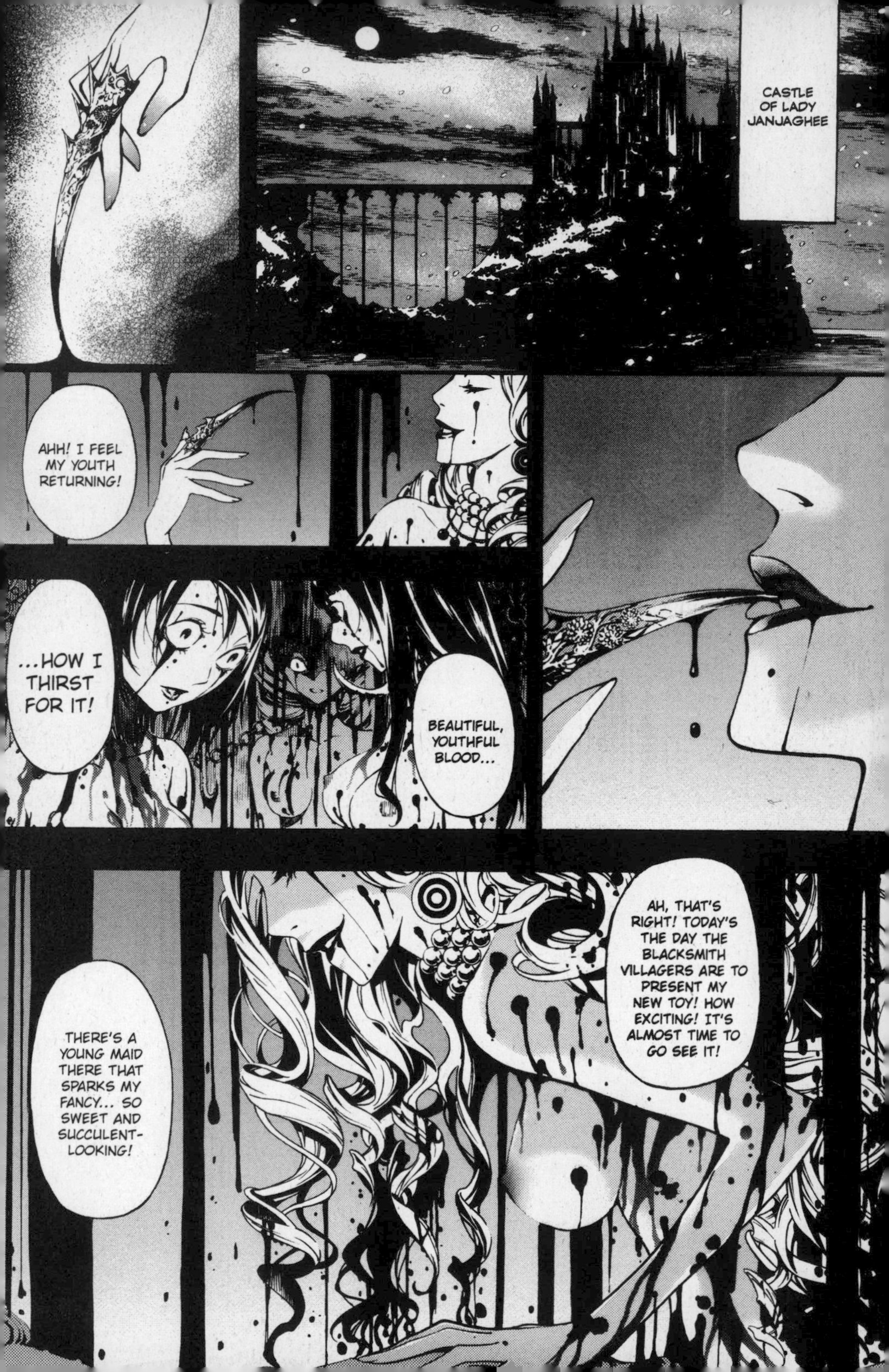
CASTLE OF LADY JANJAGHEE
AHH! I FEEL MY YOUTH RETURNING!
BEAUTIFUL, YOUTHFUL BLOOD...
...HOW I THIRST FOR IT!
AH, THAT'S RIGHT! TODAY'S THE DAY THE BLACKSMITH VILLAGERS ARE TO PRESENT MY NEW TOY! HOW EXCITING! IT'S ALMOST TIME TO GO SEE IT!
THERE'S A YOUNG MAID THERE THAT SPARKS MY FANCY... SO SWEET AND SUCCULENT-LOOKING!

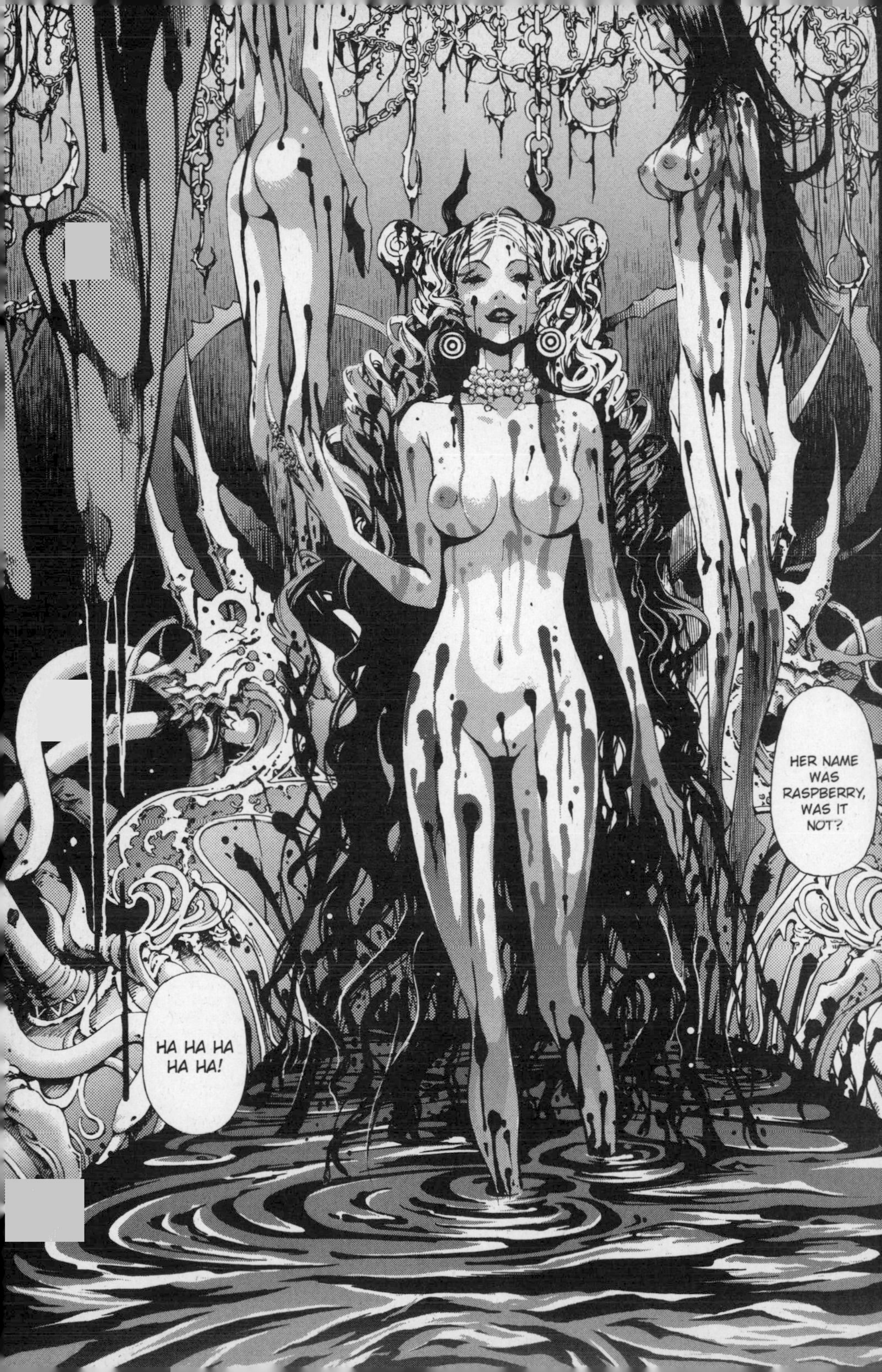
HER NAME WAS RASPBERRY, WAS IT NOT?
HA HA HA HA HA!

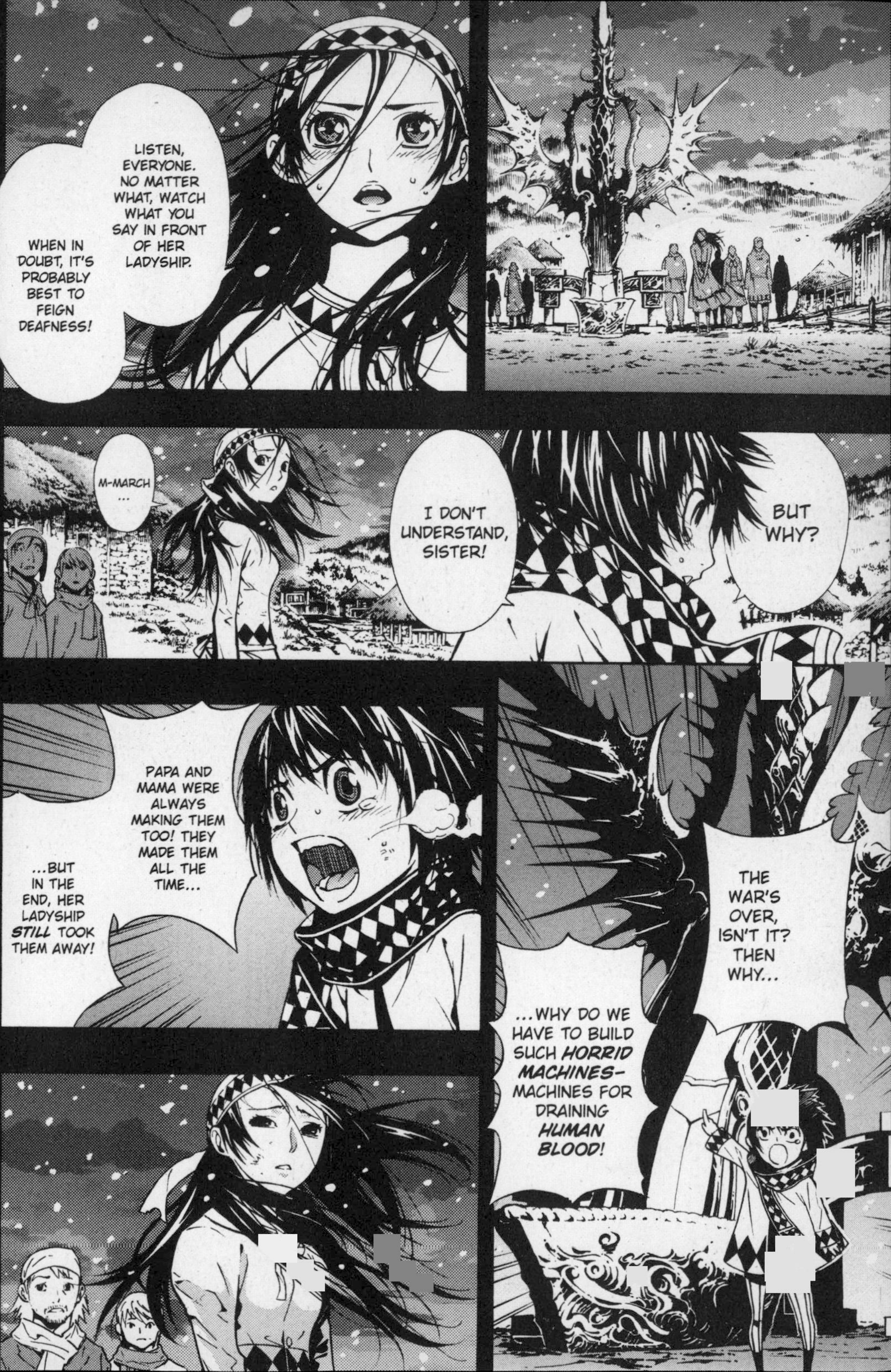
LISTEN, EVERYONE. NO MATTER WHAT, WATCH WHAT YOU SAY IN FRONT OF HER LADYSHIP.
WHEN IN DOUBT, IT'S PROBABLY BEST TO FEIGN DEAFNESS!
BUT WHY?
I DON'T UNDERSTAND, SISTER!
M-MARCH ...
THE WAR'S OVER, ISN'T IT? THEN WHY...
...WHY DO WE HAVE TO BUILD SUCH ***HORRID MACHINES***- MACHINES FOR DRAINING ***HUMAN BLOOD***!
PAPA AND MAMA WERE ALWAYS MAKING THEM TOO! THEY MADE THEM ALL THE TIME...
...BUT IN THE END, HER LADYSHIP ***STILL*** TOOK THEM AWAY!

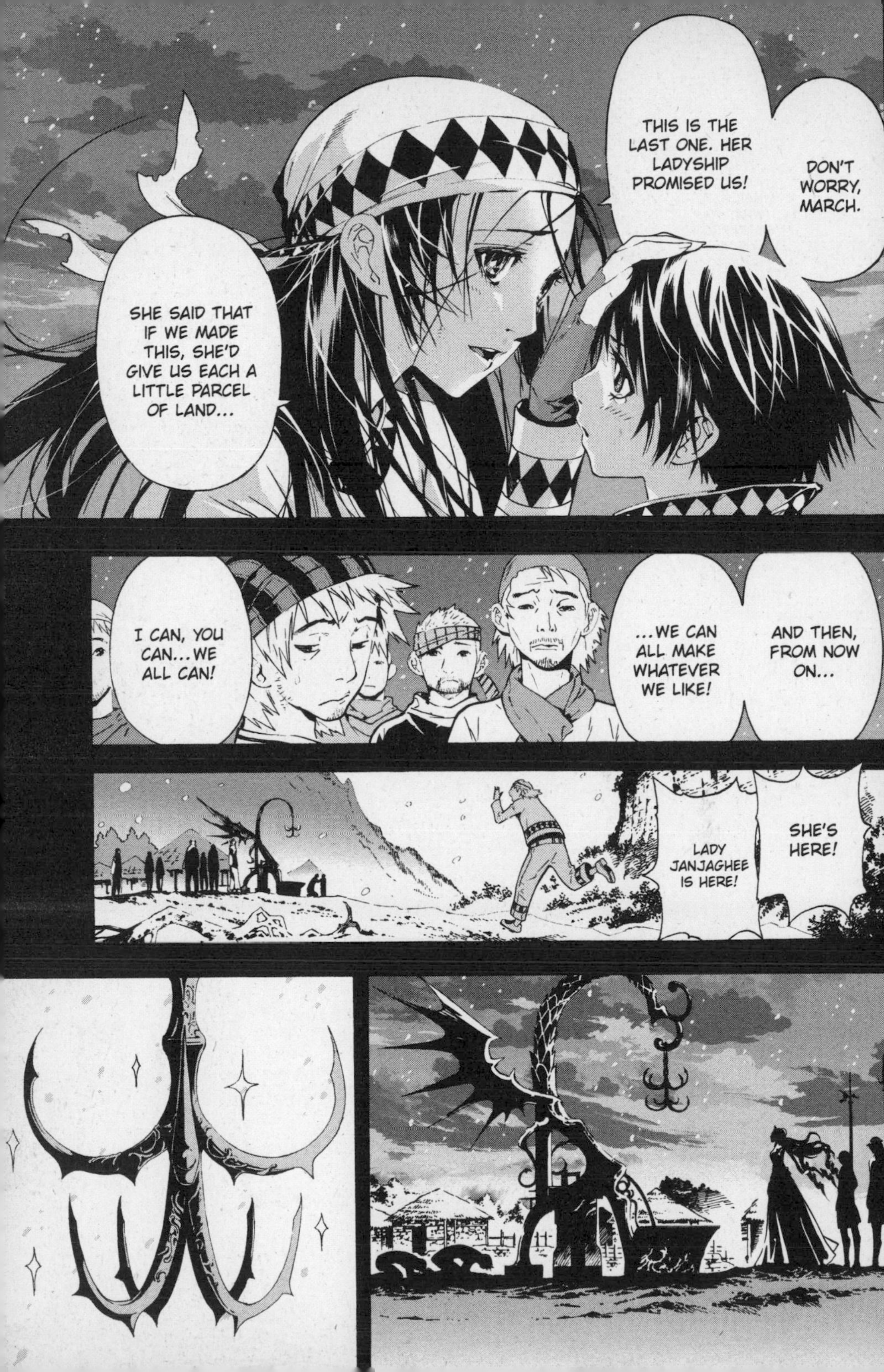
DON'T WORRY, MARCH.
THIS IS THE LAST ONE. HER LADYSHIP PROMISED US!
SHE SAID THAT IF WE MADE THIS, SHE'D GIVE US EACH A LITTLE PARCEL OF LAND...
AND THEN, FROM NOW ON...
...WE CAN ALL MAKE WHATEVER WE LIKE!
I CAN, YOU CAN...WE ALL CAN!
SHE'S HERE!
LADY JANJAGHEE IS HERE!

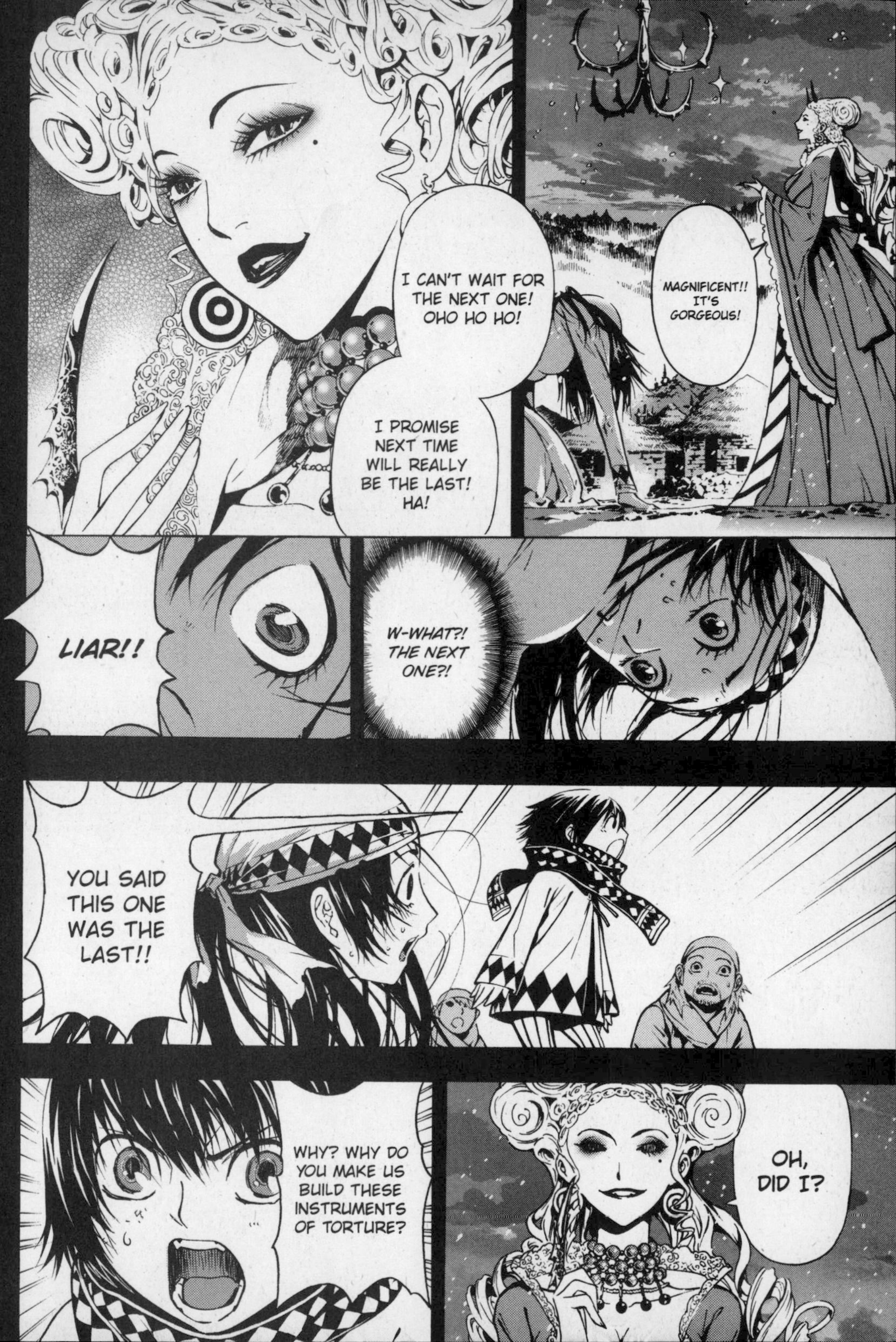
MAGNIFICENT!! IT'S GORGEOUS!
I CAN'T WAIT FOR THE NEXT ONE! OHO HO HO!
I PROMISE NEXT TIME WILL REALLY BE THE LAST! HA!
W-WHAT?! THE NEXT ONE?!
LIAR!!
YOU SAID THIS ONE WAS THE LAST!!
OH, DID I?
WHY? WHY DO YOU MAKE US BUILD THESE INSTRUMENTS OF TORTURE?

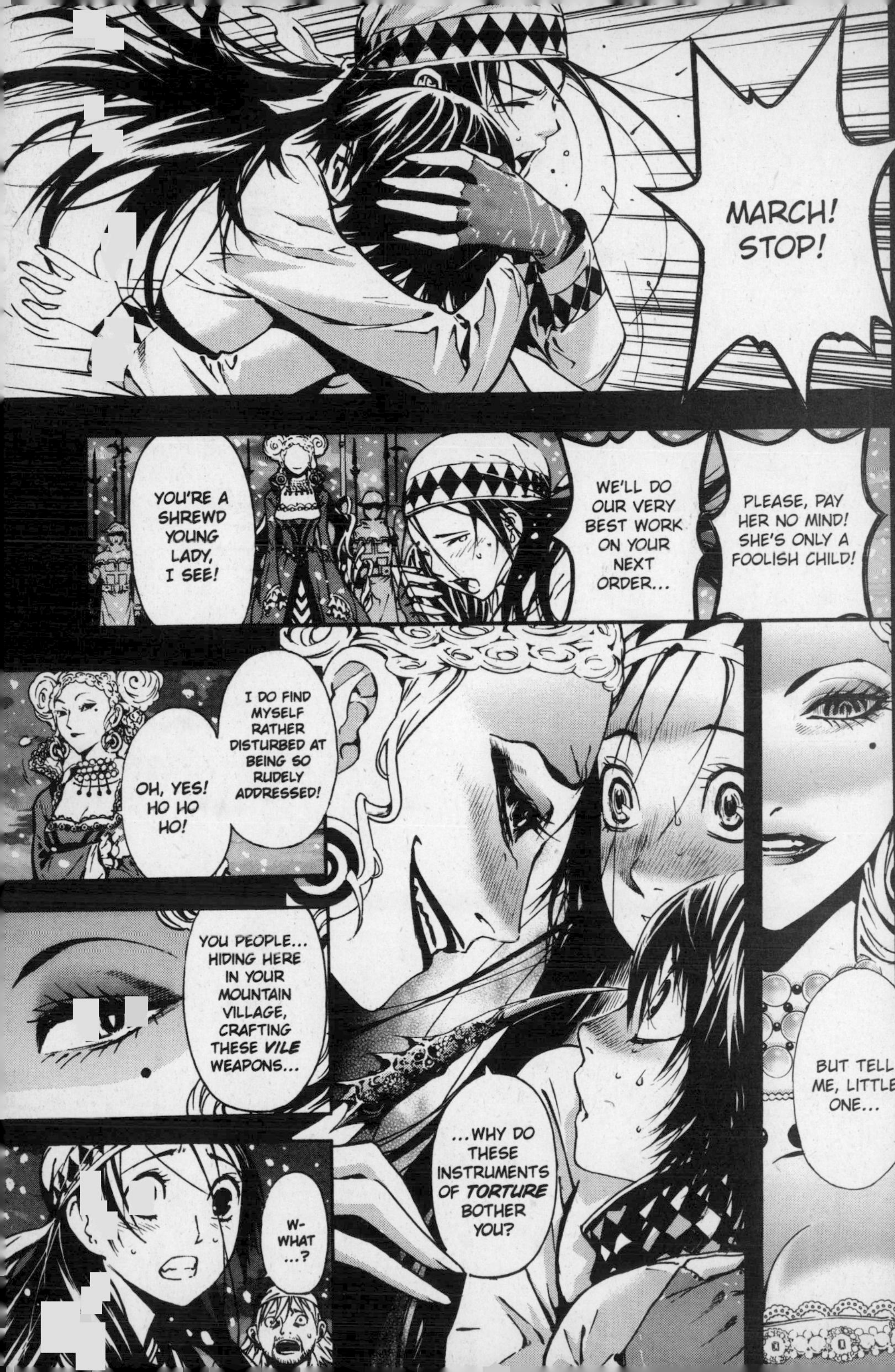
MARCH! STOP!
PLEASE, PAY HER NO MIND! SHE'S ONLY A FOOLISH CHILD!
WE'LL DO OUR VERY BEST WORK ON YOUR NEXT ORDER...
YOU'RE A SHREWD YOUNG LADY, I SEE!
BUT TELL ME, LITTLE ONE...
YOU PEOPLE... HIDING HERE IN YOUR MOUNTAIN VILLAGE, CRAFTING THESE *VILE* WEAPONS...
...WHY DO THESE INSTRUMENTS OF *TORTURE* BOTHER YOU?
I DO FIND MYSELF RATHER DISTURBED AT BEING SO RUDELY ADDRESSED!
OH, YES! HO HO HO!
W-WHAT...?

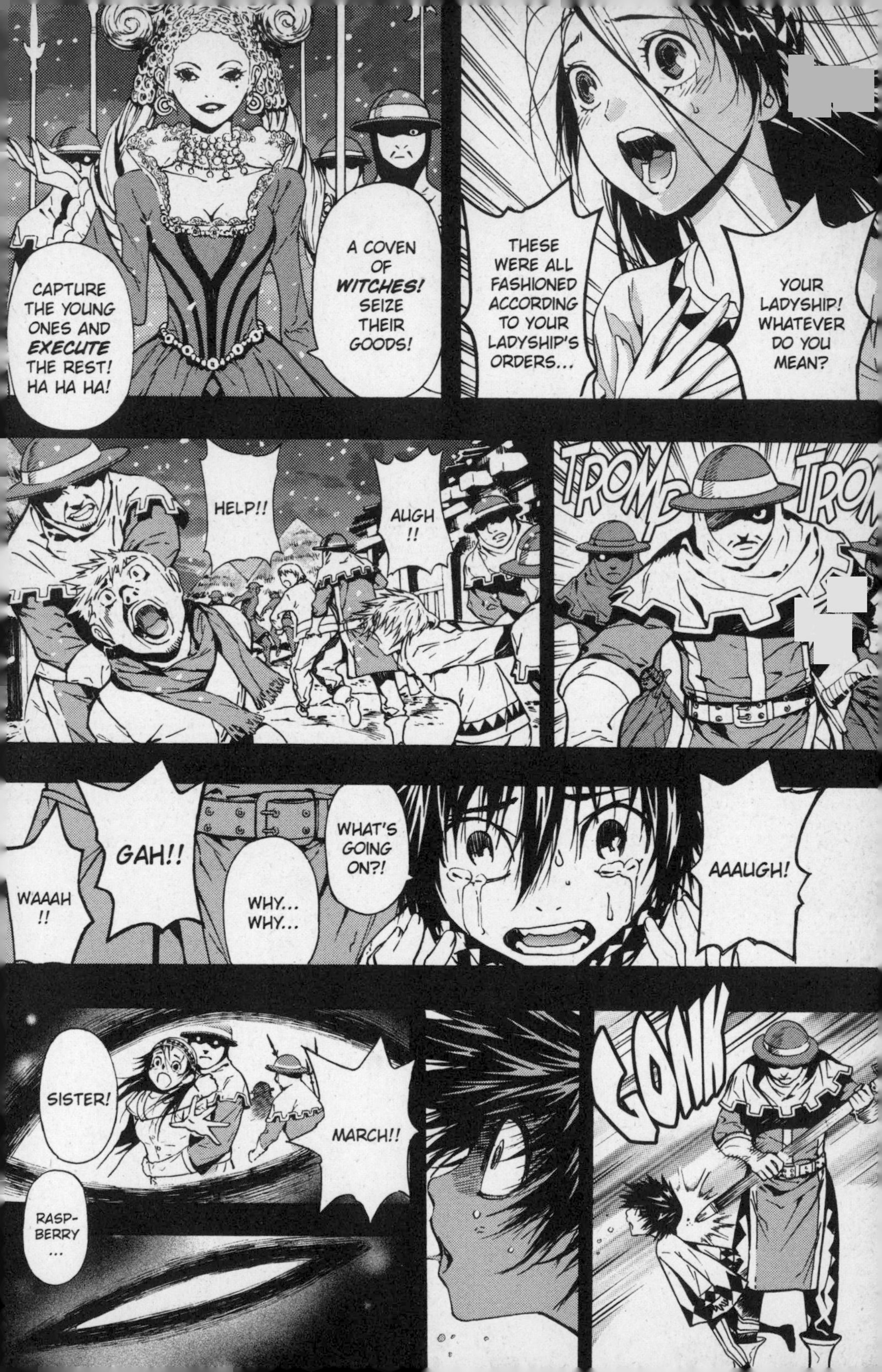

YOUR LADYSHIP! WHATEVER DO YOU MEAN?
THESE WERE ALL FASHIONED ACCORDING TO YOUR LADYSHIP'S ORDERS...
A COVEN OF **WITCHES!** SEIZE THEIR GOODS!
CAPTURE THE YOUNG ONES AND **EXECUTE** THE REST! HA HA HA!
TROMP
TROM
AUGH!!
HELP!!
AAAUGH!
WHAT'S GOING ON?!
WHY... WHY...
GAH!!
WAAAH!!
CONK
MARCH!!
SISTER!
RASPBERRY...

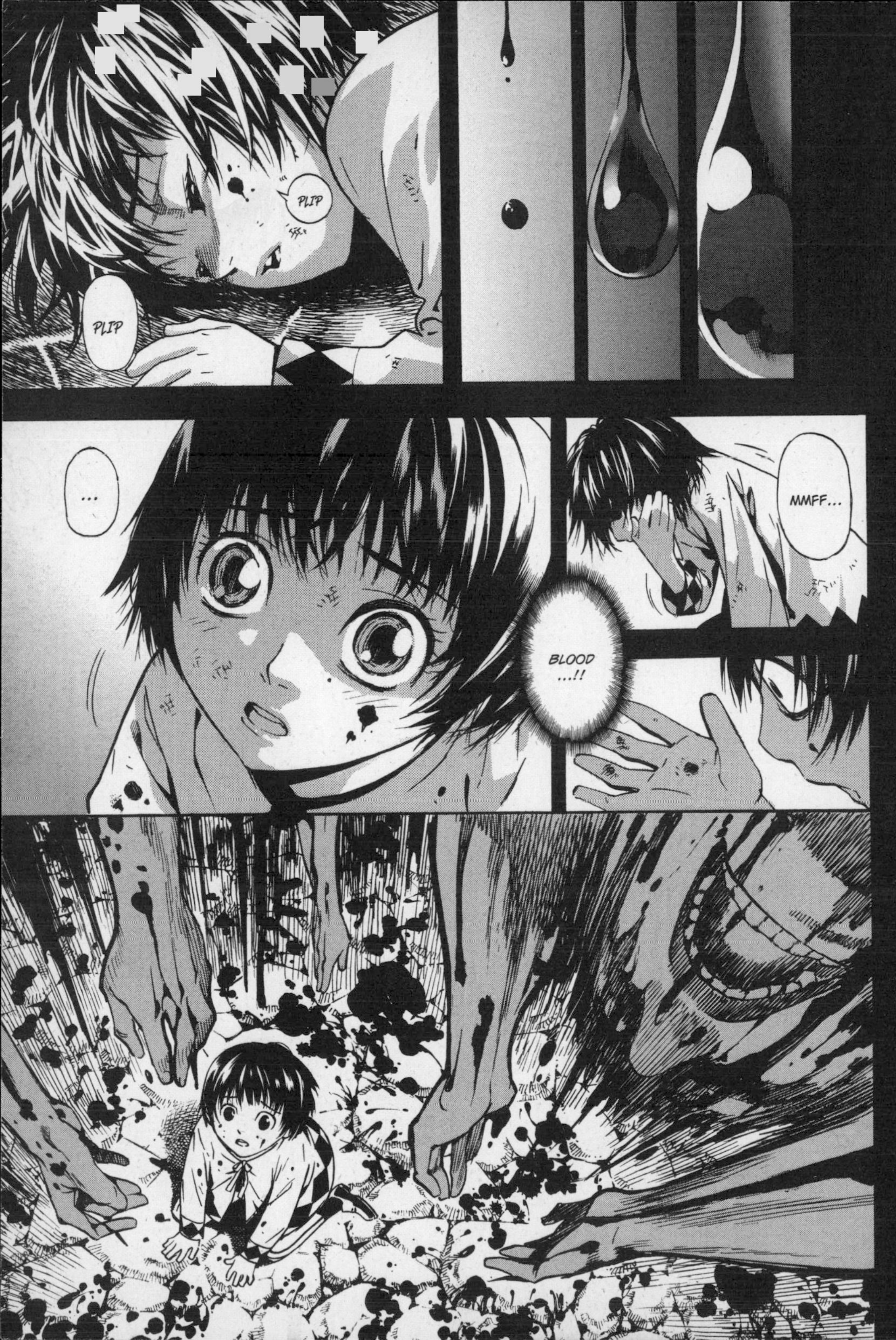
PLIP
PLIP
MMFF...
BLOOD ...!!
...

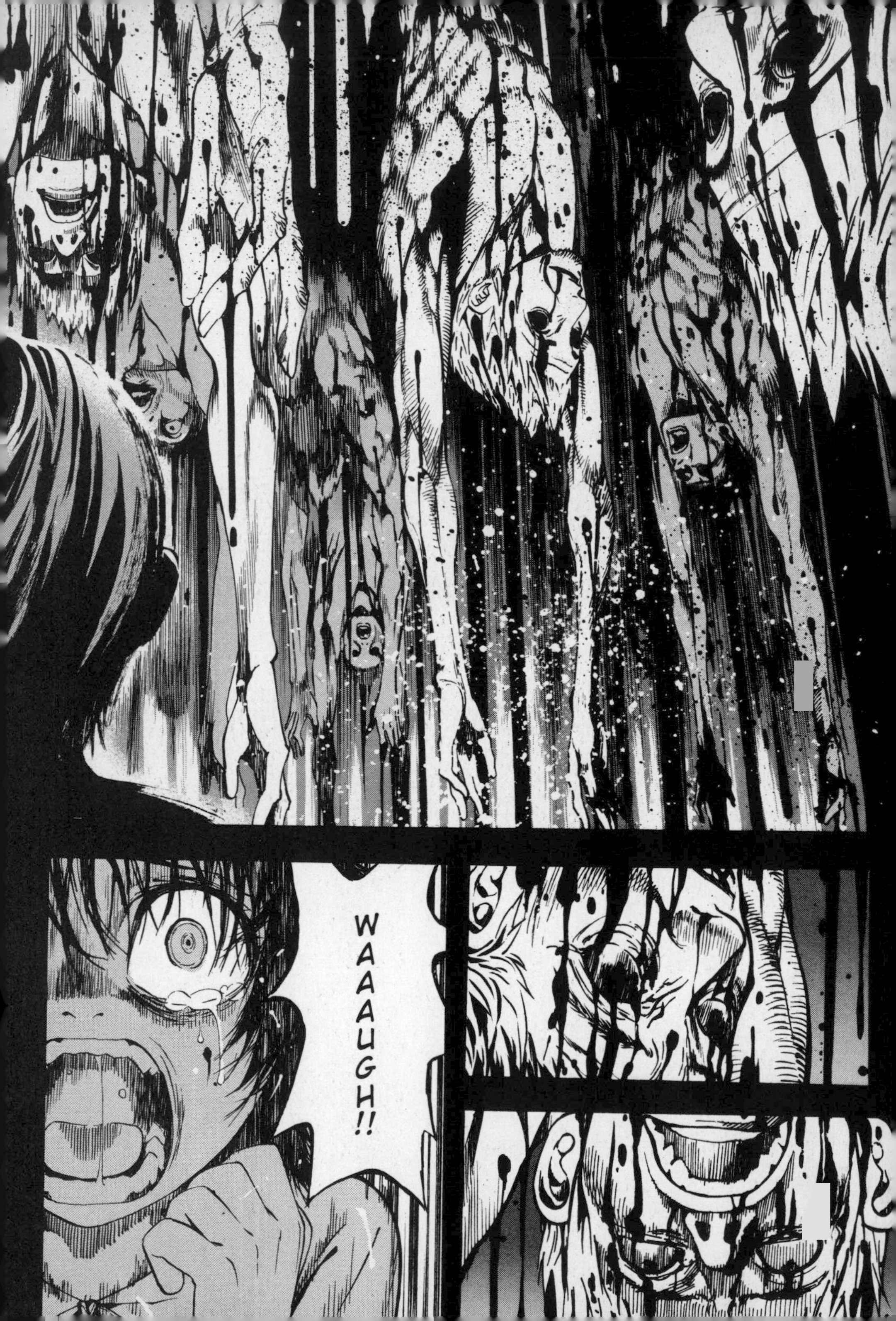
WAAAAUGH!!

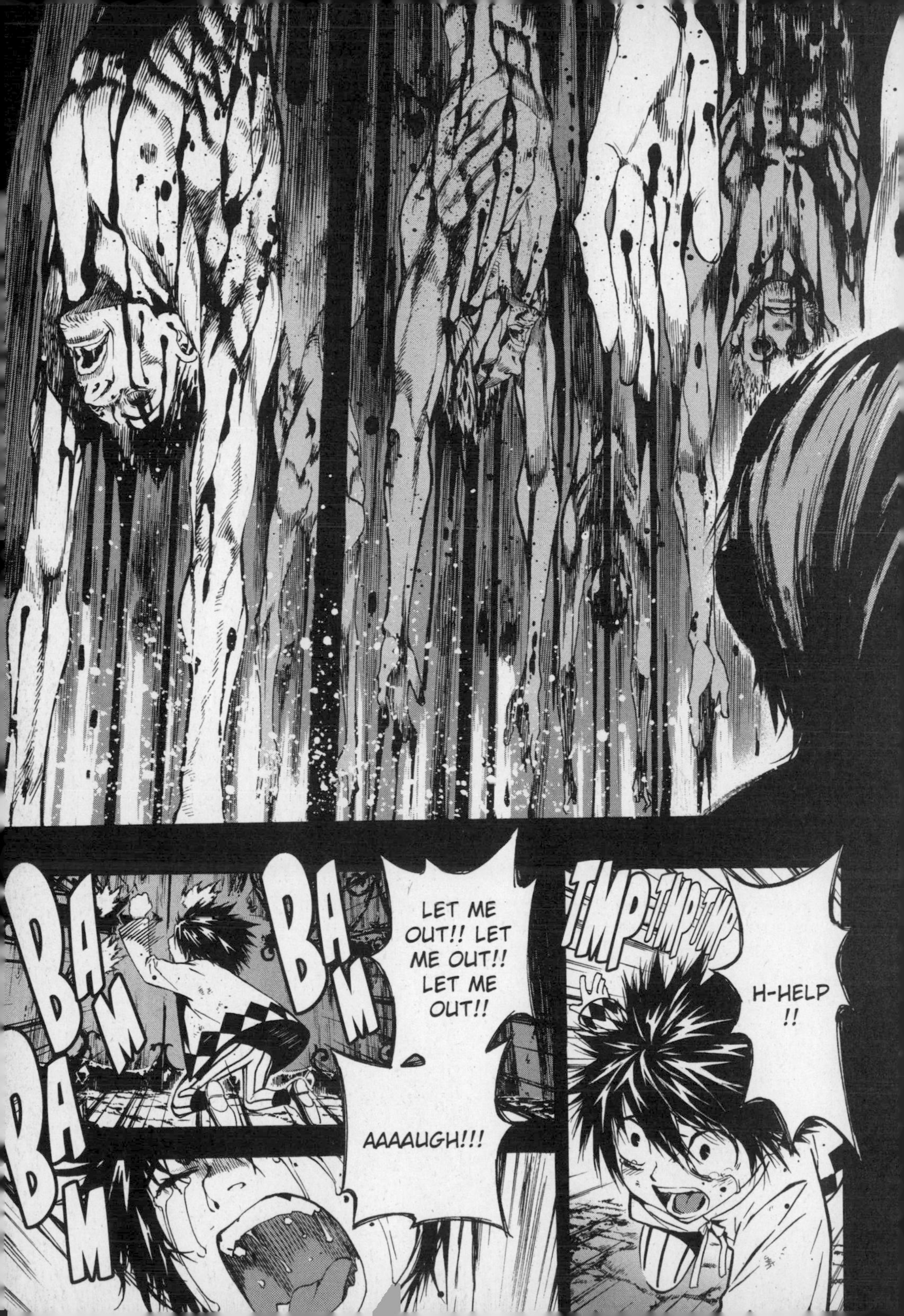
TMP TMP TMP
H-HELP !!
LET ME OUT!! LET ME OUT!! LET ME OUT!!
BAM
BAM
AAAAUGH!!!
BAM
BAM

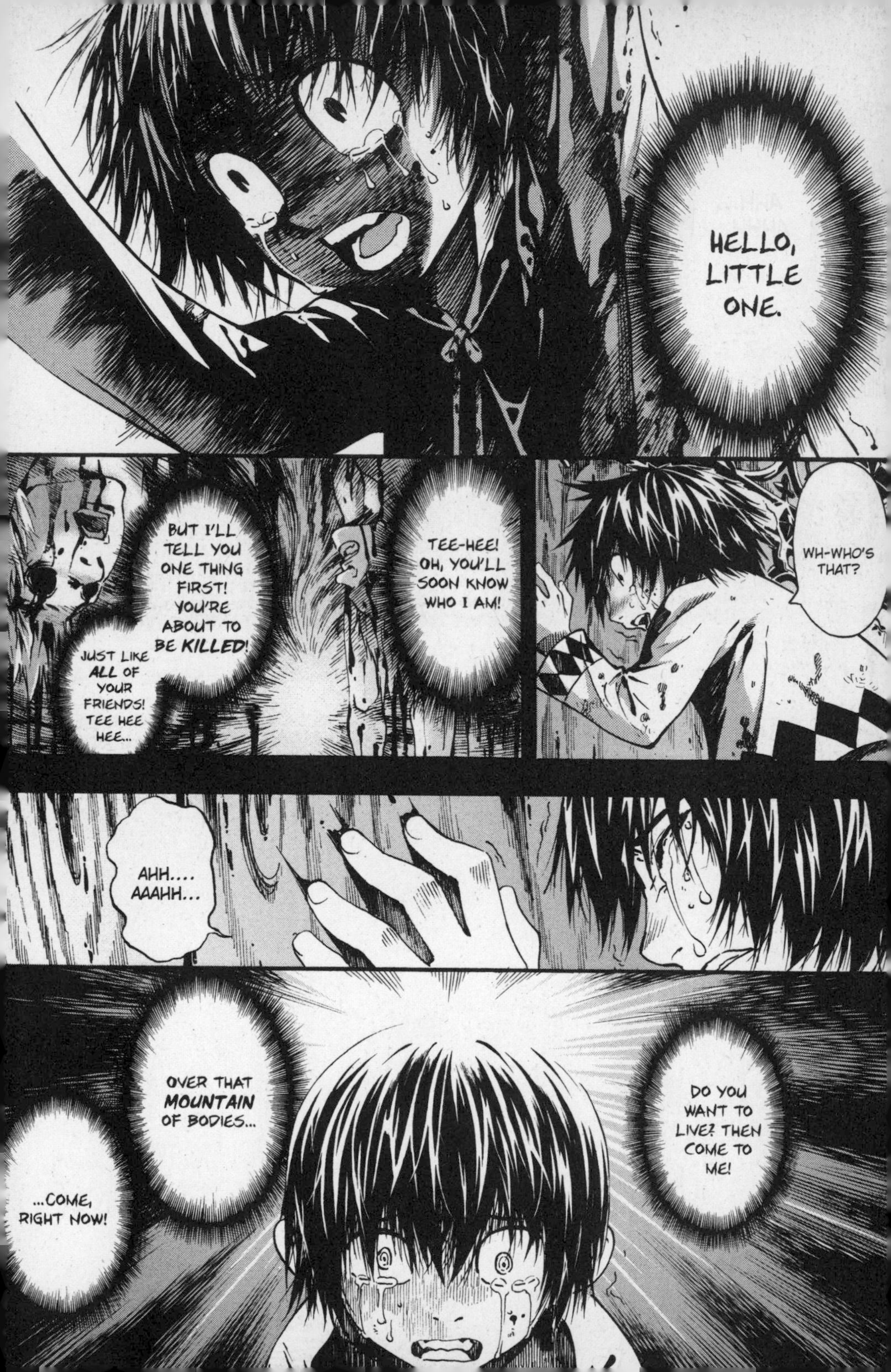
HELLO, LITTLE ONE.
WH-WHO'S THAT?
TEE-HEE! OH, YOU'LL SOON KNOW WHO I AM!
BUT I'LL TELL YOU ONE THING FIRST! YOU'RE ABOUT TO BE **KILLED**!
JUST LIKE **ALL** OF YOUR FRIENDS! TEE HEE HEE...
AHH.... AAAHH...
DO YOU WANT TO LIVE? THEN COME TO ME!
OVER THAT **MOUNTAIN** OF BODIES...
...COME, RIGHT NOW!

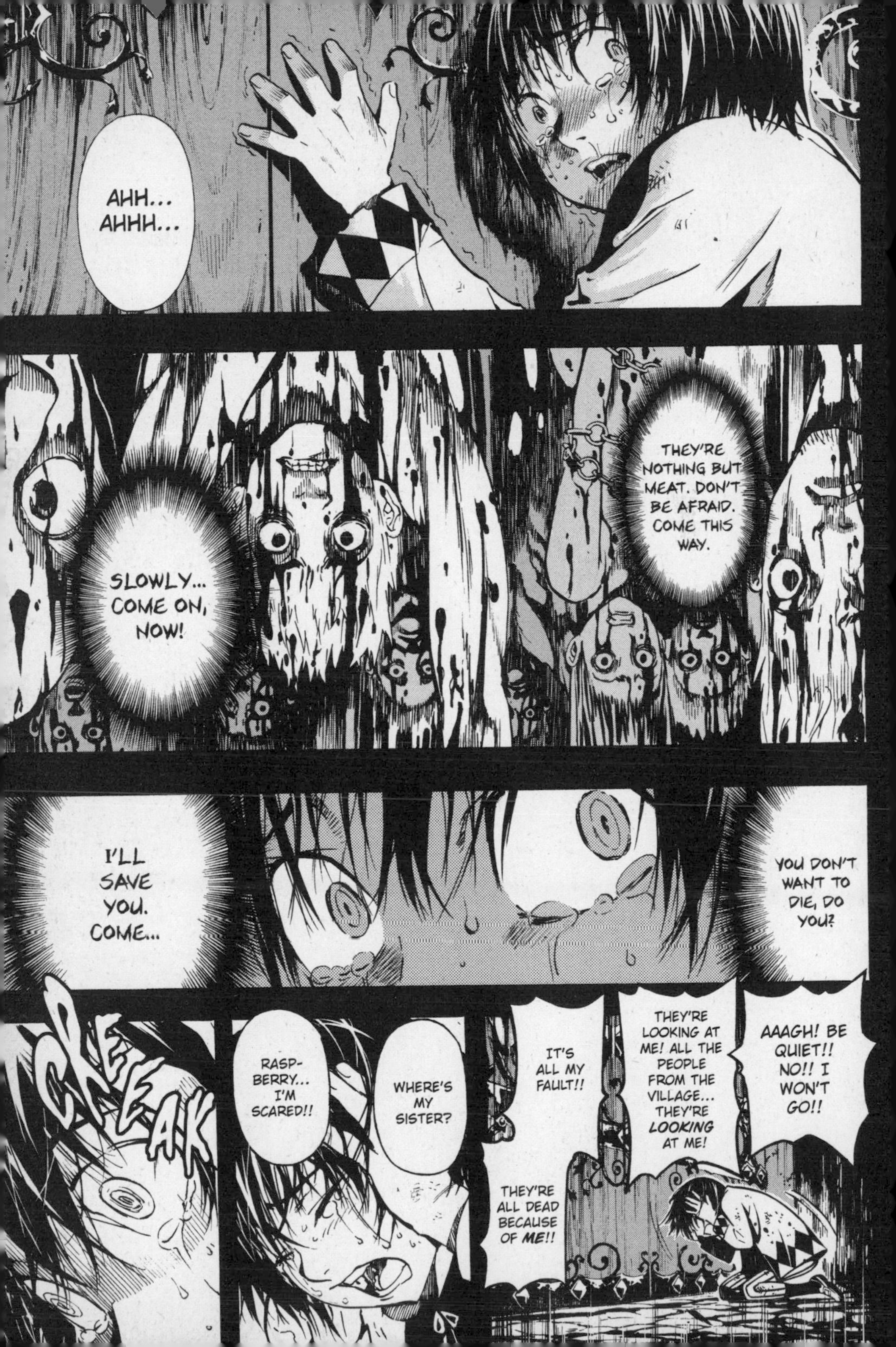
AHH... AHHH...
THEY'RE NOTHING BUT MEAT. DON'T BE AFRAID. COME THIS WAY.
SLOWLY... COME ON, NOW!
YOU DON'T WANT TO DIE, DO YOU?
I'LL SAVE YOU. COME...
AAAGH! BE QUIET!! NO!! I WON'T GO!!
THEY'RE LOOKING AT ME! ALL THE PEOPLE FROM THE VILLAGE... THEY'RE *LOOKING* AT ME!
IT'S ALL MY FAULT!!
THEY'RE ALL DEAD BECAUSE OF *ME*!!
WHERE'S MY SISTER?
RASP-BERRY... I'M SCARED!!
CREEAK

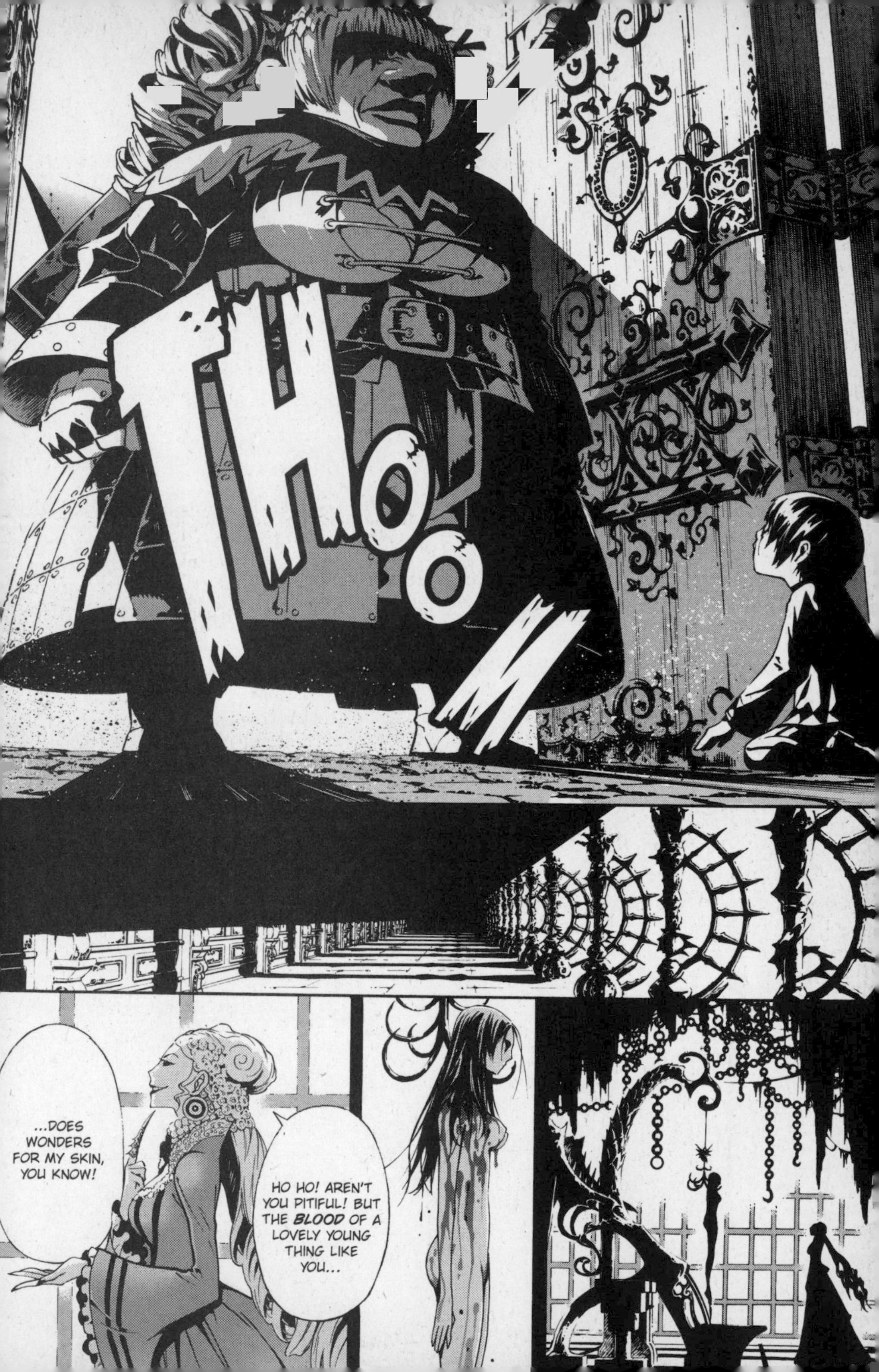
THOOM
HO HO! AREN'T YOU PITIFUL! BUT THE *BLOOD* OF A LOVELY YOUNG THING LIKE YOU...
...DOES WONDERS FOR MY SKIN, YOU KNOW!

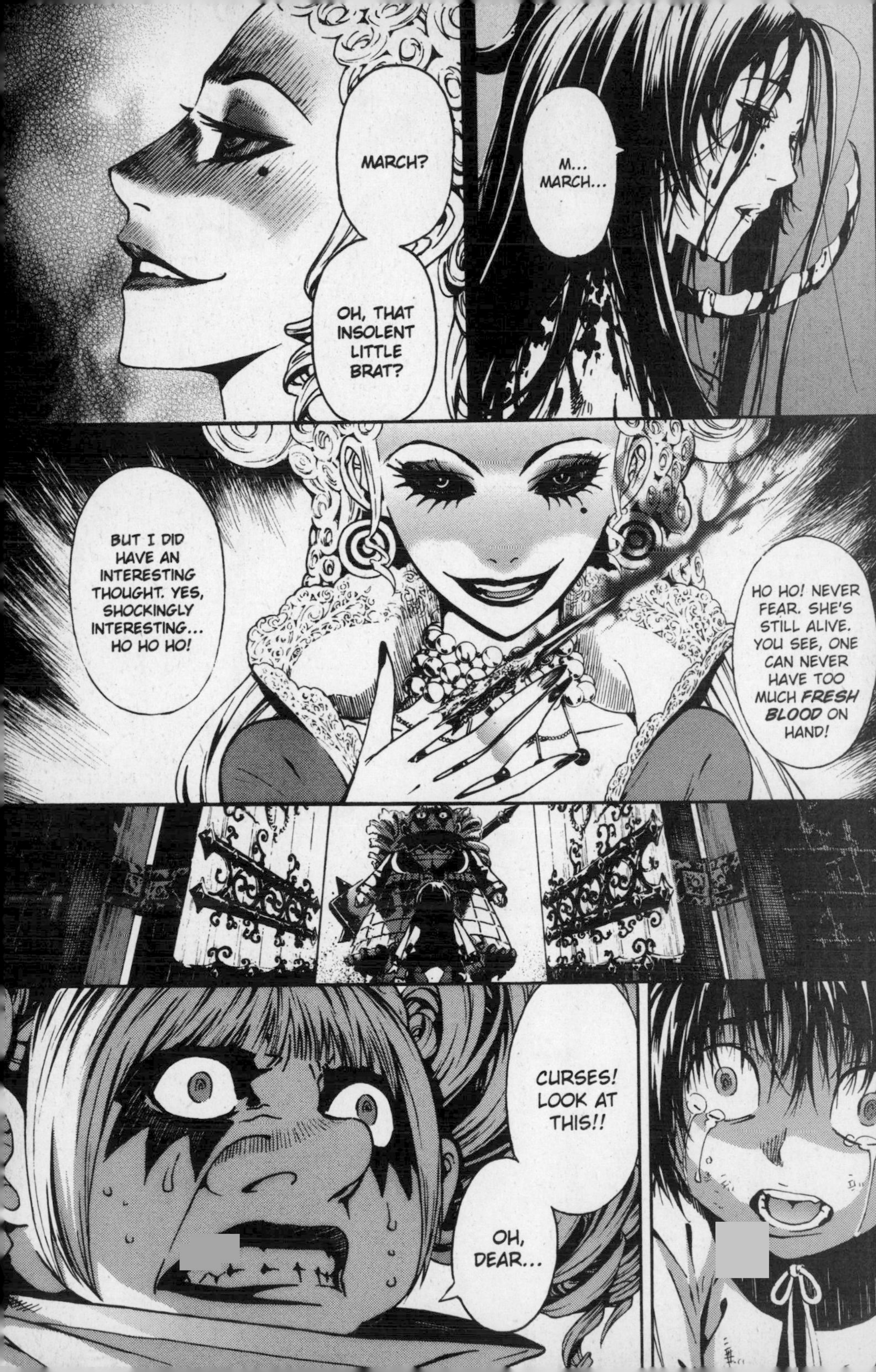
M... MARCH...
MARCH?
OH, THAT INSOLENT LITTLE BRAT?
HO HO! NEVER FEAR. SHE'S STILL ALIVE. YOU SEE, ONE CAN NEVER HAVE TOO MUCH **FRESH BLOOD** ON HAND!
BUT I DID HAVE AN INTERESTING THOUGHT. YES, SHOCKINGLY INTERESTING... HO HO HO!
CURSES! LOOK AT THIS!!
OH, DEAR...

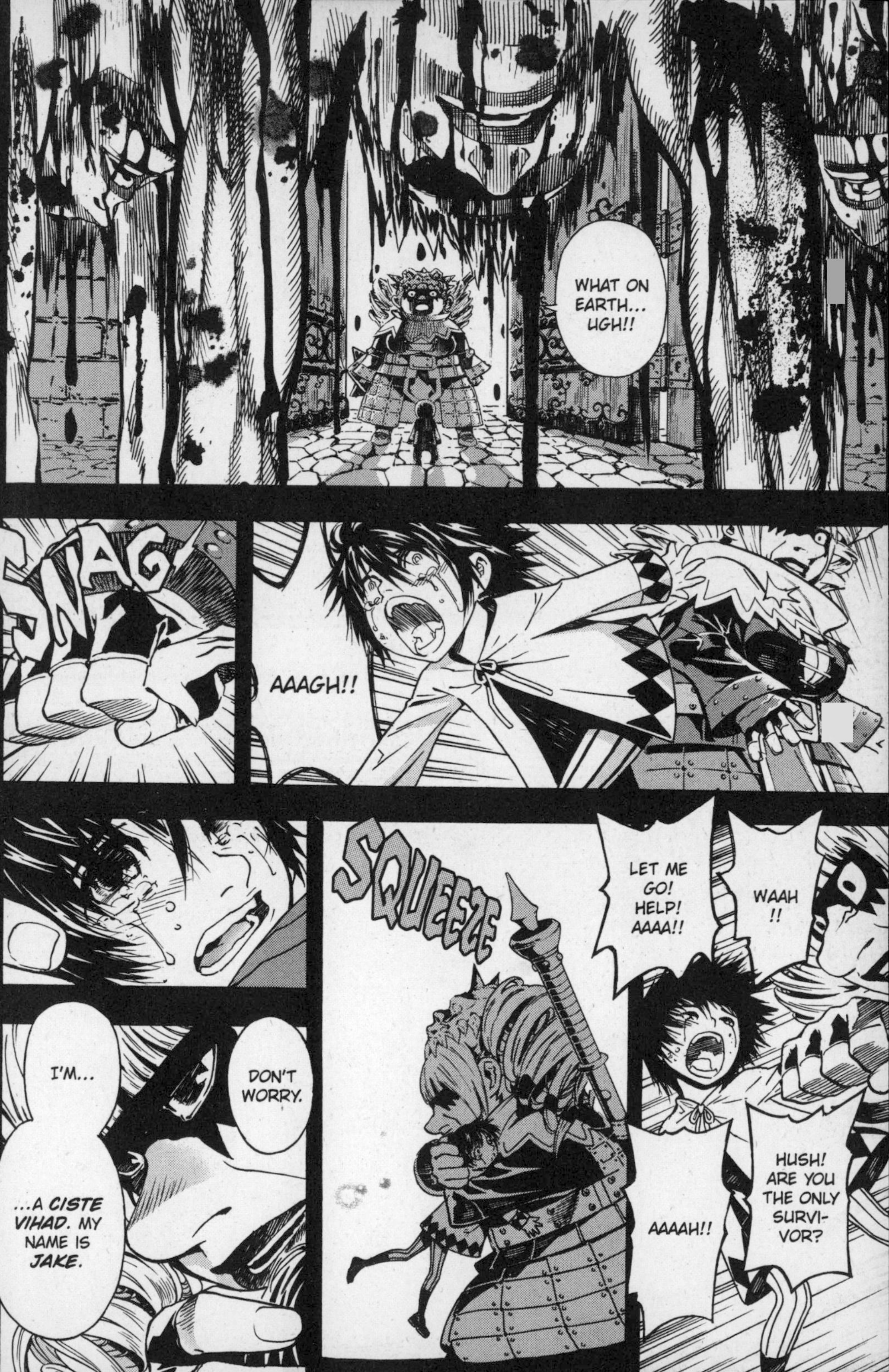
WHAT ON EARTH... UGH!!
AAAGH!!
SNAG
WAAH !!
LET ME GO! HELP! AAAA!!
SQUEEZE
HUSH! ARE YOU THE ONLY SURVI- VOR?
AAAAH!!
DON'T WORRY.
I'M...
...A *CISTE VIHAD*. MY NAME IS *JAKE*.

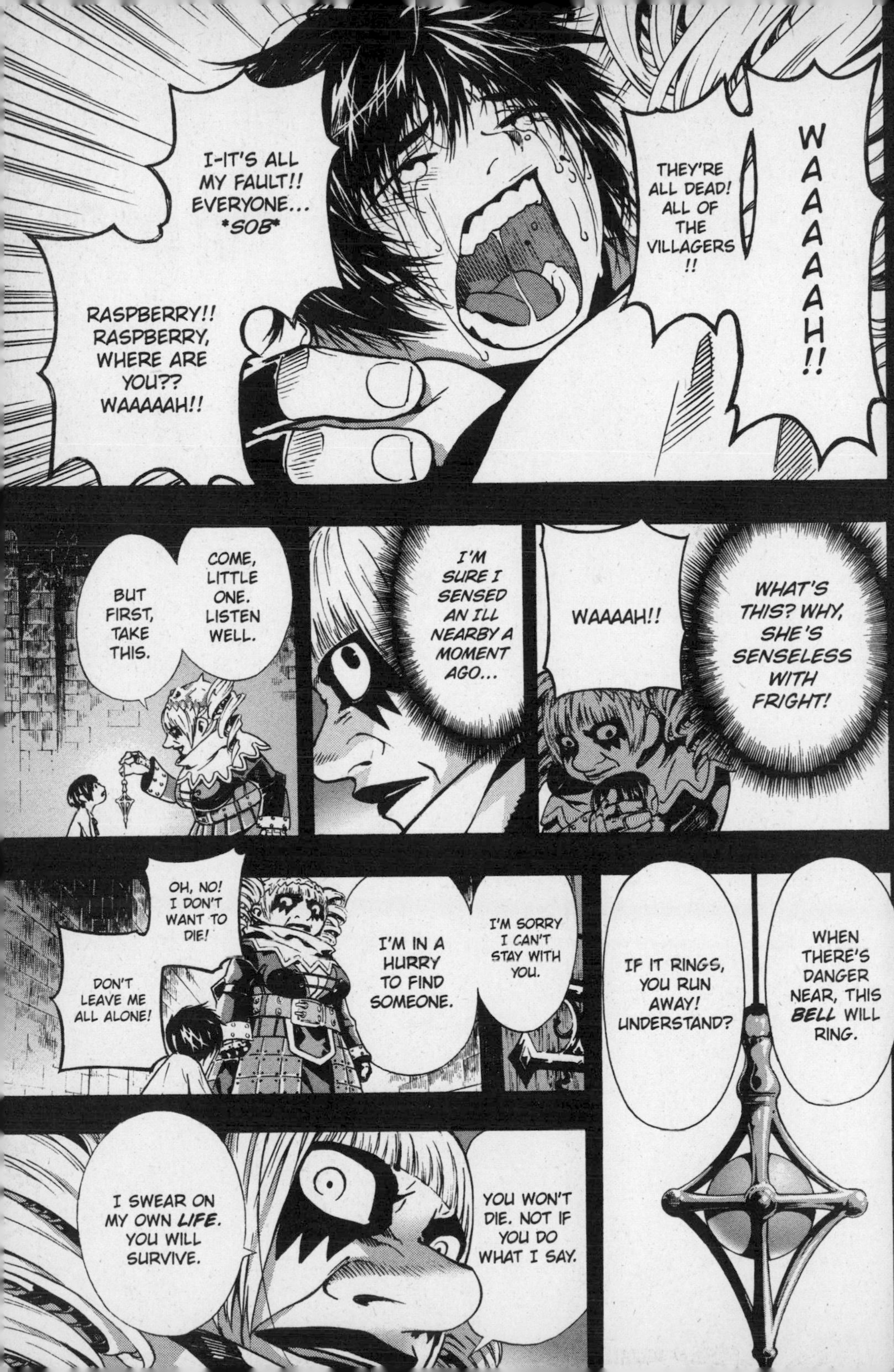
WAAAAAAH!!
THEY'RE ALL DEAD! ALL OF THE VILLAGERS !!
I-IT'S ALL MY FAULT!! EVERYONE... *SOB*
RASPBERRY!! RASPBERRY, WHERE ARE YOU?? WAAAAAH!!
WHAT'S THIS? WHY, SHE'S SENSELESS WITH FRIGHT!
WAAAAH!!
I'M SURE I SENSED AN ILL NEARBY A MOMENT AGO...
COME, LITTLE ONE. LISTEN WELL.
BUT FIRST, TAKE THIS.
WHEN THERE'S DANGER NEAR, THIS BELL WILL RING.
IF IT RINGS, YOU RUN AWAY! UNDERSTAND?
I'M SORRY I CAN'T STAY WITH YOU.
I'M IN A HURRY TO FIND SOMEONE.
OH, NO! I DON'T WANT TO DIE!
DON'T LEAVE ME ALL ALONE!
YOU WON'T DIE. NOT IF YOU DO WHAT I SAY.
I SWEAR ON MY OWN LIFE. YOU WILL SURVIVE.

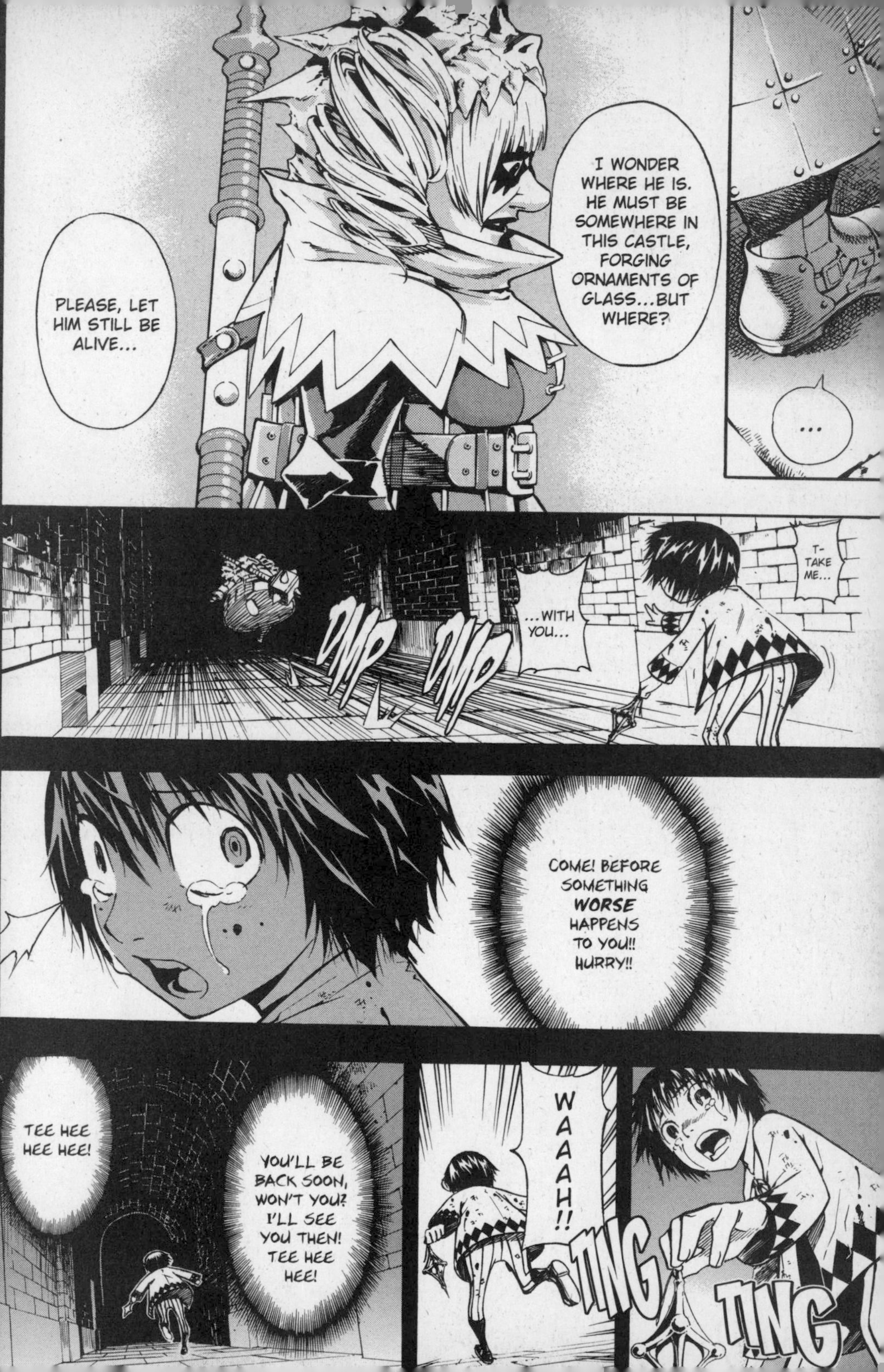
...
I WONDER WHERE HE IS. HE MUST BE SOMEWHERE IN THIS CASTLE, FORGING ORNAMENTS OF GLASS...BUT WHERE?
PLEASE, LET HIM STILL BE ALIVE...
T-TAKE ME...
...WITH YOU...
DMP
DMP
COME! BEFORE SOMETHING WORSE HAPPENS TO YOU!! HURRY!!
TING
TING
WAAAAH!!
TING
TEE HEE HEE HEE!
YOU'LL BE BACK SOON, WON'T YOU? I'LL SEE YOU THEN! TEE HEE HEE!

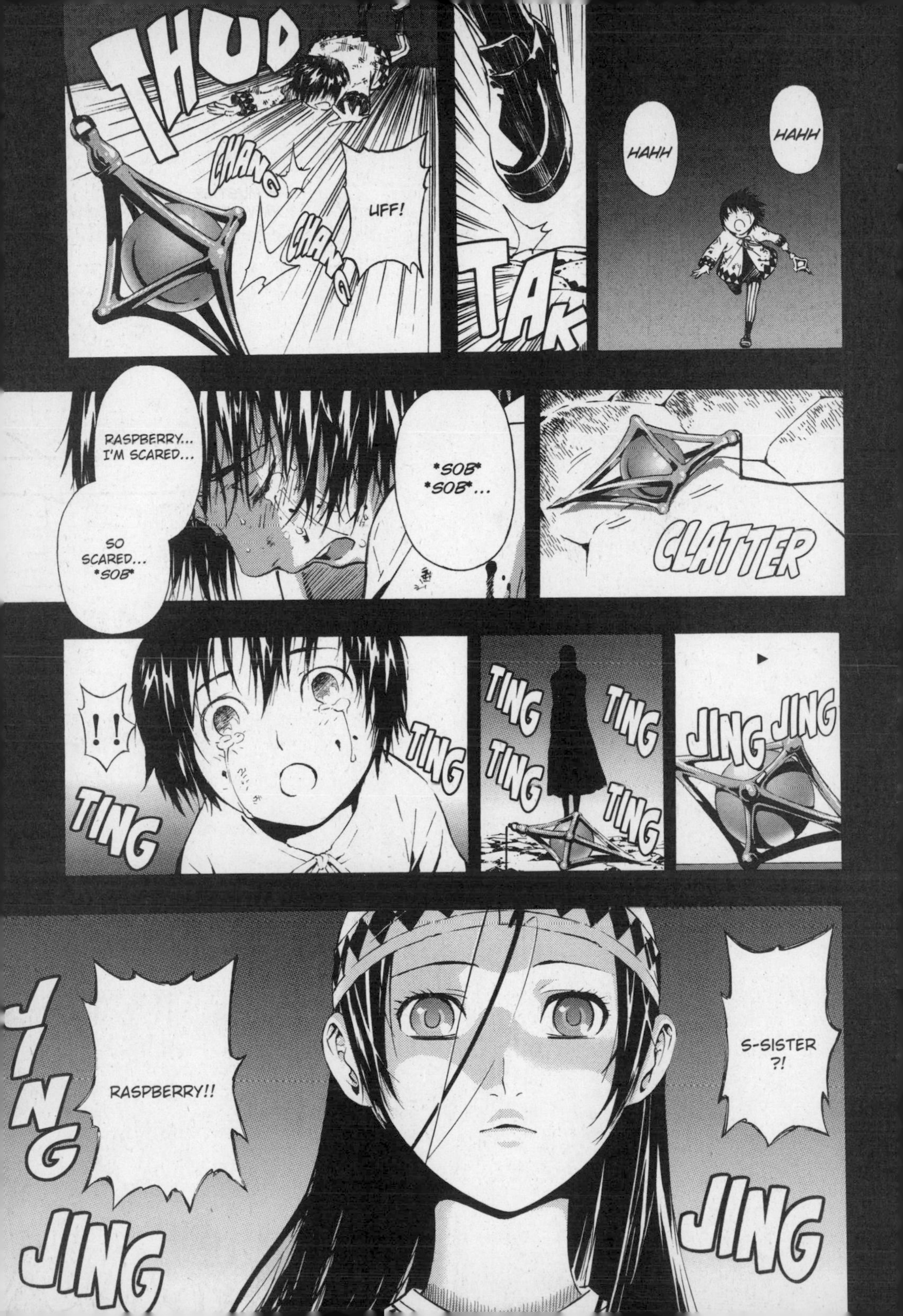
HAHH
HAHH
TAK
UFF!
THUD
CHANG
CHANG
CLATTER
SOB *SOB*...
RASPBERRY... I'M SCARED...
SO SCARED... *SOB*
JING JING
TING TING
TING TING
TING
!!
TING
S-SISTER ?!
JING
RASPBERRY!!
JING JING

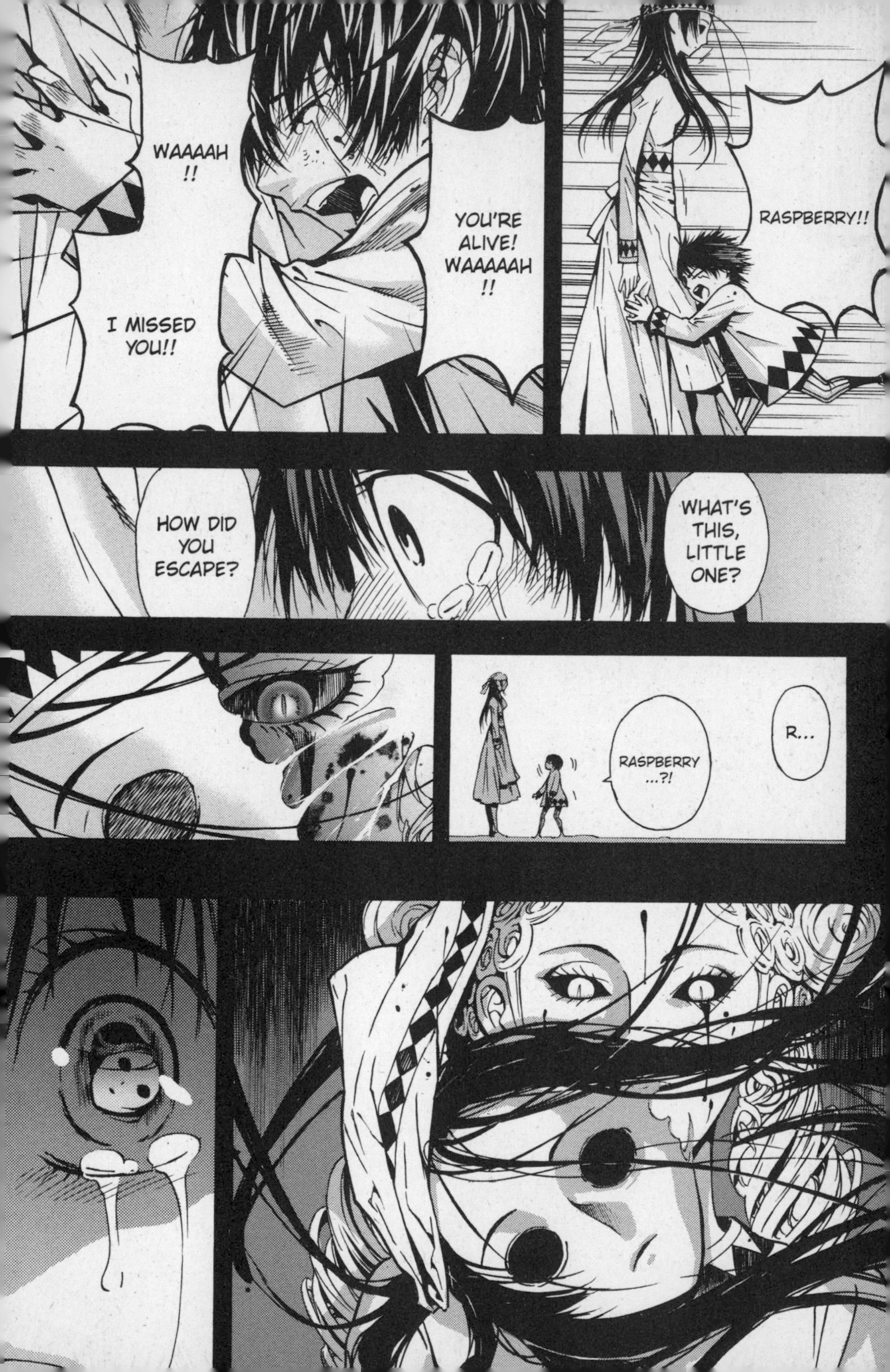
RASPBERRY!!
YOU'RE ALIVE! WAAAAAH !!
WAAAAH !!
I MISSED YOU!!
WHAT'S THIS, LITTLE ONE?
HOW DID YOU ESCAPE?
R...
RASPBERRY ...?!

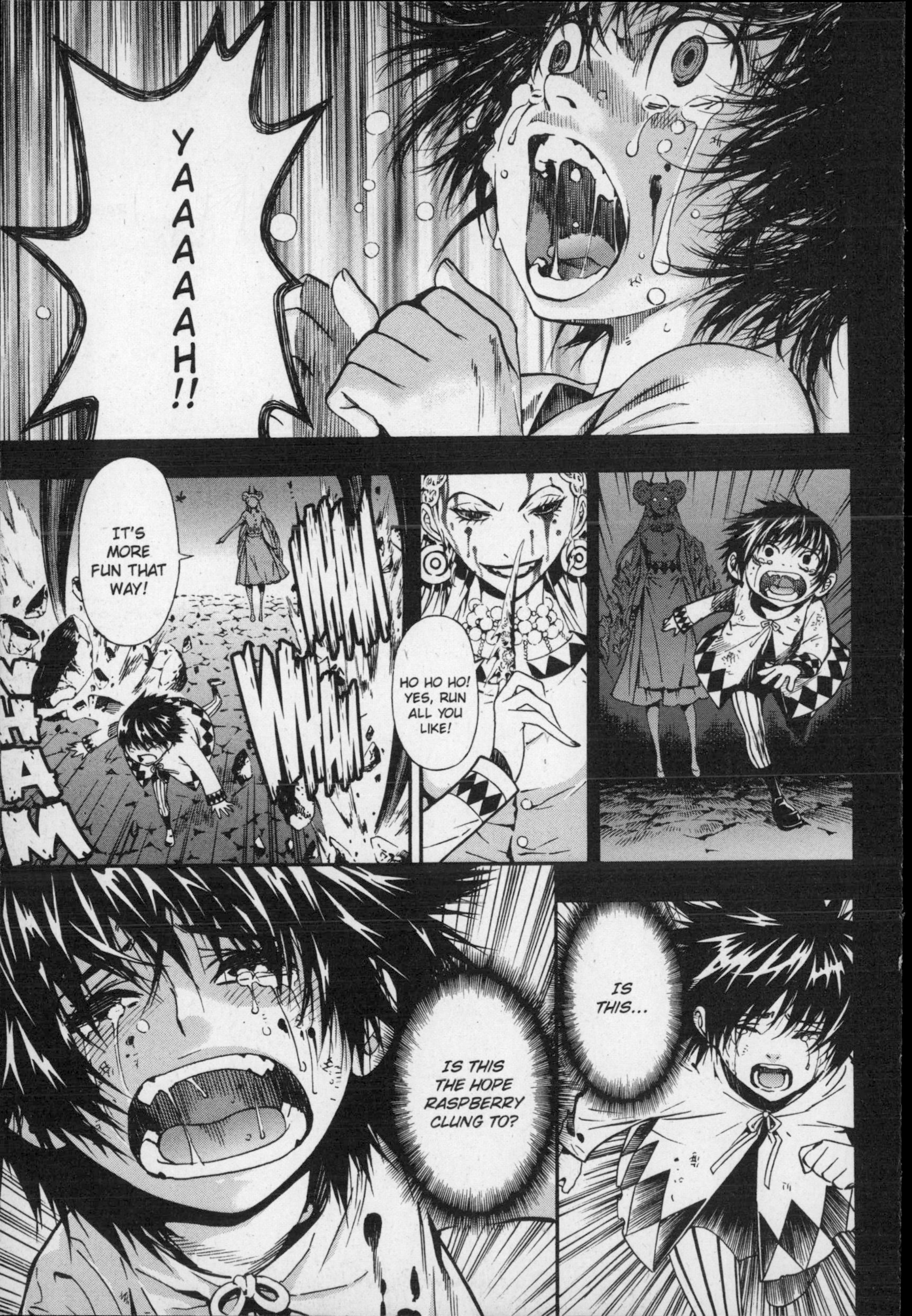
YAAAAAAH!!
HO HO HO! YES, RUN ALL YOU LIKE!
IT'S MORE FUN THAT WAY!
IS THIS...
IS THIS THE HOPE RASPBERRY CLUNG TO?

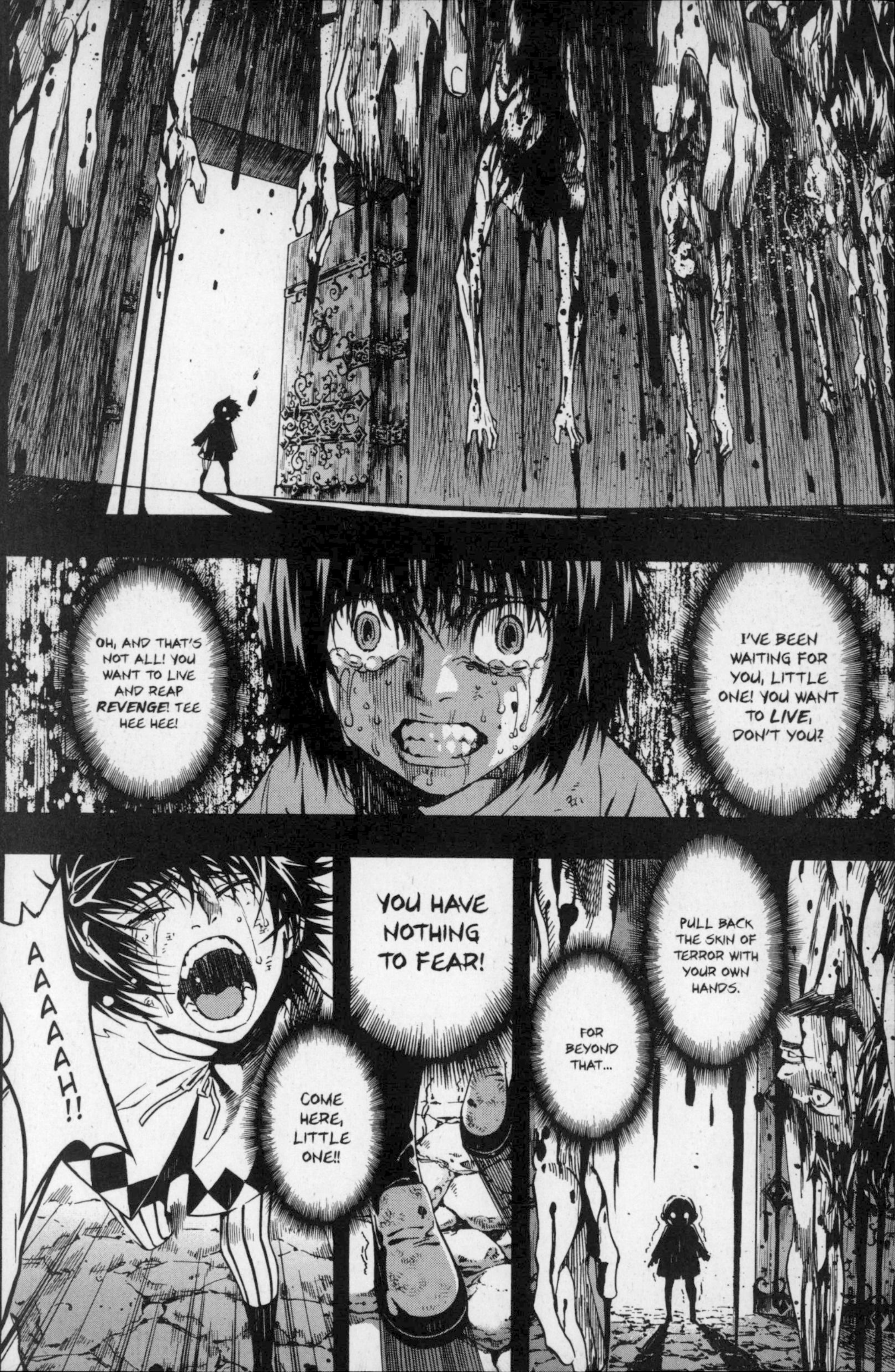
I'VE BEEN WAITING FOR YOU, LITTLE ONE! YOU WANT TO LIVE, DON'T YOU?
OH, AND THAT'S NOT ALL! YOU WANT TO LIVE AND REAP REVENGE! TEE HEE HEE!
PULL BACK THE SKIN OF TERROR WITH YOUR OWN HANDS.
FOR BEYOND THAT...
YOU HAVE NOTHING TO FEAR!
COME HERE, LITTLE ONE!!
AAAAAAH!!

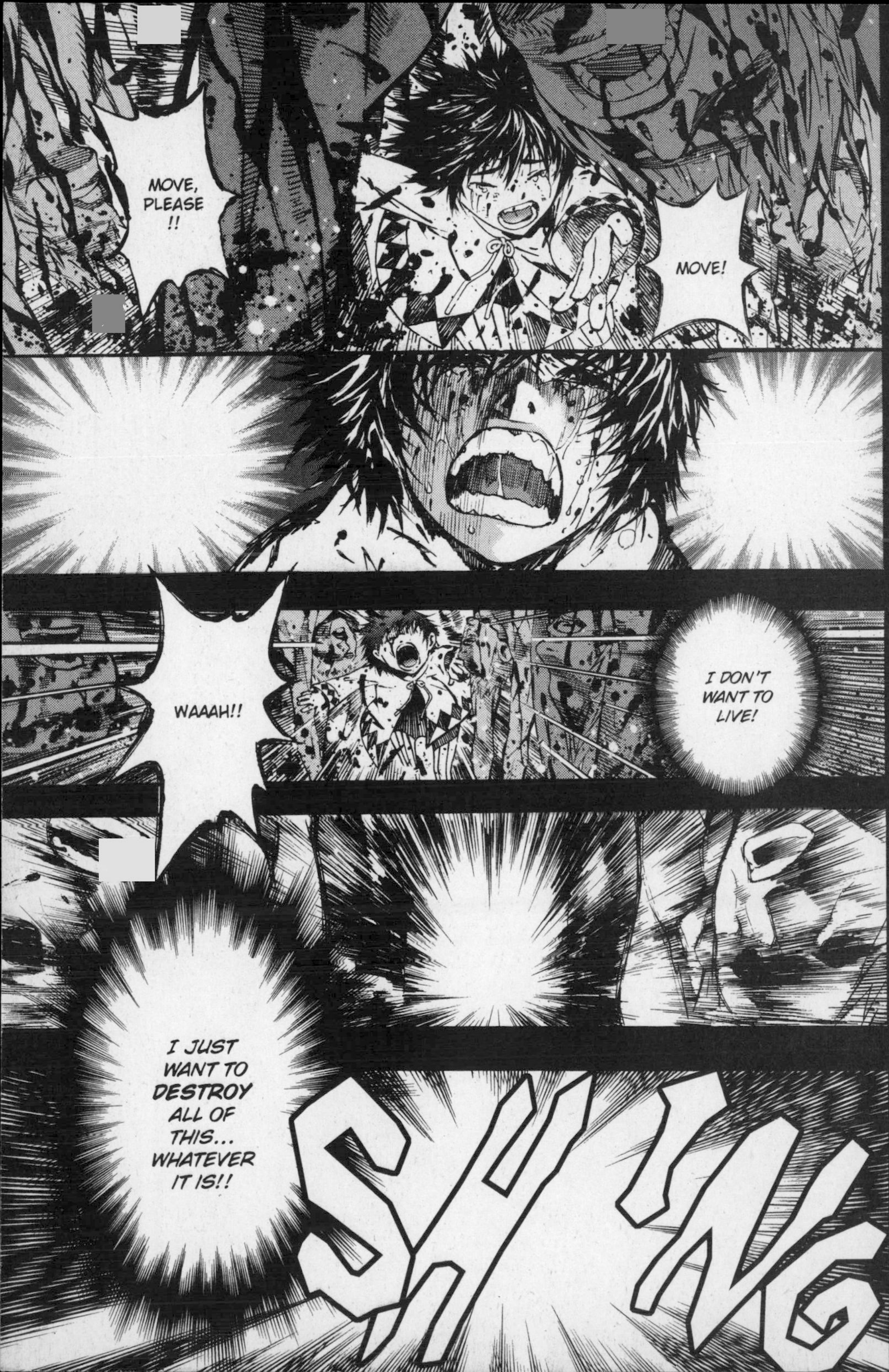
MOVE!
MOVE, PLEASE !!
I DON'T WANT TO LIVE!
WAAAH!!
I JUST WANT TO DESTROY ALL OF THIS... WHATEVER IT IS!!
SHING

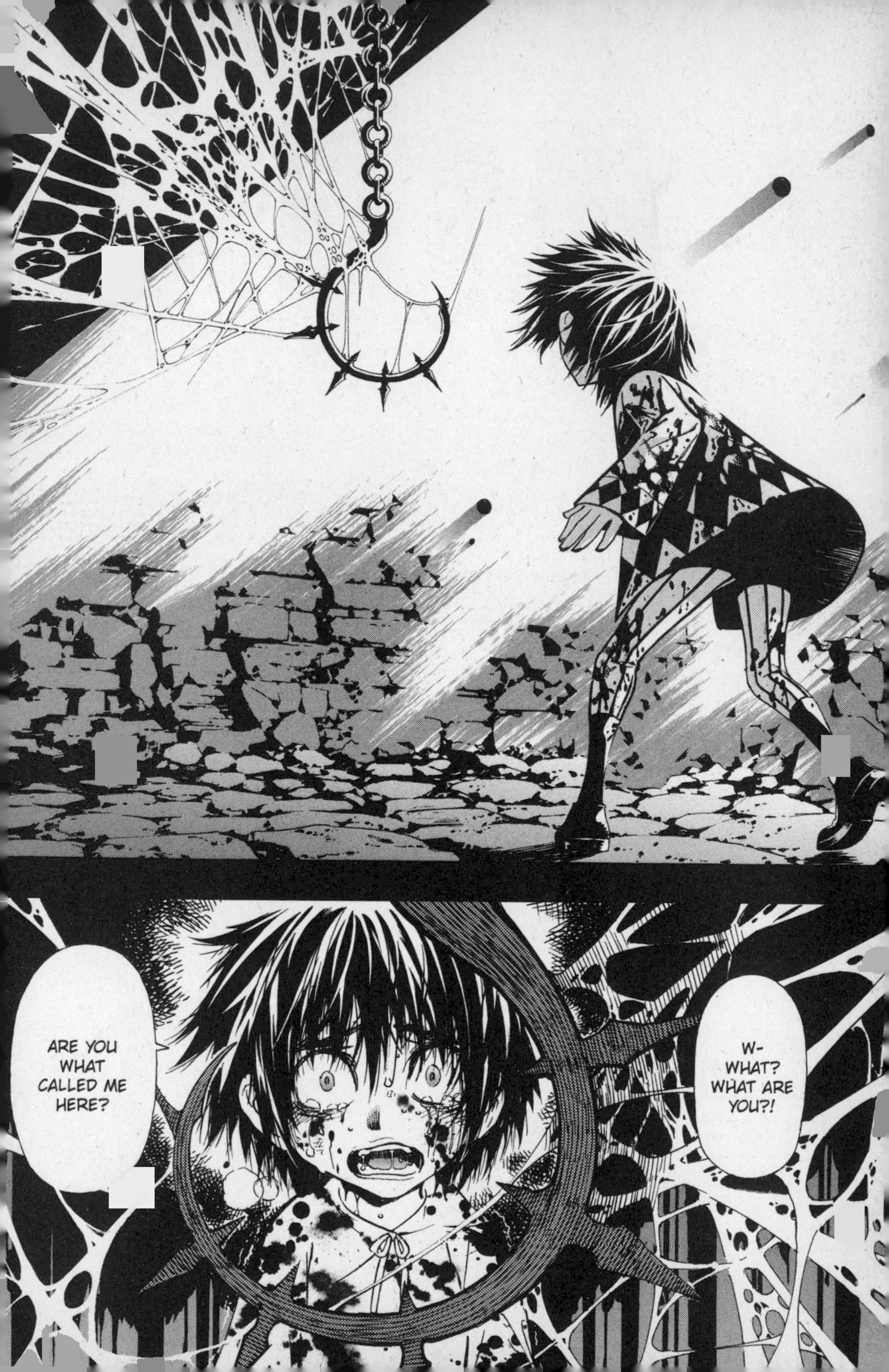
W- WHAT? WHAT ARE YOU?!
ARE YOU WHAT CALLED ME HERE?

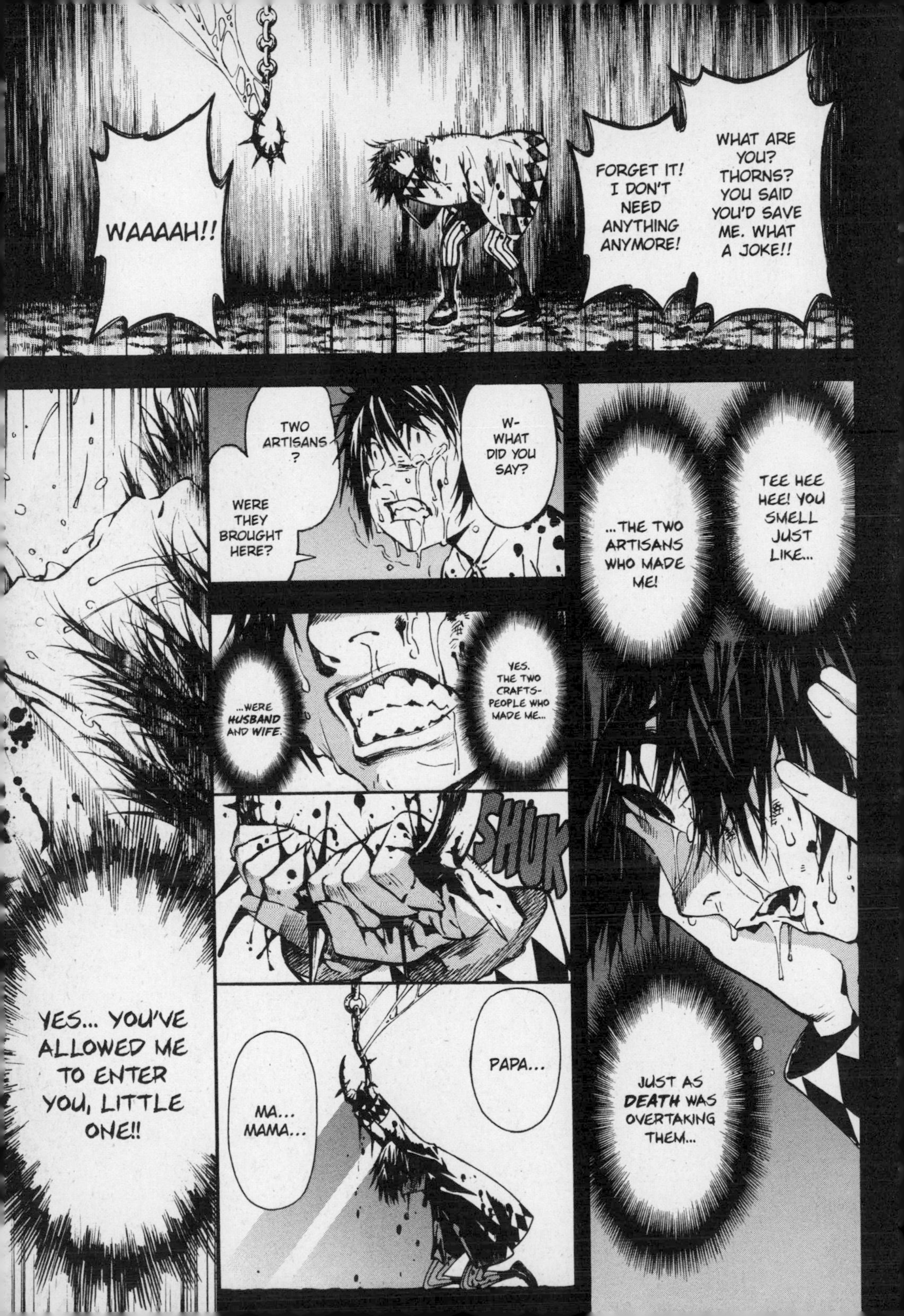
WHAT ARE YOU? THORNS? YOU SAID YOU'D SAVE ME. WHAT A JOKE!!
FORGET IT! I DON'T NEED ANYTHING ANYMORE!
WAAAAH!!
TEE HEE HEE! YOU SMELL JUST LIKE...
...THE TWO ARTISANS WHO MADE ME!
JUST AS DEATH WAS OVERTAKING THEM...
W- WHAT DID YOU SAY?
TWO ARTISANS?
WERE THEY BROUGHT HERE?
YES. THE TWO CRAFTS-PEOPLE WHO MADE ME...
...WERE HUSBAND AND WIFE.
SHUK
PAPA...
MA... MAMA...
YES... YOU'VE ALLOWED ME TO ENTER YOU, LITTLE ONE!!

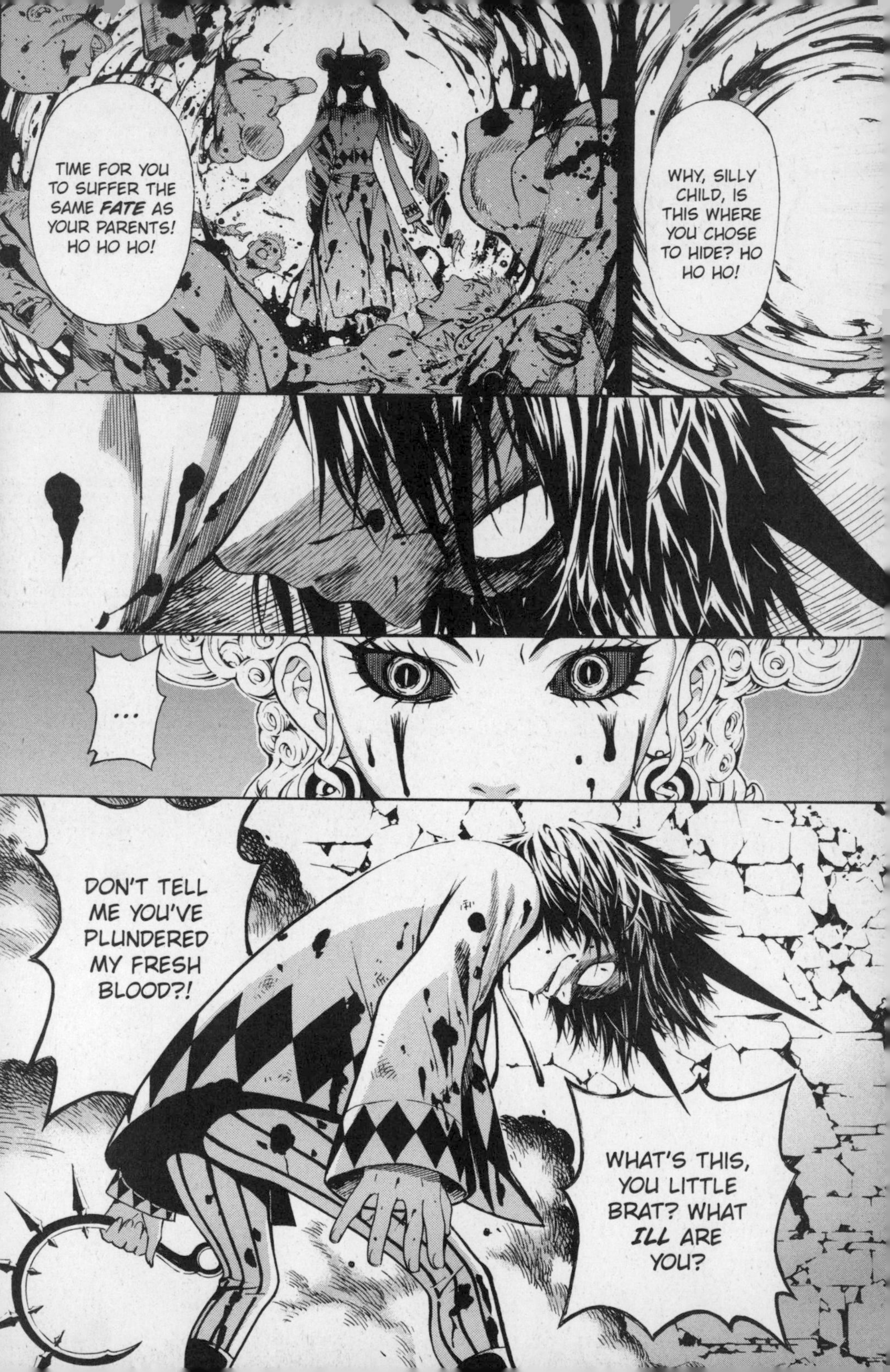
WHY, SILLY CHILD, IS THIS WHERE YOU CHOSE TO HIDE? HO HO HO!
TIME FOR YOU TO SUFFER THE SAME *FATE* AS YOUR PARENTS! HO HO HO!
...
WHAT'S THIS, YOU LITTLE BRAT? WHAT *ILL* ARE YOU?
DON'T TELL ME YOU'VE PLUNDERED MY FRESH BLOOD?!

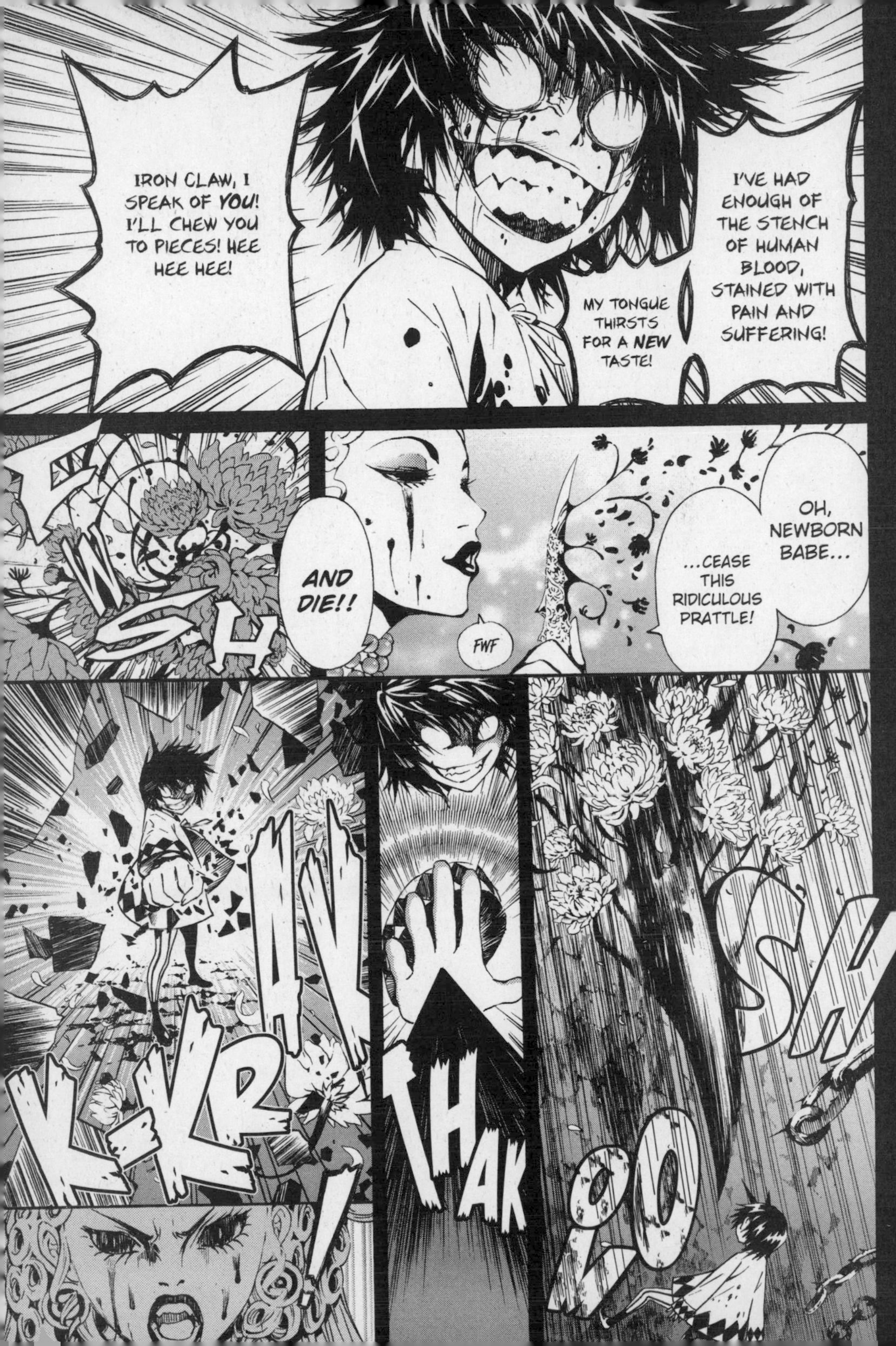
I'VE HAD ENOUGH OF THE STENCH OF HUMAN BLOOD, STAINED WITH PAIN AND SUFFERING!
MY TONGUE THIRSTS FOR A NEW TASTE!
IRON CLAW, I SPEAK OF YOU! I'LL CHEW YOU TO PIECES! HEE HEE HEE!
OH, NEWBORN BABE...
...CEASE THIS RIDICULOUS PRATTLE!
FWF
AND DIE!!
FWSH
SHOO
THWAK
K-KRAW!

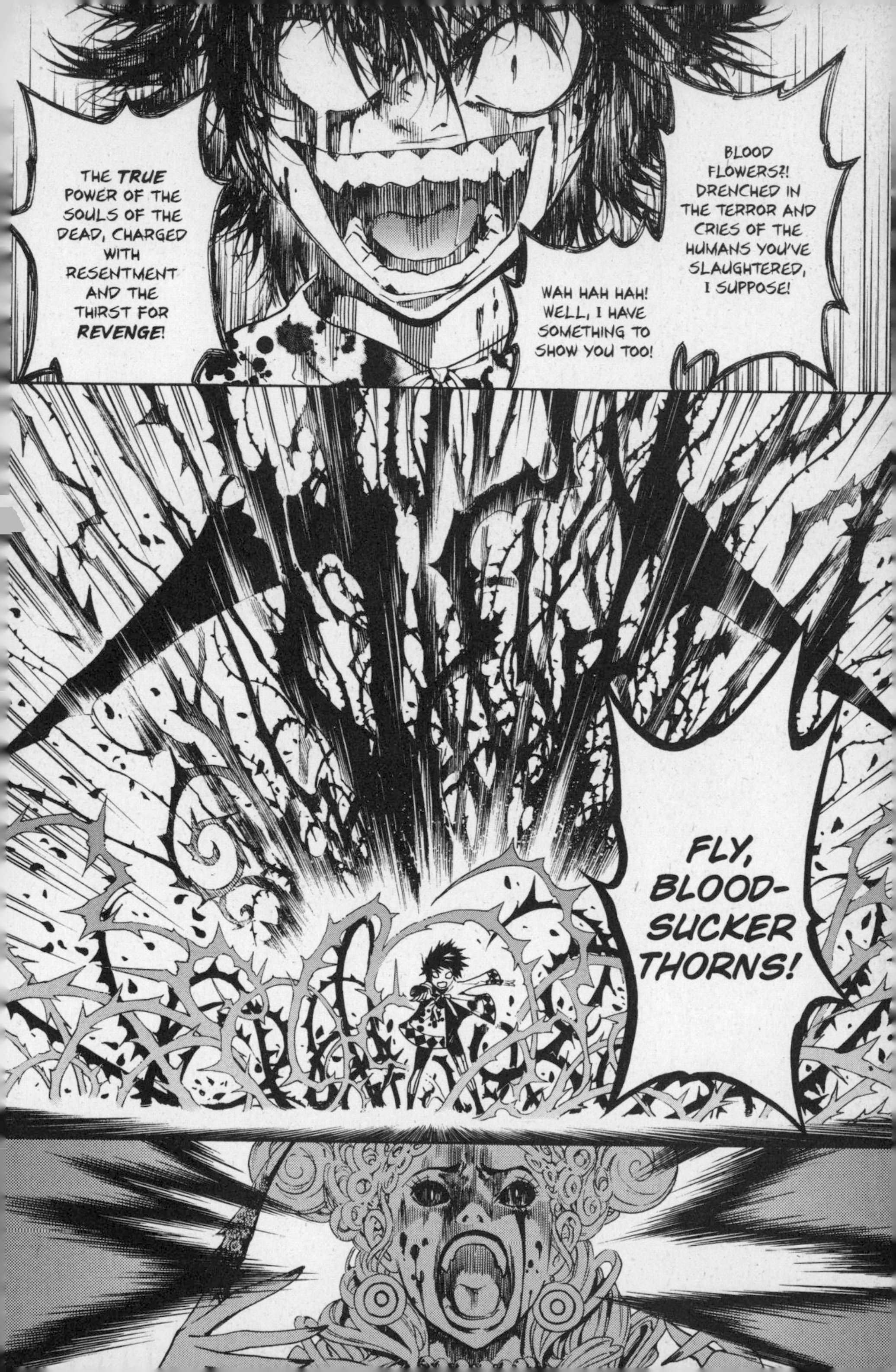
BLOOD FLOWERS?! DRENCHED IN THE TERROR AND CRIES OF THE HUMANS YOU'VE SLAUGHTERED, I SUPPOSE!
WAH HAH HAH! WELL, I HAVE SOMETHING TO SHOW YOU TOO!
THE TRUE POWER OF THE SOULS OF THE DEAD, CHARGED WITH RESENTMENT AND THE THIRST FOR REVENGE!
FLY, BLOOD-SUCKER THORNS!

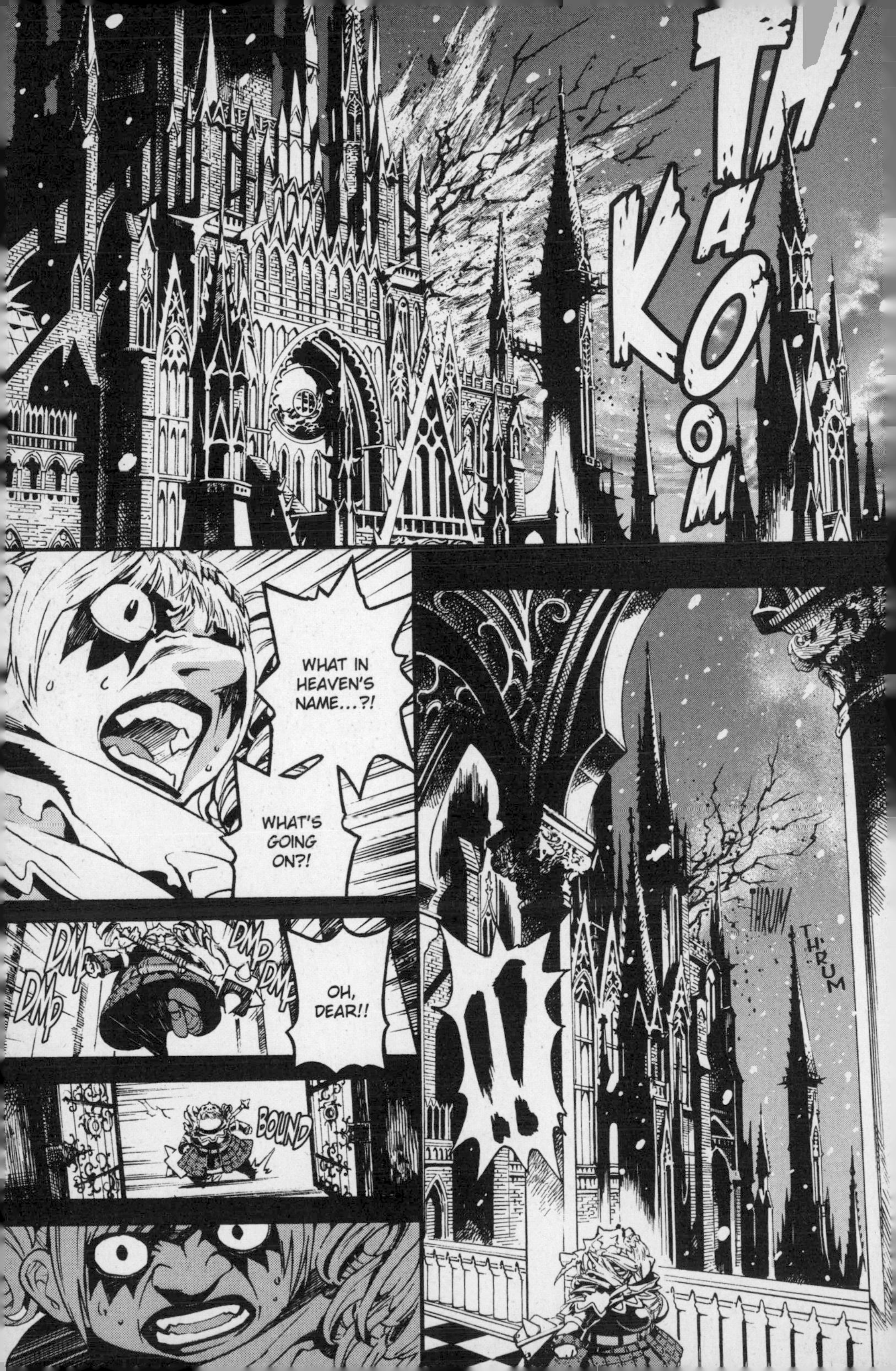
TH
KAOOM
THRUM
THRUM
WHAT IN HEAVEN'S NAME...?!
WHAT'S GOING ON?!
OH, DEAR!!
DMP DMP
DMP DMP
BOUND

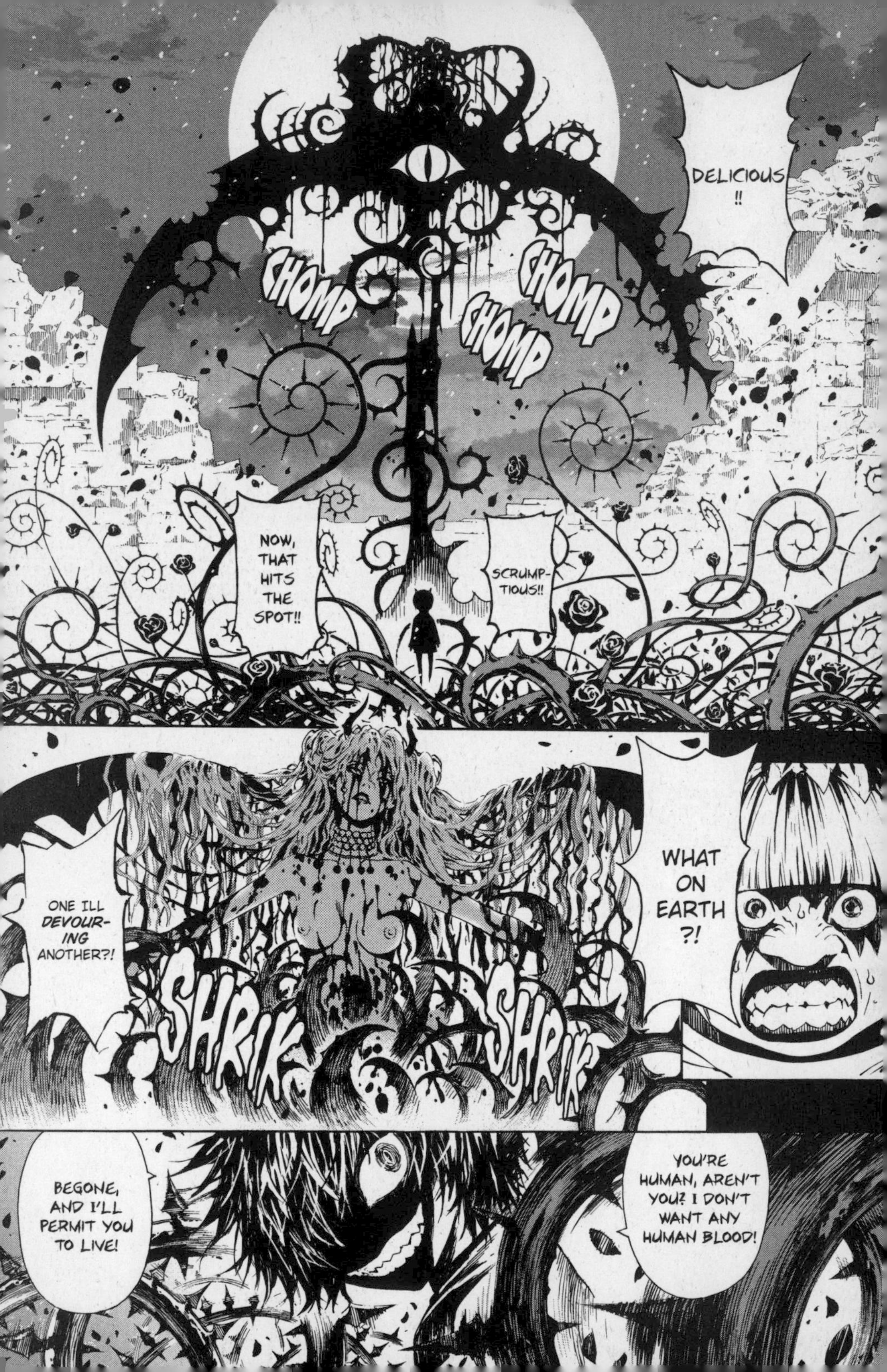
DELICIOUS!!
CHOMP
CHOMP
CHOMP
SCRUMP-TIOUS!!
NOW, THAT HITS THE SPOT!!
WHAT ON EARTH?!
SHRIK
SHRIK
ONE ILL *DEVOURING* ANOTHER?!
YOU'RE HUMAN, AREN'T YOU? I DON'T WANT ANY HUMAN BLOOD!
BEGONE, AND I'LL PERMIT YOU TO LIVE!

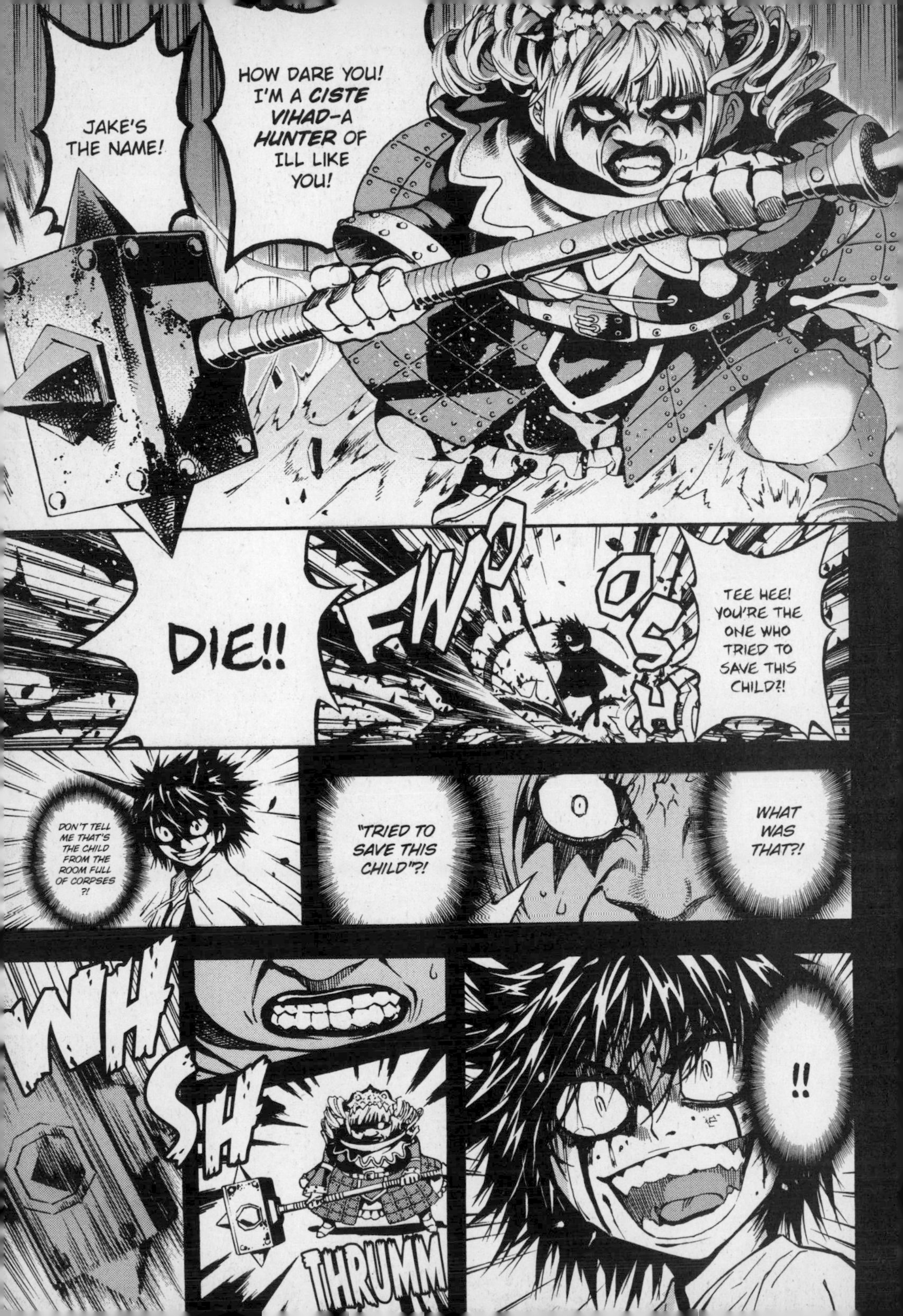
HOW DARE YOU! I'M A *CISTE VIHAD*—A *HUNTER* OF ILL LIKE YOU!
JAKE'S THE NAME!
TEE HEE! YOU'RE THE ONE WHO TRIED TO SAVE THIS CHILD?!
FWOOSH
DIE!!
WHAT WAS THAT?!
"TRIED TO SAVE THIS CHILD"?!
DON'T TELL ME THAT'S THE CHILD FROM THE ROOM FULL OF CORPSES ?!
!!
THRUMM
WHSH

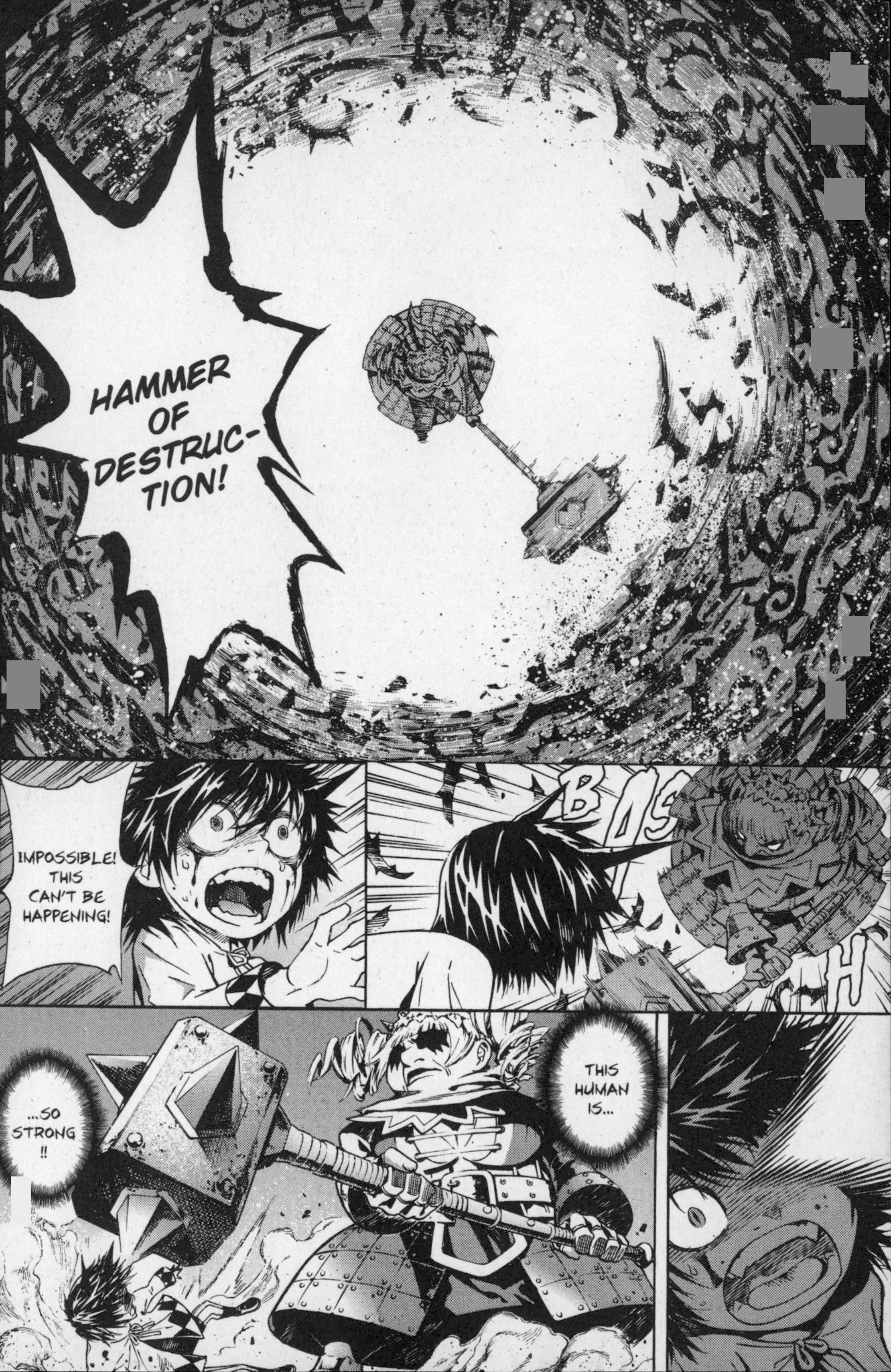
HAMMER OF DESTRUC-TION!
IMPOSSIBLE! THIS CAN'T BE HAPPENING!
THIS HUMAN IS...
...SO STRONG!!

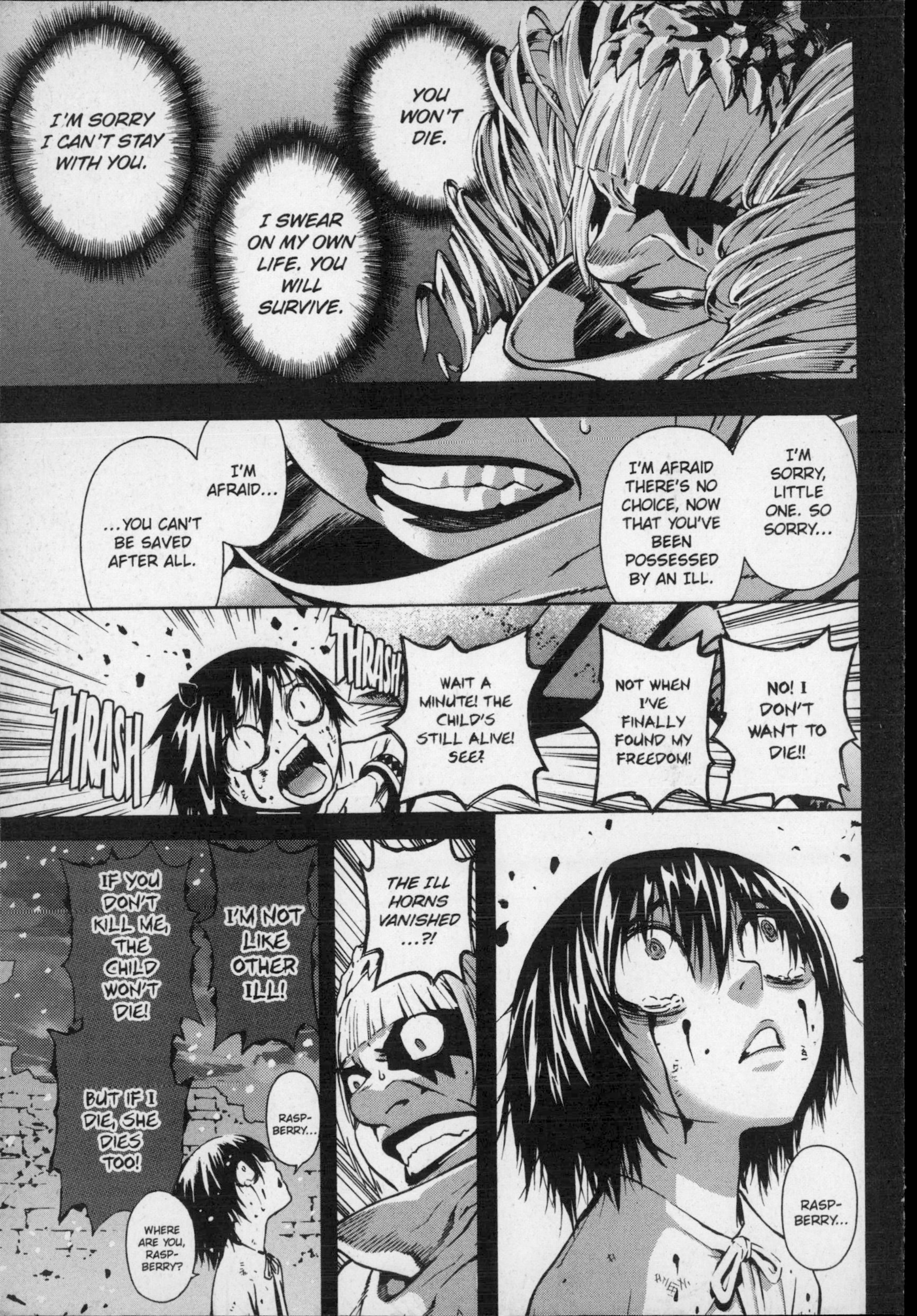
YOU WON'T DIE.
I SWEAR ON MY OWN LIFE. YOU WILL SURVIVE.
I'M SORRY I CAN'T STAY WITH YOU.
I'M SORRY, LITTLE ONE. SO SORRY...
I'M AFRAID THERE'S NO CHOICE, NOW THAT YOU'VE BEEN POSSESSED BY AN ILL.
I'M AFRAID...
...YOU CAN'T BE SAVED AFTER ALL.
NO! I DON'T WANT TO DIE!!
NOT WHEN I'VE FINALLY FOUND MY FREEDOM!
WAIT A MINUTE! THE CHILD'S STILL ALIVE! SEE?
THRASH
THRASH
RASPBERRY...
THE ILL HORNS VANISHED ...?!
RASPBERRY...
I'M NOT LIKE OTHER ILL!
IF YOU DON'T KILL ME, THE CHILD WON'T DIE!
BUT IF I DIE, SHE DIES TOO!
WHERE ARE YOU, RASPBERRY?

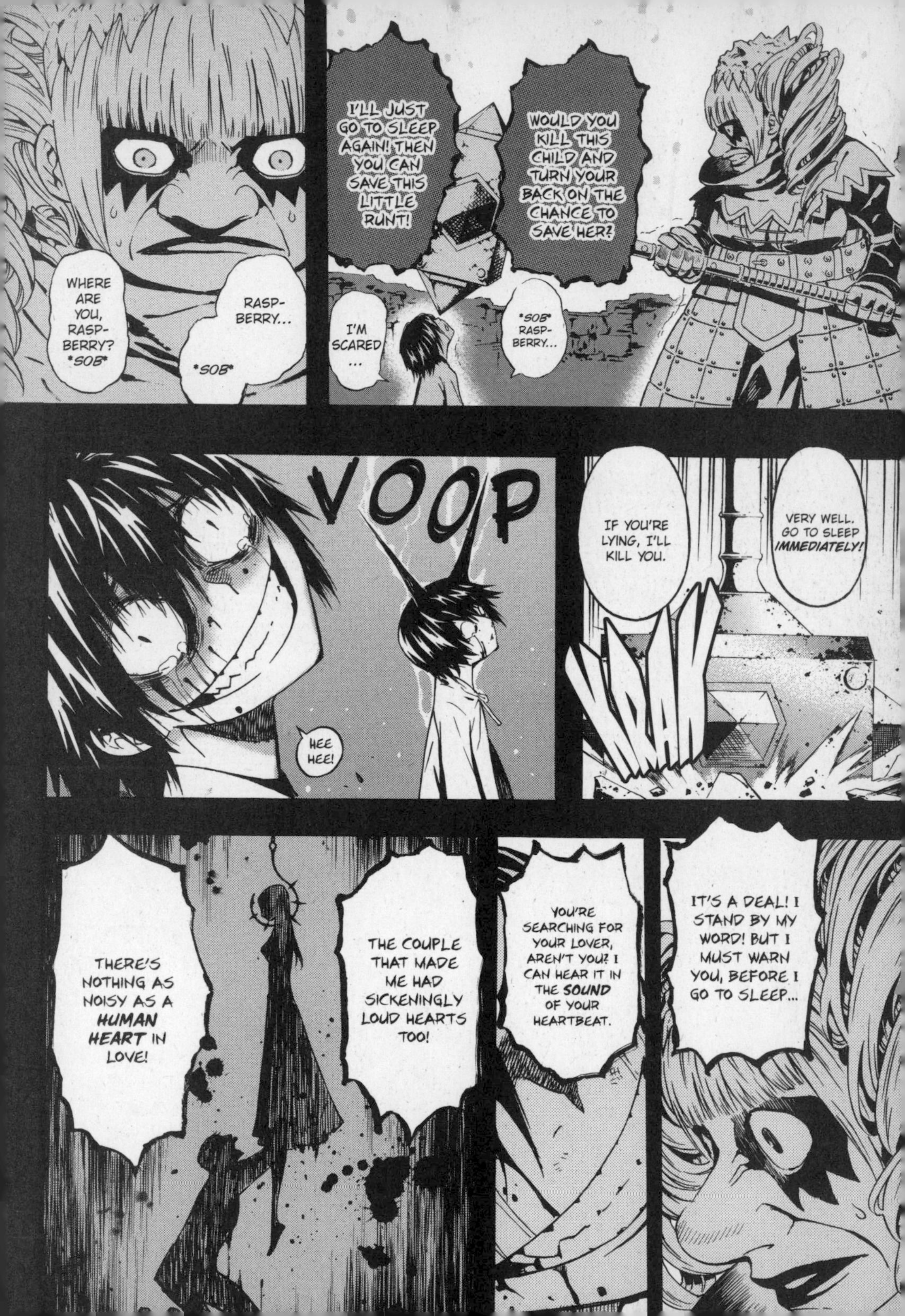
WOULD YOU KILL THIS CHILD AND TURN YOUR BACK ON THE CHANCE TO SAVE HER?
I'LL JUST GO TO SLEEP AGAIN! THEN YOU CAN SAVE THIS LITTLE RUNT!
SOB RASPBERRY...
I'M SCARED ...
RASPBERRY... *SOB*
WHERE ARE YOU, RASPBERRY? *SOB*
VERY WELL. GO TO SLEEP IMMEDIATELY!
IF YOU'RE LYING, I'LL KILL YOU.
VOOP
HEE HEE!
IT'S A DEAL! I STAND BY MY WORD! BUT I MUST WARN YOU, BEFORE I GO TO SLEEP...
YOU'RE SEARCHING FOR YOUR LOVER, AREN'T YOU? I CAN HEAR IT IN THE SOUND OF YOUR HEARTBEAT.
THE COUPLE THAT MADE ME HAD SICKENINGLY LOUD HEARTS TOO!
THERE'S NOTHING AS NOISY AS A HUMAN HEART IN LOVE!

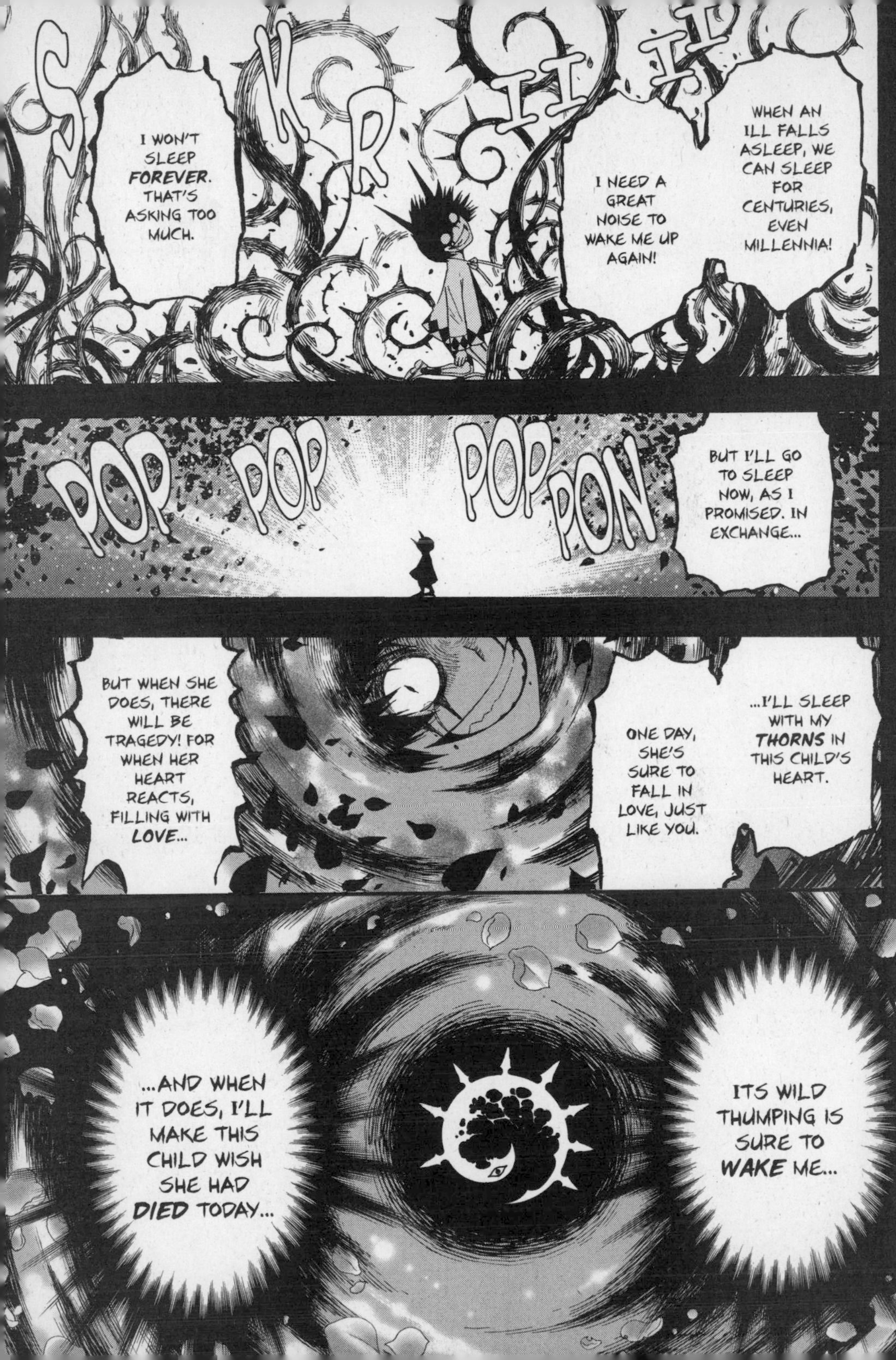
SKRIIII
WHEN AN ILL FALLS ASLEEP, WE CAN SLEEP FOR CENTURIES, EVEN MILLENNIA!
I NEED A GREAT NOISE TO WAKE ME UP AGAIN!
I WON'T SLEEP **FOREVER**. THAT'S ASKING TOO MUCH.
BUT I'LL GO TO SLEEP NOW, AS I PROMISED. IN EXCHANGE...
POP POP POPPON
...I'LL SLEEP WITH MY **THORNS** IN THIS CHILD'S HEART.
ONE DAY, SHE'S SURE TO FALL IN LOVE, JUST LIKE YOU.
BUT WHEN SHE DOES, THERE WILL BE TRAGEDY! FOR WHEN HER HEART REACTS, FILLING WITH **LOVE**...
ITS WILD THUMPING IS SURE TO **WAKE** ME...
...AND WHEN IT DOES, I'LL MAKE THIS CHILD WISH SHE HAD **DIED** TODAY...

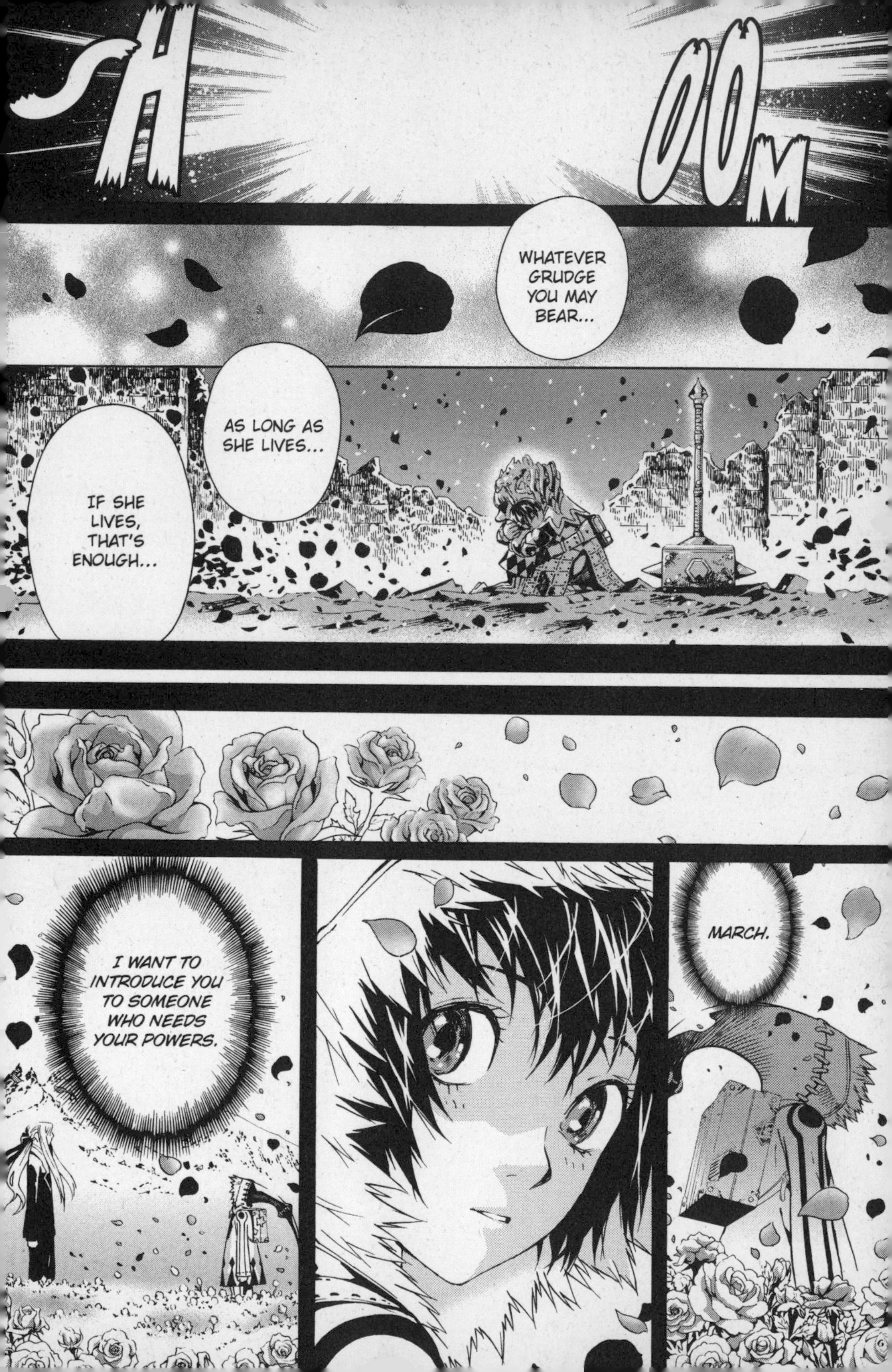
SH OOM
WHATEVER GRUDGE YOU MAY BEAR...
AS LONG AS SHE LIVES...
IF SHE LIVES, THAT'S ENOUGH...
MARCH.
I WANT TO INTRODUCE YOU TO SOMEONE WHO NEEDS YOUR POWERS.

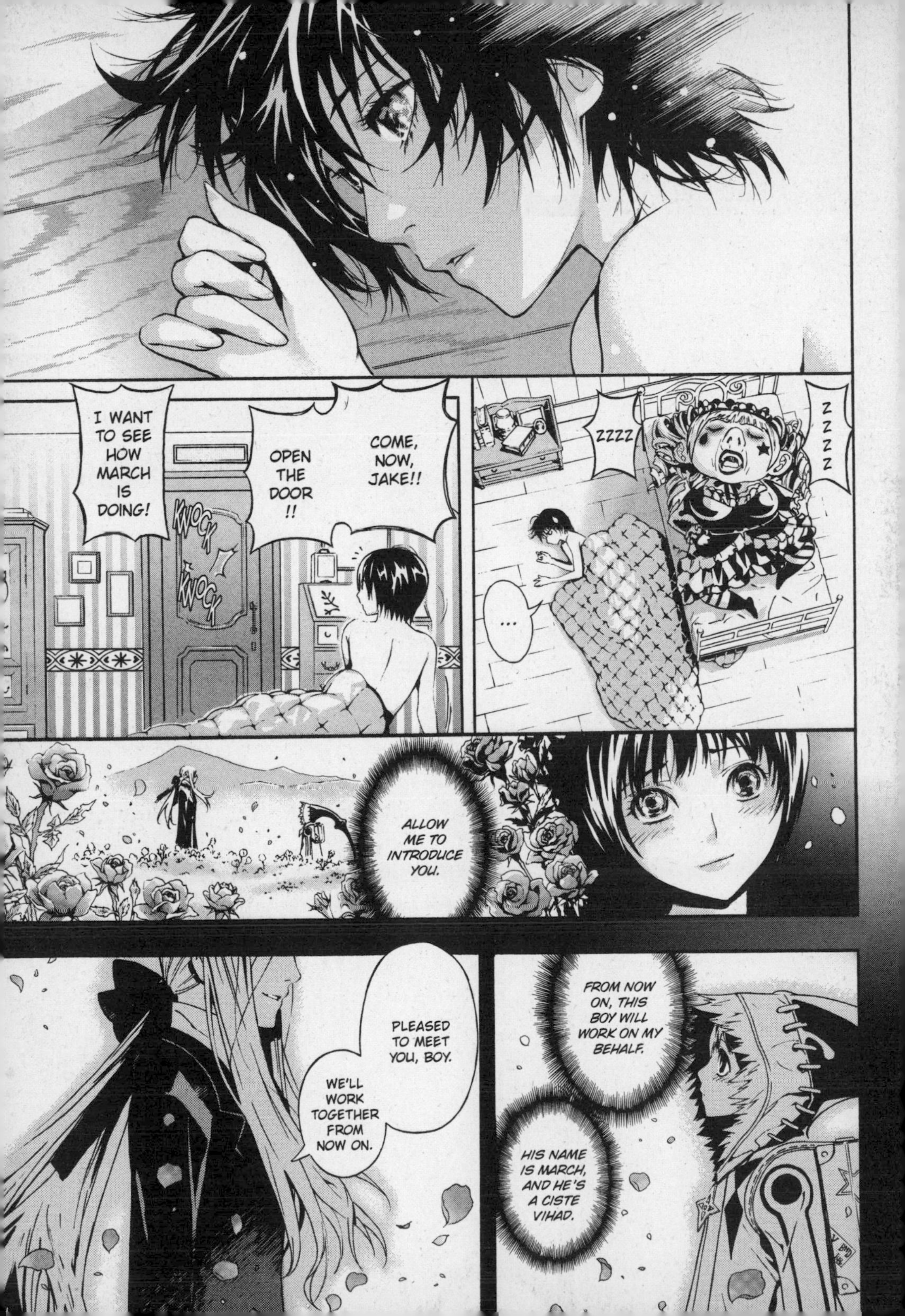
Z Z Z Z
ZZZZ
...
COME, NOW, JAKE!!
OPEN THE DOOR !!
I WANT TO SEE HOW MARCH IS DOING!
KNOCK KNOCK
ALLOW ME TO INTRODUCE YOU.
FROM NOW ON, THIS BOY WILL WORK ON MY BEHALF.
HIS NAME IS MARCH, AND HE'S A CISTE VIHAD.
PLEASED TO MEET YOU, BOY.
WE'LL WORK TOGETHER FROM NOW ON.

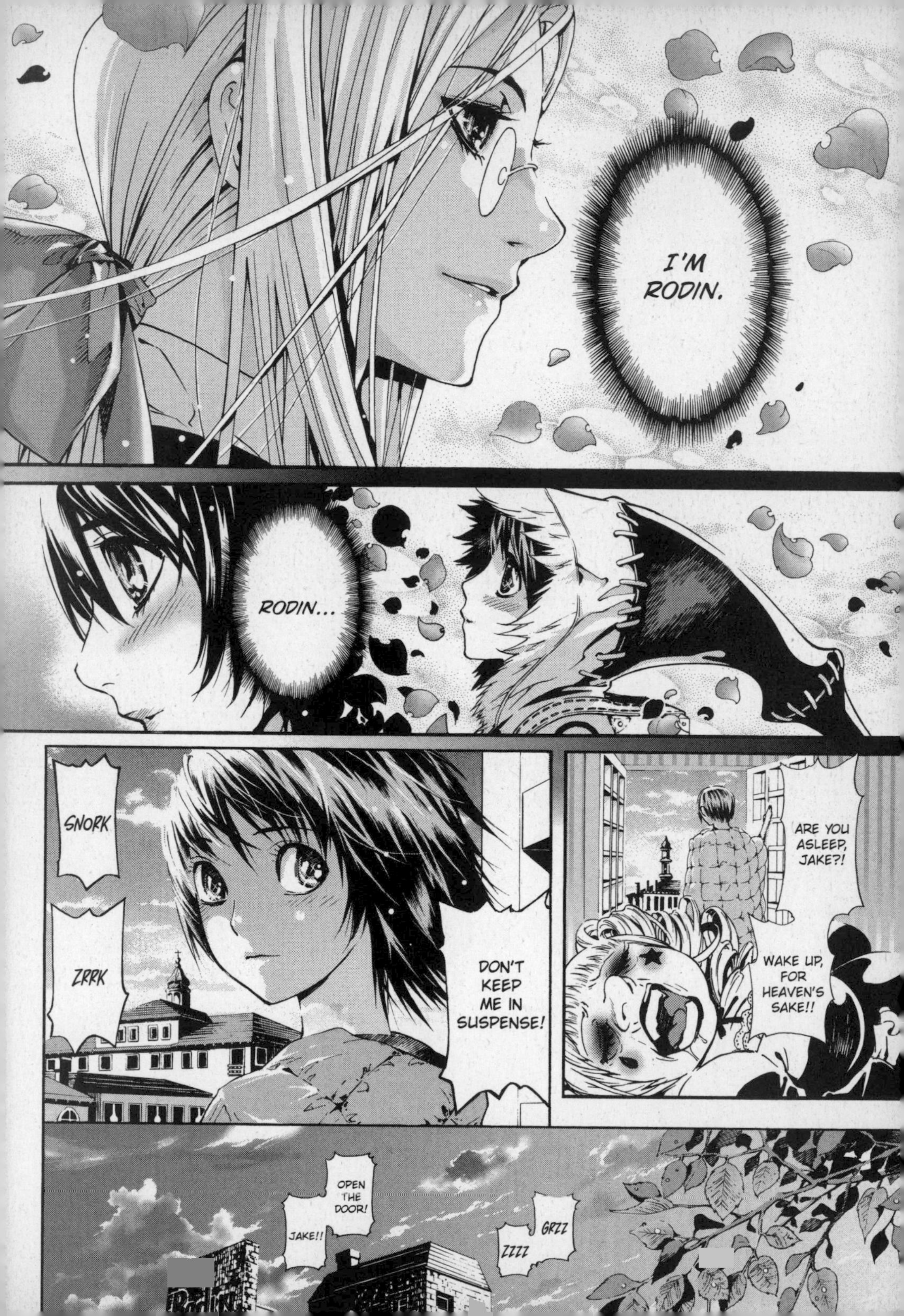

I'M RODIN.
RODIN...
ARE YOU ASLEEP, JAKE?!
WAKE UP, FOR HEAVEN'S SAKE!!
SNORK
DON'T KEEP ME IN SUSPENSE!
ZRRK
GRZZ
ZZZZ
OPEN THE DOOR!
JAKE!!

BONUS MANGA: KIM HYUNG MIN

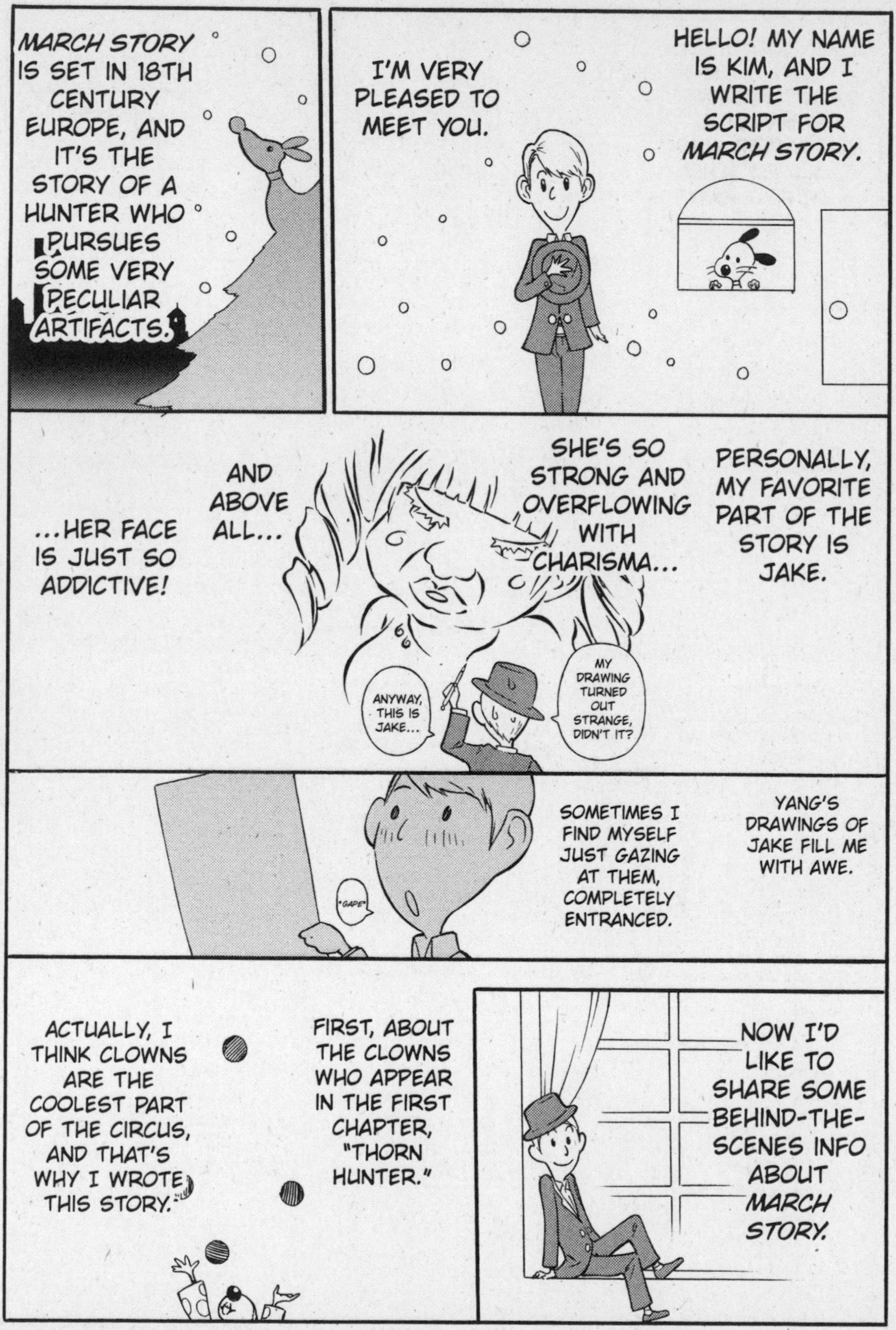

HELLO! MY NAME IS KIM, AND I WRITE THE SCRIPT FOR MARCH STORY.
I'M VERY PLEASED TO MEET YOU.
MARCH STORY IS SET IN 18TH CENTURY EUROPE, AND IT'S THE STORY OF A HUNTER WHO PURSUES SOME VERY PECULIAR ARTIFACTS.
PERSONALLY, MY FAVORITE PART OF THE STORY IS JAKE.
SHE'S SO STRONG AND OVERFLOWING WITH CHARISMA...
AND ABOVE ALL...
...HER FACE IS JUST SO ADDICTIVE!
MY DRAWING TURNED OUT STRANGE, DIDN'T IT?
ANYWAY, THIS IS JAKE...
YANG'S DRAWINGS OF JAKE FILL ME WITH AWE.
SOMETIMES I FIND MYSELF JUST GAZING AT THEM, COMPLETELY ENTRANCED.
GAPE
NOW I'D LIKE TO SHARE SOME BEHIND-THE-SCENES INFO ABOUT MARCH STORY.
FIRST, ABOUT THE CLOWNS WHO APPEAR IN THE FIRST CHAPTER, "THORN HUNTER."
ACTUALLY, I THINK CLOWNS ARE THE COOLEST PART OF THE CIRCUS, AND THAT'S WHY I WROTE THIS STORY.

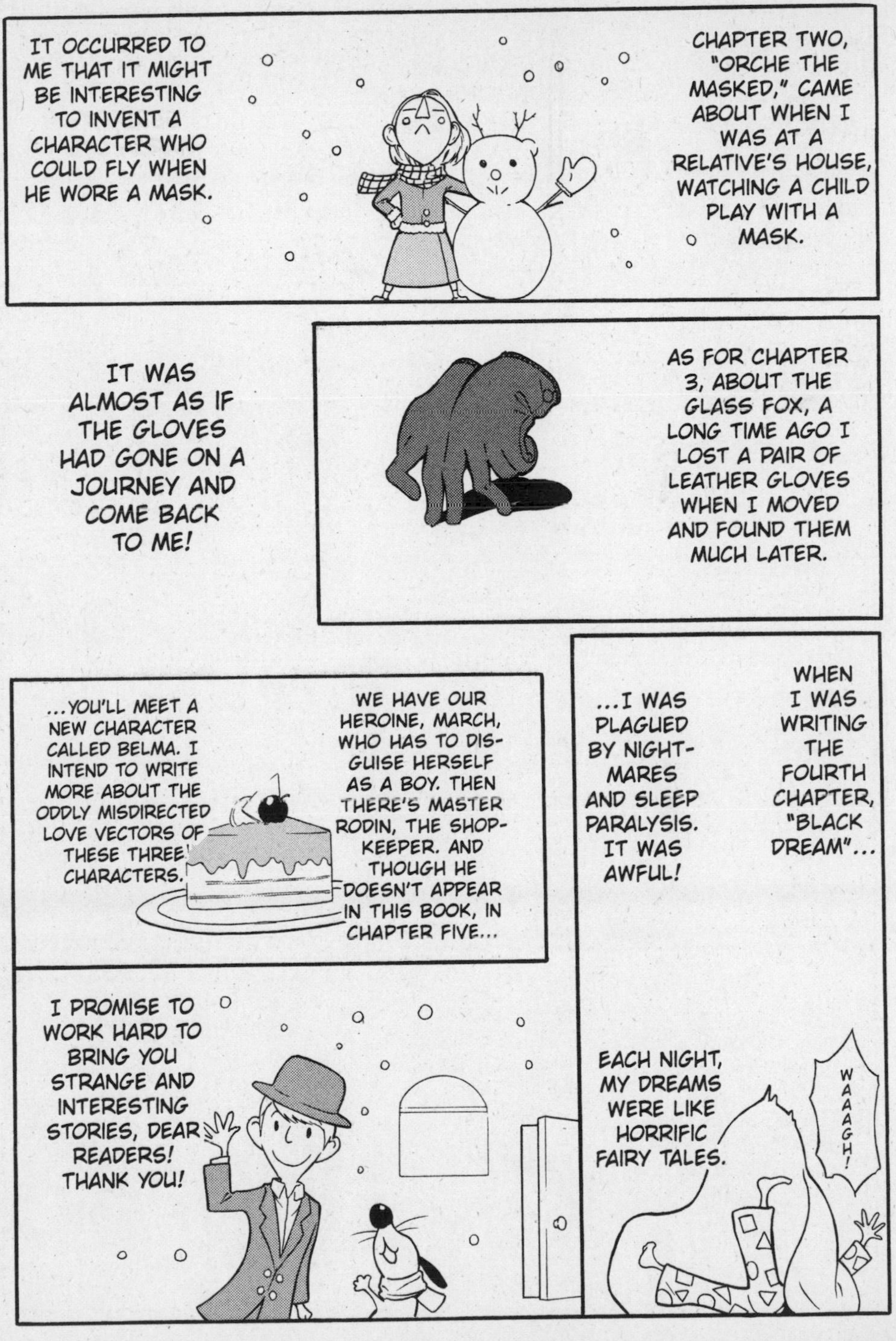
CHAPTER TWO, "ORCHE THE MASKED," CAME ABOUT WHEN I WAS AT A RELATIVE'S HOUSE, WATCHING A CHILD PLAY WITH A MASK.
IT OCCURRED TO ME THAT IT MIGHT BE INTERESTING TO INVENT A CHARACTER WHO COULD FLY WHEN HE WORE A MASK.
AS FOR CHAPTER 3, ABOUT THE GLASS FOX, A LONG TIME AGO I LOST A PAIR OF LEATHER GLOVES WHEN I MOVED AND FOUND THEM MUCH LATER.
IT WAS ALMOST AS IF THE GLOVES HAD GONE ON A JOURNEY AND COME BACK TO ME!
WHEN I WAS WRITING THE FOURTH CHAPTER, "BLACK DREAM"...
...I WAS PLAGUED BY NIGHT-MARES AND SLEEP PARALYSIS. IT WAS AWFUL!
EACH NIGHT, MY DREAMS WERE LIKE HORRIFIC FAIRY TALES.
WAAAAGH!
WE HAVE OUR HEROINE, MARCH, WHO HAS TO DIS-GUISE HERSELF AS A BOY. THEN THERE'S MASTER RODIN, THE SHOP-KEEPER. AND THOUGH HE DOESN'T APPEAR IN THIS BOOK, IN CHAPTER FIVE...
...YOU'LL MEET A NEW CHARACTER CALLED BELMA. I INTEND TO WRITE MORE ABOUT THE ODDLY MISDIRECTED LOVE VECTORS OF THESE THREE CHARACTERS.
I PROMISE TO WORK HARD TO BRING YOU STRANGE AND INTERESTING STORIES, DEAR READERS! THANK YOU!

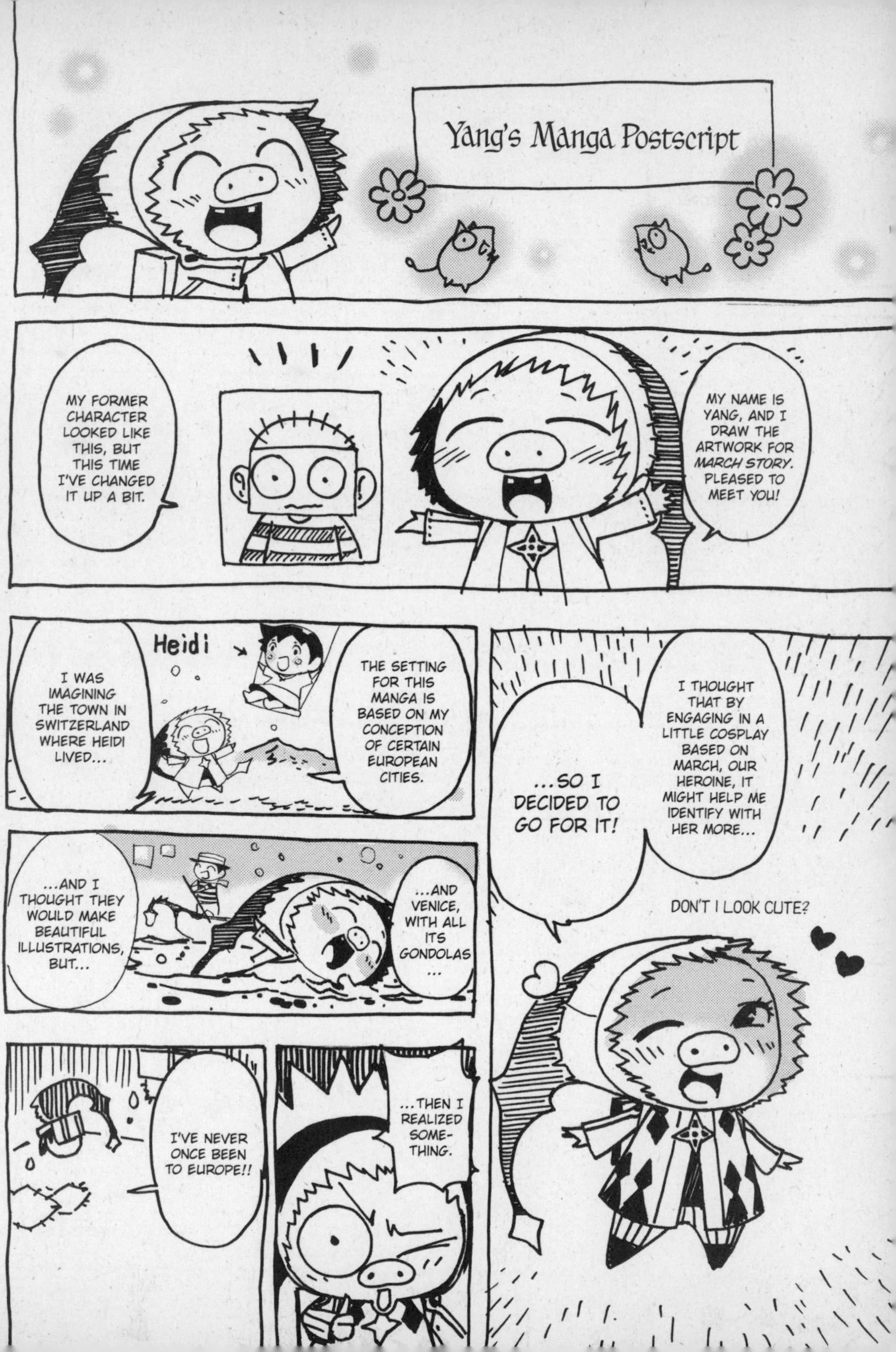
Yang's Manga Postscript
MY NAME IS YANG, AND I DRAW THE ARTWORK FOR *MARCH STORY*. PLEASED TO MEET YOU!
MY FORMER CHARACTER LOOKED LIKE THIS, BUT THIS TIME I'VE CHANGED IT UP A BIT.
I THOUGHT THAT BY ENGAGING IN A LITTLE COSPLAY BASED ON MARCH, OUR HEROINE, IT MIGHT HELP ME IDENTIFY WITH HER MORE...
...SO I DECIDED TO GO FOR IT!
DON'T I LOOK CUTE?
THE SETTING FOR THIS MANGA IS BASED ON MY CONCEPTION OF CERTAIN EUROPEAN CITIES.
Heidi
I WAS IMAGINING THE TOWN IN SWITZERLAND WHERE HEIDI LIVED...
...AND VENICE, WITH ALL ITS GONDOLAS ...
...AND I THOUGHT THEY WOULD MAKE BEAUTIFUL ILLUSTRATIONS, BUT...
...THEN I REALIZED SOME-THING.
I'VE NEVER ONCE BEEN TO EUROPE!!

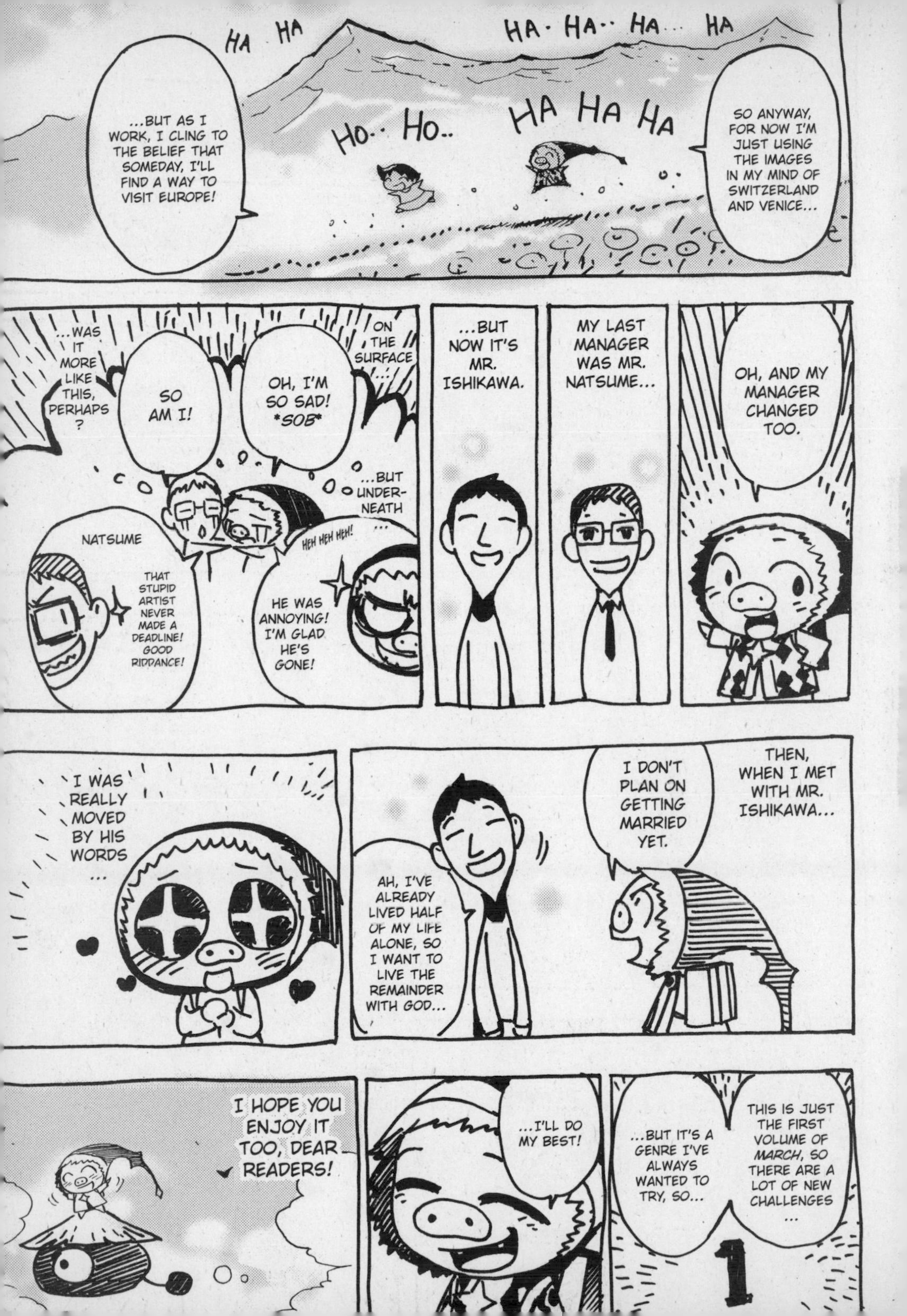
SO ANYWAY, FOR NOW I'M JUST USING THE IMAGES IN MY MIND OF SWITZERLAND AND VENICE...
HA· HA·· HA··· HA
HA HA HA
HO·· HO··
HA HA
...BUT AS I WORK, I CLING TO THE BELIEF THAT SOMEDAY, I'LL FIND A WAY TO VISIT EUROPE!
OH, AND MY MANAGER CHANGED TOO.
MY LAST MANAGER WAS MR. NATSUME...
...BUT NOW IT'S MR. ISHIKAWA.
ON THE SURFACE...
OH, I'M SO SAD! *SOB*
SO AM I!
...WAS IT MORE LIKE THIS, PERHAPS?
...BUT UNDERNEATH...
HEH HEH HEH!
HE WAS ANNOYING! I'M GLAD HE'S GONE!
NATSUME
THAT STUPID ARTIST NEVER MADE A DEADLINE! GOOD RIDDANCE!
THEN, WHEN I MET WITH MR. ISHIKAWA...
I DON'T PLAN ON GETTING MARRIED YET.
AH, I'VE ALREADY LIVED HALF OF MY LIFE ALONE, SO I WANT TO LIVE THE REMAINDER WITH GOD...
I WAS REALLY MOVED BY HIS WORDS...
THIS IS JUST THE FIRST VOLUME OF *MARCH*, SO THERE ARE A LOT OF NEW CHALLENGES...
...BUT IT'S A GENRE I'VE ALWAYS WANTED TO TRY, SO...
1
...I'LL DO MY BEST!
I HOPE YOU ENJOY IT TOO, DEAR READERS!

KYUNG IL YANG

Kyung Il Yang was born March 26, 1970. His debut work, *Soma Shinhwa Jeongi*, appeared in *Weekly Shonen Champ* in Korea. Notable works include *Zombie Hunter* (original story by Kazumasa Hirai) and *Shin Angyo Onshi (Blade of the Phantom Master*, original story by In Wan Youn). Yang also works on *Defense Devil*, currently serialized in *Weekly Shonen Sunday*.

HYUNG MIN KIM

Hyung Min Kim was born in Jinju, Korea, on December 29, 1978. In 2002 he entered the manga world, and in 2007 he debuted as an original storywriter with *March Story*, published in *Sunday GX*.

MARCH STORY

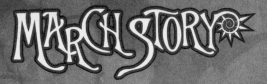

MARCH STORY
Volume 1
VIZ Signature Edition

Story by **HYUNG MIN KIM**
Art by **KYUNG IL YANG**

Original Japanese edition "MARCH STORY" published by SHOGAKUKAN Inc.

Logo design by Bay Bridge Studio

Translation & English Adaptation / Camellia Nieh
Touch-up Art & Lettering / John Hunt, Primary Graphix
Design / Frances O. Liddell
Editor / Mike Montesa

Printed in the U.S.A

Published by VIZ Media, LLC
P.O. Box 77010
San Francisco, CA 94107

10 9 8 7 6 5 4 3 2 1
First printing, October 2010

VIZ SIGNATURE

www.viz.com

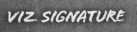

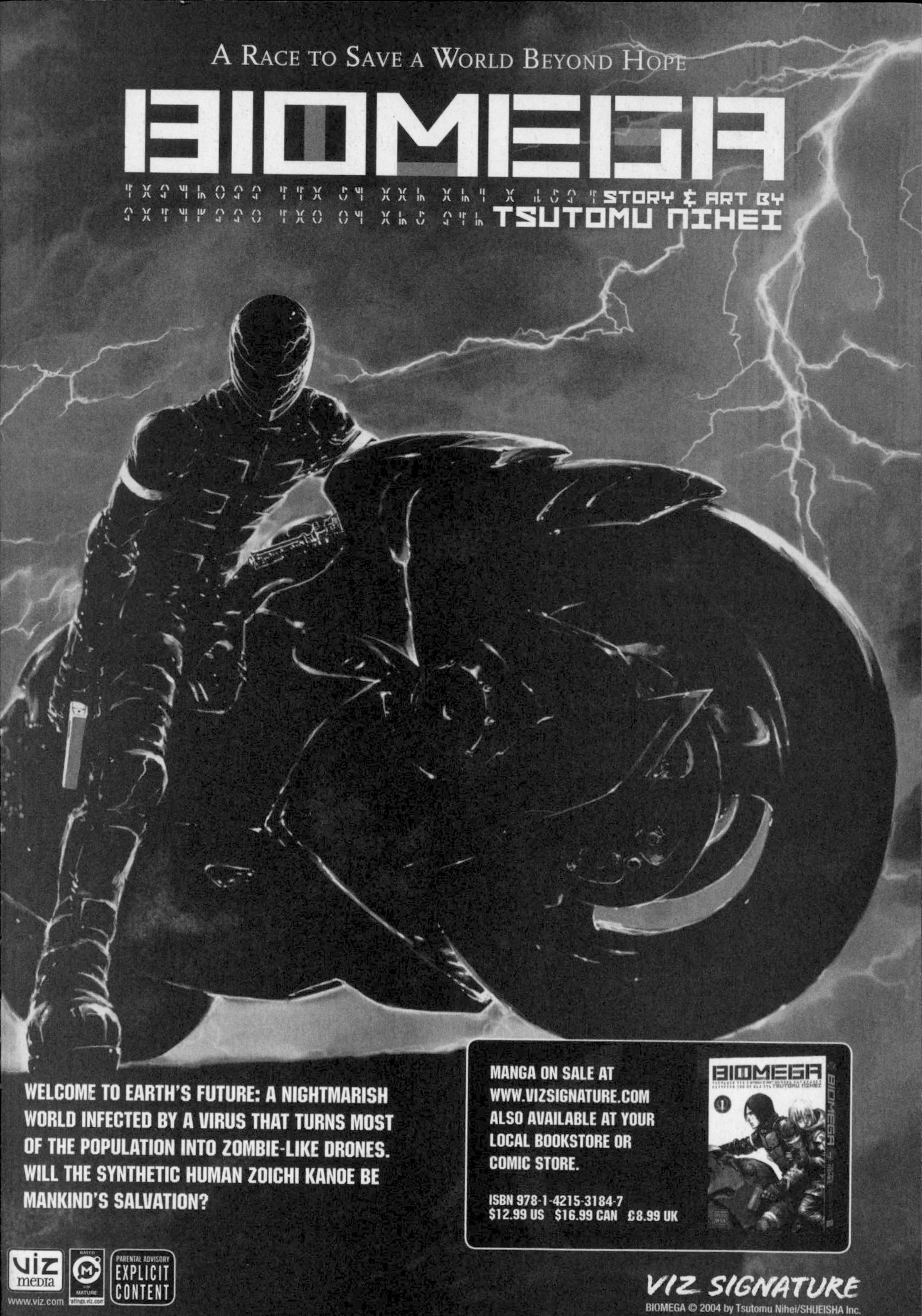
A Race to Save a World Beyond Hope
BIOMEGA
STORY & ART BY
TSUTOMU NIHEI
WELCOME TO EARTH'S FUTURE: A NIGHTMARISH WORLD INFECTED BY A VIRUS THAT TURNS MOST OF THE POPULATION INTO ZOMBIE-LIKE DRONES. WILL THE SYNTHETIC HUMAN ZOICHI KANOE BE MANKIND'S SALVATION?
MANGA ON SALE AT WWW.VIZSIGNATURE.COM
ALSO AVAILABLE AT YOUR LOCAL BOOKSTORE OR COMIC STORE.
ISBN 978-1-4215-3184-7
$12.99 US $16.99 CAN £8.99 UK
BIOMEGA
viz media
www.viz.com
PARENTAL ADVISORY
EXPLICIT CONTENT
VIZ SIGNATURE
BIOMEGA © 2004 by Tsutomu Nihei/SHUEISHA Inc.

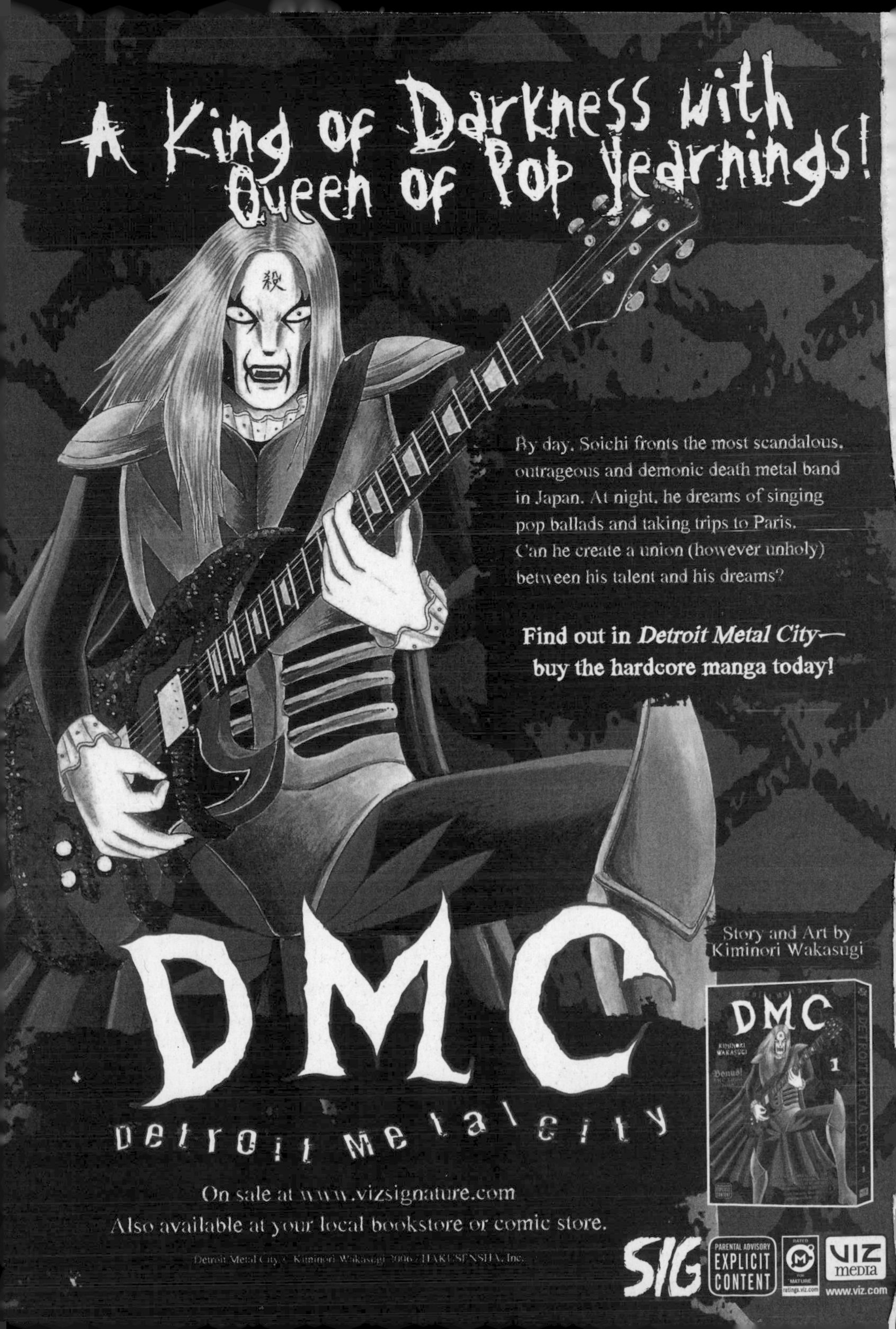

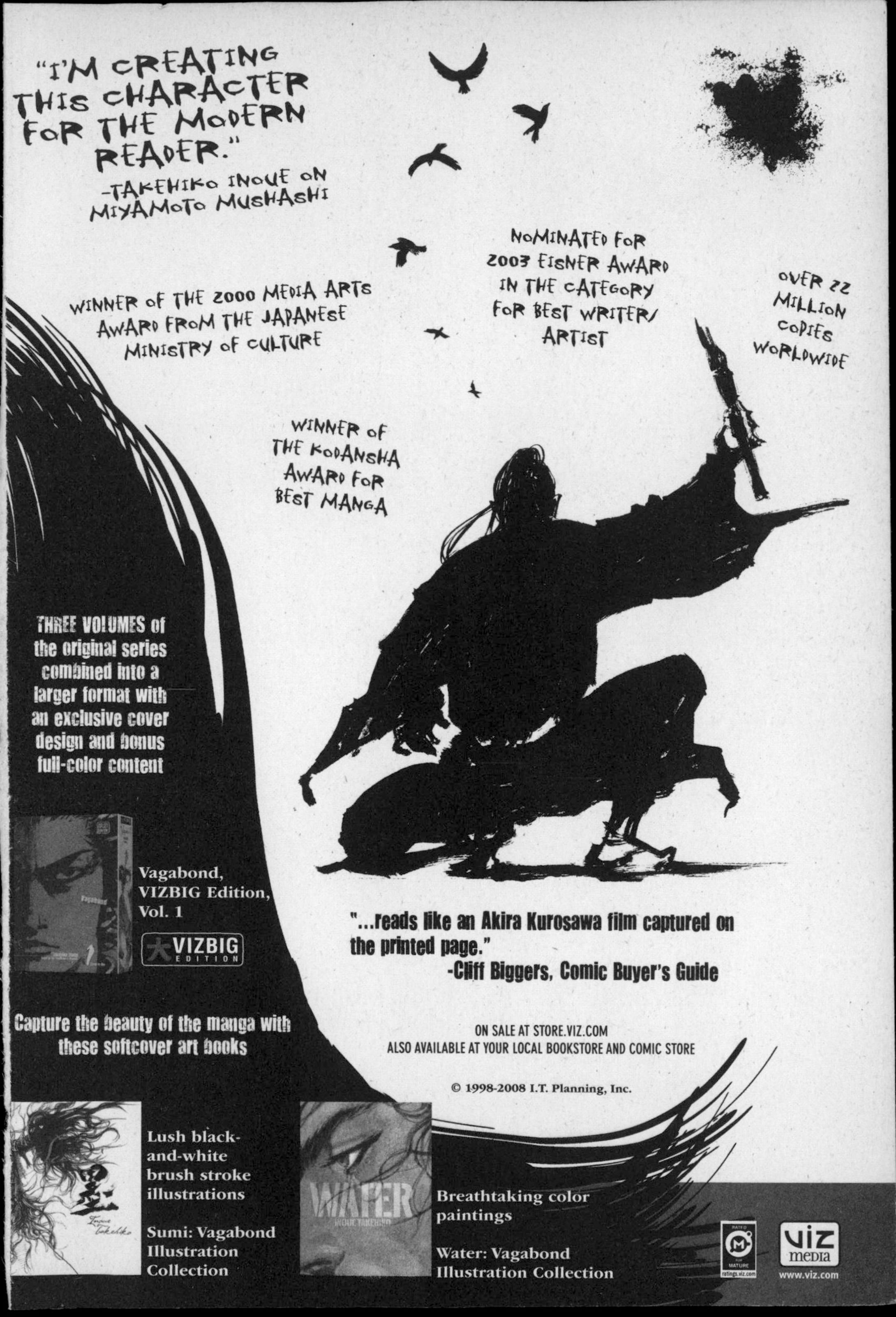
"I'M CREATING THIS CHARACTER FOR THE MODERN READER."
-TAKEHIKO INOUE ON MIYAMOTO MUSHASHI
NOMINATED FOR 2003 EISNER AWARD IN THE CATEGORY FOR BEST WRITER/ ARTIST
WINNER OF THE 2000 MEDIA ARTS AWARD FROM THE JAPANESE MINISTRY OF CULTURE
OVER 22 MILLION COPIES WORLDWIDE
WINNER OF THE KODANSHA AWARD FOR BEST MANGA
THREE VOLUMES of the original series combined into a larger format with an exclusive cover design and bonus full-color content
Vagabond, VIZBIG Edition, Vol. 1
VIZBIG EDITION
"...reads like an Akira Kurosawa film captured on the printed page."
-Cliff Biggers, Comic Buyer's Guide
ON SALE AT STORE.VIZ.COM
ALSO AVAILABLE AT YOUR LOCAL BOOKSTORE AND COMIC STORE
© 1998-2008 I.T. Planning, Inc.
Capture the beauty of the manga with these softcover art books
Lush black-and-white brush stroke illustrations
Sumi: Vagabond Illustration Collection
WATER
Breathtaking color paintings
Water: Vagabond Illustration Collection
RATED M FOR MATURE
ratings.viz.com
viz media
www.viz.com